THE ENGLISH WOMAN IN HISTORY

1   2

3   4

5   6

PLATE I   ENGLISH QUEENS

1 and 2. Silver pennies of the Canterbury moneyer EOBA, *c.* 790, with the portrait of Queen Cynethryth, the consort of Offa. No. 1 acquired before 1838; No. 2 from the Tyssen and Banks Collections and an eighteenth-century find at Eastbourne. [*Both coins enlarged 2½ times.*] See pp. 2–3. 3. Gold ryal (15s. piece) of Mary I of England, dated 1553. From the Barré Charles Roberts Collection (1810). [*Actual size.*] 4. Gold ryal of Elizabeth I of England, *c.* 1583. From the T. B. Clarke-Thornhill Collection (1934). [*Actual size.*] 5. Silver medal with portrait of Princess Mary on the occasion of her marriage, in 1677, to William of Orange: unknown artist. From the Edward Hawkins Collection (1860). [*Actual size.*] 6. Gold five-guinea piece of Queen Anne, dated 1703. From the Bank of England Collection (1878). [*Actual size.*] *From coins and medals in the British Museum.*

The English Woman
in History

DORIS MARY STENTON

Introduction by Louise A. Tilly

First published by SCHOCKEN BOOKS 1977

Library of Congress Cataloging in Publication Data

Stenton, Doris Mary Parsons, Lady.
    The English woman in history.

    Reprint of the ed. published by Allen & Unwin,
London and Macmillan, New York; with new introd.
    Includes index.
    1. Women—Great Britain—History.   I.   Title.

[HQ1593.S83 1977]   301.41′2′0941   77-75291

Manufactured in the United States of America

INTRODUCTION

Women's history has a history. Although the last five years have seen a rebirth of interest in the history of women, the field is not new. First published twenty years ago, Doris Mary Stenton's *The English Woman in History* surveys nearly the whole of the English past, from Anglo-Saxon times to the nineteenth century. Stenton concludes, as her problem shifts from the paucity of sources in the early period to the richness of the modern period: "The succession of women eminent in literature and affairs was never broken. . . . They deserve a salute today" (p. 349). Her work is a richly documented salute. Optimistic, it emphasizes political rights and institutions in their social setting, and it conceives of change embodied in great women and their ideas and deeds.

At the same time, it touches on several themes which the new wave of women's history has developed further. These themes are: the effects of life cycle on women's status, rural/urban differences in status, the unevenness of change in political and economic domains, and networks of support among women.

Women's history has had to seek out new kinds of sources in order to answer questions about women, who are rarely to be found in political chronicles or historical accounts of diplomacy and war. The key to this search lies in turning to the more intimate areas of life—to property holding, family relationships, work and education—as areas of investigation, to biography and autobiography and other personal records as sources.

Stenton's meticulously prepared research is valuable to today's historian, student, and general reader as a model exploration of sources. In it we see the historian delight in ferreting out illustrative primary sources. Since Stenton was a historian of the early medieval period, her use of sources is especially interesting in the early chapters on the Anglo-Saxon Woman and the Feudal Lady, and in the chapters on country women from the Conquest to the nineteenth century.

What kinds of sources does Stenton tap? They are all sources about and by individual women who actually lived in past time. She eschews literary sources, whether sagas, poetry, or novels. She uses contemporary narratives for framework, from Tacitus, the Roman observer of the Germanic tribes (of which the Angles and Saxons were two), to the later chroniclers and travelers' reports. For the early period she finds information in laws, charters and wills, and even place names. The study of place names for clues as to the origins of settlements and property relationships was developed as a historical method by Lady Doris Mary Stenton and Sir Frank Merry Stenton, among others. Here we see a master of the art at work. The name of Bamburgh, she tells us, is derived from "Bebbe's fort," after a Northumbrian queen, while Goodwood comes from a piece of woodland belonging to a woman called Godgifu. The proportionate importance of female names found in place names leads Stenton to deduce an important role for women as landholders in old English rural society. The artifacts of the early feudal period, after the Norman Conquest of 1066, are another sensitively used source. Stenton integrates information from coins, medals, and seals with portraits with that culled from the characters and records of monasteries, the wills of men and women, and the proceedings of manorial courts to give texture and life to a little known period. She uses a source as well known as the fifteenth-century Paston letters, interpreting them from a different perspective. Instead of focusing on William Paston and John, his son, Stenton describes the lives of Agnes and Margaret, their wives, of Elizabeth, John's sister, and of Margery and Anne, John and Margaret's daughters. The family relationships of women in various stages of their life cycles are illuminated by these passages in which wife-husband, mother-daughter, sister-brother, and mother-in-law-daughter-in-law connections are examined.

Stenton's sources become more comprehensive with the passing of time. For the seventeenth century, she can compare Puritan sermons about the role of women with tracts about the education of women, love letters, diaries, and biographies written by women. Aphra Benn, who earned her livelihood by writing plays and novels, is but the first of the increasingly numerous women writers and intellectuals from the seventeenth century on about whom Stenton tells us. Thus, since her sources are *written* records about and by individuals, Stenton writes primarily about wealthy and/or educated women and women of politically important families.

In keeping with her optimistic, evolutionary framework, Stenton starts with a rather grim picture of marriage in the feudal age:

> In an age when child marriage was part of the accepted social habit the personal choice of the child partners could hardly be consulted. The marriage of an heiress was felt to be the lord's concern since he must needs take the homage of her husband. No lord should be asked to take the homage 'of an enemy or of a person unsuitable in some other way.' . . . it is rare to find evidence in this age that anything which can be called romance went with the hard practical business of making a marriage contract. Between the greedy desire of lords and parents to make marriage a means of increasing an estate in land and the prurient attitude of the medieval Church towards love between man and woman romance had little chance. [pp. 44–45]

In Chapter XI, we read that, after centuries of injustice, political change began in the nineteenth century as a mature parliamentary system began to expand rights for new groups, of which women were one. Cases like that of Caroline Norton are cited:

> The inequality of the law which governed the relations between husband and wife had been exposed by a lawyer more than two hundred years before. His advice to wives to appeal to Parliament for relief was premature in 1632, but it remained the fact that only legislative action could correct the law's injustice to married women. The exposure by Caroline Norton (1808–77) of her own sad story was hardly necessary to make plain the need for action, but lawyers would perhaps have moved more slowly if Mrs.

Norton had borne her troubles in silence ... [p. 333]. A society which aimed at a general reform of abuses in the law had been formed in 1844 as the Law Amendment Society. Ten years later, a young woman of twenty-seven, Barbara Leigh Smith, persuaded the society to consider the disabilities of married women [p. 336].

The outcome, of course, was legislation changing the status and choice of married women. A law permitting divorce was passed, and then

in 1882 married women were given for the first time since the Norman Conquest rights of separate ownership over every kind of property. Four years before this momentous Act London University had opened its degrees to women [p. 348].

She concludes her study with the late nineteenth century advance toward equality in property rights and expanded access to education for women. The vote is still some forty years in the future, but its groundwork is prepared.

Stenton's political framework takes public institutions and legal rights as the touchstone of women's position and status. Thus, the chief criterion of emancipation which she seeks is "full participation in the rights and duties of the social order." From this perspective, women were in a position roughly equal to that of men in Anglo-Saxon England. The Norman Conquest ended this "rough and ready partnership" with men because of the military base of feudal political arrangements. Feudalism gave political rights to those who pledged military support, and women were gradually excluded from political life. The church reinforced the subjection of wives to their husbands through its teaching. The Reformation did little to change this legal situation, but the growing emphasis on women's education led to questioning and revision of the legal status of women in the time of triumph of English liberalism, the nineteenth century. Stenton, then, concludes that, within her political perspective, there is a positive evolution of status as rights expand with modern times and feminism emerges as a liberal ideology. Her historical method focuses primarily on women's political and legal status, and changes in this arena are laid to broad changes in educational opportunity, which in turn initiate the development of female consciousness. Women (and men) developed and articulated a feminist critique of the injustice in the treatment of women that led to change in the political arena.

Interestingly enough, although Stenton wrote long before the recent growth of methodological sophistication in women's history, she foreshadowed many of its themes. For example, although she does not use individual life histories or scraps of life histories in the style of "collective biography" which has developed in recent historiography, she uses some of its concepts. Collective biography takes women as a social group and collects uniform data concerning various aspects of the lives of numerous individuals in order to delineate a profile of a "typical" woman. In order to do this, both class and life cycle categories must be carefully controlled. Stenton is limited to upper-class women because of her choice of sources, but she is fully aware of life cycle effects. For example, she notes, "daughters ... may have been unhappy in youth but if they married and survived their husbands they often enjoyed ... an independence and importance which must have sweetened the sorrows of age" (p. 97). With the possible exception of the Anglo-Saxon period, the norm in all of Stenton's long time-period was that a woman would marry, bear children, and live out her life with a husband who had legally sanctioned rights over her and their children. A certain proportion of women never married, but Stenton does not think spinsters were very numerous. She notes, "the high death-rate in the Middle Ages and on almost to within living memory greatly reduced the number of unmarried and unoccupied women" (p. 100). Nevertheless, she devotes some pages to women in convents, and she examines the legal position of the *femme sole*. Recent demographic studies, for the period after 1500 at least, suggest that permanent celibacy was more common, especially in landowning families, than Stenton believed. Stenton provides a tempting sample of sources for a more systematic treatment of the single woman in a society where marriage was the normative expectation.

Being single, furthermore, was a stage in every woman's life, and the interest of the story lies in what women did in that stage, how long it lasted, whether they reentered 'single' status when widowed, and so on. Stenton provides many life histories which show that even upper class women who married were unlikely to live their entire lives after marriage in the normative pattern. Although most women would be married and mothers at some point in their adult lives, high mortality meant that most or all of a woman's children might die before she did and that she might outlive one or even several husbands. How did the expectations and behavior of women vary as they passed in and out of normative roles over their lifetimes as the deaths of parents, children, and spouses changed their position and choices? Widowhood for women with wealth and resources could be a time of independence and influence; this cannot be generalized, however, to women in other classes for whom widowhood meant vulnerability, poverty, and dependence. Orphanhood for both rich and poor young women was likely to bring a time of dependence and vulnerability. Reduced likelihood of widowhood and orphanhood went along with improved life expectancy in the nineteenth century and later. Women had better chances to live longer, healthier lives. Yet, paradoxically, they also had fewer possibilities of moving out of the expected life cycle. The acceptance of social behavior like birth control and divorce made that possible again.

Stenton is quite aware of the fact that the history of institutions and legal rights is only part of the picture. She notes, "The law is clear enough and the Church's view is clear enough. But men and women are never ruled in their personal relationships by law alone or by the Church alone" (p. 98). Stenton comments here on the important economic role of women in agricultural households: "It is probably not far from the truth to say that the nearer the household was to the land, the stronger the ties between man and wife, the more nearly were they on equal terms" (p. 98; see also pp. 104, 113 for similar statements). This equality is based on economic need, for "No farmer could get along without a wife," and not on any ideology about male/female relationships. This is undoubtedly true, and it serves as a reminder that behavior and prescriptions may be quite different matters.

Stenton argues further along, however, that the preaching of the church and its ideological structures eventually invaded even the relatively egalitarian English countryside. She notes Mrs. Cappe's report of 1787 of a visit to her home village in Yorkshire in which the visitor remarked on the contemptuous treatment of women by men. Stenton explains, "the homilies have brought forth their inevitable fruit. The countryman has at last 'a supreme contempt for women'" (p. 114). How can this interpretation be reconciled with Stenton's political framework, which sees expanding consciousness of rights in the eighteenth century, and with her recognition of a kind of equality in peasant households, close to the land? Here a focus on economic change can help, a focus which separates changes in economic structure from changes in political rights. Stenton is correct in noting that women were more involved economically in the peasant agricultural economy than in the urban manufacturing sector, and this involvement may indeed have given them a measure of equality with men. However, there was a long-term change in women's economic activity as labor and resources in the English economy as a whole shifted from agriculture to manufacturing and commerce through the process of industrialization. Not only did manufacturing become the dominant economic activity of the society, but the scale, too, of both agriculture and manufacturing grew enormously, from the middle of the eighteenth century on. Economic participation and political rights did not change contemporaneously and in the same direction. In the same period in which consciousness of the inferior legal status of women was growing among urban, middle class, educated feminists, fewer and fewer women were to be found in the position of wife of a small-holding agriculturalist— the position which Stenton finds most conducive to an informal equality between the sexes. There was a decline in women's contribution to production which went along with the increased productivity based on increased scale. As the scale of industry and of agriculture grew, women were less likely to be active producers, in city or country.

Two other aspects of this economic change we call industrialization were the decline of the domestic mode of production and its replacement by the industrial mode and the rising importance of individual wage earning. The apparent loss of respect for women which

Mrs. Cappe noted in Yorkshire at the end of the eighteenth century was connected to the disappearance of the joint economic enterprise of husbands, wives, and children in relatively small productive units. The period saw a rise of wage-earning, landless laborers who lived in households where the division of labor was differentiated and men were the chief wage earners.

The economic perspective reminds us that the expansion of political and civil rights for women and the growth of institutional protection for women's position is not the whole story, just as Stenton points out. More women were needed as workers when household production was the dominant form of production and individual productivity was low. One conclusion is that industrialization was disadvantageous in the short run to women because it diminished possibilities for economic contribution by them.

Over the long run, the growth of scale in agriculture freed some women from farm work, and wealthier rural women were no longer active participants in agricultural production. Similar trends occurred in the differentiating urban economy, which also increased in scale. The developing economy of England no longer needed every hand engaged in the production of necessities, and new, non-productive occupations became more numerous. Writing as a profession and teaching as a profession distinct from religious ministering both emerged in the late seventeenth and eighteenth centuries. Both were primarily male professions, but women, who by choice or by necessity were either permanently or temporarily forced to earn their living, sometimes took up these professions as ways to support themselves. These women were exceptions, and the spread of education to which they contributed was very slow.

The decline of household production together with growing industrialization meant, over the very long run, the emergence of new kinds of jobs for women which required minimal education and literacy. These were the "tertiary" white collar occupations such as teacher, nurse, clerk, and so on, which expanded spectacularly only at the end of the nineteenth century. It was only then that female education spread and became the rule rather than the exception. The experience of increasing numbers of women as individual, wage-earning workers over at least part of their life cycles (married women in England did not benefit from the expansion of tertiary occupations) promoted the development of legal categories and rights for women which matched their current behavior.

Another theme which has been more fully developed by recent women's history is that of networks among women. On the one hand, Stenton shows that many of the early feminists and educators shared a common milieu and friendships. On the other hand, she notes that some women refused such connections. For example, she writes of Lady Hester Stanhope: "It was unfortunate for Lady Hester that she had no one to teach her that a woman needs friends of her own sex" (p. 274). Interestingly, she shows that the women who led the fight for reform of English laws affecting the status of women were not the women who made high personal achievements on their own, like Florence Nightingale or Harriet Martineau. The latter, for example, viewed the women's movement from a position of arrogant self-reliance. She was "a woman strong enough to make her own way but lacked imaginative insight into the feelings of others ..." (p. 340). Florence Nightingale "disclaimed all interest in the movement to widen opportunities before women. 'I am brutally indifferent to the rights and wrongs of my sex,' she wrote to Harriet Martineau in 1858" (p. 343). So, in addition to the unevenness of change in the economic and political spheres noted above, Stenton shows that consciousness is not always directly correlated with economic or political gains. The women whose feminist consciousness was awakened in nineteenth century England were educated and middle class. Their movement was built on female solidarity, but relatively few of them worked for a living.

Stenton was a trail blazer. She sought out forgotten sources relating to individual women and reexamined more familiar sources in order to uncover long overlooked facts. Her book is a rich tapestry of life stories which provide raw material for other kinds of history than the institutional history she does so well. For the medieval and early modern periods, Stenton has given a view of English women that is both deep and sweeping. For the long expanse of time from Anglo-

Saxons to Victorians, she provides us with a chronicle of the political evolution of women's rights and the interplay of this process with educational change. For this extraordinary contribution we are still in debt to Lady Doris Mary Stenton, historian.

1977   LOUISE A. TILLY

PREFACE

My purpose in writing this book has been to display the place women have held and the influence they have exerted within the changing pattern of English society from the earliest down to modern times. This book, therefore, can only begin with the famous description of the women of the Germanic tribes written by the Roman historian Tacitus. It ends, save for an occasional excursion, with the publication of *The Subjection of Women* by John Stuart Mill in 1869. The evidence for more recent generations is so voluminous, and so many studies of individual women of this age have appeared that to carry my survey farther would have thrown the book out of focus. The material from which I have drawn my evidence is contemporary with the people of whom I write in the successive chapters of this book. Contemporary narrative history, the early laws, charters, and wills throw sometimes surprising light on the women of the early period of our history. The records of courts of justice, both the royal courts and those of the manor, grants of land, and wills are invaluable for the Middle Ages, and before they have ended the stream of correspondence has begun. The Paston letters have been a quarry for generations of historians. They are an astonishingly rich and lively source, and for their date they stand almost alone. Nevertheless, as the years pass the material soon becomes embarrassingly ample, and I have been able to use diaries, memoirs, and letters, sermons, and tracts dealing directly or incidentally with my subject.

All the women the reader will meet in these pages were real people who lived and worked in the England of their day. In my search for material I have deliberately avoided the romantic literature of the Middle Ages, coloured as it is throughout by an artificial embellishment of life. Nor have I used the novels of a later period. The active imagination of the novelist produces creatures who seem for a moment to live more vividly than the real people of history, for they are tailored to fit a story, and the inconsistences and contradictions of real life are ironed out. The comments of Lady Mary Wortley Montagu, quoted in this book, upon her contemporary, Samuel Richardson, and his famous *Pamela* should be read by every historian who is tempted to drive home a point by quoting a character from fiction. The historian's own insight may possibly be stimulated by reading the work of novelists contemporary with his period, but he should not draw it into evidence. I have therefore deliberately refrained from citing the phantoms who appear in novels however brilliant the writing or convincing the circumstances may seem.

The period covered by this book is so long and the literature so vast that careful consideration of my plan was necessary. It was obviously impossible to deal on equal terms with every female activity, nor were they all equally relevant to my design. I had no desire to set out an orderly catalogue of female excellence. In particular, there seemed little that I could say with advantage about women artists or writers of plays, poems, or novels, or about actresses. Since the days of Aphra Behn women have shone in increasing numbers as imaginative writers. Between the birth of Aphra Behn in 1640 and the death of Eliza Haywood in 1756 the female novelist was forged. Aphra Behn, Mrs. Manley, and Mrs. Haywood, who belonged to three successive generations, established a lasting tradition. None of them, so far as I know, has left a diary behind her. Other women of parts, who might have been cited, have doubtless been overlooked because their works do not happen to have come my way. I have only recently been introduced by Professor Bruce Dickins to Agnes Beaumont, a slightly younger contemporary of Aphra Behn, whose brief story of the troubles which fell on her because she insisted on riding pillion behind John Bunyan to a religious meeting at Gamlingay is an astonishingly vivid piece of natural writing by the daughter of a small farmer, who lived in a two-roomed cottage and spent most of his time 'serving the cows'. Agnes Beaumont is relevant to my argument because the capacity of a farmer's daughter to make an exciting story out of her own experiences is another proof of my contention that the education of girls in the seventeenth century was not always as ineffective as some writers seem to believe.

For my purpose it is fortunate that the period for which the evidence is fullest is also the period which is best known. The political influence of the great ladies of the nineteenth century has always been appreciated. Many of their names are almost household words. It would have been a waste of space to talk of them here. Fortunately, too, much excellent modern writing has been devoted to individual women of this age. Miss M. G. Jones's life of Hannah More, Mrs. Cecil Woodham-Smith's life of Florence Nightingale, and Lady Stephen's life of Emily Davies are three cardinal works which between them go far to display the whole field of activity open to the exceptional woman between 1770 and 1900. For these and other books I record my gratitude. For the rest, I have tried throughout this book to allow the women of whom I write and the men who have written about them to speak for themselves in precise quotations drawn from the best edition of their works available to me. I have recorded in footnotes the exact reference to each quotation.

The impulse towards writing this book came many years ago from the contrast between the masterful and independent Anglo-Saxon ladies of whom my husband talked, and the legally dependent, although still masterful ladies whom I met in the plea rolls and charters of the twelfth and thirteenth centuries. With the possibility that I might some day write this book my husband and I have for many years watched the catalogues and searched the shelves of antiquarian booksellers for anything which might throw light on any part of the subject. The search has added spice to many of our holidays. I am grateful to Mr. Rayner Unwin for asking me to write this book for publication by his firm, and for his patience, help, and encouragement while the work was in progress. Until I applied myself seriously to the task of writing and extended my researches well beyond the period for which I had been trained I had no idea how clear a pattern would emerge. It is satisfactory to an historian who boldly undertakes a survey of a wide sweep of history if he finds that his subject falls into shape, so that a clear line of development can be discerned. I began with a lively interest in the Middle Ages, but as I progressed down the centuries my interest and my excitement grew.

My thanks are due to all those whose encouragement has helped me to persevere in the task of writing this book. But I owe particular thanks to Mr. E. Smith, formerly Registrar of the University of Reading, who put me on the track of several important books and lent me many from his own library; to Dr. Dorothy Whitelock, who gave me a collection of books about women and the women's movement in the late nineteenth century which has been of great service; to Professor Bruce Dickins, who showed me the Duchess of Newcastle's books given by her to the library of Corpus Christi College, Cambridge; to Mr. R. H. M. Dolley, who provided photographs of Cynethryth's silver pennies and chose the other coins illustrated in the Frontispiece; to Mr. Charles Clay for obtaining for me *The Lives of Lady Anne Clifford* printed in 1916 for presentation to the Roxburghe Club; to Mr. G. R. Fletcher for a new photograph of

Lady Anne Clifford's tomb; to Mr. H. C. Johnson, who introduced me to the Book of the Queen's Wardrobe now in the Public Record Office and enabled me to obtain an illustration of a page recording gifts of second-hand dresses to certain ladies of the bedchamber and their signatures acknowledging their receipt of them; to Miss P. M. Barnes for exploring the great collections at the Record Office for appropriate illustrations; to Mr. Baillie Reynolds for help in obtaining the photograph of Blanche Parry's tomb in Bacton church; to Mr. H. W. Edwards, antiquarian bookseller of Ashmore Green, who has lent me several seventeenth-century books too expensive for my purchase; to Mr. Arnold Muirhead, antiquarian bookseller of St. Albans, who has not only filled my shelves from his ample stock, but has lent me items from his own remarkable library of first editions. Miss Vera Douie, Librarian of the Women's Service Library, has introduced me to many seventeenth- and eighteenth-century books in the possession of the Fawcett Society and called my attention to items in second-hand catalogues. I am most grateful to her for her help and advice. To Miss Mary Kirkus, Librarian of the University of Reading, I owe more than I can easily express. From the time when she and Miss Kathleen Major, my husband and I spent a holiday together at Oakham and occupied a wet Sunday afternoon discussing the possible plan of this book she has plied me with material and watched the catalogues on my behalf. To her staff in the University Library, imbued with something of her own spirit, I offer my thanks for much ungrudging help. My husband has accompanied me through every stage of this long journey.

WHITLEY PARK FARM,   D. M. S.
READING,
25 *March* 1956

CONTENTS

ILLUSTRATIONS

THE ENGLISH WOMAN IN HISTORY

CHAPTER I

The Anglo-Saxon Woman

One who attempts to trace through the centuries of English history
evidence of the place allowed by English men to English women in the
world of their day must begin investigations in Anglo-Saxon England.
A dark age of disaster and destruction separates Saxon England from
Roman Britain. The Saxons and Angles who overran the Roman province
brought to this country their own social conceptions. To reconstruct
them is impossible, but enough is known about them to suggest that the
Saxon warrior of the first century after Christ had regarded his wife
as his equal partner in the struggle for existence. In his famous description
of the German women of this age, the Roman historian, Tacitus, may
well have wished to point a moral for the lascivious ladies of the capital,
but the detailed knowledge behind his account of the various Germanic
peoples entitles his opinion to respect. He described the Germans as
almost the only barbarians content with one wife, though he observed
that women were willing to accept polygamous marriage with men of
the highest nobility. The German husband gave dower to his wife, oxen,
a horse and bridle, a shield, and spear or sword. She, in return, brought
some piece of armour to her husband. She was warned by the very
rites with which her marriage began that she came to share hard work
and peril; that her fate would be the same as her husband's in peace and
in war. According to Tacitus, tradition related that some battles lost, or
almost lost, were saved by the women, 'by the urgency of their prayers
and the baring of their breasts'. The Germans felt that 'in their women
was something holy which made them able to look into the future and
they scorned neither to consult them nor to follow their advice'. The
peoples of whom Tacitus wrote lived some four hundred years before the
Angles and Saxons made any settlements in Britain, but they were the
stock from which the first English women sprang.

Tacitus refers to the ancient songs which he calls the only form of record known to the Germans. The songs have perished, but some impression of their character may be gathered from English poems reflecting the conditions of an earlier time which were written in the seventh or eighth century. They are interesting to the historian of English women because they give a glimpse, if nothing more, of the great ladies of the Heroic Age, when the Germanic tribes were moving towards settlement within the borders of the Roman Empire. In their natural setting of the great hall, which was the centre of early social life, these ladies appear as figures of grace and dignity, overseeing the entertainment of the guests, or rewarding a poet who had recited acceptable verses before the company. They met tragedy with courage, and bore an honourable part in the conflict of loyalties which might arise at any time within the circle of their kinsmen. They stand for an ideal of civilized behaviour in a violent age.

In all periods of Anglo-Saxon history a great lady could take part in public affairs so effectively that her name was long remembered. Nothing beyond the name is known of the Northumbrian queen Bebbe who left her name to Bamburgh—'Bebbe's fort'—but only a woman who was outstanding in her day could have been permanently associated with this commanding site. The Anglo-Saxons seem to have had no fixed objection to a woman's government, for a widowed queen of Wessex is said on good authority to have ruled her husband's people for a year after him, late in the seventh century. Even in her husband's lifetime a queen could behave high-handedly. The Anglo-Saxon Chronicle records that in 722 Æthelburg, wife of Ine, King of Wessex, 'destroyed Taunton, which Ine formerly built'. The story that must have lain behind this entry is lost, but the entry would be meaningless if the queen had not been acting on her own initiative. In contrast to these dim figures, Cynethryth, wife of Offa, King of the Mercians (757–96), stands out as an individual in her own right. Offa himself was a great king, who came near to uniting all England under his own rule. He was a dangerous enemy to all who set themselves up against his line, and his wife passed into legend as the type of a tyrannous queen. The details of her tyranny, if such it were, have vanished. She is alive today because coins were struck in her name and with her portrait—by many centuries, the earliest portrait of an English woman. She was singularly fortunate in the skill of the die-cutter who produced these remarkable profiles. Even through the medium of a small silver penny, the impression of a vivid personality is given by the delicate features, the large eye, and the abundant hair, generally unconfined by diadem or fillet. No queen consort in later centuries was ever allowed to issue coins in her own name. The only king who has recognized his consort's existence on his own coins is Henry VIII, on whose gold crowns K R stands for Katherine of Aragon, A R for Anne Boleyn, and I R for Jane Seymour.

A reputation for tyranny far worse than that of Cynethryth became attached to her daughter Eadburg, wife of Beorhtric, King of Wessex. According to Asser, the contemporary biographer of King Alfred, she behaved in a manner odious to God and man. If she could not remove her enemies from power by accusing them to the king, she poisoned them. In the end, the poison which she had prepared for a young man high in the king's favour was drunk in error by the king as well as by the youth so that they both died. As she could no longer remain in Wessex after her husband's death, she went oversea, with a vast treasure, to the court of the Emperor Charles the Great. She bore many gifts to the Emperor, who in Asser's story asked her whether she would prefer to marry him or his son, who was standing beside him on the dais. Unwisely, Eadburg chose his son, because he was the younger. The Emperor refused to let her marry him, but gave her a large monastery of nuns. Since she behaved worse as an abbess than she had behaved as a queen, the Emperor cast her out to live in poverty and wretchedness. Writing in 893, Asser said that he had spoken to many people who had seen her in her last miserable years, begging for alms daily at Pavia, attended by a little slave-boy.

Asser tells this story in order to explain what he calls a 'perverse' West Saxon custom which denied the title of queen to the king's wife. The custom, he says, had arisen because of Eadburg's evil conduct. The story has obviously been coloured by West Saxon hatred of a Mercian princess, but it cannot be a mere invention. The fact that the wife of a King of Wessex was not accorded the name of queen was known in France forty years before Asser wrote his life of Alfred. So far as can be seen, it was not until the late tenth century that the wives of the Kings of Wessex—by that time, Kings of England—once more received the name and state of queens. Until then, and occasionally for long afterwards, the king's wife was known as the Lady, and his mother, naturally, but less happily, as the Old Lady.

While Alfred was reigning in Wessex, the midland kingdom of Mercia was destroyed by an invasion of Vikings who took its eastern half for their own settlement. The western half, which remained to the English, came to be ruled by a nobleman named Æthelred, who looked to King Alfred for support and received his daughter Æthelflæd in marriage. As ruler of Western Mercia jointly with her husband, and after his death in 911 in her own name as Lady of the Mercians, she was unswervingly loyal to her father's house. It was the use which she made of the military forces of the western midlands which enabled her brother Edward, King of Wessex, to enforce his authority upon all the Viking armies in England south of the Humber. She may fairly be counted among the few English women who in any period have permanently influenced the course of history.

As a woman who could carry out successful campaigns in her own person she stands alone. Her method was to protect her own country by fortifying strategic points, and then to assault the nearest fortresses in enemy hands. Even before her husband died she had repaired the Roman walls of Chester. Some of the fortresses of her own building, such as Warwick and Stafford, soon became important as centres of local trade and government. But the most remarkable feature of her operations is the fact that she conducted them at the head of a military household such as had surrounded the kings of the Heroic Age. The work involved hard fighting. A contemporary records that at her capture of Derby, four retainers 'dear to her' were killed inside the gates, and the surrender of Leicester 'peaceably, through God's help' is carefully noted in contrast. When she died, at Tamworth in the summer of 918, she was on the verge of a still more notable success, for a little while before, the men of York had solemnly promised to accept her lordship. It is not surprising that her reputation survived the Norman Conquest, to be commemorated by the Anglo-Norman chronicler Henry of Huntingdon in Latin verse. It was also natural that the Jacobean poet and dramatist Thomas Heywood, compiling a *History of Women* when Henry's work had recently been printed, should paraphrase in English verse his poem in praise of Æthelflæd.

No other woman of the Saxon time stands out so clearly at the centre of affairs. But a century later, the conquest of England and Norway by Cnut of Denmark opened an even wider career to a remarkable English woman with whom he had contracted an irregular marriage during the warfare of his youth. She was the daughter of a nobleman with a large estate in Northamptonshire and was commonly known as Ælfgifu 'of Northampton'. Her association with Cnut survived his respectable marriage with the Duke of Normandy's sister, and she kept Cnut's confidence up to the end of his life. She bore him two sons, the elder of whom he made King of Norway, under her regency. She governed Norway with such severity that the years of her rule, ended at last by a successful revolt, became proverbial in the north as a synonym for an evil time. After the death of Cnut, she returned to England, and prevailed upon the leading noblemen of the country to recognize her second son, Harold, surnamed 'Harefoot', as king. With this her story ends; no chronicler recorded her death, nor has any description survived of the young woman from Northamptonshire who was remembered as a tyrant by the fiercest of European peoples.

The wives, daughters, and mistresses of kings had more chance of making their mark than women even a few stages lower in the social scale. Nevertheless, there were women outside the royal circle whose names are still familiar. Some of them were remembered for their religious foundations, like the wealthy Staffordshire lady, Wulfrun, who founded a minster in her *heah tun*, or chief manor, and is kept in memory by the name of Wolverhampton. Others have reached an undesirable form of immortality through stories which gathered round their names in the Middle Ages. Neither Leofric, Earl of Mercia, who was one of the few statesmen of his time, nor Godgifu, his wife and partner in all good works, have contributed anything beyond their names to the grotesque invention of Lady Godiva's ride through Coventry. Now and then, though all too rarely, an epithet attached to a woman's name in her own generation tells something of her personality. The lady named Eadgifu, with land in seven counties, whom Domesday Book describes as 'the rich', 'the fair', or 'the fair and rich', cannot have been commonplace, and may well have been formidable to those who knew her.

But the achievements of the ladies who have left a mark of their own upon the world tell less about the general position of women in society than the names of undistinguished women which have become attached to villages, hamlets, and farms. The intensive study of place-names during the last fifty years has produced a surprising number of examples which show women in possession of land, or anticipating the position held in later times by the lady of a manor. The relationship between the ordinary inhabitants of a village and the woman from whom its name is derived can never be defined, and probably varied widely between one place and another. Nothing definite can be said about the rights which Wulfrun enjoyed over her *heah tun* of Wolverhampton or the Anglo-Danish lady, Tola, over the Dorset village known from her name as Tolpuddle. What names of this kind place beyond dispute is the position of local predominance which Anglo-Saxon custom allowed to individual women in the Anglo-Saxon state[1].

An interest of another kind belongs to the far more numerous names which associate women with the common features of the countryside—woods and clearings, springs and brooks. Their general meaning is clear enough. The original Goodwood must have been a piece of woodland belonging to a woman called Godgifu. Taken one at a time these names prove little beyond the bare fact that a particular woman at one time possessed a particular piece of property. But when a large collection of them has been brought together it gives an overwhelming impression of the important place which women must have held in Old English rural life. The commonest names of this type are those which end in the element 'ley', the modern form of the Anglo-Saxon word *leah*, a clearing. Many of these clearings belonged to men and were called after them, but a remarkable number bear the names of women. Audley and Balterley in Staffordshire, Aveley in Essex, Kimberley in Norfolk, Habberley and Wilderley in Shropshire were originally the clearings belonging to women named Ealdgyth, Bealdthryth, Ælfgyth, Cyneburg, Heathuburg, and Wilthryth. The list has been made at random, and if account were taken of field names, it could be extended almost indefinitely. The reduction of woodland to cultivation was perhaps the most important of all the processes which converted the Britain of the Saxon settlements into the England of Edward the Confessor. In this work, so far as can be seen, women took part on equal terms with men.

By the end of the sixth century, the English peoples were sufficiently established in Britain for the Pope to organize a mission for their conversion. Augustine and his companions landed in Kent in 597. Before Augustine died, King Æthelbert had caused the laws of his people to be written out in the English language. It was afterwards said that he was following the example of the Romans in thus writing down his laws, which certainly give the impression of a carefully thought out code. The Kentish people were still very primitive in their ways of life. Their Christianity was new, and had hardly affected their ancient customs and

---

[1] See F. M. Stenton, 'The Place of Women in Anglo-Saxon Society', *Transactions of the Royal Historical Society*, 4th series, vol. xxv, 1943, pp. 1–13.

outlook. Their society was extremely complicated, but if the slaves are left out of the reckoning, the differences between one class and another were insignificant in comparison with the fundamental distinction between men noble by birth or through service to the king and peasants cultivating their ancestral family-lands. A century later it was easy to tell from the speech and bearing of a man whether he were of noble or of peasant birth[1]. The difference must have been as clearly marked in the days of King Æthelbert. But gentle or simple, all the king's free subjects were countrymen living simply on the produce of their estates or farms.

There is more proportionately about women and their place in society in the laws of Æthelbert than in those of any other Anglo-Saxon king[2]. Their virtue was protected by an elaborate scale of penalties. 'If a man lies with a maiden belonging to the king he shall pay 50 shillings compensation. If she is a grinding slave he shall pay 25 shillings; if she is of the third class 12 shillings. . . . If a man lies with a nobleman's serving maid, he shall pay 12 shillings compensation. . . . If a man lies with the serving maid of a ceorl', that is a free farmer, 'he shall pay 6 shillings; if with a slave of the second class, 50 sceattas; of the third class, 30 sceattas'[3]. The 'sceatta' was roughly equivalent to the later silver penny. In each of these cases, the money went, not to the woman, but to the person— king, nobleman, or 'ceorl'—whose protection had been flouted. The same principle governs two laws relating to free women. The first provides that the ravisher of 'a free woman with long hair' shall pay to her guardian 30 shillings as compensation[4]. The wording of this law shows that the woman in the case was understood to have been a consenting party. The second law simply states that injury, of whatever kind, to a free maiden must be paid for at the same rate as injury to a free man[5]. The king at this point is looking back to a long and detailed list of injuries for which compensation has already been provided in the laws, and is making this tariff generally applicable to women as well as men.

Æthelbert's laws make an honest, though not in all respects a success- ful attempt to define the law governing the relations between husband

---

[1] Bede, *Historia Ecclesiastica*, lib. iv, cap. xx.
[2] They can be studied most conveniently in *The Laws of the Earliest English Kings*, edited and translated by F. L. Attenborough, Cambridge, 1922. Many of the laws can be read in translation in *English Historical Documents*, vol. i, ed. Dorothy Whitelock, London, 1955.
[3] Laws of Æthelbert, 10, 11, 14.   [4] *Ibid.*, 73.   [5] *Ibid.*, 74.

and wife. In trying to find the exact meaning of these laws it must always be remembered that the men who wrote them down were unpractised in the art of expressing their meaning in written words. To set out the rules which governed such a complex social relationship as marriage was never easy. Some of the laws seem to suggest that a wife was regarded as a man's most valuable piece of property. She must be purchased. 'If a man buys a maiden the bargain shall stand, if there is no dishonesty. If there is dishonesty, she shall be taken back to her home, and the money is to be returned'[1]. Again, 'if a man forcibly carries off a maiden, he shall pay 50 shillings to her owner and afterwards buy from the owner his consent. If she is betrothed at a price to another man, 20 shillings shall be paid in compensation'[2]. This attitude is most clearly expressed in the law which declares that 'if a free man lies with the wife of another free man he shall pay the husband his "wergild", and buy a second wife with his own money, and bring her to the other man's home'[3]. The wergild was the price a man's kin could exact from his slayer, and the amount was dictated by the dead man's place in the social scale. It was both convenient and usual for a serious offence to be atoned for by payment of the sum at which the offender's own life was valued. There is something much older than Christianity in this law—which would make the adulterer buy with his own money a new wife for the man he has betrayed— something of which Christianity could not approve, but to which it must for the moment submit.

The ancient Germanic feeling that a marriage was a bargain which, like any other bargain, could be broken by the mutual consent of the contracting parties and might well be broken by one alone is expressed clearly in Æthelbert's laws. 'If a wife wishes to depart with her children, she shall have half the goods. If the husband wishes to keep the children, she shall have a share of the goods equal to a child's'[4]. So far the meaning seems plain. The next law is particularly interesting because it touches a question which was still vexing lawyers in the heart of the Middle Ages: 'If she does not bear a child, the father's relatives shall have her goods, and the morning gift'[5]. The 'morning gift' was the present given by the husband to his wife in the morning after their marriage night. It was reported in a famous law-suit of about 900 that a lady had sold land in Wessex stating that it was fully in her power to do so, 'because it was her

[1] Laws of Æthelbert, 77.   [2] Ibid., 82 and 83.
[3] Ibid., 31.   [4] Ibid., 79 and 80.   [5] Ibid., 81.

morning gift'[1]. If a woman's power in regard to land which had been given her on the morning after her marriage was so complete as this, it is not unnatural that the land should pass to her relatives if both she and her husband died without heirs.

A remarkable group of these cryptic laws relates to the position of widows. One of them runs: 'If a woman bears a living child she shall have half the goods left by her husband if he dies first'[2]. Another law attempts a classification of widows, and sets out the sums due for violating the right of protecting her dependants enjoyed by a widow of noble birth, and by widows said to be of the second, the third, and the fourth class[3]. Yet another law regulates the compensation due from a man who 'takes a widow who does not belong to him' to the man who is her lawful guardian[4]. The importance, and, too often, the exact meaning of laws like these are disguised by their laconic wording, and by the frequent use of archaic phrases which are never found again. But they show that at the turn of the sixth and seventh centuries there existed in Kent a large body of law defining the position of women in society, protecting them from violence, and safeguarding their honour.

Other codes of law were issued while Kent was still an independent kingdom. The laws of the joint kings, Hlothhere and Eadric, belong to the winter of 684–5. In the eighty years which had passed since Æthelbert's laws were written down considerably greater ease of expression has been achieved. The intention in the mind of the legislator is brought out much more clearly by the longer sentences of these later laws. In only one law are women concerned, but it is an important one. 'If a man dies leaving a wife and a child, it is right that the child should accompany its mother; and one of the father's relatives who is willing to act shall be given him as his guardian to take care of his property until he is ten years old'[5]. Here there is nothing primitive, except the conception that maturity was reached at the age of ten. The law suggests a singularly humane and civilized outlook; the child's need of his mother is recognized and the woman's need of protection in looking after the child's land.

There is nothing specifically Christian in the attitude to women revealed in the first two codes of English laws. Augustine himself cannot have

---

[1] *Select English Historical Documents*, ed. F. E. Harmer, Cambridge, 1914, pp. 31 and 61. See also below, p. 22, for a widow granting her morning gift to Christ Church, Canterbury.   [2] Æthelbert, 78.   [3] *Ibid.*, 75.   [4] *Ibid.*, 76.
[5] Hlothhere and Eadric, 6.

regarded some of Æthelbert's rules about marriage with favour. But a partially converted people cannot have been expected to change their ancestral attitude to this fundamental matter in a moment. Marriage as a bond which could be broken only by death was an alien conception to the Germanic peoples. Nor had they any rigid rules against the marriage of near kinsfolk. The harsh conditions of life, the possibility that one or the other partner might be carried off by raiders into slavery, even into another country, made men regard the marriage contract as one which could be broken when need arose. One of the many problems with which the Greek scholar Theodore had to deal when he came to England as Archbishop of Canterbury in 669 was the reconciliation of native English and of Christian views of marriage. In his first general council of the English Church he forbade incest, the abandonment of wives for any other reason than adultery, and the remarriage of offenders. But he found it impossible to impose any rigorous code of marriage law on the half-converted English of his day. He allowed remarriage after one year to a woman if her husband was condemned to penal slavery, and after five years to a man whose wife, 'despising him', had left him. He allowed remarriage after five years to a husband or wife whose partner had been carried off into hopeless captivity. It is uncertain what he thought about the situation which would arise if the captive returned. Neither was he definite on the question whether the man or woman whose partner had entered religion might marry again. This was a burning question in the highest ranks of society, where many women felt a strong call to the religious life. In 672 Æthelthryth, wife of King Ecgfrith of Northumbria, with the encouragement of high ecclesiastics, secured from her most reluctant husband permission to lead the life of a nun. She was still living when her husband married again[1].

Archbishop Theodore died in 690 and the men who succeeded him as leaders of the Church in England were less tolerant of lingering heathen marriage customs. In 695 the third code of Kentish laws was issued by King Wihtred. They relate almost exclusively to ecclesiastical matters. No less than four of them refer to unlawful marriages. Men are to abandon them and repent. Foreigners who will not do this 'shall depart from the land with their possessions and their sins'[2]. Natives of the land who are recalcitrant are to be excluded from the communion of the Church

---

[1] See Dr. Plummer's note in his edition of Bede's *Historia Ecclesiastica*, vol. ii, p. 236.
[2] Wihtred, 4.

without being subject to the forfeiture of their goods. Penalties were set for nobles and peasants who should in future enter into such unions. A priest who consents to such a union, neglects to baptize the sick, or is so drunk that he cannot discharge this duty is to abstain from his ministrations, pending the bishop's decision. No definition of an unlawful union is given in the laws. That was a matter for the Church. Nor do the laws set any penalty on the woman. In one only of Wihtred's laws is a woman directly mentioned. When appointing a penalty for a married man who has been sacrificing to devils, it exempts his wife from a similar penalty if she knew nothing of his crime[1]. The wife is not felt to be so much in her husband's power that her guilt can be assumed from his.

The first laws issued by a West Saxon king come from the reign of Ine and were issued at about the same time as those of Wihtred of Kent. Ine's code is a long one. It contains seventy-six laws, many of them with several dependent clauses, but women receive little attention. The laws of Ine contain the same assumption as the Kentish laws, that a wife is generally purchased. This is clearly shown in the law which provides that if a man buys a wife and the marriage does not take place the bride's guardian shall return the bridal price and as much again and give appropriate compensation to the man who has given his personal security that the marriage will take place[2]. As in Kent the fatherless infant was left in his mother's care: 'If a husband has a child by his wife and dies, the mother shall have her child and bring it up, and every year 6 shillings shall be given for its maintenance—a cow in summer and an ox in winter; the relatives shall keep the family home until the child reaches maturity'[3]. A man who 'steals without the knowledge of his wife and children shall pay a fine of 60 shillings, but if he steals with the knowledge of all his household, they shall all go into slavery'[4]. 'If a husband steals a beast and carries it into his house and it is seized therein, he shall forfeit his share of the chattels, his wife only being exempt, since she must obey her lord. If she dare declare with an oath that she has not tasted the stolen meat, she shall retain her third share of the chattels'[5]. Here is the first occasion when the wife's duty to obey her husband as her lord is openly and firmly enunciated in English law. It is not fanciful to see in this statement the first indication that the Pauline view of the relationship between husband and wife is beginning to affect the conceptions on which society rested.

Christianity was an eastern religion and the subjection of the woman

[1] Wihtred, 12.   [2] Ine, 31.   [3] Ibid., 38.   [4] Ibid., 7.   [5] Ibid., 57.

to the man was preached with conviction by its most important early convert, St. Paul. To him women were temptation. 'He that is unmarried careth for the things that belong to the Lord, how he may please the Lord: but he that is married careth for the things that are of the world, how he may please his wife'. To St. Paul marriage was the means of preventing sin. 'Nevertheless, to avoid fornication, let every husband have his own wife, and let every wife have her own husband'. 'It is better to marry than to burn'. To St. Paul the woman was without question subject to her husband and every woman must live in subjection. 'The head of every man is Christ; and the head of the woman is the man; and the head of Christ is God'. 'Let your women keep silent in the churches for it is not permitted to them to speak; but they are commanded to be under obedience, as also says the law. And if they will learn anything, let them ask their husbands at home: for it is a shame for women to speak in the church'. 'Let women learn in silence with all subjection. But I suffer not a woman to teach, nor to usurp authority over the man, but to be in silence'. 'Wives submit yourselves unto your own husbands, as it is fit in the Lord'. To St. Paul the marriage bond was indissoluble. 'And unto the married I command, yet not I, but the Lord, let not the wife depart from her husband: but, and if she depart, let her remain unmarried, or be reconciled to her husband: and let not the husband put away his wife'. Such teaching was alien to the traditions of the primitive society of the Anglo-Saxon world.

The Pauline conception of the place of women in society was fortunately slow to impress itself on the minds of English men and women. Anglo-Saxon women were for a time undoubted gainers by the conversion. Christianity opened to the English people new worlds of the mind as well as of faith. Many of the men who preached the Christian faith were eminent scholars. The establishment of schools was part of their duty, for men must be trained for the service of the Church. Archbishop Theodore is the last known pupil of the schools of Athens. He brought to England a living tradition of Greek learning. Hadrian, his companion, was a learned monk from the schools of North Africa. Some fragments of ancient learning had been preserved in the Irish Church when Britain fell to the Saxon invaders, and were brought to England by Irish missionaries. That many women came to share in this new learning is proved by the writings which some of them have left to the present day, and by the traditions which have been preserved of others. Learning in this age could only be pursued in communities united by a religious purpose. By the middle of the seventh century women had begun to take vows of religion, and within a generation, monasteries governed by women had become a characteristic feature of English religious life. So far as can now be seen, none of these houses was founded exclusively for women. The association of communities of men and women in a single monastery raised many problems of organization and discipline. It is a tribute to the efficiency with which they were faced that only one house of this kind—Coldingham beyond the Tweed—is known to have given grounds for scandal. The one principle observed everywhere in the government of these double monasteries was the subjection of both communities to the rule of an abbess. The authority thus allowed to a woman is a remarkable illustration of the respect in which women were held in Anglo-Saxon society, and it was unshaken by criticism aimed at it from the highest quarters. Archbishop Theodore declared that it was unseemly for men to rule women in religion, or women, men, but he added 'let us not destroy that which is the custom in this country'[1].

The most famous of these women was a Northumbrian lady of royal descent named Hild, the foundress and ruler of a large double monastery at Whitby. Few English women have ever exercised a more far-reaching influence on the world they knew. Her reputation brought her visitors from far and wide for advice and help. But it is the educational work carried out under her direction which sets her apart from other women of her rank and calling. In an age when the spread of Christianity in England was hindered by the fewness of priests, many of Hild's monks were brought to a degree of learning adequate to the priesthood. Bede, the greatest of Anglo-Saxon historians, states that he had known five bishops, each of whom had been educated at Whitby in her time[2]. No record of her personality has survived, but it is at least clear that she was sensible and sympathetic when Cædmon, a cowherd on her estate, suddenly found himself capable of composing sacred verse. It was with her encouragement that he became the first religious poet in the English language[3].

The organization of these double monasteries differed from one to another. In some, the nuns and monks seem to have had a common

---

[1] Haddan and Stubbs, *Councils*, vol. iii, p. 195.
[2] Bede, *Historia Ecclesiastica*, ed. Plummer, lib. iv, cap. xxi.
[3] *Ibid.*, lib. iv, cap. xxii.

church but in others each community was rigidly separate from the other. A description of Wimborne in Dorset under the Abbess Tette, sister of King Ine of Wessex, has been preserved in the life of the most famous daughter of that house, Leofgyth, or Leoba, Abbess of Tauberbischofsheim. From its beginnings the foundation at Wimborne had consisted of two monasteries, each surrounded by high stout walls, one monastery for men and the other for women. A woman was never allowed to enter the monastery of the men, nor a man that of the nuns, except only the priests, who entered the nuns' church to perform the office of mass, but left the church to return to their own house immediately the service was over. Once a nun had retired from the world into the nunnery she was never allowed to go out into it again save for a good reason with the abbess's advice. The abbess herself, when she needed to make arrangements or give orders about outside affairs, spoke through a window[1].

A story told in this life about a harsh prioress of Wimborne gives a sinister glimpse of life within the walls of the monastery. On account of her zeal for discipline this nun was often made prioress and frequently appointed dean. She maintained so rigid a discipline that she aroused the hatred of most of the nuns and particularly of the younger nuns. Even to the last hour of her life she never made any amends to them, but died as unyielding as she had lived. After she was buried a mound was raised in the accustomed manner above her grave. As soon as the young nuns saw the place where she was buried they cursed her cruelty, nay more, they leaped on to the mound and, trampling it as if it were the dead corpse, they reproached the dead woman with the most bitter insults to relieve their mortification. The Abbess Tette restrained them, but was shocked to see that the mound heaped over the grave had sunk to about half a foot below the top of the grave. She regarded this as a sign of God's judgment against the woman buried there. She called the nuns together and admonished them and implored them to join her in prayer for the dead woman. She enjoined on them a fast of three days. When the fast was over the abbess went into the church with the nuns and prayed for the dead nun. As she prayed the tomb gradually filled up with soil and when she ceased it was level with the top[2]. This must have been one of the stories of her youth that Leoba liked to tell in old age when she was an abbess in Germany.

Leoba came of a noble West Saxon family and from birth was dedicated

---

[1] *English Historical Documents*, vol. i, ed. Whitelock, p. 719.   [2] *Ibid.*, pp. 720–1.

to the religious life. She was educated not at Wimborne, as the author of her life says, but at Minster in Thanet, another double monastery, at that time ruled over by an abbess named Eadburg. At the time when Leoba was growing up the zeal of a people whose own conversion was scarcely beyond living memory was moving many Englishmen to work as missionaries among the heathen of Germany and the Low Countries. The most eminent of them was the West Saxon, Wynfrith, known in religion as Boniface. He was born shortly before 675 and began his work as a missionary in 716, when he was already one of the best-known churchmen in Wessex. In 722 the Pope consecrated him bishop to the Germans and ten years later he received the title and office of archbishop. Throughout his life Boniface kept in touch with his English friends and many of them followed him to Germany. Leoba wrote to Boniface soon after he became archbishop, describing herself as 'the lowest handmaid of those who bear the light yoke of Christ'. She reminded him of his former friendship with her father, Dynne, now eight years dead, and asked that he would pray for Dynne's soul. She also commended to his memory her mother, Æbbe, his kinswoman, who was still alive, but in poor health. Leoba herself, she reminded him, was her parents' only child, and she desired that she might have Boniface as her brother. She had 'taken care to send this little gift', not that it was worthy of his attention, but to remind him of her. She asked him to correct the 'rusticity' of her letter and sent him four lines of Latin verse. She has learned the art of verse, she says, from Eadburg, 'who unceasingly searches out the divine law'[1].

Boniface asked Tette, Abbess of Wimborne, to send Leoba to him in Germany and he made her abbess of a monastery which he had established at Tauberbischofsheim in Bavaria. Under her rule the house prospered. Women taught by her were sought as teachers by other houses in those parts and many of her pupils themselves became abbesses. Before Boniface set out on his last mission to Frisia in 754, a mission from which he did not expect to return, he sent for Leoba to come to him at Fulda, and asked her to stay in Germany to the end. He commended her to the bishop 'and the older monks who were present, admonishing them to care for her with honour and reverence, and affirming it to be his wish that after death her body should be laid next to his bones in the same grave, so that they might await together the day of resurrection who had in their

---

[1] *Letters of Boniface and Lull*, ed. M. Tangl, Berlin, 1916, pp. 52–3.

lives served Christ with like vow and zeal'[1]. Leoba lived until 780 and was buried near Boniface at Fulda.

There were other nuns among the 'very great multitude' of people who followed Boniface to Germany. It was an English nun named Hygeburg of the monastery at Heidenheim who wrote down the recollections of Willibald, Bishop of Eichstätt, the first Englishman known to have travelled in the Near East. Her work has been described as 'the earliest extant book of travel written by an English pen'[2]. It is also the first book written by an English woman. Willibald, a West Saxon and a kinsman of Boniface himself, made a pilgrimage to Rome in 720 and carried out from there a greater pilgrimage to Jerusalem and the Holy Land. His adventures, told in his old age to his fellow country-woman, give a unique picture of the relations between Christians and Moslems in the generation after the conquest of Syria by the Arabs.

Despite the dangers and difficulties of travel many English women desired to make the pilgrimage to Rome in the eighth century. In the course of a long letter to Boniface written between 719 and 722 the Abbess Eangyth, 'unworthy servant of the servants of God, undeservedly bearing the name of abbess', and Heaburg, called Bucge, her only daughter, lamented the difficulties in the way of their pilgrimage to Rome. Poverty pressed upon them and the king's hostility, because they were 'accused before him by those who envied' them. They were burdened also with 'the service of the king and queen, of the bishop and the reeve, and of great men and their companions'. They complained that they had no son nor brother, no father nor uncle. Eangyth had no kin save one sister and a mother, very old, and a brother's son, who was unhappy 'because our king holds his people in hatred'. For all these and similar causes their life was hard to live. They had sought long for a familiar friend and had found one in Boniface. 'And if God should give, as by his angel, . . . that we should come into those lands and make that pilgrimage to the place where thou dwellest, and if we could hear the living words from thy mouth, how sweet would thy eloquence be, my lord, beyond honey or the honeycomb in our mouths'. They go on to say how much they desire to visit Rome and there seek 'pardon for their sins as many have done and still do; and I especially', that is, Eangyth, 'who am bowed down with age and have committed many sins in my life. And of this my

[1] *English Historical Documents*, vol. i, p. 724.
[2] W. Levison, *England and the Continent in the Eighth Century*, Oxford, 1946, p. 43.

desire and plan, Wale, formerly my abbess and spiritual mother, knew, but my only daughter', that is, Bucge, 'is still young and has not yet found this desire'. Like Leoba, the writers were diffident about their Latin style, which they called 'rustic and uncultured'[1].

Bucge herself, in due course, became an abbess in Kent, and wrote to Boniface for advice about making the pilgrimage to Rome. In his reply, written before 738, he addressed her as 'most loved lady and sister, in the love of God to be preferred above all other women', and continued 'I do not presume myself either to forbid you to journey abroad or strongly urge it. But I will tell you how it strikes me. . . . If you cannot in any way find peace of mind at home because of worldly cares, you may perhaps find it on pilgrimage, as our sister Whitburg has done. She has written to tell me that she has found at St. Peter's threshold the peace that she long desired. But she advises me—for I wrote to her about you—that you should wait until Rome is free from the attacks of the Saracens, and until she, God willing, has invited you. And this seems best to me. Make ready the things you will need for your journey and wait to hear from her, and then do what the goodness of the Lord commands'[2]. In course of time Bucge visited Rome and there talked with Boniface himself. When she returned to her own monastery she bore messages from Boniface to the King of Kent, whom she summoned to speak with her there. Between 748 and 754 the king wrote to Boniface, sending him gifts and asking in return for two falcons of a sort which were very difficult to acquire in Kent[3].

Before the end of his work in Germany Boniface had come to doubt the wisdom of encouraging women to go on pilgrimage. In the course of a long letter to the Archbishop of Canterbury he asked him to forbid women to undertake pilgrimages, and further suggested that secular princes should also forbid the practice 'because for the greater part the pilgrims perish, few remaining unharmed'. There were, he said, very few cities on the road to Rome 'in which there is not an adulteress or harlot of the English race; which is a scandal and shame to your whole church'[4].

But no fears of pirates or of the manifold dangers of the way could prevent Englishmen and women from journeying to Rome. Two kings of Wessex, Cædwella (689) and Ine (725), had gone there to die, and more than a hundred years later Burgred of Mercia retired there with his wife,

---

[1] *Letters of Boniface*, pp. 21–6.   [2] *Ibid.*, p. 48.
[3] *Ibid.*, pp. 229–31.   [4] *Ibid.*, p. 169.

driven from his country by the invasion of the heathen Danes. His widow died at Pavia some twenty years after their flight from Mercia. Frithugyth, the wife of King Ine's successor, went on pilgrimage to Rome with Bishop Forthhere of Sherborne in 737. Since they both witnessed a royal charter to the bishop himself in 739 it is clear that, like Bucge, they went and came in safety[1]. Several documents survive showing individuals making arrangements for their pilgrimage. The women who wrote of it to Boniface were members of noble West Saxon families. Like Frithugyth herself, they would not have made the journey without adequate escort and a sufficiency of money to pay the cost of travel and food.

Early in the ninth century a Kentish nobleman, Æthelnoth, with Gænburg his wife, made a joint will before the Archbishop of Canterbury, his priest, and a representative of the king. They recorded that whichever of them should live the longer should have the estate at Eythorne, Kent, and that if they had a child, the child should succeed to it, but that otherwise the land should go to the archbishop, who should pay for it, distributing its value for the good of the testators' souls. They added that if one or both of them should 'wish to go south', that is, should go on pilgrimage to Rome, the archbishop should buy the land[2]. This Kentish nobleman clearly saw nothing incongruous in the possibility that he or his wife might wish to go on pilgrimage separately. That women could make their own arrangements for financing a pilgrimage is shown by a ninth-century charter recording that a widow named Werthryth had sold for this purpose an estate which had come to her under her husband's will[3].

Up to the end of the Anglo-Saxon period women as well as men were setting out on pilgrimage. An East Anglian nobleman named Ketel made his will between 1052 and 1066. His wife, Sæflæd, was dead and he was about to set out to Rome with his stepdaughter, Ælfgifu. They had made an agreement about the land they both owned at Onehouse, Suffolk; 'whichever of us shall live the longer, is to have as much land as the two of us have there. And if death befall us both on the way to Rome, the estate is to go to Bury St. Edmunds for me, for Sæflæd and for Ælfgifu, but all the men are to be free'[4]. The last surviving Anglo-Saxon will was ✓

---

[1] *Crawford Charters*, ed. A. S. Napier and W. H. Stevenson, No. 1, pp. 1-3. The editors accepted the date 739 and regarded the charter as genuine, note, pp. 37 ff.

[2] *Anglo-Saxon Charters*, ed. A. J. Robertson, Cambridge, 1939, pp. 4-7.

[3] Birch, *Cartularium Saxonicum*, vol. ii, no. 537, p. 155.

[4] *Anglo-Saxon Wills*, ed. Dorothy Whitelock, Cambridge, 1930, pp. 90 and 91.

made by a Lincolnshire nobleman and his wife, Ulf and Madselin, after the battle of Hastings had been fought. They made their will at the moment of their departure for Jerusalem. It is possible that they were moved to go so far by conditions in their conquered land. The phrase 'if I do not come home', which occurs twice in this short will, shows that Ulf and Madselin had no illusions about the perils which faced them[1].

The dangers of pilgrimage were the less intimidating in that life in England itself was never safe for long together. In reading the singularly humane writings of Bede and the letters of the highly articulate men and women which passed between England and Germany in the eighth century, it is hard to believe that the writers are separated from us by more than twelve hundred years. In the ninth century their civilization was on the defensive against the heathen which surrounded Europe on the north, east, and south. If it had not been for King Alfred it would have been destroyed altogether in England before the attacks of the Danish invaders. His defence of Wessex and his determination to provide books for his people and see that they could read them saved something on which future generations could build again. The demoralization which resulted from the presence of a heathen army in England for years on end forms the background of a letter of 878 from the Pope to the Archbishop of Canterbury. 'Touching those whom you affirm to leave their own wives against the command of the Lord, we enjoin that no man leave his wife or wife her husband, except for the cause of fornication. If anyone separates for this cause, he or she is to remain unmarried or they are to be mutually reconciled; since, as our Lord says, "what God hath joined let not man put asunder". If a man does this and is not ready to make amends by due penance, let him remain separated from the fellowship of the Church. Neither are you to permit anyone to marry within his own kindred'[2]. Such injunctions were not readily observed.

A similar hint of demoralization appears in the laws of King Alfred which penalize the abduction of nuns and the raping of girls under age. An attack on the chastity of a nun was punished by the exaction of twice the amount of money due for a similar attack on a lay woman[3]. Alfred declared that if a man took a nun from a monastery without the permission of the king and the bishop he should pay 120 shillings, half to the king and half to the bishop and the lord of the church to which the nun

[1] *Anglo-Saxon Wills*, pp. 94–7.
[2] *English Historical Documents*, vol. i, p. 812.   [3] Alfred, no. 18.

belonged. If the escaped nun outlived her abductor the king refused to allow her to inherit anything of his property, nor should their children inherit. If any of their children were slain the 'wergild' due to the mother's kin should go to the king, but the father's kin should be paid the share due to them[1]. It may fairly be taken as a sign of King Alfred's care for youth that a man who raped a girl under age should henceforward pay the same amount of money as he would have paid for a similar offence had she been of full age[2].

Throughout the Old English period the laws show that it was the king's duty to protect the widow and the fatherless. There was, indeed, general commiseration with their sad lot. Under King Athelstan (924–39) the men of London exempted 'poor widows, who have no land and no one to work for them' from a yearly tax of four pence that was being levied for the common purposes of the city and its neighbourhood[3]. The royal attitude was clearly expressed by King Æthelred II (979–1016), who declared that 'all widows who lead a respectable life shall enjoy the special protection of God and the king. And each of them shall remain without a husband for a year, after which she may decide as she herself pleases'[4]. The laws imply that the widow, even though she might need protection, was free to make her own decisions as to her future life.

In contrast to these passages which stress the widow's need of protection, there may be set a narrative which shows a widow defying the law and all the power of the state. A Kentish gentleman named Wulfbold had for many years kept possession of an estate which did not belong to him, in spite of a peremptory summons from the king to surrender it, four times repeated. At last the king in council passed a sentence of forfeiture upon him, but he disregarded it, and died in possession of the property, leaving his whole estate to his widow. After this, a cousin of Wulfbold took possession of one of the properties which he had been holding, whereupon Wulfbold's widow with her child 'went there and killed him and his fifteen companions'. The story ended in 996 with a renewed sentence of forfeiture, and a grant of all the property to the king's mother[5]. The name of Wulfbold's widow is never mentioned in the story.

From a time which by then was immemorial kings had been co-oper-

[1] Alfred, no. 8.   [2] Ibid., no. 29.
[3] VI Athelstan, 2. Attenborough, pp. 158, 159.
[4] The Laws of the Kings of England from Edmund to Henry I, edited and translated by A. J. Robertson, Cambridge, 1925, pp. 84, 85, V Æthelred, 21.
[5] Anglo-Saxon Charters, pp. 128–31.

ating with the Church in developing a law of marriage which should be consonant with Christian principles. In seventh-century Kent King Wihtred had imposed ecclesiastical penalties on those guilty of unlawful unions, although he had ruled that the goods of the guilty should not be confiscated[1]. The so-called laws of Edward and Guthrum, which can now be attributed to Æthelred II, declare that 'in the case of incestuous unions the king shall take possession of the male offender and the bishop of the female offender, unless they make compensation before God and the world, as the bishop shall prescribe according to the gravity of the offence. If two brothers or two near relatives lie with one woman, they shall pay as compensation, with all promptness, whatever sum may be approved... according to the gravity of the offence'[2]. Elsewhere, Æthelred more than once admonishes 'all Christian men carefully' to 'avoid unlawful unions and duly observe the law of the Church'[3]. Legislation in this sense was by no means a dead letter. The village of Helperby, Yorkshire, is known to have been forfeited to the Archbishop of York by two brothers who had one wife[4].

When Cnut of Denmark had made himself king of both the Danish and English peoples in England (1016–35), he issued a great code of law covering the whole land. Whenever possible he based his laws on those of his English predecessors, but he dealt with many matters which they had not touched, and he carried further many subjects with which they had already dealt. He strengthened with heavy penalties the law by which Æthelred had forbidden widows to marry within a year after their husbands' death[5]. Even if the widow had been married by force she is to lose all her possessions, unless she will leave her second husband 'and return home and never afterwards be his'. No widow is to be too hastily consecrated as a nun[6]. The king had a financial interest in preventing the hasty remarriage of widows or their immediate withdrawal from the world, for at least in aristocratic circles the widow was responsible for the 'heriot' due to the king from her late husband's estate. In origin, the heriot was the equipment for war given by a lord to a retainer and returnable to the lord on the retainer's death. Its military origin was still apparent in the eleventh century. The heriot of an earl, for

[1] Above, pp. 10–11.   [2] Attenborough, pp. 104, 105.
[3] V Æthelred, 10. Robertson, pp. 82, 83, and VI Æthelred, 11. Ibid., pp. 94, 95.
[4] Birch, Cart. Saxon, vol. iii, p. 578.
[5] V Æthelred, 21, 1, Robertson, pp. 84, 85.
[6] II Cnut, 73 and 73a, Robertson, pp. 210–13.

example, was eight horses, four saddled and four unsaddled, four helmets, four coats of mail, eight spears and eight shields, four swords, and two hundred gold coins[1]. But it was already beginning to take on the character of a death-duty upon the property of men with no particular responsibilities in war. Among the peasantry it survived the Middle Ages themselves, to become one of the incidents of copyhold tenure[2]. Before the Norman Conquest it was graduated in accordance with the dead man's rank, but it was everywhere a heavy charge on the property which he had left. In emphasizing the widow's responsibility for the payment, Cnut allows her to meet it at any time within twelve months, 'if it has not been convenient for her to pay earlier'[3].

The king's acceptance of a heriot was a visible sign that the dead man had ended his life in the king's full peace and favour. A remarkable document written shortly before 999 shows a widow proffering her husband's heriot to the king in order that his name might be cleared from a charge of treason. An Essex gentleman named Æthelric of Bocking had died under suspicion of plotting to receive King Swein of Denmark into England some years before. In his will, Æthelric had set out the heriot—sixty gold coins, a sword with its belt, two horses, two round shields, and two spears—which should pass at his death to King Æthelred. He also left estates to the cathedral monastery of Canterbury and to other churches. When he was dead, his widow—whose name is never given—brought his heriot to King Æthelred, who was then holding a great council at Cookham in Berkshire, but before accepting it, the king reopened before the council the charge under which Æthelric had lain. At last, persuaded by the Archbishop of Canterbury who acted as the widow's advocate, and by a prominent nobleman, the king allowed her to grant her own morning gift to the church of Canterbury 'for the sake of the king and all the people', and then withdrew the charge of treason against her husband, so that his will might stand. The document was written while the council was in session. To a modern reader, its interest does not lie in the estates which were its chief concern, but in its picture of a widow defending

---

[1] II Cnut, 71a, Robertson, pp. 208, 209.

[2] See below, p. 88. An example of the heriot paid by a woman customary tenant in the manor of Sonning, Berkshire, in the seventeenth century can be given: At the court held on 20 April 1621, the jurors reported the death of 'Margaret Palmer, widow, a customary tenant by copy of court roll of one messuage and one virgate of land called Hatch house ... whence there falls due as heriot, one cow worth 23s. and 4d.' Court Rolls of the manor of Sonning, in private hands. [3] II Cnut, 73a, 4. Robertson, pp. 212, 213.

her husband's reputation before an assembly drawn, as the document itself records, 'from far and wide, from West Saxons and Mercians, Danes and Englishmen'[1].

The greatest of all authorities on the Anglo-Saxon laws has described Cnut as 'setting himself on the side of the oppressed; strangers, men without kindred, the unfree, and women'[2]. The most striking illustration of his attitude to women is the law which reads: 'No woman or maiden shall ever be forced to marry a man whom she dislikes, nor shall she ever be given for money, unless the suitor wishes to give something of his own free will'[3]. For the first time, the law denies the right of anyone to sell a woman. Cnut is also careful to define the legal position of a woman whose husband has been proved guilty of theft. The wife shall be clear of guilt unless the stolen goods had been put under her lock and key. 'But', the law continues, 'it is her duty to guard the keys of the following:—her storeroom and her chest and her cupboard. If the goods have been put in any of these, she shall be held guilty'[4]. Cnut points out that a wife cannot forbid her husband to bring anything into his cottage. But there is no unqualified assertion such as Ine had made three hundred years before that a woman must obey her husband as her lord.

The record of a marriage settlement from the earliest years of Cnut's reign shows the kind of arrangement that could be made for this purpose between two families of high rank. 'Here in this document', it runs, 'is declared the agreement which Godwine made with Brihtric when he wooed his daughter. In the first place, he gave her a pound's weight of gold to induce her to accept his suit, and he granted her the estate at Street and whatever belongs to it, and a hundred and fifty acres at Burmarsh and also thirty oxen and twenty cows and ten horses and ten slaves'. The agreement was made at Kingston in Surrey before King Cnut, and attested by the Archbishop of Canterbury and the Abbot of St. Augustine's with the monastic communities of which they were the heads, and by the sheriff and a number of other Kentish gentlemen whose names are recorded in the deed. 'And when the maiden was brought from Brightling' eleven men whose names are given came forward as security for the agreement. The terms of the settlement were written out three times, and a copy was laid up in each of the two great churches at

[1] *Anglo-Saxon Wills*, pp. 42–7.
[2] F. Liebermann, *Die Gesetze der Angelsachsen*, vol. iii, p. 197.
[3] II Cnut, 74.   [4] II Cnut, 76.

Canterbury. Brihtric, the maiden's father, had the third copy[1]. The essential fact at the heart of all this formality is the financial independence assured to the bride by the bridegroom before the marriage ceremony had taken place.

This settlement is one among many personal records written in Old English—deeds, reports of law-suits, and wills—which illustrate the position of women in society. The most important, though by no means the earliest of them, is the will of King Alfred. In a long document, written as though the king himself were speaking, he set out his intentions in regard to the vast estate in land which was at his own disposal. He named the properties which should go to each of his sons and daughters, his other kinsmen and his wife. He desired those to whom he was bequeathing land not to leave it away from his own family on their death unless they themselves had children. In that case, he expressed a preference for the land to pass to a male child 'so long as there be any capable of holding it'. 'My grandfather', he said, 'bequeathed his land to the spear-side, not to the spindle-side. If therefore I have given to any woman what my grandfather acquired, and my kinsmen wish to have it while the woman lives, they are to buy it back from her. My kinsmen must pay for such land because they are taking other property of mine which I may give to the female line or the male line as I will'[2]. It was King Alfred's grandfather, King Egbert, who set Wessex on the way towards supremacy in England. It seems probable that Egbert, wishing to secure the domin-ance of his own line among the noble families of Wessex, sought to consolidate the lands of the house in the male side. The extreme care with which King Alfred tried to bring his own bequests into conformity with his grandfather's wishes suggests that King Egbert had at this point been departing from traditional West Saxon practice.

More than fifty wills written in English have survived from this last period of the Anglo-Saxon state. These documents are not wills in the modern sense. They are rather post-obit gifts made with the consent of the king. Only the very greatest families were allowed to dispose of their land in this way, and each will is the result of a special concession on the king's part. Dr. Dorothy Whitelock has printed thirty-nine of these wills in one volume with translations and notes to each document[3]. Of these

[1] *Anglo-Saxon Charters*, pp. 150-1.
[2] *Select English Historical Documents*, ed. F. E. Harmer, no. xi.
[3] *Anglo-Saxon Wills*, Cambridge, 1930.

no less than ten are made by women and three more of them are made jointly by a man and his wife. In none of these wills is there any indication that the testator has any preference for land to go to the male rather than the female line. Nor is there any hint that in leaving land to a woman the testator is leaving it to a religious house of which the woman named is the head. Land is bequeathed to a woman as though it were the most natural thing in the world to leave it in that way. The bequests to women are not subject to the failure of male heirs. The impression these wills give is that men and women were equally concerned to provide for all their children without regard to sex. Many of these wills have survived because some church was made the residuary legatee and therefore had an interest in preserving a copy of the will. There must have been many similar dispositions of which no evidence has survived.

A widow of noble birth named Wynflæd made her will about 950. She owned many estates in Wessex, in Berkshire, Wiltshire, Hampshire and Dorset. She left the better of her offering cloths and her cross to the church, and two silver cups to the community for use in the refectory, but it is not clear which church. She had a nun's vestments, but she had other clothes, caps, gowns, a bracelet, a brooch, and headbands. It is possible that after her husband's death she had taken a vow of chastity and lived in close association with a religious community. She still held her lands and could dispose of them at her will. Some estates she left unconditionally to her daughter Æthelflæd: others to her son Eadmer. An estate at Faccombe, Hampshire, which was her morning gift, she left to her son Eadmer for his life. If his sister, Æthelflæd, outlived him it was to go to her for her life and afterwards to Eadwold, Eadmer's son. Wynflæd requested her son to relinquish either the estate at Coleshill or that at Adderbury to his son Eadwold as soon as he was old enough to hold land. Both estates were to go to Eadwold after Eadmer's death. Her engraved bracelet and brooch Wynflæd left to Æthelflæd. Eadmer had a daughter Eadgifu, as well as a son. No estates in their entirety were left to her, but Wynflæd left her two skilled slaves, a woman weaver and a seamstress. She left her the stock and bondmen on two estates and certain household goods. Eadgifu also was to share all the broken horses with her brother Eadwold. Other people appear in the will as recipients of bequests, but whether they were of Wynflæd's family is uncertain. Wynflæd arranged for many people, mostly women who are mentioned by name, to be set free after her death and she expressed the hope that for her soul's sake her children would free any other people of hers who had fallen into slavery as a punishment for crime. She left to Æthelflæd everything which was not specifically bequeathed, 'books and such small things', and she hoped that Æthelflæd would be mindful of her soul[1].

At some time between 984 and 1016 a lady named Wulfwaru made her will leaving certain goods 'to St. Peter's monastery at Bath for my poor soul and for the souls of my ancestors from whom my property and my possessions came to me'. Nothing is known, apart from the will, of Wulfwaru or of her two sons, Wulfmer and Ælfwine, or of her two daughters, Goda and Ælfwaru. To her elder son she left two estates 'with meat and with men and all tilth'. She divided another estate equally between her elder son and her younger daughter: 'and they are to share the principal residence between them as evenly as they can, so that each of them shall have a just portion of it'. To her younger son she left three estates and to her elder daughter one estate; all were left 'with meat and with men and all tilth'. She divided her goods—gold, brooches, cups, tapestry, women's attire, and bedclothes—between her children, indicating what each was to have. To her four menservants she left a band of twenty mancuses of gold and to her household women, in common, 'a good chest well decorated'. This will is well drafted and gives the impression that the woman who made it was eminently fair and just. If she left less land to her daughters than to her sons, it was probably because their husbands had land of their own[2]. A woman who inherited land seems to have been free to leave it among her children as she wished and in accordance with their need.

It was not even incumbent upon a woman to leave any of her land to her sons. One of the most revealing documents which has survived from Cnut's reign is the account of a lawsuit in the shire court of Hereford. The bishop and the earl were present and several of the greatest men in the kingdom at that time, Thurkil the White, who was concerned in the case, and Tovi the Proud, who had come there on the king's business. The sheriff and all the thegns—that is, all the men of position—in Herefordshire were also present. A certain Edwin came and sued his own mother for land, namely Wellington and Cradley. The bishop asked whose business it was to reply for his mother, and Thurkil the White spoke up and said that it was his business, if he knew her case. Since he did not know the case, three thegns were instructed to ride from the meeting to

---

[1] *Anglo-Saxon Wills*, pp. 10–15.   [2] *Ibid.*, pp. 62–5.

the place where the lady was and ask her what claim she had to the lands for which her son was suing her. 'Then she said that she had no land that in any way belonged to him, and she was very angry with her son, and she called before her Leofflæd, Thurkil's wife, her kinswoman, and before the three thegns, said "Here sits Leofflæd my kinswoman, to whom, after my death, I give both my land and my gold, my robes and my raiment and all that I have". And she then said to the thegns: "Be thegns, and duly announce my message to the meeting before all the good men, and tell them to whom I have given my land and all that I have, and to my own son nothing; and ask them to be witnesses of this". And they did so; they rode to the meeting and told all the good men what she had laid upon them. Then Thurkil the White stood up in the meeting and asked all the thegns to give his wife the land, free and quit, which her kinswoman had granted her, and they did so. Then Thurkil rode to St. Æthelbert's minster at Hereford, with the consent and witness of all the people, and had it recorded in a gospel book'[1]. It is curious that this dominant lady remains anonymous.

Most of the wills and charters which have survived from the last age of the Anglo-Saxon state come from the English part of Anglo-Saxon England. The Scandinavian peoples who had settled in the further midlands and the north in King Alfred's time were heathen barbarians. Their descendants could only be absorbed by slow degrees into the Christian society of the land. The sagas which come from Iceland and the Scandanavian homeland indicate that the women of the Viking world could be as fierce and masterful as their men. For a long time there were Englishmen who spoke of the Danes in England as barbarous, and of their women as people of disgusting social habits. Even so, the critics imply that there were many in England who did not scorn to copy the filthy habits of the Danes. Little is known at first hand about the women of Danish England. Women of Danish name and undoubted Danish descent appear, though rarely, as ladies of villages in those parts. Raventhorpe in Lincolnshire takes its name from a woman named Ragnhildr, and Gunthorpe by the Trent, from a woman named Gunnhildr. It may be added that the most uncompromising assertion of a married woman's independence that has survived from Anglo-Saxon England comes from the East Riding of Yorkshire. In 1086, a Yorkshire jury recorded that a woman bearing the Danish name Asa 'had her land separate and free from the lordship and power of Bernulf her husband even while they lived together, so that he

[1] *Anglo-Saxon Charters*, pp. 150–3.

could make neither gift nor sale of it, nor could he forfeit it. Moreover, after their separation she withdrew with all her land, and possessed it as lady'.

Enough has been said to show that in Anglo-Saxon England men and women lived on terms of rough equality with each other. Inevitably for a period so remote from today, the evidence available to historians is incomplete and patchy. The women whose wills and letters have survived all belonged to noble families. But the women who had personal control of their store room, their box, and their cupboard were the wives of the free farmers of the countryside. The Anglo-Saxon way of life was broken by the Norman Conquest. William the Conqueror was concerned neither to destroy nor to protect ancient English habits of life. Nevertheless, feudal law enforced by a conqueror meant the end of many things in England, not least among them the independent status of the noble English lady.

CHAPTER II

Feudal Law and the Feudal Lady
1066–1660

Through the six hundred years that lie between the Norman Conquest and the Restoration of Charles II noble English ladies lived in a world governed by feudal law. As a conqueror William I could change ancient English practices of inheritance to suit the rules of law under which he and his followers had been born and bred. The rule of primogeniture aimed at preserving the integrity of an estate held of the king and thus enabling its holder to perform the service due from it to the crown. Daughters and younger sons were therefore dependent on their father's bounty. Their portions caused many family quarrels. When sons failed the inheritance was divided among the daughters. It was regarded as 'less than lawful and more than just' when the earldom of Gloucester was carried intact by one of three sisters to her husband, John, brother of Richard I[1]. The feudal world was essentially a masculine world. Its society was organized for war in which women were expected to take no part. In this lies the essential difference between the Anglo-Saxon and the Anglo-Norman outlook. Even in the eleventh century Englishmen preferred the arts of peace to those of war, whereas war had created the Norman state.

The large number of charters recording grants of land by women in the early feudal age might at first sight suggest that women still occupied in Anglo-Norman society much the place that they had held in Saxon days. It is, indeed, true that they could hold land in their own right. They could inherit it from their ancestors. They could sell it or give it in reward to their servants. They could give land to a religious house. They could plead and be impleaded for their land in the courts of law. Nevertheless, in a military society it was inevitable that those who could

[1] *Historia Rerum Anglicarum Willelmi parvi . . . de Newburgh*, ed. H. C. Hamilton, London, 1856, vol. ii, p. 8.

not fight should take a second place to those who fought. The superiority of men over women became part of the unchallengeable order of ideas. The influence of the Church, with its unquestioning acceptance of the Pauline view of women's place, made in the same direction. The great ladies of the Anglo-Norman world had no public duties. They were summoned neither to the army nor to the king's council. They could not be jurors[1] or judges. There seems to have been no legal basis for the idea of the perpetual guardianship of women[2], but the minor was in the guardianship of her father or lord and the wife in the guardianship of her husband. A woman generally passed from father or lord to husband long before she reached the age of twenty-one. Not until she became a widow was an heiress likely to be out of guardianship.

Again and again the legal records of the age use words or phrases implying the absolute subjection of the wife to her husband. She was 'under the rod' or 'under the power' of her husband. She 'could not gainsay' her husband even when he was selling land which she had inherited from her father. She could not plead in court without her husband. She could make no will without her husband's consent. 'It is adjudged', said the justices who were hearing pleas at Northampton in 1202, 'that since the wife in her husband's lifetime has nothing of her own nor can she make any purchase with her own money, let Peter and Maud have their seisin of that land which Gerard, whose heir Maud is, bought with his own money'. The jurors had been so rash, or so foolish, as to say that they did not know whether Gerard bought the land at stake 'with his own money or the money of his wife'[3].

It is true that occasionally the wife's subordination to her husband could turn to her advantage. The great lawyer, Henry of Bracton, who wrote an account of the practice of the royal courts of justice in the middle of the thirteenth century, was interested in a case he found in a roll compiled in 1226. A Yorkshire man and his wife had brought an action to recover land in their lord's court. The first writ they brought seems to have been genuine, but another was needed and they forged it. When this writ was brought into court it was at once apparent that it had been forged, for the work was badly done. There was no particular reason for

---

[1] Save when a question of pregnancy was raised in court. Then a jury of matrons was appointed to examine the woman who claimed to be with child.

[2] F. Pollock and F. W. Maitland, *History of English Law*, 2nd ed., 1898, vol. ii, p. 437.

[3] *The Earliest Northamptonshire Assize Rolls*, ed. D. M. Stenton, Northamptonshire Record Society, vol. v, 1930, Case no. 450, p. 57.

forging the writ, except to save a journey to Westminster to get it. The writ was a common form writ, issued as a matter of course, but it had to be fetched by the litigant himself. His unwillingness to take the journey cost him his life, for he was hanged for forging the king's seal. 'But his wife was freed, whether cognizant of the crime or not', said Bracton, 'because she was under the rod of her husband'[1].

Nevertheless, although law and custom put the wife under her husband's power and gave her land, goods and money to him there are signs of an uneasy social conscience on this point. Many twelfth-century charters record the gift or sale of land which had come to the grantor by marriage. The purchaser of such land often gave the wife of the seller some personal gift, a ring or brooch, or a sum of money. The fact of the wife's consent to a sale of land is often noted in the charter. The buyer was less concerned with abstract justice than with the possibility that his bargain might be questioned when the seller himself had died. It is significant that the judges, who at the end of the twelfth century were fashioning the common law, had given some thought to the position of the wife whose husband wished to sell her land. If a husband made a final concord before the king's judges by which any of his wife's land passed to another person she was examined separately as to whether she agreed to the terms and her name was included with her husband's in the record of the transaction. The judges also made it possible for a woman in her widowhood to bring an action against the buyer and recover the land. She had to say that it was sold by her husband 'whom in his lifetime she could not gainsay'. King John was even ready to allow a married woman to plead on her own behalf because she satisfied him that her husband, in collusion with the plaintiff, intended to lose her land by default. The clerk who recorded the case said that the king was 'moved by pity'. It was not until 1285 that a woman was given statutory right to intervene in a plea when her husband deliberately defaulted so that she was in danger of losing her inheritance[2]. This was seventy-five years after King John's decision.

The question whether a married woman was allowed to make a valid will is of some interest in view of the medieval belief that to die without

---

[1] *Bracton's Note-Book*, ed. F. W. Maitland, Cambridge, 1887, Case no. 1847, vol. iii, p. 646. Bracton, f. 414.

[2] By the second statute of Westminster, c. 3. The wife could 'pray to be received to defend her right'. T. F. T. Plucknett, *Legislation of Edward I*, Oxford, 1949, p. 123.

making a will was not only unwise, but positively sinful. A detailed description of the last illness and death of Archbishop Hubert Walter in 1205 has been preserved because he had been accused of this last crime, intestate death. The wills which could be made at this period did not touch land, as in Anglo-Saxon times, for all land was held of some lord to whom it reverted on the holder's death without heirs. The heir to land should be known, for as one law writer says 'only God can make an heir'. The heir could expect to receive his father's land only after he had paid a sum of money to his lord called a relief. Men could make wills of their chattels, money, household goods, clothes, jewels, stock, and farm implements. Many of them were probably verbal wills made on the death-bed where the priest's presence secured the fulfilment of the dying man's will. Women must naturally have wished to enjoy the sense of security which the making of a will gave to the death-bed.

Few early wills survive, but incidental references show that great ladies were in the habit of making them. In 1184 the king's justiciar authorized the payment of money from a husband's estate to his widow's executors in order that they might carry out her will[1]. No one doubts, however, that a widow could make her will. It was felt in the twelfth century that a married woman should be able to make a valid will of such things as she had made her own by use, her jewels and clothes, and also of the share of her husband's goods which would be hers on his death. A man's goods were generally held to fall into three parts at his death, the wife's part, the children's part, and the dead's part, that is, the share which was given to religious purposes for the good of the dead man's soul. The Great Charter of 1215 recognized that it was for the Church to supervise the division of the dead man's goods by his executors. Bracton declared that 'for decency's sake'[2] a woman should not make her will in her husband's lifetime without his consent, but it is unlikely that a woman who felt herself on the point of death would not make at least a verbal disposition of her goods. Among the wills preserved at Lincoln is a will of a widow made in 1283. It is discussed in a later chapter[3].

A number of early documents survive which show women near to death trying to provide for their souls' health. 'I, Avice daughter of Randulf the sheriff, with the spontaneous consent of Lettice my eldest daughter and of R. de Novo foro her husband and of their heirs, and of

---

[1] *ad faciendam divisam ipsius*, Pipe Roll 30 Henry II, p. 134.
[2] f. 60b, *propter honestatem*.
[3] Pp. 86-7.

Mabel my second daughter and her heirs, and of Aubreye my third daughter and R. de Sancto Quintino her husband and their heirs, have given and granted to the church of St. Mary of Blyth and the monks serving God there William son of Geoffrey of Markham and his heirs and one bovate of land rendering 6 shillings yearly to the said monks, that bovate, namely, which this W. held of me, for the safety of my soul and the souls of all my predecessors, in perpetual alms, quietly, peaceably, and free from all secular service, in wood, in field, in pastures and in feedings and in all liberties belonging to the said land, saving the service of the lord king. And so I have assigned this alms for the refreshment of the monks on the anniversary of my burial so that through their intercession my spirit may be refreshed in the skies with celestial food and drink'[1]. Randulf son of Ingleram had been sheriff of Nottinghamshire and Derbyshire in 1155 and Avice was his heir. She in turn was succeeded by three daughters, whose consent, with that of their husbands and heirs, she sought before making this provision. The husband of her second daughter, Mabel, was evidently dead before his mother-in-law came to make her final gifts for her soul's health. This is not a will. Nothing is said of chattels, debts or executors. Its effect must have been to transfer the rent due from William son of Geoffrey of Markham to religious ends. The monks of Blyth must render the service due to the crown from this land, but the rent of 6 shillings a year was free for their refreshment on the anniversary of Avice's funeral. She must have made her disposition before the end of the twelfth century.

A document similar in intention, but more carefully drawn and bearing a date, was issued by Amicia of Croft in Leicestershire. Her deed was addressed 'to all seeing or hearing these letters', and informed them that 'with the consent and will of William Basset my son and heir, I have given and granted with my body and confirmed by this present charter, for the safety of my soul and of my children, and for the safety of the souls of my predecessors and successors to God and the church of blessed Mary of Eaton [Nuneaton, Warwickshire] and the nuns of the order of Fontévrault there serving God half my mill of Sapcote with all its appurtenances in pure and perpetual alms, save two shillings which ought to be paid to the church of Sapcote in tithes. . . . I will also that they have and hold the aforesaid half of the aforesaid mill freely and quietly and peaceably in pure and perpetual alms with all appurtenances and liberties

---

[1] British Museum, Harl. MS. 3759, f. 80b.

of me and my heirs for ever. I will also that this my gift, which in my last and spontaneous will I have made at Sapcote on the Friday next before the Nativity of blessed Mary in the eighteenth year of the reign of King John, shall remain firm and stable for ever, so that if I shall ever make any other gift with my body it shall be held for nothing and as broken; and for the greater security I have set my seal to the present writing'[1]. This grant, made on 8 September 1216, again lacks the characteristic signs of the last will. There are no executors appointed, no legacies indicated, nor does the grantor direct that her debts shall be paid. But she calls the document her 'last and spontaneous will'. Gifts of this kind had long been recognized by the king's court, which had ruled under Henry II that a gift made in a last will should stand if it were made with the heir's consent[2].

Neither Avice, daughter of Randulf the sheriff, nor Amicia of Croft, mentioned her husband in her deed, and it may be presumed that they were both widows when the gifts were made. Later it would have been a matter of course for a widow making such a deed to say that she was living in her 'free widowhood'. The common law defined precisely what both widows and widowers might expect from the possessions of their deceased partner. It was more generous to the husband than to the wife. If a wife had borne her husband a child and died before him, all the land which the couple had held during the marriage in right of the wife remained to her husband for his life. The custom by which he thus profited was known as 'the courtesy of England'. Even if the child did not survive infancy the husband held 'by the courtesy' and excluded his wife's heirs from the land. Most lawyers held that the child must have 'given forth some voice or cry arguing life and natural humanity' for the husband to enjoy his courtesy. An Elizabethan writer says that 'if it bellowed, bleated, brayed, grunted, rored, or howled, there accrued no courtesie by getting such an uncivill urchin'. Many law suits came of this rule[3].

A wife who survived her husband could expect to receive in dower a third part of her husband's estate. Sometimes she was dowered with specific lands at the church door on her wedding day. In this case she could enter those lands immediately on her husband's death. Such a settlement at the church door in the sight of the congregation was not,

---

[1] British Museum, Add. Chart. 47615.
[2] *Glanvill, De Legibus et Consuetudinibus Regni Angliæ*, ed. Woodbine, Yale, 1932, p. 97.
[3] *The Lawes Resolutions of Womens Rights*, London, 1632, p. 88.

however, necessary to secure for the widow a third of all lands her husband had held at any time during the marriage. But if dower had not been formally assigned in this way the widow had to wait for her dower until she received it from her husband's heir. Sometimes he was slow to give her dower and the widow could then bring an action in the royal courts to secure it. From an early date the king had himself provided a remedy in his own court for widows unable to obtain their dower[1]. The widow's 'thirds' as they came to be called were often a heavy burden on an estate out of which provision had also to be made for younger sons and daughters before what was left of the inheritance went to the eldest son. It was not unusual for an estate to be maintaining the widows of more than one generation at the same time.

The widow's dower was accepted as a fixed charge throughout the feudal age. But the growing practice of making settlements at the time of marriage lessened the uncertainty which the traditional dower created. It became the law that dower was not due on lands held jointly by husband and wife. In the highest ranks of society the widow by the end of the Middle Ages usually talked of her jointure rather than her dower.[2] The elaborate and carefully drawn marriage settlements which secured the wife's future made her no less desirable to a second husband than the simple 'thirds' of earlier generations. Widows were always eagerly sought in marriage. The provision made by their father which had helped to make them desirable to their first husbands had been increased by what their first marriage had earned them. In the days before the Great Charter the widows of the king's tenants in chief were a source of considerable profit to him. He could extort money from them for permission to live unmarried or to marry a second or third husband of their own choice. He could give their marriage as a reward to one of his servants.

One of the greatest ladies in twelfth-century Anglo-Norman society was Hawisa, Countess of Aumale in her own right. Her marriage to the Earl of Essex at Pleshey, Essex, in 1180 was the great social event of the year, and was described in his chronicle by Ralf de Diceto, Dean of St. Paul's. It seemed to him a presage of their future happiness that the wedding

---

[1] *Glanvill*, Book vi.

[2] It was still possible in the seventeenth century for a widow to 'sue out her thirds' if no settlement had been made. Lady Anne Clifford noted in her diary in May 1617: 'This time my Lord's Mother did first of all sue out her thirds which was an increase of trouble and discontent to my Lord'. *The Diary of the Lady Anne Clifford*, ed. V. Sackville-West, London, 1923, p. 68.

took place on the day of St. Felix, 14 January[1]. The earl died at Rouen on 12 December 1189, leaving no heir. A lady in possession of the great Aumale inheritance in Normandy, the Aumale estates in England which included the greater part of Holderness, and a third of the lands of the earldom of Essex, was a rich prize. Richard I gave her in marriage to William de Forz of Oleron, a Poitevin, who was one of the commanders of his crusading fleet. Such a husband was far beneath the countess in rank and she was forced into compliance by the seizure and sale of the stock on her manors on behalf of the crown[2]. A contemporary monastic chronicler, in recording this marriage, described Hawisa as 'a woman almost a man to whom nothing masculine is lacking save virility'[3]. It may be that this great lady resented and was known to resent the subordinate position to which even the richest woman in her own right must submit. Her household was organized on almost royal lines. As early as 1181 she granted a large estate at Eastwell to Garendon Abbey, Leicestershire, by charter witnessed not only by a group of men, but also by the lady Aanor of Walden, Mabel de Oseville, Beatrice de Gueres, Avice, Beatrice de Berneres, and Maud of Hastings, who were clearly her maids in waiting[4]. Hawisa's third and last husband, Baldwin de Béthune, died in October 1212. The king at once forced her to offer him 5,000 marks for 'her inheritance and her dowers and that she be not distrained to marry'. She had paid £1,000 of this enormous sum before the end of the financial year[5]. Before she herself died on 11 March 1214 she confirmed her earlier gift to Garendon. She described herself in this charter as 'established in my liege power after the death of my lord Baldwin de Béthune and after I have made fine with the lord king touching my right and inheritance'. This charter, again, is witnessed by the men about her, two abbots, a chaplain, the sheriff, and three others and again the witness list concludes with the names of ladies: 'Alice de Fountains, Richenda, and Clemency my maidens' [6]. No other lady of her age and rank speaks so clearly to us across the centuries.

[1] *The Historical Works of Master Ralf de Diceto*, ed. W. Stubbs, Rolls Series, 1876, vol. ii, p. 3.　　　　　　　　　　　　　　　　[2] *Pipe Roll 6 Richard I*, p. 163.

[3] *Chronicon Ricardi Divisiensis*, ed. J. Stevenson, London, 1838, p. 11.

[4] Hist. MSS. Commission, Rutland Report, vol. iv, p. 6.

[5] *Pipe Roll 14 John*, p. 37.

[6] *Sir Christopher Hatton's Book of Seals*, ed. Lewis C. Loyd and D. M. Stenton, Oxford, 1950, no. 444. Only occasionally were women's charters witnessed by women. The Rievaulx cartulary preserves the record of a confirmation to the abbey by a Yorkshire woman

Despite the new feudal subservience forced upon the greatest ladies of the land after the Norman Conquest it was still possible for individual women to make enough impression on their world for their names to be remembered. William I, Henry I, and Henry II each allowed his queen to act as regent in his absence. Henry I's daughter, Matilda, wife and then widow of the Emperor Henry V of Germany, was married to the heir of Anjou by her father in the hope that she might secure the union of Normandy and Anjou as well as succeed to the throne of England. She came within measurable distance of winning the crown, and lost all chance of it because of her own proud and haughty temper. Like the wife of her rival, King Stephen, she herself took part in the struggles for power. It is clear that women could ride as well as men, plan campaigns, and direct the defences of a castle. In 1075 Emma, wife of the rebel Earl of Norfolk, was left in her husband's castle of Norwich while he escaped oversea. She held the castle until she was given a safe-conduct to leave the country. Twenty years later the wife of the rebel Earl of Northumbria only surrendered Bamburgh Castle to William II because he threatened to blind her husband, whom he had captured. Nichola de la Haia, the wife of Gerard de Camville, Sheriff of Lincoln, had brought to her husband the hereditary office of constable of Lincoln Castle. With him she was besieged in Lincoln in 1191, and twenty-five years later, as a widow, she herself held the castle against the king's rebels.

The greatest of all these ladies was Eleanor, duchess in her own right of Aquitaine, divorced wife of Louis VII of France and wife of Henry II. She had more influence on the course of history than any other great lady of her time. Her intrigue with Raymond of Antioch while she was on crusade with her first husband encouraged him to seek a divorce, for though she had brought Aquitaine to the crown of France she had borne no son to inherit the kingdom. The Church gave Louis VII a divorce on the grounds of consanguinity. Eleanor's subsequent marriage to Henry, Duke of Normandy, carried Aquitaine to the English royal house and made inevitable the long history of war between France and England. To Henry II Eleanor bore son after son whom she supported in their

of a hide of land which was part of her dower. She swore to observe the terms of the charter in the hand of Bertha, wife of Rannulf de Glanville, then sheriff. The charter was witnessed by Rannulf himself, his clerk, and five other men as well as by 'Bertha *vice comitissa*, Maud her daughter, Maud, daughter of Tockeman, Eda wife of Brian the clerk, Helewisa their daughter and Othild wife of Godwin Givenout', *Rievaulx Cartulary*, Surtees Society, vol. 83, 1889, p. 62.

rebellions against their father. Her husband could only control her by keeping her in prison. On his death she at once recovered her liberty and 'set out holding her royal court from city to city and castle to castle as it pleased her. And having sent messengers through all the counties of England she commanded all captives to be released from captivity, since she knew from experience that captivity was grievous to man and that it was a joyous refreshment of the spirit to emerge from it'[1]. Without doubt she had learned wisdom in captivity for until her death in 1204 she did much to secure her sons in their hereditary possessions.

In the twelfth century the king and his officers classed widows with the heirs and heiresses in the king's wardship as profitable sources of wealth on which the king must be kept fully informed. In 1185 Henry II sent a company of judges round the land to enquire into 'ladies, boys, and girls' who should be in the king's hands. Some part of the returns compiled before these judges has survived. The careful particularity which notes down the age of each widow and heir, the value of the holding and all information about it which might interest a prospective purchaser reflects a harsh age. There is nothing romantic about a society which produced such entries as the three following which relate to the Rutland ladies at the moment in the king's hand and available for re-marriage:

'Roheis de Bussey, who was the daughter of Baldwin fitz Gilbert, is in the gift of the lord king and is aged sixty. Her land in Essendine is worth £10 with this stock, namely three ploughs and a hundred sheep, but the sheep are lacking. She has two daughters as heirs. One is the wife of Hugh Wake and the other of John de Builli.

'Alice de Bidun, sister of William Mauduit, is in the gift of the lord king, and is aged fifty. Her land in Morcott with appurtenances is worth £10 a year with one plough which is there. She has four daughters; the eldest Hugh of Glympton has through the gift of the lord king, the second Miles de Beauchamp, the third Richard de Beauchamp, the fourth Geoffrey son of Geoffrey. In addition to the rent she has taken from the land since her husband's death 24 shillings in aid.

'Alice de Beaufow, widow of Thomas de Beaufow, is in the gift of the lord king. She was the daughter of Waleran de Oiri and niece of Nigel son of Alexander. She is twenty and has one son as heir, who is two. Her land in Seaton is worth £5:6:8 with this stock, namely two ploughs, a

---

[1] *Gesta Regis Henrici secundi Benedicti abbatis* (Howden), ed. W. Stubbs, Rolls Series, 1867, vol. ii, p. 74.

hundred sheep, two draught animals, five sows, one boar, and four cows. In the first year in which the land has been in her hand she has received in rent 36 shillings and 10 pence and two pounds of pepper, and apart from the rent her tenants have given her 4 shillings and three loads of oats'[1].

Boys and girls who would inherit land were generally married as children, but the Church recognized that a marriage between two children below the age of consent might be broken when they were old enough to consummate the marriage. The age of consent for boys was held to be fourteen, and for girls, twelve[2]. In Edward I's reign it was established that a girl's father could not take an aid from his tenants to help pay the expenses of her wedding until she was seven years old. Such financial help could only be taken for the marriage of an eldest daughter, and for her marriage it could be taken once only. This rule remained in force until feudal tenures were abolished in 1660 and even at the end of the feudal period it was not unusual for a girl to be married in her middle 'teens.

The roll of ladies, boys, and girls gives a glimpse of many twelfth-century families. A simple example is the family of La Veile. Roger, son of Richard La Veile, was six and was the heir of an estate at Erpingham, Norfolk, worth £50 a year. He was in the custody of his mother and 'paternal uncles'. His mother was aged thirty and had two other sons and five daughters[3]. A more elaborate nexus of family relationship surrounded Eugenia Picot, daughter and co-heiress of Ralf Picot of Milton, Kent. She had married first William Malet, a household officer of King Henry II. In 1170 he died, leaving her dowered with lands in Cambridgeshire. She was then married to another royal servant, Thomas fitz Bernard, the king's chief forester[4], who died not long before the roll was made up in 1185. 'She had three sons by Thomas fitz Bernard and one daughter; the eldest son is ten, the middle eight, and the third three'. The king had given Eugenia's daughter, Maud, in marriage to the infant heir of John de Bidun, but in 1185 her husband was already dead, leaving her a widow of ten in the custody of her mother, who was holding her land. Eugenia's eldest son was, at ten, already married to an heiress of five, who with her land, an Essex manor, was in the charge of her mother-in-law. Eugenia herself, twice married and twice widowed, was thirty. Her

---

[1] *Rotuli de Dominabus*, Pipe Roll Society, 1st series, vol. xxxv, 1913, p. 45.
[2] F. W. Maitland, *History of English Law*, vol. ii, p. 390.
[3] *Rotuli de Dominabus*, pp. 54, 56.
[4] *Magister forestarius et justiciarius per totam Angliam*, Benedict, vol. i, p. 323.

daughter Maud, already a widow in 1185, is known to have lived until 1255 when she died at the age of eighty[1].

It will be noticed how careful the Justices were to record the family to which these ladies belonged. When a man chose his wife he allied himself to her kindred. Sometimes when the lady was not daughter or sister of someone whom everybody knew the clerks were content to say, as they did of 'the wife of Peter de Peleville', that she 'is born of knights'[2]; or, as they said of Mary, widow of Guy Lestrange, that 'she is born of knights and barons'[3]. Mary herself was said to be forty and to have had three lords, that is, to have been married three times. 'Her dowers and marriage portion lie in divers counties'. The unnamed wife of Peter de Peleville was said to be forty-six, which, if accurate, is remarkable, for she was said to have a son not yet a year old[4]. Peter had left an elder son aged twenty-four, who was a leper in the king's wardship, and two marriage-able daughters, one fourteen and the other five. Precision in the matter of ages was difficult to secure. Roheis de Bussey, whom the Rutland jurors thought was sixty, was described as only fifty in Lincolnshire. The jurors tried to be as precise as possible in recording the ages of the younger women, but they seem content to describe an elderly lady as fifty or sixty and an old lady as sixty or seventy or even eighty. It was of impor-tance to the intending purchaser of a widow's marriage to have some guide to the length of time for which he might expect to enjoy the lady's dower from her former husbands. All the evidence goes to show that women in the twelfth century, if they escaped the perils of childhood and childbirth, could live as long as many women do today.

Many old ladies of the Middle Ages looked to religious houses to provide comfort for their latter days. An elaborate arrangement made by Maud de Mundeville survives to illustrate the sort of bargain which a great lady could make with a religious house of men. Maud was the daughter and heiress of Nigel de Mundeville and had been given in marriage to Rualon d'Avranches by Henry I[5]. She gave to St. Andrew's Priory, Northampton, the village of Sywell with all its appurtenances, as well in wood as in plain, and the church, granting it to them absolutely, except for four virgates and a half which she gave with her daughter to the church of Elstow'. She stipulated also that 'Hamo the chaplain shall have the church of Sywell

---

[1] *Rotuli de Dominabus*, pp. xxxvii, 55, 87.
[2] *Ibid.*, p. 53.   [3] *Loc. cit.*   [4] *Ibid.*, p. 52.
[5] *The Domesday Monachorum of Christchurch, Canterbury*, ed. David C. Douglas, London, 1944, pp. 42–3.

and shall hold it freely and quietly. On such condition and agreement',
the record continues, 'that when the lady Maud shall wish to come to the
religious habit she shall receive the habit of religion in the same house, and
she shall have with her one nun, whom she shall choose, and likewise
four servants whom she shall choose. She and the lady whom she has with
her shall have suitable food, namely they shall receive the food of two
monks and their four servants the same as four of the prior's household
servants. If the lady she chooses shall die before her, in accordance with
her judgment and will she shall have another with her whom she shall
choose. If the lady Maud shall die first the monks shall grant her lady
suitable food so long as they see that her life is worthy'. The monks
promised that if any other lady should retire to their house she should not
live in Maud's lodgings contrary to her will. They also promised that if
Maud should fall ill so that she could not come to the monastery 'one of the
brethren should go to her and do for her the service due to a sister'. With
the consent of the prior and all the brethren Maud retained five marks a
year from the village of Sywell for her own use to be paid in two annual
instalments, stipulating that if the estate did not bring in five marks the
monks 'will make up the amount from their own table of St. Andrew'.
Finally Maud granted to the priory the services which she had from two
men, Gerard and William, providing that the men shall be free and quit
by doing those services, as they had been in her own day. Maud's son and
heir, as the only loser by this transaction, confirmed his mother's agreement in a formal deed dated 'in this year of the incarnation, 1147, King
Stephen reigning in England, in the times of Eugenius the Pope'[1].

The religious life or marriage were the only alternatives considered by
a gentleman in the feudal age as provision for his daughters. If he wished
to find husbands of their own rank for them he must provide each with an
adequate marriage portion. Surviving legal instruments by which such
settlements were secured show that fathers found this a heavy drain on
their resources. Occasionally a great man was forced to marry a daughter to
one of his own tenants, reducing the service which had previously been
done by the tenant to himself[2]. It was inevitable that fathers should look to
nunneries for relief. At the beginning of the feudal age there were only
nine fully established nunneries in England. The feudal baronage added
many more to this number as the Middle Ages went on. There was a

---

[1] These two documents were copied into the cartulary of St. Andrew's Priory, B.M.
Cott. Vesp. E xvii, f. 199 and dorse.   [2] Book of Seals, no. 298 and n, p. 205.

curious mixture of genuine religious fervour with a strong sense of the advantage of having a family nunnery in many of these foundations. The old Saxon houses, like Shaftesbury or Wilton, were more richly endowed than any of the post-Conquest nunneries, although a few houses, like Godstow, Oxfordshire, or Elstow, Bedfordshire, were better off than most of the other recent foundations. The nuns of Godstow earned the especial patronage of Henry II because they gave shelter to the corpse of his mistress, Fair Rosamund Clifford[1]. At the end of the Middle Ages the richest house was Syon Abbey, founded in the fifteenth century near London, where the court could visit it by water.

Nunneries were in general small. At the time of the dissolution a considerable number had fewer than ten inmates. The fashionable Syon, which far outnumbered any other house, had only fifty-one. Although numbers had fallen in all English nunneries towards the end of their history, there is no evidence that they were ever high[2]. After the monasteries had been long dissolved people looked back to them regretfully when they wondered how to educate and provide for their daughters[3]. The misery of a young girl placed in a nunnery because her father could not afford to buy her a husband had been long forgotten. Even now it must not be overstressed. Children, both boys and girls, often received part of their earliest education from nuns, so that the life of the cloister was familiar from early youth. Parents were glad to leave young children in the safe custody of nuns for weeks or even months together. Nuns were driven to accept the charge for purely financial reasons. Their endowments were often insufficient for the needs of the house, nor were nuns always good managers of their resources. It was little that the average nun could teach, beyond perhaps the alphabet and manners. Bishops disliked nuns taking children into their house, particularly as there was often nowhere but the nuns' own chamber for them to sleep[4].

It would be possible to collect from medieval wills and from charters granting land 'in free marriage' with a daughter the terms of many marriage settlements. In 1383 Sir William Fraunk, who held a number of Lincolnshire manors, provided that if his son died without issue his eldest

[1] *Benedict*, vol. ii, pp. 231–2.

[2] The large numbers attributed to the houses of the Gilbertine Order at the end of the twelfth century were due essentially to the reputation of the founder and cannot long have survived him.   [3] See below, pp. 183–4.

[4] All these points are discussed by Eileen Power, *Medieval English Nunneries*, Cambridge, 1922.

daughter, Elizabeth, should be married to a gentleman who would take her father's arms and receive his lands. His other daughters were to be made nuns in houses of good repute or married in accordance with their degree, the expenses of these operations being born by the estate. Each daughter who became a nun was to enjoy during her life forty shillings a year towards her maintenance and clothing[1]. William Copuldike, of Harrington, Lincolnshire, willed in 1504 that his daughter Elizabeth should have a hundred marks for her marriage portion, but 'if she be disposed to be a woman of religion I will she have twenty marks or more as it should be thought reasonable by the discretion of myne executors'. If Elizabeth died before marriage or became a nun her sister Cecily was to have fifty marks of the money which would have been Elizabeth's marriage portion[2]. It was cheaper to place a girl in a nunnery than to get her married, but there is little suggestion that parents often tried to force girls into religion against their will.

A case in which the plaintiff alleged that this had been done came before the king's court of justice in 1207. A certain Alice Clement sued her sister's son for a considerable estate in Wroxton and South Newington, Oxfordshire, which she asserted was her own share of her father's inheritance. Her nephew and his father, Alice's brother-in-law, replied that Alice had no right to the land because she was a nun and had been excommunicated for leaving her nunnery of Ankerwyke after being a nun there for fifteen years. They even produced letters of excommunication issued by the judges appointed to hear the case by the Pope, and letters from two Popes confirming her excommunication. Alice replied that these documents should not dispose of her claim because when she was five years old her sister's husband and her sister herself placed her with the nuns of Ankerwyke 'and she was there three years. Then, as she was taught, she asked to be made a nun, but afterwards, when she came to years of discretion, she abandoned the habit'. She married Alan of Woodcote and appealed to Pope Innocent III, who appointed judges delegate to try the case. They 'absolved her from the petition of the nuns of Ankerwyke' by the authority of the Pope, who confirmed their action by his letters. The end of the action is not recorded, for King John summoned it to be heard before himself[3]. But that Alice was enabled to secure at least a portion of her

[1] *Book of Seals*, no. 486, p. 336.
[2] *Lincoln Wills*, vol. i, ed. C. W. Foster, Lincoln Record Society, vol. v, 1914, pp. 20–2.
[3] *Curia Regis Rolls*, ed. C. T. Flower, vol. v, pp. 79–80.

inheritance is shown by the final concord made between her and her nephew in 1224[1].

Occasionally cases heard before the king's judges seem to suggest that women were indifferent as to whether they entered a nunnery or married, provided they did one or the other. At York in 1219 the jurors found it hard to say whether a man had been dispossessed 'unjustly and without judgment' of a free tenement in the city because the land in question was the inheritance of a certain Agnes who gave it to him on condition that he either found her a good husband within three years or put her in some religious house. If he did this he should keep the land, but if not it should return to Agnes. She lived in his house for three years and more and he neither arranged a marriage for her nor put her into religion. After she had lived there for fully fifteen years she returned to her own land[2]. Since the property lay in York it seems very likely that Agnes was the daughter of a York citizen, who might well have been content from the social point of view for his daughter to mingle with the daughters of the feudal aristocracy in a religious house. In the early years of the thirteenth century it might not have been so easy to put a citizen's daughter into a nunnery or marry her into a county family as it would have been at the end of the Middle Ages.

In an age when child marriage was part of the accepted social habit the personal choice of the child partners could hardly be consulted. The marriage of an heiress was felt to be the lord's concern since he must needs take the homage of her husband. No lord should be asked to take the homage 'of an enemy or of a person unsuitable in some other way'[3]. One of the judicial scandals of the twelfth century was made possible because of this rule that the lord's consent was required for the marriage of an heiress. A contemporary Yorkshire chronicler preserved the story of the young Yorkshireman, Gilbert of Plumpton, whom he describes as 'of noble stock'. In 1184 Gilbert was deprived of his land and taken to Worcester where he was condemned to death because he had carried off and married an heiress in the king's wardship whom the Chief Justiciar had intended to give in marriage to his own steward. Gilbert was saved from death on the gallows at the last moment by the intervention of the

---

[1] *The Feet of Fines for Oxfordshire*, ed. H. E. Salter, Oxfordshire Record Society, vol. xii, pp. 60, 61.
[2] *Rolls of the Justices in Eyre, Yorkshire*, ed. D. M. Stenton, Selden Society, vol. 56, pp. 78–9.
[3] *Glanvill*, pp. 109–10.

Bishop of Worcester encouraged by 'a great crowd of men and women crying out that Gilbert was a just man and the innocent ought not to suffer these things'. The matter came to the king's ears and Gilbert was reprieved, but he was imprisoned until after Henry II's death in 1189, for he had broken feudal law and accepted custom by marrying one of the king's wards without permission[1]. The story ended happily, for Gilbert's brother purchased from Richard I both his brother's freedom and permission for him to have his wife again with the land[2].

The outcry against the treatment of Gilbert of Plumpton and the bishop's success in preventing his judicial murder suggests that such scandals were unusual. But it is rare to find evidence in this age that anything which can be called romance went with the hard practical business of making a marriage contract. Between the greedy desire of lords and parents to make marriage a means of increasing an estate in land and the prurient attitude of the medieval Church towards love between man and woman romance had little chance. The law of marriage all over medieval Europe was the law of the Roman Church, not the law of any individual state. The unnatural admiration of virginity professed by medieval ecclesiastics had very ill effects. To represent marriage as valuable only as a means of avoiding sin for those too weak to remain virgin inevitably lowered the esteem of the married state. The failure of the Church to declare that only public marriage in the face of the congregation by an ordained priest was lawful marriage meant the encouragement of secret marriages. Although the practice of publishing the banns of marriage was laid down by the Church at the end of the twelfth century and gave opportunity for the exposure of any previous engagement by either party, secret marriages were still lawful, and were still made. Moreover, the Church's rules on the subject of consanguinity were a frequent cause of stumbling, partly because of their grotesque elaboration and partly because the Church insisted that the physical union of a man and woman, irrespective of any ceremony, created a blood relationship. 'When we weigh', wrote F. W. Maitland, 'the merits of the medieval Church and have remembered all her good deeds, we have to put into the other scale as a weighty counterpoise the incalculable harm done by a marriage law which was a maze of flighty fancies and misapplied logic'[3]. It is a testimony

---

[1] *Benedict*, vol. i, pp. 314–16.
[2] *Pipe Roll 2 Richard I*, p. 66.
[3] *History of English Law*, vol. ii, p. 389.

to the essential sanity of the medieval English people that respect for honest marriage was not killed before the end of the Middle Ages.

Broken marriages are by no means a modern phenomenon. It is indeed possible that they were more frequent in an age of child marriages than in modern times. A noble lady, whose name appears only as M., appealed for help to Pope Alexander III in the 'seventies of the twelfth century. She belonged to the Lincoln diocese. Her story was that when she was a little girl she was given in marriage to R., who was a knight, but she remained in her parents' home. After three or four years the relations of both parties began to say that the marriage ought to be dissolved for consanguinity. Disturbed by this her husband fetched her by force from her parents' home and kept her like a prisoner for three years. Then she escaped back to her own home. She was now pregnant. Her relatives brought a plea touching the validity of the marriage in the court of the Bishop of Lincoln. The husband appealed to the Archbishop of Canterbury, as papal legate, asking for the restitution of his wife. The archbishop enjoined that the husband should provide for his wife who should be put in some nunnery or other suitable place for the birth of her child. The husband would not agree, but with drawn sword pursued his wife into the church of St. Margaret, Lincoln, where she had taken refuge and forced her to agree to settle their differences by the advice of two men chosen by him and two by her, rather than pursue the plea in the ecclesiastical court. The Pope instructed the Bishop of St. Asaph to enquire carefully into the truth of the story. If the husband had thus forced his wife to agree to abide by the judgment of four friends, she should be absolved from her promise. The case of consanguinity should then be heard and settled. Since the woman seemed to be afraid of her husband, the bishop should prevent the husband seeking out his wife before the case was heard[1]. The end of the story is not preserved.

It was not difficult to get a marriage annulled in the Middle Ages, if the expense of going to the Church courts could be met[2]. Precontract was frequently alleged as a reason for divorce. Nor was it difficult to find that a marriage between people of position was within the prohibited degrees if one of the parties wished to bring it to an end. The marriages of William

---

[1] *Papal Decretals relating to the diocese of Lincoln*, ed. W. Holtzmann and E. W. Kemp, Lincoln Record Society, vol. xlvii, 1954, pp. 44–7.

[2] The famous Anesty case was made possible by the annulment of a marriage about the year 1143, 'English Society in the Early Middle Ages', *Pelican History of England*, vol. iii, pp. 36–8.

de Roumara, grandson of the first Earl of Lincoln, were considered by Pope Celestine III in 1191-2. William married first a lady called Alice, whose parentage is unknown. This marriage was annulled for consanguinity, and William married Philippa, daughter of the Count of Alençon. The case came before the Pope because William secretly confessed to the Bishop of Lincoln that his conscience pricked him because, at the suggestion of his first wife, he had allowed the marriage to be dissolved on the grounds of kinship although he knew that there was no such tie of blood between them. The Pope declared that, although William was troubled in mind, he must not desert his second wife. The bishop must impose penance on him for agreeing to the separation against his conscience, and as an additional penalty William must not deny conjugal rights to his second wife, but must regard himself as having lost the right to demand them of her[1].

Despite the efforts of the Church to uphold the sanctity of marriage and punish adultery it was common for men to maintain mistresses. In the twelfth century the kings set a bad example. Both Henry I and Henry II had more mistresses than one and Henry I recognized an amazing number of illegitimate children. Like Charles II in a later generation he had no scruples about raising them to high position in the land. Two of his sons were created earls and the rest were well provided for[2]. One of the daughters married the King of Scots and one became an abbess. To have been the mistress of Henry I was no impediment to a good marriage. Sybil Corbet, mother of the Queen of Scots and the Earl of Cornwall, married the son and heir of the king's chamberlain. Isabella, daughter of the Count of Meulan, married the first Earl of Pembroke. Edith, daughter of the Lord of Greystoke, Cumberland, married Robert d'Oilli, one of the king's constables and a leading tenant in chief in Oxfordshire. Pride in illegitimate royal birth reaches its height when Geoffrey, Archbishop of York, bastard son of Henry II, called himself 'son of the king' upon his archiepiscopal seal[3].

Chance has preserved evidence of the care of several medieval barons for their mistresses or the children they had borne them. Thomas son of Richard, lord of Cuckney, Nottinghamshire, when about to set out on crusade in the middle of the twelfth century gave 'to Ailiva and her younger

---

[1] *Lincoln Decretals*, pp. 56-7.
[2] *Complete Peerage*, 2nd ed., vol. xi, Appendix D, 'Henry I's Illegitimate Children', pp. 105-21.   [3] Hist. MSS. Com., Hastings Report, vol. i, p. 121.

daughter by me the land of her father which he held for the service of one bovate, and Reginald, her own brother, with his land which he also held for the service of one bovate'. Ailiva was to hold this gift of the Hospital of Jerusalem by the rent of 12 pence a year until Thomas's return from the Holy Land, and if he did not return she was to hold it for ever by the rent of 2 shillings for the grantor's soul and the souls of his father and mother[1]. A Norman lord can here be seen providing for his English mistress and their children by the gift of her father's villein land and her own brother with his holding. Later in the century Amalric son of Ralf, in one of the earliest known post-Conquest wills, left ten marks of silver to his children born of a mistress. Henry II confirmed his will in 1180[2]. In the middle of the thirteenth century Philip son of Roger Pantulf gave to Denise of Warwick and the children begotten by himself on her 'three half virgates of land in Long Lawford, Warwickshire, with the men sitting on that land and all their issue and all their chattels'. Denise and her children were to hold by the rent of a pair of white gloves worth a halfpenny or one halfpenny at Easter[3].

No case reveals more clearly the medieval baron's attitude to marriage than one which came before the court of Edward I in 1302. William Painel and Margaret his wife claimed Margaret's dower from the heir of her former husband John de Camoys. Less than twenty years before, Parliament had laid down that a woman who eloped from her husband and stayed with her adulterer should have no dower unless her husband was reconciled with her[4]. To William Painel's claim it was therefore objected that Margaret had eloped with him. In reply William and Margaret produced a solemn charter by which John de Camoys quit-claimed to William Painel Margaret his wife with all her goods and chattels. John de Camoys had died in 1298 and William Painel had thereafter married Margaret. William and Margaret also produced in court certificates from the Archbishop of Canterbury and the Bishop of Chichester bearing witness that the couple had been charged with adultery in Court Christian and had proved their innocence by compurgation. Margaret's oath-helpers had been a number of ladies, married and unmarried, among them a prioress. William and Margaret also offered to put themselves on a jury as to whether they had committed adultery or

---

[1] Bodleian Library, Nottinghamshire Charters, 2.
[2] B. M. Egerton MS. 3031, f. 38 and 38b.   [3] *Book of Seals*, no. 269, p. 188.
[4] The Statute of Westminster II, 1285.

not. Maitland printed in full in his *History of English Law* the judgment of
the king's court delivered in this case. The measured dignity with which
the judges set aside the plaintiffs' claim rebukes alike the greedy and
shameless plaintiffs and the incompetent archaism of the ecclesiastical
courts[1].

A marriage which was probably arranged by the woman herself under
unusual circumstances lies behind the otherwise commonplace record of a
grant of land to Leicester Abbey in the early thirteenth century. Wigan
de la Mara confirmed to the abbey 'for the safety of my soul and the soul
of Maud Trussel my wife and the souls of all our ancestors and successors,
in pure, free, and perpetual alms, one carucate of land in the village of
Theddingworth, which the aforesaid Maud gave me for my homage and
service when I deraigned her inheritance for her by the duel'[2]. The plea to
which this charter refers was brought against Maud Trussel by two men
and two women for a knight's fee in Theddingworth. It was ended in 1201
by a final concord which gave the knight's fee to Maud Trussel after the
judicial duel had been 'pledged, armed and fought'[3]. These two documents
are of special interest as the only known evidence for the marriage of a
woman of rank to a man of rank who had acted as her champion in a trial
by battle.

The power of kings and other lords to arrange the marriages of women
in their gift was limited by a social convention that neither a man nor a
woman should thus be given to a partner of lower rank. Such a marriage
was regarded as 'disparagement'. Like all conventions of this kind it was
often broken in practice. Its breach was one of the grievances for which
the barons tried to get a remedy in the Great Charter in 1215. They demanded that heirs shall be so married that they shall not be disparaged, and that
by the counsel of their next of kin[4]. When at last the king was brought to
grant the Charter he conceded that 'heirs shall be married without
disparagement, so that before the marriage is contracted the heir's next of
kin shall be informed'[5]. The slight change in wording between the barons'
demand and the king's concession shows that not all the barons had hoped
for had been won. But at least they had secured a general promise that
heirs in the king's wardship shall not in future be disparaged. They had

---

[1] *History of English Law*, vol. ii, pp. 395–6.
[2] Public Record Office, Aug. Off. Misc. Books 43, no. 187.
[3] P.R.O. Feet of Fines, Leicestershire, 121/3/63.
[4] Articles of the Barons, cl. 3.
[5] Magna Carta, cl. 6.

also pledged themselves to the same concession in regard to the marriages of heirs who held land of them.

The king's control over the heirs and heiresses of his tenants in chief continued until feudal tenures were swept away in 1660. They were then an anachronism. In Tudor times the court of wards had been established to ensure that the crown made full profit from its care of young heirs and heiresses and its right to arrange their marriages. In these last generations of feudalism the king's right to the wardship and marriage of heirs was a cause of anxiety to parents, as the will of Sir Simonds D'Ewes of Stow Langtoft, Suffolk, bears witness. Sir Simonds was one of that eminent company of antiquaries who illumine the seventeenth century. He made his will in 1639 and in it entreated and desired his beloved wife 'that she would purchase of the King or his officers the wardship of our children, whether I leave a male or female heir at the time of my decease under age, which, that it may be compassed without borrowing upon usury, let money be raised by the sale of my household-stuff and goods, . . . or else let some farms be let out for some terms of years, for a fine paid down and a small rent reserved; so that she buy the said wardship to the only use and benefit of our heirs successively, one after another, and that she take especial care to provide for their security before she enter into treaty for her second marriage'[1].

Widows were more fortunate than children in 1215. The king then promised that the widow on her husband's death 'shall immediately and without difficulty have her marriage portion and her inheritance, nor shall she give anything for her dower or her marriage portion or her inheritance which she and her husband held on the day of his death, and let her remain in her husband's house forty days after his death, within which let her dower be assigned to her'[2]. This was an important promise which carried with it the admission that the land the wife had brought to her husband remained her right, a right that was in no wise broken by the fact that her husband had held that land as his own during their marriage. In 1215 the king was forced into agreeing that widows should no longer fall completely into the king's power on their husbands' death. 'No widow', the king promised, 'shall be distrained to marry while she wishes to live without a husband, provided that she will give security that she will not marry without our consent, if she holds of us, or without the assent of

---

[1] *The Autobiography and Correspondence of Sir Simonds D'Ewes*, ed. J. O. Halliwell, London, 1845, vol. ii, pp. 153–4.   [2] Magna Carta, cl. 7.

the lord of whom she holds, if she holds of another'[1]. These promises mark a tentative beginning of the emancipation of English women from the legal subservience which had followed the Norman conquest.

Ladies who had purchased freedom to live as widows from King John and ladies whom he had sold to a second or third husband must wryly have said that the king's charter had come too late for them. As recently as 1214 he had married off his own first wife, whose marriage to him had been annulled in 1200, to the young Earl of Essex in return for the promise of a large sum of money which the earl did not live to pay[2]. It was left, a burden on his estate, to be settled in time by his successors. The earl was killed in a tournament in 1216 and his widow and her lands were put into the custody of Hubert de Burgh, the Justiciar, who promptly married her himself, though seemingly the marriage was secret. The countess died shortly afterwards. Even after the issue of the charter in 1215, the king could not refrain from disposing of a young widow as a reward to the mercenary captain, Faukes de Breauté. Margaret, daughter and coheiress of Warin fitz Gerold, the king's chamberlain, had been married as a child to Baldwin the heir of the Earl of Devon. Baldwin died before his father on 1 September 1216, when he was certainly no more than sixteen and may have been less. Margaret had borne him a son, who in due course became Earl of Devon[3]. She bitterly resented her forced marriage to Faukes de Breauté, and when he rebelled and was exiled in 1224 she obtained an annulment of the marriage from the Pope. She survived, a widow, until 1252. In recording her death in that year Matthew Paris took the opportunity of preserving a verse made on the marriage:

> 'Law joined them, love and the concord of the bed.
> But what sort of law? What sort of Love? What sort of
>   concord?
> Law which was no law. Love which was hate. Concord
>   which was discord'[4].

The records of the first half of the thirteenth century do not suggest that many noble widows at once took advantage of the king's promise that they could live unmarried if they so wished. To control a great inheritance

[1] Magna Carta, cl. 8.
[2] *Memoriale Fratris Walteri de Coventria*, ed. W. Stubbs, Rolls Series, 1873, vol. ii, p. 225.
[3] *Complete Peerage*, 2nd ed., vol. iv, pp. 316, 318.
[4] *Matthew Paris Chronica Majora*, ed. H. R. Luard, Rolls Series, 1880, vol. v, p. 323.

consisting of estates which might be scattered over many shires was not easy. Robert Grosseteste, Bishop of Lincoln, wrote a little tract on the way to manage a great estate for the benefit of a noble widow, Margaret, Countess of Lincoln, whose first husband, John de Lacy, Earl of Lincoln, died on 22 July 1240[1]. He advised her to begin by finding out exactly what lands of hers were let and the terms of the leases. She should find out the exact acreage of all her manors and whether they were adequately stocked. At harvest great care must be exercised over loading and storing the corn and deciding what must be kept for bread and beer through the year and what, if any, can be sold. The lady herself must keep control of her granges. She must at Michaelmas plan out her year's movements, so that she could live economically on the produce of her estates, but not impoverish any manor by staying in it too long. Those things which must be bought, such as wine, wax, and clothes, could be best bought at the fairs; for the manors in the eastern counties, Boston fair; for the Winchester lands, Southampton fair, and for the west country estates, Bristol fair; for cloth, St. Ives was best. The lady must control her household servants, make them courteous to her guests, clean and tidy in her presence, and well behaved at meals. She should herself see to the disposal of the food given in alms. The lady should sit in the middle of the high table where she can best keep watch on the service of both food and drink. She should aim at inspiring fear and reverence in her household. It is perhaps not surprising that the countess did not long remain a widow, bearing alone this burden of responsibility. Before April 1242 she had married the Earl of Pembroke, who died in 1245. Before June 1252 she had married a certain Richard of Wiltshire as her third husband. She died during March 1266[2].

If a great lady wished to live unmarried in the first half of the thirteenth century she either took the veil and entered a nunnery or became an anchoress, retiring completely from the world. The most famous anchoress of the thirteenth century was Loretta, widow of the Earl of Leicester, who died in 1204. Loretta was one of the three daughters of William de Braiose, lord of the honour of Bramber in Sussex and of an important lordship on the Welsh marches. Her father, after being one of King John's intimate friends and counsellors, fell into disgrace and at last died in exile. Her mother and elder brother disappeared under mysterious circumstances in one of the

[1] *Walter of Henley's Husbandry, together with an anonymous husbandry, seneschaucie and Robert Grosseteste's Rules*, ed. E. Lamond, Introduction by W. Cunningham, London, 1890, pp. xlii and 122 ff.   [2] *Complete Peerage*, 2nd ed., vol. vii, pp. 679-80.

royal castles where they were imprisoned. At the end of 1207 Loretta
made an agreement with the king that she would neither marry nor enter
the religious life for a year from St. Andrew's day, 30 November. Later
she seems to have fled from England for her lands were in the king's
hands. Her sister Margaret probably also fled to France with her husband.
Her sister Annora was put in prison. Loretta returned to England before
King John died, but she did not retire from the world to her cell at
Hackington, Kent, until about 1220. Annora, who married a lord on the
Welsh marches, also became an anchoress after her husband's death in
1227. Her refuge was at Iffley near Oxford. These ladies were able to live
a simple life in a modest two- or three-roomed house, attended by a
couple of servants, with a manservant to look after their business. They
disposed of their property and were fed by the alms of people of position.
Although an anchoress had left the world and could not go out into it
again, she could talk to visitors through her window. Loretta died at
Hackington on 4 March in 1266 or one of the following years. She had
lived through the barons' war and had been consulted not long before she
died about the rights and liberties which belonged to the Earl of Leicester
as steward of England. She was described as the 'recluse of Hackington',
but it was well remembered that she also was 'formerly Countess of
Leicester'[1].

Ela, Countess of Salisbury, a contemporary of Annora and Loretta, also
retired from the world after the death of her husband. She was the daughter
and heiress of the Earl of Salisbury and had carried the title and lands to her
husband, William Longsword, an illegitimate son of Henry II. She was
married to him in 1198, when she was about twelve years old. Her
husband died in 1226 after Ela had borne him four sons and four daughters.
The earl had joined the crusaders at Damietta early in Henry III's reign.
Rumours of his death while returning home brought his wife an unwelcome offer of marriage from the nephew of Hubert de Burgh, the king's
Justiciar. The countess refused him with scorn for she had already heard
that the rumours of her husband's death were false. On his return the earl,
whose health had been broken by his experiences, complained to the king
of the low fellow who had tried to marry his wife adulterously. The
Justiciar was forced to buy his favour by giving him precious horses and
rich gifts. When they had come to terms the Justiciar entertained the earl

[1] F. M. Powicke, 'Loretta, Countess of Leicester', in *Historical Essays in Honour of James
Tait*, Manchester, 1933, pp. 247–72.

to dinner, at which it was suspected the earl was given poison, for he died soon afterwards[1]. In 1232 his widow built a house for Augustinian nuns at Lacock in Wiltshire, where she took the veil in 1238. In the following year she became abbess and held that office until 1257 when ill health obliged her to retire. She died and was buried at Lacock in 1261[2]. A woman of this type was admirably placed as the head of a religious community. Although no longer in the world she was of it, able through her connections with the society she had left to further the interests of her house.

As the thirteenth century wore on and the privileges won by the Great Charter were again and again confirmed the crown could no longer bring the weapon of distraint into play against a widow who would not take a husband at the royal suggestion, as Richard I had done against the Countess of Aumale. The king could still sell or give away the marriage of a widow and the fine which would be due from her if she married without the consent of her overlord, but if she chose to live as a widow neither king nor suitor could stop her doing so. Family pressure, however, probably caused many widows to marry again. Moreover, in war-time a man who had bought a widow's marriage from the king might try to make his bargain effective by force. Isabella de Forz[3] complained of being pursued about the country with horses and arms on this account, so that she had to take refuge in Wales, but for all that she preserved her widowed estate[4]. There are signs that widows were beginning to realize the independence of their position. Matthew Paris describes how another Isabella, the widowed Countess of Arundel, bearded the king 'in his chamber' to complain that the heir of one of her tenants had been taken into the king's wardship because he held a little land of the crown. When she approached him the king at first showed her an agreeable countenance, but afterwards, blaming her with rather bitter words, he gave her nothing of what she asked. 'Wherefore she, although a woman, answered fearlessly, not like a woman, "Oh, my lord king, wherefore do you turn your face from justice? In your court now that which is just cannot be obtained. . . . You set yourself between God and us, but neither yourself nor us do you rule well. . . .".' The king, sneering and grinning, called out in a high voice and asked the

[1] *Roger of Wendover*, ed. H. O. Coxe, London, 1842, vol. iv, pp. 113–14 and 116–17.

[2] *Complete Peerage*, 2nd ed., vol. xi, pp. 381–2.

[3] Widow of the Count of Aumale, who was grandson of the Countess Hawisa, see pp. 35–6 above and p. 55 below.

[4] F. M. Powicke, *Henry III and the Lord Edward*, Oxford, 1947, vol. ii, pp. 707–8.

countess if the barons of England had made a charter with her and made her their advocate because of her eloquence. The countess, 'although she was young, yet not in a childish way', reminded the king of the charter which his father had made and he himself had granted and confirmed[1]. The Earl of Arundel had married Isabella when he was about nineteen in 1234. He died without issue in 1243. His widow survived him for nearly forty years. She died in 1282.

The way in which a widow could come into control of a vast complex of estates by the operation of the laws of inheritance and dower is well illustrated by the life of Isabella de Forz, Countess of Aumale. She was born in 1237 and married the Count of Aumale in 1249 at the age of twelve. She was widowed in 1260, and for the rest of her life held in dower a third of the great Aumale inheritance. In 1262 she inherited from her brother the earldom of Devon which carried with it, as it had throughout the Norman and Angevin period, the lordship of the Isle of Wight. Thereupon Isabella assumed the title of 'Countess of Aumale and Devon and Lady of the Island'[2]. She had acquired a territorial position which the crown, stronger under Edward I than it had ever been before, could only regard as too great for a subject. The Isle of Wight, in particular, both Henry III and, after him, Edward I had desired. Isabella's son and heir died at the age of sixteen in 1269. Her only surviving child, a daughter, was married at ten to the king's younger son, but she died at fifteen in 1274. Edward I then tried to buy Isabella's inheritance from her, but not until she was on her death-bed in November 1293 did the bargain go through. Even then the sale was confined to the Isle of Wight which was at last separated from the earldom of Devon. A remote kinsman, for whose interests Isabella had little care, acquired the other lands of the earldom and with them the title of earl[3].

There is ample evidence in legal records that the great ladies of the twelfth and thirteenth centuries were as interested as their husbands and sons in preserving or increasing the estates which had come to them by inheritance or marriage. Earls and barons and their ladies rarely appeared in person in court to prosecute or defend their actions for land. Attorneys answered on their behalf and the earliest members of the legal profession gained profit and experience in the give and take of the interminable law-

[1] *Matthew Paris Chronica Majora*, vol. v, pp. 336–7.
[2] *Complete Peerage*, 2nd ed., vol. iv, p. 322 *n*.
[3] F. M. Powicke, *Henry III and the Lord Edward*, pp. 707–9.

suits brought as readily by noble ladies as by their husbands. If the land at issue were claimed as a wife's inheritance she, as well as her husband, must be represented in court. Like their husbands, ladies had their own seals to authenticate their letters and grants of land.

At this time it was usual for a seal to bear a representation of its owner. A great man of the period generally appeared in full armour riding a spirited horse, with his arms well displayed on shield and horse cloth. The great lady was generally shown standing, sometimes facing front, sometimes turning to right or left. Her seal was therefore not round but oval. It is never possible to tell whether the lady portrayed on a seal were beautiful or not, but something of her style of dress and something also of her interests can be seen. Margaret, Countess of Lincoln and Pembroke, is shown wearing a long dress, a fur cloak, and a flat head-dress. Ela, Countess of Salisbury, is wearing a long dress girt at the waist, and a fur cloak[1]. The Countess Hawisa of Aumale is wearing a long dress without cloak or head-dress. The dresses sometimes look almost moulded to the figure, with a straight long skirt. Sometimes the skirt flared at the feet. At the end of the twelfth century the tight sleeves were stressed by a long floating piece of drapery hanging from the wrists. Ladies all through this period enjoyed the sport of hawking and many appear on their seals holding a hawk or falcon on one hand or the other. The Countess Hawisa holds one on her left hand. Occasionally, like Maud, widow of Sir William of Hartshill, ladies have small dogs shown on their seals. Maud is standing with a small dog at her feet and another in her arms[2]. The interest in heraldry, which was growing in strength all through and long after this period, is reflected in ladies' seals, as in those of their husbands. Sometimes the lady is shown holding up shields of arms[3]. Sometimes heraldic devices invade even her clothes and are shown as ornaments on her dress[4]. Occasionally a lady allowed herself to appear on horseback on her seal. Mabel of Gatton in the thirteenth century is shown riding sideways in a long dress with a hawk on her left hand[5].

As the Middle Ages went on, comfort and privacy increased. The hall ceased to be the centre of the life of a great household, for rooms with large open fireplaces and chimneys to carry off the smoke added to the attraction of life indoors and of such indoor occupations as reading and

[1] *Catalogue of Seals in the Department of Manuscripts in the British Museum*, 1892, vol. ii, nos. 6676, 6678.   [2] *Ibid.*, no. 6658.
[3] *Ibid.*, no. 6573.   [4] *Ibid.*, no. 6695.   [5] *Ibid.*, no. 6648.

writing Long before the Middle Ages were over most people of position could write a good letter, though their spelling was generally erratic. By the fifteenth century individual great men were collecting books and making libraries. They were patrons of learning, responsive to the stirrings of thought and feeling which preceded the full renaissance. Their ladies shared their tastes and sometimes shared the education which trained them, but no great lady of the last generations of the true Middle Ages has left anything that comes near literature behind her[1]. They lived through a civil war which destroyed the heads of many noble families, for it degenerated ito a series of family feuds rather than war. It bred treachery and insecurity, which itself bred treason trials and executions.

The reign of Henry VII (1485–1509) marks the beginning of a new age in English history. He drew whatever hereditary right he possessed to the crown through his mother, Margaret Beaufort, Countess of Richmond, to whom the Lancastrian claim to the throne and the Lancastrian wealth descended. She was content that the right should pass through her to her son. 'My oune suet and most deere Kynge and all my worldly joy' as she addressed him in a letter which she signed as 'your faythfull trewe bedewoman and humble modyr, Margaret R.' (that is, Richmond)[2]. Her austere and delicate features can be seen in those of her son and again in the face of her great-grandchild, Queen Elizabeth.

The women of Tudor England were still very near the Middle Ages. The new learning which many of them professed could not at once change the fundamental outlook of all women. For all that some women could turn Greek into Latin and both of them into English and back again the real interest of most women remained, as it always had been, their land and household. The law they lived under was still feudal. Among all the frail and fashionable young scholars of the age a woman like Elizabeth Talbot, Countess of Shrewsbury, stands like a rock of medieval common sense, as strong as Queen Elizabeth herself[3]. To all later generations

[1] There is no other evidence for the existence of Juliana Berners, said to be Prioress of Sopwell, than the *Explicit*, which closes the treatise on hunting in the *Boke of St. Albans* 'Explicit dame Julyans Barnes in her boke of huntyng'. Wynkyn de Worde's version runs 'Explicit dame Julyans Bernes doctryne in her boke of huntynge'. For a careful discussion of this lady and the value of the statements about her see *The Boke of St. Albans by Dame Juliana Berners*, London, 1905. Introduction by William Blades, pp. 7–13.

[2] *Original Letters Illustrative of English History*, ed. Henry Ellis, London, 1824, vol. i, pp. 46–8.

[3] Information here given is derived from J. Hunter, *Hallamshire* (1811), pp. 62–96; E. Lodge, *Illustrations of British History*, vol. ii.

Elizabeth Talbot, wife of Gilbert, sixth Earl of Shrewsbury, has remained Bess of Hardwick, who brought the Cavendishes to Derbyshire and was the mother of two sons who founded respectively the dukedoms of Devonshire and Newcastle. She was the fourth daughter and coheiress of John Hardwick, whose ancestors for five generations had been lords of the manor of Hardwick, near Tibshelf, Derbyshire. On both sides she came of Derbyshire country stock. She was born in 1518 and at the age of fourteen married Robert Barlow, of Barlow in Dronfield, in that county. This excellent, if undistinguished, marriage made her fortune, for her marriage settlement secured her husband's lands to herself and her heirs. Robert Barlow died within a year of the marriage, so that his widow at fifteen came into control of his estate. It is a pity that 'this beautiful and discreet woman'[1] Elizabeth Barlow has left no account of her thoughts during the sixteen years she remained a widow, for it must have been then that her character was formed.

In 1549 at Bradgate, Leicestershire, 'at two o'clock after midnight', she married Sir William Cavendish, who came of a Suffolk family, but sold his lands in the south and purchased lands in Derbyshire so that his wife might live among her own people. He is the only one of all her husbands by whom she had children. Three sons and three daughters of hers by him lived to grow up. Sir William began to build Chatsworth, but died in 1557 leaving it for his widow to finish. She soon married again, and again made sure that her settlement secured her husband's lands to her own heirs, if she had no issue by him. Her third husband was Sir William St. Loe of Tadmarton, Oxfordshire, who was captain of the guard to Queen Elizabeth. When not in attendance at court he lived in Derbyshire and when he died his whole estate passed to his widow to the exclusion of daughters by a former marriage. The widowed 'Lady St. Low had not survived her Charms of Wit and Beauty'[2]. Her successive marriages had enriched her so much that she was a valuable matrimonial prize. She accepted the addresses of the Earl of Shrewsbury, but only after she had secured the marriages of her own eldest son to the earl's daughter and her own youngest daughter Mary, aged twelve, to the earl's second son, Gilbert, his eldest son being already married. Queen Elizabeth welcomed the marriage and soon found a way of using some of the earl's wealth.

[1] White Kennet, *A Sermon preach'd at the Funeral of the Right Noble William Duke of Devonshire . . . with some Memoirs of the Family of Cavendish*, London, 1708, p. 65.
[2] *Ibid.*, p. 67.

Before the end of 1568 she had determined that Mary Queen of Scots
should be put into his custody. He could entertain the queen and her
attendants without expecting full reimbursement of his expenses from
the crown. His recent marriage to a lady known for her beauty, her wit,
and the resolution of her character would protect him from falling under
the influence of his prisoner.

For sixteen years the Queen of Scots remained in the custody of the
Earl of Shrewsbury. Long before the end of this time he had quarrelled
bitterly with his wife. In 1574 she endangered her husband's standing with
the queen by securing a marriage between her daughter, Elizabeth
Cavendish, and Charles, Earl of Lennox, brother-in-law of Mary Queen
of Scots. The Countess of Lennox and her son had been entertained for
five days by the Countess of Shrewsbury at Rufford on their way north,
and in that time the marriage was made. It was indeed flying high, for the
countess's new son-in-law was a grandson of Margaret Tudor, Queen
Elizabeth's aunt. The queen sent the Countess of Shrewsbury to prison in
the Tower of London for three months and the earl had some difficulty in
explaining how he had come to allow his wife to make the match. He had
no scruple in blaming her for the affair. The only issue of the marriage was
the Lady Arabella Stuart, who was left an orphan when she was four years
old. The Countess of Shrewsbury took charge of the infant, 'my dearest
juyll Arabella', as she described her when writing to the queen's ministers
to ask for a larger allowance for her maintenance[1]. But the early affection
waned and the Lady Arabella was cut out of her grandmother's will.

Bess of Hardwick was not an easy woman to live with. Her early
widowhood and her success in her marriage treaties induced in her a
tyrannical spirit which grew stronger with the years. Her last husband's
early affection for her had gone long before his death. She pestered him to
remove with his charge to her house at Chatsworth and left him to settle
there herself in 1583. She even told Queen Elizabeth that the earl was too
friendly with the Queen of Scots. Bitter recriminations passed between
husband and wife, so that at last the queen intervened to patch up a
reconciliation between them. But it was too late. The earl had fallen under
the domination of one of his female servants, a certain Eleanor Britton.
The countess spent large sums of money building houses in her own
country-side. At Chatsworth, Oldcoates, Worksop, and Bolsover she had
been at work in her fourth husband's lifetime. After his death in January

[1] Ellis, *Original Letters*, 2nd series, vol. iii, p. 65.

1591 she built a splendid mansion at Hardwick, completed in 1597. There she spent her fourth widowhood and there she died[1]. Historians have uttered bitter words about this strong-minded woman: 'She was a woman of a masculine understanding and conduct; proud, furious, selfish, and unfeeling. She was a builder, a buyer and seller of estates, a money lender, a farmer, a merchant of lead, coals, and timber: when disengaged from these employments, she intrigued alternately with Elizabeth and Mary, always to the prejudice and terror of her husband. She lived to a great old age, continually flattered, but seldom deceived, and died in 1607, immensely rich without a friend'[2]. Edmund Lodge, who wrote these words in 1791, had made full use of the papers of the Talbot family and based his judgment on them. But a man who could use the phrase 'of masculine understanding' as a term of reproach to a woman could never appreciate Bess of Hardwick. The key to her character and career lies in her sixteen years of widowhood, beginning when she was only fifteen. She then tasted liberty and she was strong enough never to relinquish it again. She kept her second and third husbands' affection. For her fourth husband she was altogether too strong.

Something of Bess of Hardwick's quality may well have been inherited by her granddaughter, Elizabeth, Countess of Kent, who was the daughter of Mary Cavendish, wife of Gilbert, Earl of Shrewsbury. A woman who could win the respect and affection of John Selden deserves attention. He had been the legal adviser of the Earl of Kent and habitually spent his vacations at the earl's seat at Wrest, Bedfordshire, where he could peacefully pursue his studies. After the earl's death without issue in 1639, Selden was reputed to have married his widow, though such a marriage was never admitted by either party. John Aubrey, who delighted in scandal, is the authority always quoted for this marriage. He describes how John Selden lived with the countess, whose servants were at his disposal[3]. When she died in December 1651 she bequeathed most of her property to Selden, who was her executor. Lady Kent was 'a lady of uncommon virtue and piety'[4] and Selden was an eminent scholar who had enjoyed the friendship and trust of the earl and countess for many years. A man and woman of such quality could afford to be indifferent to the gossip which floated round the town. Lady Kent appears in the

---

[1] On 13 February 1608, *D.N.B.*

[2] *Illustrations of British History*, vol. i, p. xvii.

[3] Quoted by Wood from Aubrey's manuscript, *Athenæ Oxonienses*, ed. Bliss, vol. iii, p. 378.   [4] Nichols, *Literary Anecdotes*, vol. viii, p. 510.

Dictionary of National Biography as an author because after her death a
collection of medical recipes was published in her name[1].

It is unlikely that Elizabeth's reign passed without many women
reflecting that it was unreasonable to subject women to the rule of their
husbands while the queen was proving the capacity of a woman to govern
a kingdom. Even among the conservative lawyers of the time there was
sympathy with their position. In 1632 there was published a book entitled
The Lawes Resolutions of Womens Rights or The Lawes provision for Women.
It purports to be 'a methodicall collection of such Statutes and Customes,
with the Cases, Opinions, Arguments and points of Learning in the Law as
doe properly concerne Women'[2]. The book was written a good many
years before publication, almost certainly during the last years of
Elizabeth. The lawyer who saw it through the press speaks of its author as
dead. He quotes no later law than one of 39 Elizabeth and describes himself
as 'having sailed between the capes of Magna Charta and Quadra-
gesima of Queen Elizabeth'[3]. He undertook the work, he says, as 'A
publique Advantage and peculiar service to that Sexe generally beloved,
and by the Author had in venerable estimation'[4]. Despite all the writer's
efforts to encourage his feminine readers by little stories and jests, the work
remains stiff reading. If the generality of ladies could cope with it
successfully in the seventeenth century there is no doubt that they were a
well-educated and able generation.

The author of this book seems to have felt assurance that women would
read him. He wrote, as he says, 'not regarding so much to satisfie the
deeplearned or searchers for subtility, as woman kind, to whom I am a
thankfull debter by nature'[5]. After reaching back to the creation of man
and woman he proceeds in his first book to show how a woman may
inherit land, when she can come out of wardship, and how she should
make a partition of land with a sister. After this he thinks that 'she should
long to be married: . . . And I did not meane when I began to produce any
vestall virgin, Nunne, or new Saint Brigid'[6]. Having set out a clear and
concise account of betrothal, marriage, and divorce, the writer goes on to
describe the provision made by the girl's father which he calls 'the condiments of love'. 'Good meats are the better for good sauce; venison craveth

---

[1] *A choice Manuall, or Rare and Select Secrets in Physick and Chyrurgery Collected and practised
by the . . . Countesse of Kent, late deceased*, 2nd ed., London, 1653.

[2] Description on the title-page, London, 1632.

[3] *Ibid.*, p. 403. The author speaks of 'the late Queene Elizabeth' on p. 402.

[4] *Ibid.*, Preface signed I. L. but unpaged.   [5] *Ibid.*, p. 3.   [6] *Ibid.*, p. 51.

wine, and Wedlock hath certaine Condiments, which come best in season at the wooing time'[1]. After he has described the law relating to land given by the woman's father in free marriage and the law touching wife's dower from her husband he concludes: 'I have held young maides now indeed somewhat long in the old endowments . . . for my desire is that they should be able to have when they are widdowes a coach, or at least an ambler, and some money in their purses'[2]. His next book deals with the results of man and wife being made one person. 'The wife must take the name of her husband, Alice Greene becommeth Alice Musgraue; She that in the morning was Faire weather, is at night, perhaps Rainebow or Goodwife Foule; Sweet heart going to church, and Hoistbrick comming home'. She must take her second husband's rank in society even though her first husband had a title and her second had not, for 'the dignitie hangeth meerely on the male side carrying the sceptre of Wedlocke'[3].

'If a Seignioresse of a manor marry her bond-man, he is made free, and where before hee was her footstoole, he is now her head and Seignior'[4]. A man may beat 'an outlaw, a traitor, a Pagan, his villein, or his wife because by the Law Common these persons can have no action: God send Gentle-women better sport or better companie'. Nevertheless, he points out, there is a writ which a woman may sue out of Chancery if she 'threatened by her husband to bee beaten, mischieved, or slaine . . . to compell him to finde surety of honest behaviour towards her and that he shall neither doe nor procure to be done to her (marke I pray you) any bodily damage, otherwise than appertaines to the office of a husband for lawfull and reasonable correction'. He suggests, however, that perhaps the wife might not be so badly off after all since there is no action which a husband can bring if his wife beats him[5]. But he goes on to point out that 'That which the husband hath is his owne' and 'That which the wife hath is the husband's'. A brief chapter on each of these texts drives home the lesson further expounded through many pages of detailed exposition illustrated by cases from old collections of law reports.

The author explains to his readers that *femme sole* means a woman of full age, unmarried or a widow, and *femme couert* means a married woman. He

<hr/>

[1] *Lawes Resolutions*, p. 72.   [2] *Ibid.*, p. 115.

[3] *Ibid.*, pp. 125–6. The author quoted the case of a writ brought by 'The Lady Anne Powes and her husband Randolph Hayward, Esquire' touching part of the inheritance of Charles Brandon, Duke of Suffolk, against the then Duke of Suffolk and his wife. The plaintiffs were forced to obtain another writ in the name of 'Randolph Hayward and his wife, late the wife of Lord Powes'.   [4] *Ibid.*, p. 128.   [5] *Ibid.*, pp. 128–9.

tells them what each may do in law. He warns the married woman that she must 'take heed of elopement' because 'a woman that leaves her husband, goeth away and abides with her adulterer, if she be convicted thereof, loseth for ever her command of dower etc'. He instanced the famous Camoys case which has already been quoted[1]. Dower was sought 'by R. H. and Anne his wife' and 'it was pleaded that the said Anne in the life of Lord Powes

> Frankly of her owne accord,
> Left her Husband and her Lord,
> And from Bednall Greene she ran
> With Mathew Rochlei Gentleman

to the parish of Saint Clements Danes, where she lived in adultery, all the life long of Lord Powes'[2]. The plaintiffs pleaded that Lady Powis had been reconciled to her husband, but this plea was rejected. 'But', says the author, 'me thinkes here wanteth equality in the law. Women go downe stile, and many graines allowance will not make the ballance hang euen: A poore woman shall have but the third foote of her Husbands lands when he is dead, for all the service she did him during the accouplement (perhaps a long time and a tedious) and if she be extravagant with a friend this is elopement and forfeiture etc. But as the saying is, men are happy by the masse, they may goe where they list I warrant yee, and because they are enforced to travell in the world, they will pay deare abroad for that which they esteeme of no value at home. Their adultrous soiournings is not discerned, they may lope over ditch and Dale, a thousand out-ridings and out-biddings is no forfeiture, but as soone as the good wife is gone, the badman will have her land, not the third, but euery foote of it'. There is no doubt here of the writer's sympathy with women. He continues: 'Have patience (my Schollers) take not your opportunitie of revenge, rather move for redresse by Parliament and in the meane season be perswaded that liberty or impunity in doing evil is no freedome or happines'[3]. Here at the turn of the sixteenth and seventeenth centuries is the first appearance

---

[1] See above, p. 48.

[2] The case was brought by Ralf Haworth, Esq., and the Lady Anne Powis his wife against John Herbert and his wife. *Dyer's Reports*, ed. John Vaillant, London, 1794, vol. ii, p. 106. Lady Powis was a daughter of Charles Brandon, Duke of Suffolk, by Anne Browne, born before the marriage of her parents. *Complete Peerage*, 2nd ed., vol. xii, pp. 458 n. and 462 n.   [3] *Lawes Resolutions*, pp. 144–6.

of the idea that Parliament was the only authority strong enough to right the wrongs of women.

It is unnecessary to follow all the argument of the learned author by which he tries to forewarn a woman of the various ways in which her husband may dispose of her land and dower and she may circumvent him. He himself declared that to go farther in 'the streame of fines and recoverie' would require 'a cunning swimmer'[1]. He was scornful of the old way of protecting the wife's interest when a husband wished to make a final concord touching land which is of her right. He warns her that she would lose all possibility of action at law if a fine has been lawfully levied by man and wife, 'where (forsooth) because a woman is examined by a Justice . . . and acknowledgeth her free consent and agreement, what cannot men get their wiues to do if they list, she shall be barred and foreuer excluded from a great many acres of ground, for a few kisses and a gay gowne. That is a fine final concord for till it be done and dispatcht, the poore woman can haue no quiet, her husband keepes such a iawling'[2]. But the author praised jointures, which he treated as a more up-to-date means of providing for a wife than dower. 'All husbands are not so unkinde or untrusty as to endamage their wiues by alienation of their lands: but contrariwise the greatest part of honest, wise and sober men are of themselves careful to purchase somewhat for their wiues, if they be not yet they stand sometimes bound by the woman's parents to make their wiues some joynture'. Very many English women, he went on to say, have wisdom enough of their own to see how much better a jointure is than dower. Lands purchased by husband and wife jointly for the wife can be enjoyed at once. Dower 'must be tarried for till the husband be dead: It must be demanded, sometimes sued for, sometime neither with suit or demand obtained'[3].

It is clear that women in Elizabeth's day were still as much 'under the rod' of their husbands, sometimes to their own advantage, as they had been when Bracton wrote[4]. 'If a man and wife commit felonie jointly, it seemeth that the wife is no felon, but it shall be wholley judged the husband's fact'. If a husband finds his wife committing felony, however, he must abandon her and his own house in order to avoid being treated as an accessory. But if a man commit felony 'his wife not ignorant of it may keep his company still notwithstanding . . . for a woman cannot bee

---

[1] *Lawes Resolutions*, p. 182.
[3] *Ibid.*, pp. 182–3.

[2] *Ibid.*, pp. 179–80.
[4] See above, p. 30.

accessory to her husband inasmuch as she is forbidden by the Law of God to bewray him'[1].

The conception that a husband is the 'lord' of his wife which coloured the feudal aspect of their relationship was far more than a literary common-place. It brought the woman who plotted against the life of her husband under the law of treason, and subjected her to the death penalty in its severest form. A woman convicted of murdering her husband was held guilty of 'petty treason' and therefore burned alive. The last English woman to suffer in this way for this crime was Catherine Hayes, executed at Tyburn in 1726. The author of *The Lawes Resolutions of Womens Rights* feels himself obliged to warn women of the words of the Act of Treasons of 25 Edward III cap. 2: 'that if any servant kill his master, any woman kill her husband, or any man secular or religious person kill his Prelate to whom he owes obedience, this is treason. . . . The Statute is but the declaration of the common law'. He rubs home the lesson by quoting a case of Edward II's time: 'A woman compasseth with her adulterer the death of her husband, they assailed him riding on the highway, beating, wounding, leaving him for dead, and then they fled: The husband got up, levied hue and cry, came before the Justices, they sent after the offenders, which were gotten, arraigned, and the matter found by verdict, the adul-terer was hanged, the woman burned to death, the husband living, the will shall be reputed as the deed, 15 Edward 2'. The author goes on to quote the case of a woman servant bringing into her mistress's house and 'to her bed-side where the mistress lay asleep a stranger who killed her mistress, the servant silent, nothing doing but holding the candle', and is clearly uncertain whether the servant has committed petty treason, since the Act does not include the word mistress as well as master. He points out that if a wife conspires with a servant, who kills his master in the wife's absence, yet she is guilty of treason, but if she conspires with a man not his servant who likewise kills her husband in her absence she is 'but barely hanged as accessorie, because the principal was but a murderer'[2]. There is nothing new in this severity. A case from King John's reign which ended in the burning of a woman for her husband's murder is only noticed in the records because her land was bought from the chief lord of the fee by one of the king's clerks[3].

In the sixteenth as in the thirteenth century the widow had the right of

---

[1] *Lawes Resolutions*, p. 206.   [2] *Ibid.*, pp. 208–9.
[3] *Pipe Roll 3 John*, pp. xv–xvi, 32.

making an appeal against her husband's murderer. In *The Lawes Resolutions of Womens Rights* the process follows a long account of the reasons which may lead a widow to marry for a second time. Naturally, though not necessarily, the author takes for his example an appeal begun by a woman who was following up the murder of her second husband. His account is severely technical, but it is introduced by a paragraph of almost incongruous vivacity. He begins by describing how the widow 'married againe to her owne great liking, though not with the applause of most friends and acquaintance. But alas what would they have her to have done, she was faire, young, rich, gracious in her carriage, and so well became her mourning apparell, that when she went to church on Sundayes, the casements opened of their owne accord on both sides the streets, that bachelours and widdowers might behold her. . . . Her man at home kissed her pantables and serued diligently, her late husband's physitian came and visited often; the Lawyer to whom she went for counsell tooke opportunity to aduise for himself. If shee went to any feast there was always one guest, sometimes two or three, the more for her sake; If she were at home the suitors ouertooke one another. . . . All day she was troubled with answering petitions'. In the end she married 'one not of the long robe, not a man macerate and dryed up with study, but a gallant gulberd lad; that might well be worthy of her had he been as thrifty as kind hearted, or half so wise as hardy and adventurous'. The end of it was that he wasted her money, was challenged to a duel and 'there my new married man was slaine; Now his wife will bring her appeale'[1]. The law which governed it need not be discussed here[2].

Even in the seventeenth century husbands and wives were living within the framework of a law which in all essentials was medieval. How should it be otherwise when the feudal incidents of wardship and marriage still prevailed? Many of the marriages arranged by parents or guardians for financial reasons doubtless turned out well enough, but much unhappiness came of others. The life-story of Frances Coke shows the penalties which a woman might suffer if she broke away from an impossible marriage. She was the younger daughter of Sir Edward Coke, the champion and exponent of the common law, by his second wife, Lady Elizabeth Hatton.

[1] *Lawes Resolutions*, pp. 331–2.
[2] It should be noted that every woman had the right to appeal anyone she suspected of her husband's death. The author was anxious to get in his account of the popular and beautiful rich widow.

This marriage had not been a success and Lady Elizabeth lived apart from her husband. She tried in vain to prevent Coke arranging a marriage between her daughter Frances and Sir John Villiers, the eldest brother of the king's favourite, the Duke of Buckingham. Buckingham wanted to find a rich wife for his brother and asked for the hand of Frances Coke, who was only fourteen and might well have expected a better match. Sir Edward Coke agreed to the marriage because he needed the support of Buckingham. Lady Elizabeth tried to find a different husband for her daughter and carried her off to a cousin's house, but Coke, aided by his sons by his first wife, seized Frances by force. Her mother took the case to the Star Chamber and was vocal in her complaints against her husband, both about the marriage and his treatment of her own property, but she could do nothing. Indeed, she was put into the custody of one of the aldermen of London and could not attend her daughter's wedding, which took place on Michaelmas Day, 1617.

To satisfy Buckingham the king made Sir John Villiers a viscount and he took the title of Purbeck from the property he hoped to come by through his wife. Lord Purbeck was of poor intelligence, sometimes falling into insanity. His wife became intimate with one of the sons of the Earl of Suffolk, Sir Robert Howard, who made no secret of his feeling for her. When she gave birth to a child in 1624 it was generally accepted that Howard was its father. Both Lady Purbeck and Howard were cited to appear before the court of High Commission on a charge of adultery. Lady Purbeck was sentenced to a heavy fine, imprisonment during pleasure, and penance barefoot and in a white sheet. She escaped, without doing penance, whether to Shropshire with Sir Robert Howard, as was later alleged, or to France, is now no matter. She undoubtedly eloped from her husband and suffered the penalties described by the anonymous writer of the lawbook for women's use. Her own money remained with her husband and his family. In 1635 she and Sir Robert Howard returned to London and were both taken again, but again she escaped, this time certainly to France. When war broke out she returned to England and died at Oxford in 1645. She was fortunate in that she had friends to help her and that Sir Robert Howard was faithful to her as long as she lived[1].

The penalties of unfaithfulness were harsh but they were balanced by

[1] The story of Frances Coke was worked out from the original documents by Laura Norsworthy, *The Lady of Bleeding Heart Yard*, London, 1935.

the independence allowed by the common law of England to every widow. The Duchess of Newcastle, who wrote a brief autobiography in order that after ages might be able to distinguish between herself and the duke's first wife[1], described in it her upbringing at St. John's near Colchester. Her mother, Lady Lucas, was left a widow soon after the duchess, her youngest child, was born. Although her husband's estate was divided between herself and her sons, and a sum of money was appointed as portions for her daughters 'yet by reason she and her children agreed with a mutual consent, all their affairs were managed so well as she lived not in a much lower condition than when my father lived. 'Tis true, my mother might have increased her daughters' portions by a thrifty sparing, yet she chose to bestow it on our breeding, honest pleasures and harmless delights', feeling that 'if she bred us with needy necessity' it might create in her children 'mean thoughts and base actions'[2]. Her mother would often complain that her family was 'too great for her weak management', and often pressed her eldest son to take it upon him, 'yet I observed she took a pleasure, and some little pride in the governing thereof. She was very skilful in leases and setting of lands, and court keeping, ordering of stewards and the like affairs. Also I observed that my mother, nor my brothers, before these wars had never any lawsuits, but what an attorney despatched in a term with small cost'[3].

Lady Fanshawe, who wrote her memoirs after her husband's death in 1668, acknowledged with thankfulness 'God's bounty' to her husband's family in bestowing 'most excellent wives on most of them, both in person and fortune'. She spoke of her own mother-in-law with particular appreciation. She was 'left a widow at thirty-nine years of age, handsome, with a full fortune, all her children provided for', but instead of marrying again, she 'kept herself a widow, and out of her jointure and revenue purchased six hundred pounds a year for the younger children of her eldest son; besides she added five hundred pounds apiece to the portions of her younger children, having nine'[4]. It was clearly regarded as a sign of peculiar virtue in a handsome young widow if she refrained from marrying again but devoted herself to the welfare of her children. For despite the independence and authority enjoyed by widows it is interesting to see how often they tempted fortune again by taking another husband.

---

[1] *Memoirs of William Cavendish, Duke of Newcastle*, ed. C. H. Firth, London, 1905, p. 178.   [2] *Ibid.*, p. 156-7.   [3] *Ibid.*, p. 165.
[4] *The Memoirs of Lady Fanshawe*, London, 1907, p. 16.

No account of the position of women in the feudal world would be satisfactory which omitted to notice the life of Anne, Countess of Pembroke (1590–1676). It is impossible to stay long in Westmorland today without hearing of the Lady Anne, for her memory still lives among the Westmorland people, many of whom bear the same surnames as those who served her in the seventeenth century. The country itself is not greatly changed. She was the sole surviving child of George Clifford, third Earl of Cumberland, and could look back on a noble pedigree stretching in the male line as far as the Norman Conquest. To the main line of the Cliffords the land of the Viponts and Vescys had come, acquisitions which had drawn them from the Welsh border to the north. Lady Anne's grandmother was a daughter of Lord Dacre of the north and was remarkable among the nobility of the day in that she had never been to London or the south in her life. Her husband had made over to her as her jointure all his Westmorland lands. Her son succeeded to the earldom at the age of eleven and was brought up by his guardian, Francis Russel, second Earl of Bedford. At nineteen he married one of his guardian's daughters, Margaret, to whom he had been betrothed in childhood. She was seventeen at the time of the marriage. Their two sons died in infancy and the Earl of Cumberland left his lands by will to his brother, to revert to his daughter the Lady Anne, if the male line failed.

From this will came trouble and litigation. Margaret, Countess of Cumberland, whose effigy survives in Appleby church, was a woman of great strength of character. She had her daughter carefully educated for the position she was to fill. The poet and historian, Samuel Daniel, was her tutor, but her father would not allow her to learn a foreign language. When the Lady Anne was fifteen in 1605 her father died. She recorded that a little before his death he expressed 'a great Beliefe that hee had his Brother's sonne would dye without issue male, and therby all his Landes would come to be myne'[1]. The Countess of Cumberland was determined that her daughter should inherit her father's estates and in 1607 she took the Lady Anne to Westmorland and began to collect the evidences necessary to substantiate her claim. All her life the Lady Anne was a keeper of diaries, a collector of evidences about the history of her family, a builder of memorials to all with whom she had connections—even to Samuel Daniel because he was her teacher, to Spenser because she loved his work. She read and re-read her diaries and annotated them. She

---

[1] G. C. Williamson, *Lady Anne Clifford*, Kendal, 1922, p. 22.

employed clerks to copy them out and help her with her compilations. The long and fruitless litigation begun by her mother in the court of wards and continued by the Lady Anne herself stimulated her pride of family and love of Westmorland. She was married in 1609 to Richard Sackville, Lord Buckhurst, who two days after the wedding succeeded to the earldom of Dorset. The marriage took her to Kent and to Knole. Her chief jointure house was Bollbroke in Sussex, but Westmorland was ever in her thoughts. In the retrospect her marriage was happy enough, though her husband was not faithful to her. 'Sometimes I had fair words from him, and sometimes foul, but I took all patiently, and did strive to give him as much content and assurance of my love as I could possibly, yet I told him that I would never part with Westmoreland upon any condition whatever'[1].

The death of the Countess of Cumberland in 1616 made no difference to her daughter's determination to win her lands. The Earl of Dorset was ready to compound for them and the king himself intervened to try to force the Lady Anne to drop her claim. The suit was of such importance that it came, as it would have come in the twelfth century, before the king himself. James I was unsuccessful, for the Lady Anne constantly declared, even in the king's presence, that she would 'never give up Westmoreland'. The king therefore awarded the land to the Earl of Cumberland in return for the payment of a substantial sum to the Earl of Dorset. After her husband's death in 1624 the countess remained a widow for six years, but in 1630, to most people's surprise, she married Philip Herbert, Earl of Pembroke and Montgomery. He was the son of the learned Countess of Pembroke[2], but if royalist propaganda is to be believed was a foul-mouthed creature with no interests beyond sport. That he was handsome seems certain. He was also a lover of fine buildings as Wilton itself bears witness. His readiness to support his wife in her claim to Westmorland, and his great position which made his support valuable, would have been enough to make her wish for the marriage. In December 1643 her cousin, the last Earl of Cumberland, died, and she entered quietly into possession under

---

[1] *The Diary of the Lady Anne Clifford*, ed. V. Sackville-West, London, 1923, p. 62, under date 5 April 1617.

[2] 'Sidney's sister, Pembroke's mother,
  Death; 'ere thou hast slain another,
  Wise and fair and good as she,
  Time shall throw a dart at Thee'.
        —From an epitaph on her ascribed to Ben Jonson.

her father's will. She was then fifty-three, but she did not hurry off to Westmorland. When she went north at last in 1649 she parted from the south for ever and stepped back into the Middle Ages.

The Lady Anne was born at Skipton Castle in Craven and she visited it on her way north in 1649. The wars had meant considerable damage, but a castle so strongly built as Skipton could not be altogether ruinous. By 1663 the work of repair was completed and the Lady Anne resided in the castle for five months in 1666. From Skipton she then went on to her other castle in Craven, Barden Tower, a fortified house rather than a castle. Today Barden is again a ruin, but the Lady Anne's inscription over the entrance greets the visitor. While the property had been in the hands of her uncle he had been able to make an arrangement with the crown so that if the land reverted to the Lady Anne for lack of male heirs Barden manor and castle should remain with his female line. But the Lady Anne kept Barden as long as she lived.

In an age when for several generations noble households had been accommodated in mansions of varying degrees of comfort, the Lady Anne chose like her medieval ancestors to live in castles. Her favourite castles were Appleby, from old days the head of the Westmorland property, and Brougham, where her father was born, her mother had died, and where she died herself. After her mother's death Brougham passed to the Earl of Cumberland, who in 1617 entertained King James I there. During the civil war many castles were destroyed and none escaped damage, but some had fallen out of use before the end of the Middle Ages. The Lady Anne found Brougham 'ruinous and desolate' and Appleby in not much better state, but it was possible to live in them while the extensive repairs and rebuildings were carried out. Brough Castle was far more decayed than Brougham or Appleby, for it had been burned down in 1521 and since then neglected. She began work there in 1649. In 1661 she was able 'to lye there' three nights and in 1666 she kept Christmas there, which, as she proudly noted, none of her ancestors had done since 1521. The fourth of the Westmorland castles, Pendragon, had also lain ruinous for more than a hundred years when the Lady Anne inherited her ancestral lands. Today its ruins look not very different from what they must have been in 1649. The valley of Mallerstang has changed little through the centuries and remains desolate and wild. Pendragon Castle had been built to prevent the Scots passing south by way of the Eden valley, and it never had a town or village beside it. The castle was called Pendragon at least as early as the fourteenth century[1]. Even as a girl the Lady Anne had thought of making it habitable again. By 1660 the work was done and she was able to 'lye there three nights together' in 1661. Thereafter she often stayed there on her way to and from her Yorkshire lands. She rebuilt Mallerstang chapel to serve the people of the valley.

By virtue of King John's charter to Robert de Vipont his successor in title was Sheriff of Westmorland. The Lady Anne appointed Thomas Gabetis her under-sheriff and always described him as 'my sheriff'. But when the judges came to Westmorland she met them herself, escorted them to Appleby, and entertained them in the castle. She gathered about her a number of 'chief officers', as she describes them, trusty servants who conducted her affairs under direction. Much of what she wrote in these days in Westmorland has been destroyed, but the monuments she put up, the memorial tablets she inserted in the walls of her castles, the churches and chapels she rebuilt, the almshouses she endowed, remain today. The most remarkable survival is the Countess's Pillar beside the highroad south of Brougham. The inscription upon it records that it was put up in January 1654 by 'ye right honorable Anne countess dowager of Pembroke etc. . . . for a memorial of her last parting in this place with her good and pious mother, ye right honorable Margaret, countess dowager of Cumberland, ye 2nd of April 1616 in memorial whereof she also left an annuity of four pounds to be distributed to ye poor within the parish of Brougham, every 2nd day of April for ever, upon ye stone table here hard by. Laus Deo'. In 1616 the Lady Anne, for it is easier to call her by the name by which she is remembered in her own country, had visited her mother at Brougham to consult her about the claim to Westmorland and her mother had come a little way with her as she journeyed south again. The annual distribution of alms has doubtless helped to preserve the Pillar, which is still a landmark today.

The most valuable source of evidence for the life of the Lady Anne was compiled under her own direction[2]. She caused three sets to be prepared of what she describes as 'my 3 great written Handbooks'. One set survived at Appleby Castle, a second at Skipton and a third at Bill Hill, Berkshire. In them are set out, after the familiar pattern of the best seventeenth-

[1] It so appears on the Gough map drawn in the fourteenth century and preserved in the Bodleian Library; see the Ordnance Survey reproduction.

[2] The 'great picture' at Appleby Castle displaying the Lady Anne with her parents, brothers, husbands, and teachers is a representation of her life and was also used by Dr. Williamson in writing his book *Lady Anne Clifford*.

century antiquarian research, the descent of each of the noble families to
which the Lady Anne belonged, with the documents copied out and their
seals carefully drawn. All the records had been collected, she recorded, 'by
the great and painfull industry' of her mother. Into these books an account
of the lives of her parents was entered and 'a summary memorial' of the
Lady Anne's own life. There is no doubt that she kept a daily diary during
the years in Westmorland, but the greater part of it has been lost. 'The
summary memorial' preserves a record of all her important visitors, the
places through which they passed in coming and going, the rooms they
slept in, the people and places they visited while they were her guests.
There has also survived a copy of part of the last diary which she ever
kept. It is a touching and intimate record of the last days of a long life.
Almost every day's entry ends with the sentence 'I went not out of my
house or out of my chamber today'. Each day, with her old diaries before
her, she lived again the happenings of sixty years ago. Almost every day
people came to see her and she notes that she kissed the women, took the
men by the hand, gave them some present, and they went away. If they
came from any distance these visitors dined in her house. She records
where they ate. It was generally 'with my folks in the Painted Room',
while their servants 'dined below in the hall'. The last entry she made was
on 21 March 1676, 'I went not out all this day'[1]. The next day she died.

   Until her death the widowed countess kept up a feudal state in the
north, moving in state from one to another of her castles attended by her
household and many Westmorland gentlemen. She was the last of a great
family and her ancestors and successors were ever in her thoughts. Long
before her death she prepared her memorial in Appleby church. It is in
character that she chose to be remembered there not by an effigy, but by
a black marble slab on which were shown the arms of all the families
connected with the Cliffords. But her mind was not always turned upon
the past. She kept up a close correspondence with her daughters, the
Countesses of Thanet and Northampton, and welcomed them and their
husbands and children to Westmorland. Her younger daughter, Lady
Northampton, died at the age of thirty-nine in 1661. She had borne three
sons, who died as children. Her only child who survived to grow up was
Lady Alethea Compton, who at the age of nine in 1670 visited her
grandmother at Pendragon Castle and again stayed for a week at Appleby
a few months before the Lady Anne's death. The Countess of Thanet was

----

[1] This diary is printed by Dr. Williamson, pp. 265–80.

more fortunate, for eleven of her children lived to grow up. She herself died in the same year as the Lady Anne.

The Lady Anne, who died on 22 March 1675, was buried on 14 April, and Edward Rainbowe, Bishop of Carlisle, her friend and neighbour, preached her funeral sermon, taking as his text, 'Every wise woman buildeth her house'. He set out the list of the 'material houses' which the Lady Anne had built, 'six Castles, seven Churches or Chappels, besides two Almshouses and other inferiour subservient Buildings, which she made, or made useful'. He reminded his hearers of the Countess's Pillar, where 'as Jacob did, she poured oyl upon this pillar, the oyl of Charity . . . to be as a precious ointment to perfume her pious Mother's Memory'. To illustrate the Lady Anne's humility, the bishop described how 'you might have sometimes seen her sitting in the almshouse which she built among her twelve Sisters (as she called them) and as if they had been her sisters indeed, or her children, she would sometimes eat her dinner with them, at their Almshouse; but you might often find them dining with her (at her Table) some of them every Week, all of them once a Month; and after meat, as freely and familiarly conversing with them in her Chamber, as if they had been her greatest Guests'. In this sermon is preserved the famous phrase of Dr. Donne: 'That she knew well how to discourse of all things, from Predestination, to Slea-silk'. From this sermon, too, comes the story that to General Harrison, who commanded the soldiers quartered in her castle during the Commonwealth, she 'boldly asserted, that she did love the King, that she would live and die in her Loyal thoughts to the King'. The bishop is also the authority for her remark that if she were to go to the Restoration court she would have 'to be used as they do ill-sighted or unruly horses, have Spectacles (or Blinkers) put before mine eyes, lest I should see and censure what I cannot competently judge of'. The bishop was describing a great lady to a congregation who had known her. To read his sermon[1] today is to bring her back to life.

[1] Printed for R. Royston, London, 1677.

PLATE II LADIES' SEALS

(See page 56)

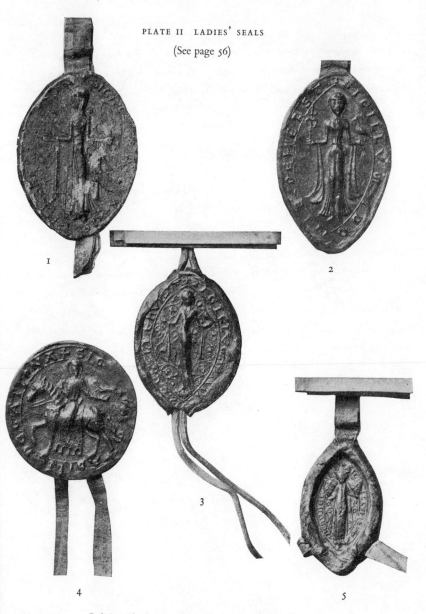

1. Rohais, wife of Gilbert de Gant, 1149–56 (B.M. Cat. vol. ii, No. 6645).
2. Idonia de Herst, late twelfth century (*Ibid.*, No. 6662).
3. Matilda de Alberville, early thirteenth century (*Ibid.*, No. 6569).
4. Mabel of Gatton, thirteenth century (*Ibid.*, No. 6648).
5. Ela de Audeley, 1274. (*Ibid.*, No. 6573).

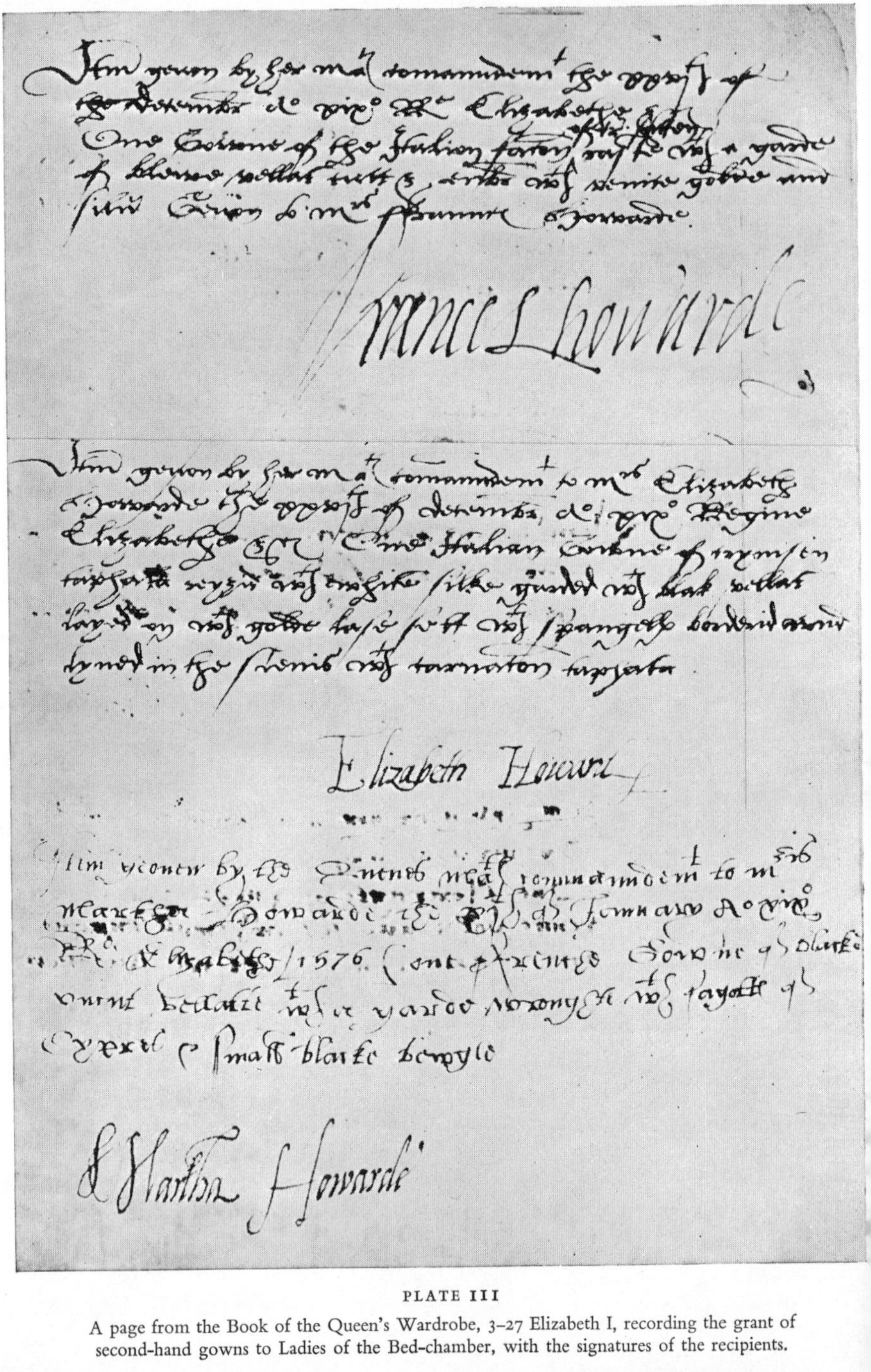

PLATE III

A page from the Book of the Queen's Wardrobe, 3–27 Elizabeth I, recording the grant of second-hand gowns to Ladies of the Bed-chamber, with the signatures of the recipients.

CHAPTER III

The Country-woman
1066–1600

The Norman Conquest came as a disaster to the higher ranks of Anglo-Saxon society. Individuals who had survived the impact of the war might be able to come to terms with the Conqueror for a portion of their estates. But their position in the social order which arose after the war was everywhere precarious, and it was only in the remoter north that the class to which they belonged came to form a distinctive element in the society of medieval England. Elsewhere, with remarkably few exceptions, the rural aristocracy of pre-Conquest days sank without a trace into the mass of the surrounding peasantry. To the peasants themselves, the effects of the Conquest were less revolutionary. The English traditions of the countryside could not be eradicated in a generation by foreign conquerors who depended for their food on the native population. Normans inevitably married English girls. English methods of local government were maintained by the king's own will, so that the courts of shire and hundred continued to do justice in the traditional English way. The new lords of English villages held private courts of justice for their men, but most of their men were Englishmen, and the manorial courts of later centuries represent without any obvious break the 'hall moots' of the Anglo-Saxon time. The women of the country-side carried on as their mothers had done before them.

The wives of English farmers have always been in a very real sense the partners of their husbands. Without the help of the women of the household it would have been impossible to look after the stock and make the butter and cheese. Women could even on occasion lend a hand in the fields. They had to make the rough cloth which dressed the members of the family from the wool of their own or their neighbours' sheep. Of the daily lives of the inhabitants of English villages in the twelfth century

little can be known, but looked at from the modern standpoint they were
certainly harsh and dreary. Over a great part of England the majority of
farmers and their wives were personally unfree. Their farm was held of
a lord and they could not leave it to seek a future elsewhere. Even in those
parts of England where there were many free peasant farmers life could
have been little different. When an unfree peasant died his land reverted
to the lord, who as a rule allowed the eldest or, in some parts, the youngest
son to take his father's place. The land of the free peasant was divided
between his sons. The succession of a number of sons in a holding too
small for division often meant a communal household farming the land
together. Whether the members of the household were free or unfree
it was the women who set the standard of its life.

The wife of the unfree peasant farmer was relatively in a stronger
position than the wife of her husband's lord. Feudal law and custom gave
the widow of quality but a third of her husband's lands, whereas ancient
custom allowed the unfree peasant's widow to hold the whole of her
husband's land so long as she did the service due to the lord. The widow's
bench, her seat by the fireside, was hers in her late husband's house as
long as she lived unmarried. Even after her sons had taken wives their
mother could not be evicted from the farmhouse of her husband. The
nine female cottagers at Stokesay, Salop, mentioned in Domesday Book,
were probably widows sitting on the few acres their husbands had formerly
held[1]. Domesday Book occasionally mentions widows among the population of a village, but there must have been many more than the clerks
troubled to record. Local custom about the position of the widow and the
rights of the sons varied from place to place, but in every farming community women were in a strong position, for their services could not be
dispensed with.

The free peasant farmers, who are found in their greatest numbers in
the counties where the Danes had settled in the ninth century, came to
follow feudal custom in regard to the amount of the widow's dower.
Among them, too, it was customary for the daughters to divide an inheritance when sons failed. These free peasant farmers often display, as late as
the early thirteenth century, their English or Scandinavian descent by the
personal names they, or their fathers, or grandparents bear. Like their
social superiors they could give away or sell their land, making a charter

[1] H. C. Darby and I. B. Terrett, *The Domesday Geography of Midland England*, Cambridge,
1954, p. 127.

as evidence of the transaction and authenticating it with their seals. Many such documents have survived, among them a considerable number made by women[1]. Robert son of Aliva of Saltfleetby, Lincolnshire, whose mother bore a common Old English name, had two daughters, named Hawisa and Maud. Maud issued a charter releasing her rights in ten acres of land at Saltfleetby to Thomas son of John of Louth, with the consent of her heirs. Her seal survives on the charter. Her sister, Hawisa, describing herself as daughter of Robert son of Ayliva of Saltfleetby, 'in her free widowhood', released the same ten acres to Thomas, and her seal also survives on her charter. Mabel widow of Robert son of Aliva, who also described herself as daughter of Aze of Yarburgh, quitclaimed to Thomas all her right in the same ten acres of land. Her seal, too, survives on her charter. Each of these women used a similar device on her seal, an inverted fleur-de-lis, and round each seal a Latin legend recorded the owner's name. All these charters come from the early thirteenth century.

Three other charters, two made by Hawisa and the third by their father's widow, Mabel, daughter of Aze of Yarburgh, help to indicate the financial standing of the family. For 10 shillings down and a yearly rent of 2 pence Hawisa granted one acre of meadow to John, son of Odo of Saltfleetby. She also released to him all the lands which he had from her or her family, namely nine acres of the land of Robert, son of Aileva of Saltfleetby. On both these charters her seal survives. Mabel released all her rights of dower in her husband's lands in Saltfleetby to Odo Galle for half a mark of silver, that is 6 shillings and 8 pence. Her seal, which was set to the document, no longer survives upon it. These are neither large acreages nor large sums of money. These women were of simple farming stock, descendants of the free men who had been farming in Lincolnshire for generations before the Norman Conquest.

It is remarkable how many of the men whose charters show that they were of Anglo-Scandinavian peasant stock describe themselves as son or grandson of a woman. Walter son of Bela of Wrangle, Swan son of Goda of Wiberton, Roger son of Wlviva of Kirkby Green, Gilbert son of Quenild, Osbert son of Edus, Robert son of Boniva of Somercotes,

[1] F. M. Stenton, 'The Free Peasantry of the Northern Danelaw', *Bulletin de la Société Royale des Lettres de Lund*, Lund, Sweden, 1926, pp. 73–185. All the charters quoted in this and the five following paragraphs are dealt with in this article, which contains a calendar of all the grants of land made by men of Anglo-Scandinavian descent in the northern Danelaw and known to the writer in 1925.

John son of Wlviva of Skidbrook, William son of Geva of Saltfleetby, Osbert son of Godiva, Robert son of Ralf son of Aldith of Saltfleetby, Alan son of Alice daughter of Hungwin, Hungwin son of Aldith, Gilbert son of Queneluva, Robert son of Queneluva, Hugh and Oggrim sons of Aluerun—all these are grantors of land, generally very little land, a perch of meadow, an acre of arable. It is sometimes held that men who are said to be the sons of women are bastards. It is also generally admitted that if a man married a lady of higher social standing than his own their children took their mother's name. When the king's Justiciar, Geoffrey fitz Peter, married the heiress of the Mandeville earldom of Essex their son and heir was styled Geoffrey de Mandeville. Neither of these conditions fits the hard-headed free peasantry of Lincolnshire. When they call themselves their mother's rather than their father's sons, it may be presumed that the land with which they are dealing came to them through their mother. To preserve her name was to assert their right and to indicate their title to their land.

It was probably this consideration which caused the grantor of a fishery in the River Witham to Kirkstead Abbey in the late twelfth century to describe himself as 'William son-in-law of Ulf of Coningsby'. The fishery had, he stated, been formerly held by the monks by the gift of his father-in-law. The monks agreed to pay a yearly rent of 12 pence or six 'sticks' of eels. William recorded in his charter the fact of his wife's consent to the grant. Three men who had married sisters at Haltham on Bain— Robert son of Suarthoued and Richolda his wife, Rainald and Ivetta his wife, William and Agnes his wife, together with Gunnild, the sister of these women—agreed in 1163 to allow the monks of Kirkstead Abbey to make a mill-dam on the River Bain, touching which there had been a dispute between them. In return for this concession, the monks gave them one mark and agreed to receive them into the fraternity of their house. The land which these four women had shared must have descended to them from their father. Although no land passed to the Abbey by this gift the men alone could not make it unless their wives and their wives' sister were also included in the deed.

Some of the grants of land made by women of peasant families suggest that much division of a small inheritance has made it impossible for the holder of the land to till it to any profit. Gunnilda daughter of Acke Mudding of Saltfleetby, released to Andrew son of Odo Galle all her right in her father's land in return for one mark of silver which

Andrew has given her 'in her great necessity'. The same Andrew Galle acquired three perches of meadow in Saltfleetby from Hawisa, daughter of Ragenild of Saltfleetby, for 10 shillings given her 'in her necessity'. Both these women owned seals which they set to their charters. Maud, daughter of Yungwin of Saltfleetby, about 1220 released to Philip, son of Odo Galle, all her right and claim in one toft and one croft and all the land that was Yungwin's for 20 shillings. Maud's seal, an ornate fleur-de-lis surrounded by a legend bearing her name, was attached to her charter by a strip of parchment cut from another document. The Galle family already in the twelfth century had begun to buy up the land of those who could no longer afford to keep it. They were still buying up such land a century later.

Among the free peasant farmers of Lincolnshire the women of the family held both by law and custom a strong place. There are many charters by which men provide modest marriage portions for their daughters. In return for a yearly rent of 2 pence Wigot of Holme about the year 1210 gave an acre and a half of meadow in the north part of his strip to Siwat son of Hugh in free marriage with Edith his daughter. Some ten years later Siwat gave to Odo Galle and his heirs an acre of this meadow in return for a yearly rent of one penny. Some years later still Siwat sold to Odo Galle's son Andrew the whole acre and a half for 20 shillings and a yearly rent of 2 pence. The value of Edith's marriage portion would therefore seem to have been 20 shillings. The duty of providing for their sisters was clearly felt to be incumbent on brothers. In the early thirteenth century Robert the priest, son of Stepi, granted to his sisters, Maud and Alice, a toft and four acres af arable land in Saltfleetby to hold for their lives at a rent of 8 pence payable to Robert's brother, Alan. If the women died before Robert, the land was to revert to him subject to the rent payable to Alan. Both men put their seals to this document. There are even indications that a sister with surviving brothers had rights by inheritance over her father's land. Three brothers, Robert, Thomas, and Thomas, the sons of Hugh son of Godric of Saltfleetby, granted by a single charter to which their three seals were appended a strip of land lying in Thornholm at a yearly rent of 2 pence. Agnes daughter of Hugh son of Godric of Saltfleetby made a separate charter releasing her right in the same strip. Among these folk of native peasant stock the ancient tradition of the rough equality between men and women had not yet been entirely forgotten.

Even in the courts of justice presided over by the royal judges country-

women can be seen appearing and speaking on their own behalf. Sometimes a woman can be seen acting for her husband. Reginald the smith
and Goda his wife brought an action against Gilbert of Howell for land
in Boothby Graffoe, Lincolnshire, in 1202. As it so happened that the case
could not be settled out of hand, Reginald appointed his wife, Goda, as
his attorney to carry on the plea[1]. A plea for dower in Barton-on-Humber,
brought by William Wine and Beatrice, his wife, was adjourned, and
Beatrice appointed her husband her attorney in case she could not herself
be present. At the same time William appointed Beatrice as his attorney
in case he could not himself be present[2]. Lest it should be thought that
only Lincolnshire country-women were considered competent to plead
in person in court an example can be quoted from Somerset. Hamo
and Christina his wife and Lucy his wife's sister brought an action in
1201 to recover land which was evidently the inheritance of the two
women. The case was adjourned from Taunton to Westminister, and
Hamo and Lucy both appointed Christina, Hamo's wife, as their attorney
to follow up the suit there[3].

The laws of Cnut, quoted in a previous chapter, had laid stress on
the domestic responsibilities of the farmer's wife. She was admonished
to keep control of the keys of her storeroom, her box and her cupboard
so that no stolen meat could be put in them, for no wife could prevent
her husband from bringing anything into his own cottage. The tradition
of the wife's control of household stores goes back to the heathen days,
when many women were buried with the hangers on which their keys
had hung from their waists. This tradition has held through the centuries.
The wives of peasant farmers in the twelfth century had little either of
jewellery or cash to put in a box, but references to a wife's box or a
woman's box occassionally occur. In 1202 a certain William of Lea said
that three men had gone to his lord's house and stolen various articles
belonging to his lord and certain things belonging to himself including
a gold brooch which was his wife's and was 'in the chest of his lord's
wife'[4]. Similarly when in 1200 the undersheriff of Buckinghamshire
wanted to put money recovered from a thief under safe keeping he took
the keys of his own wife's chest and put the money in it[5]. The ladies who

---

[1] *Earliest Lincolnshire Assize Rolls*, Case 1133, p. 200.   [2] *Ibid.*, Case 434, pp. 75–6.
[3] *Pleas before the King or his Justices*, vol. ii, Selden Society, vol. 68, Case 678, p. 200.
[4] *Earliest Lincolnshire Assize Rolls*, Case 731, p. 126.
[5] *Pleas before the King or his Justices*, vol. i, Case 3121, p. 299.

owned these two chests were country-women of rather higher social standing than the wives of the peasant farmers among whom they lived. But Christina Arnold, who in 1293 accused a man in the manor court of King's Ripton of beating her, breaking her box, and ejecting her from her house was a customary tenant of the manor[1]. The houses of Emma at the Water and Duva at the Water, both customary tenants at Ashton, Wilts, were broken into in 1262. In each case the woman's chest was broken and robbed. Duva had a bushel of wheat in hers[2].

The best evidence for the position of women in the village communities of medieval England comes from the records of proceedings in the manorial courts. Every court-roll provides ample evidence of women farming independently the holdings of their former husbands and engaging in litigation on their own behalf. Women were frequently fined for breaches of manorial custom. At Tooting, Surrey, in 1246, Maud widow of Robin and Mabel widow of Spendelove were fined 6 pence each because they had encroached on the lord's land[3], and in 1247 Lucy Rede was in court because her cattle had strayed on to the lord's pasture[4]. At Ruislip in 1246 Isabella widow of Peter had to pay 18 pence because her son, John, had trespassed in the lord's woods[5]. At Wantage, Berkshire, in 1247 Aileva gave up her holding to her son who was allowed to enter upon it on payment of 20 shillings to the lord. On the same court-day Hugh son of Adam paid 2 shillings for permission to hold 'a certain parcel of land' which Christina widow of Peter of the churchyard had leased to him[6]. The rent of the land was two hens a year. The Abbot of Bec's court at Weedon Beck, in Northamptonshire, can be seen in 1248 arranging the division of a small farm between two sisters, Juliana and Goda the daughters of Saer. Juliana was unmarried, but Goda was the wife of William Snell, who had taken possession of the whole inheritance. The court arranged that Juliana should have a barn with an open space before it and two strips of the land for ploughing[7].

From the standpoint of the lord's court, these men and women were customary tenants, personally unfree. They could not give their daughters in marriage without the lord's consent. The widow of a customary tenant could not marry without the consent of the lord. Fines for marriages made without permission formed a small, but steady item of manorial

---

[1] *Select Pleas in Manorial Courts*, ed. F. W. Maitland, Selden Society, vol. 3, 1888, p. 112.
[2] *Ibid.*, pp. 181–2.   [3] *Ibid.*, p. 8.   [4] *Ibid.*, p. 12.
[5] *Ibid.*, p. 8.   [6] *Ibid.*, pp. 10, 11.   [7] *Ibid.*, p. 17.

income. In 1248 Ragenilda, widow of Robert le Beck, paid 2 shillings at Ruislip because she had married again without licence, and she offered to pay in all 5 shillings if she recovered possession of her late husband's holding by verdict of the manorial jury[1]. She appeared and spoke on her own behalf, her new husband taking no part in the plea. It is possible that he had come from another manor. The jury gave their verdict in Ragenilda's favour. In 1247 at Wantage, William Iremonger gave 6 shillings and 8 pence for permission to marry a widow and enter the tenement which her husband had formerly held[2]. A glimpse into a cottage home at Weedon Beck in 1288 is given by an entry recording that Richard Loverd rendered into the lord's hands a cottage with its appurtenances and that Emma Loverd, his daughter, rendered into the lord's hands one acre of arable land, and that Hugh Coverer was put in possession of both cottage and land. Hugh gave the lord 5 shillings for licence to enter the land and marry Emma, and he undertook to board Richard as well as he boarded himself and give him each year one garment and one pair of linen drawers and one pair of boots and slippers[3].

Country-women in great number added to their resources by brewing and selling ale. They often broke the rules governing its quality and the size of the measures by which they sold it. Every court roll provides evidence of this profitable trade, which seems to have been entirely in women's hands. The following women were presented on a single court-day at Hemingford Abbots, Huntingdonshire, in 1278. The entry runs: 'Simon son of Roger and Reginald son of Peter, ale-tasters, say that Katherine Ingol has broken the assize of beer. Therefore she is in mercy, 12 pence, surety, Thomas the smith. From the wife of Thomas Amable for the same, 18 pence, surety, William at the stile. From Christina Osmund for the same, 12 pence, surety, Thomas Almar. From the wife of Nicholas Trappe, 6 pence, surety, William at the stile. From the wife of John Gunild for the same, 6 pence, surety, John Aunzered. From Emma Cat for the same, 6 pence, surety, John Aunzered. From the wife of John Coe for the same—she is poor—surety Reginald Almar. From the wife of Anger at the bank for the same and for bad ale, 12 pence, surety, Henry son of Roger. From the wife of John Noble because she broke the assize, 18 pence, surety, her husband. From Alice Cot nothing, because she kept the assize and brewed once only. From Beatrice Mutun because she has continually broken the assize, nothing, because she is the man—

---

[1] *Select Pleas in Manorial Courts*, p. 14.   [2] *Ibid.*, p. 11.   [3] *Ibid.*, p. 32.

homo—of Sir Reginald de Grey'[1]. The independent position of the country-woman is well illustrated by this entry. The woman herself, and not her husband, is charged with the fine. The description of the hardened offender Beatrice Mutun, as 'the man of Reginald de Grey', simply means that her fine is due to the lord of another manor than that for which the court was held. Now, as in the thirteenth century, the village of Hemingford Grey adjoins the village of Hemingford Abbots.

The treatment of women varied somewhat from manor to manor, as did the relations between the lord and his servants and the customary tenants. Everywhere the lord assumed the right to take a fine from girls who bore illegitimate children. Sometimes the clerk simply records that certain girls are charged with *lerewita*, the Anglo-Saxon word meaning the fine payable for fornication. Sometimes the clerk notes that a girl has borne an illegitimate child and records the amount of the fine she owes the lord. On one court-day at Chatteris in 1272 no fewer than eight girls were fined, most of them paying 6 pence, but one of them 12 pence. Several of these girls, among them one called Matilda the fool, were pardoned payment because of their poverty[2]. The courts of the Church were responsible for maintaining a watch over the morals of the laity and occasionally the roll of a manorial court takes notice of the fact that a customary tenant has been fined in the Church court for adultery. In 1290 at Gidding, Huntingdonshire, the jurors reported that Richard Dyer, a married man, had been convicted of adultery and 'lost the lord's chattels'. The fine which was due from him was pardoned[3].

All lords of manors took a fine from their tenants for permission to give their daughters in marriage, but the Abbot of Ramsey showed an unusual interest in the remarriage of widows. At Wistowe in 1294 Sarah Bishop, described as 'a young widow', was ordered to marry 'before the next court-day'[4]. As a churchman it is possible that the abbot was as concerned with the morals of an unprotected widow as he was with securing the present—*gersuma*—due to him for permission to make the marriage. In 1288 the abbot's court at Shillington summoned Agnes Payn, a widow, 'to provide herself with a husband', but she did not appear in court, having set out to Evesham. She was ordered to find a husband before Christmas, but there is no evidence that she ever came

---

[1] *Select Pleas in Manorial Courts*, p. 89.
[2] *Court Rolls of the Abbey of Ramsey*, ed. W. O. Ault, Yale, 1928, pp. 265–6.
[3] *Select Pleas in Manorial Courts*, p. 97.   [4] *Court Rolls of Ramsey*, p. 211.

back from Evesham[1]. It is more remarkable that the abbot's court is obviously choosing the men who shall become the widows' husbands. The record of proceedings on Saturday, 14 July, at Chatteris concludes with a list of men, each of whom is directed to marry a particular widow. Each of the women is described by the name of her former husband: John Jawe, for example, is matched with 'the wife of Geoffrey Spark'[2]. Agnes Sempol, whose holding consisted of eight acres of land, was unwilling to comply with the lord's commands. She first appeared on the roll as a widow in the court held at Chatteris on 2 August 1289, when she found two sureties that she would 'provide herself with a husband before the next court-day, or satisfy the lord abbot'. Thomas son of Christina Cade was said to be 'ready to take and lead Agnes Sempol to wife'. In the following May, Agnes was still unmarried. The clerk recorded that she gave the lord 12 pence 'to have respite until Michaelmas to choose herself a husband who can defend the eight acres of land'[3].

The Abbot of Ramsey was more peremptory than most lords in his treatment of widows, but the economic condition of the widow among his unfree tenants was a matter of interest to every lord. It was essential that on every holding there should be someone capable of doing the heavy work on the land. On one court-day at Ashton, Wilts, in 1262 the widow of Richard of Gayford agreed to pay a fine of 20 shillings for her husband's land, and found two sureties that she would pay the money and render the services due. On the same day the widow of Ralf the miller of Luvemede promised 18 pence by way of fine and found sureties that she would pay the money and perform the services due. Her sureties also undertook to see that she kept up the house and tenement properly. A third widow appeared on the same day: Duva widow of Roger at the Water promised to pay a fine of 20 shillings, and found sureties that she would pay the money, perform the services due, and well and honestly maintain the house and the land[4]. The robbery of a bushel of wheat from Duva's box has been mentioned above. It was not always easy for a widow to keep her land in good heart. Aileva of Rougham was a freeholder of twelve acres of land at Rougham, Norfolk, in 1202. Her land lay untilled because of her poverty and in consequence her lord leased it to a certain Thomas Blund and his son. Aileva, being a free

---

[1] *Court Rolls of Ramsey*, p. 195.   [2] *Ibid.*, p. 270.   [3] *Ibid.*, pp. 277, 279.
[4] *Select Pleas in Manorial Courts*, p. 183.

tenant, was able to recover her land in the king's court, although she had to employ an attorney to represent her at Westminster, where she was awarded damages of 8 shillings and 9 pence[1].

Though the women who married within the manor generally stayed on in their husband's house after his death, unmarried daughters, like unmarried sons, often ran away from their native village to seek a living elsewhere. Their lord might try to recall them, but they rarely came home again. Matilda Siggeword and Matilda and Alice White ran off from Ingoldmells, Lincolnshire, in 1303[2]. The court ordered that they should find pledges to appear but there is no reference to them again on the rolls. Stark poverty was often the reason for the disappearance both of girls and boys from their homes. There are occasional references in plea rolls to women who have become robbers, generally living with some man following the same occupation. Hawisa, a female robber of Norfolk, was concerned with the murder of a servant of the Earl of Arundel and successfully underwent the ordeal. John Barate, who loved Hawisa, was less fortunate, for he died in prison[3]. Emma Brunfustian preyed on the inhabitants of Northamptonshire. She was said to go 'daily to the market of Daventry and Northampton' and to be 'of the worst repute so that she kills men and leads robbers to rob houses'. She was reported to be kept by Adam Falc, 'likewise of the worst repute'. With a number of other men, one of whom was called Hudde the forger, Emma robbed merchants at Stamford fair[4]. The medieval English woman who took to highway robbery was a sordid, rather than a romantic figure.

The twelfth and thirteenth centuries were a period of increasing wealth. The ravages of the Norman Conquest were being made good even before Domesday Book was compiled. By the end of the twelfth century there were men of substance in every part of England living on their estates and maintaining households which were centres of modest hospitality. Every country house was a farmhouse of greater or less dignity. Seven neighbours were present in Simon of Kyme's hall at Bullington when a man was murdered at its door[5]. Many village girls could earn

[1] *Earliest Northamptonshire Assize Rolls*, Case 817, pp. 140–1.
[2] *Court Rolls of the Manor of Ingoldmells*, ed. W. O. Massingberd, London, 1902, p. 28.
[3] *Pleas before the King or his Justices, 1198–1202*, vol. ii, p. 9.
[4] *Earliest Northamptonshire Assize Rolls*, Cases 696 and 707, pp. 113–15.
[5] *Earliest Lincolnshire Assize Rolls*, Case 1461, p. 262.

their livings by working in the household of the richer men in their neighbourhood. The equipment of the home of a knight of the shire in the early thirteenth century was simple enough, but it must have taken the labour of many women to maintain.

What sort of household goods the knight's lady had at her disposal is hard to guess. The articles most commonly stolen were cloaks, tunics, hoods, linen sheets, towels, and food. Cloth was frequently stolen, sometimes from private houses, but more often from merchants and packmen. Wool, too, was stolen from the very backs of sheep. A Lincolnshire knight, Andrew of Edlington, was in 1202 accused of entering his uncle's house as he lay dying and seizing four swords, four hatchets, two bows, fifteen arrows, two linen sheets, and five yards of linen cloth, as well as the title-deeds to the property[1]. It may be presumed that these things were the most valuable contents of the house. There is little evidence of comfort in such lists at this date.

Before the end of the thirteenth century a lady would own much more household equipment, though she was still poorly supplied by modern standards. Christina widow of John son of William of Long Bennington, Lincolnshire, made her will in 1283 and an inventory of her goods was attached to it[2]. She lived at Bennington and farmed her dower lands. She owned a mare worth 6 shillings, which was her best beast. She therefore left it to the church of Bennington as her mortuary. Apart from the mare her stock consisted of two cows, a horse, two young oxen, five pigs, and a hundred and twenty sheep. She had straw in the yard, hay, malt, wheat, barley, and peas to bequeath. Her farm cart, which she describes as 'bound with iron', she left to be sold for the benefit of the poor. Her furniture consisted of a table, a chest 'bound with iron', four leaden vessels, two napkins, two towels, a cauldron, a brass pot, two small brass pots, two possets, two pans, one basin, one washing-bowl, six carpets[3], fourteen linen sheets, three pillows, three blankets, a coverlet, one feather bed, and twelve yards of linen cloth. Curiously enough no seats, forms or stools are mentioned They may be included under 'all the utensils of the house both brass and wood not separately bequeathed', which she left to two beneficiaries. There is no hint in the inventory of what they

---

[1] *Earliest Lincolnshire Assize Rolls,* Case 594, p. 105.

[2] *Lincoln Wills,* vol. i, ed. C. W. Foster, Lincoln Record Society, vol. v, 1914, pp. 2–4.

[3] The Latin word for carpets at this date means not carpets but covers, that is some sort of rug or table-cloth.

were. Her wardrobe was good, but not extensive. She had a blue furred super-tunic, that is a blue cloak trimmed with fur for cold weather. She had a shift, a frock, a blue mantle, a cloak, and a wimple, that is a head-dress. She also had a tunic of 'watchet' and a robe of brown cloth 'which has been in use'. This must have been her daily wear, but it was worth bequeathing separately in the will. No boots or shoes were apparently worth leaving.

Christina was a country lady of local standing in south Lincolnshire. She had little cash to leave, no more than £7 in silver pennies. To keep much money in a country house would have been an invitation to robbers. It was best to buy a few more sheep or a piece of plate with extra money. For the good of her soul Christina left a number of small bequests, 12 pence, 6 pence, or 3 pence to the churches in the neighbourhood, including the minsters of Lincoln and Southwell. She left similar sums to two bridges, and remembered in like manner the friars, lepers, the sick, and orphans. The length of her will is increased by the fact that she left her six score sheep in ones, twos, threes, or fours to her kinsfolk, friends, servants, and their children. To Laurence, who is simply thus described, she left ten sheep and half the crop of her land. Since 1235 widows were permitted to bequeath to whom they wished the crops standing on their dower land[1]. It is probable that Laurence was her son and her husband's heir. She left a horse, two oxen, a cow, and twelve sheep to a certain Nicholas Raum, with the proviso that they should be at the disposition of Laurence until the end of ten years. Her malt and corn she distributed in bushels among a number of people who seem to have been her menservants and maid-servants. If there were any residue she desired that it should be distributed among the poor of Bennington. Christina must have been the great lady of the village, in life a dominant figure, who meant her will to be felt ten years after her death.

The life of the farmer's wife did not change greatly through the Middle Ages. Political troubles, even the civil wars of the fifteenth century, affected it less than the recurrent visitations of pestilence and famine. The populations of whole villages were wiped out by the virulent outbreaks of the mid-fourteenth century. If some of the inhabitants escaped the pestilence they were too few to carry on the cultivation of the old open fields. Lincolnshire, in the early Middle Ages one of the most prosperous parts of the country, was grievously afflicted, and the Wolds bear many

---

[1] Statute of Merton, cap. 2.

traces of villages lost because of the plague. But, if plague brought death to many it put a premium on the labour of the survivors, who, despite statutory attempts to keep wages at their old levels, were certainly paid far more than their ancestors had enjoyed. Village households which came safely through the Middle Ages to the sixteenth century were more prosperous than those of a couple of centuries before. The customary tenant farmers were no longer serfs working so many days a week on their lord's land. Most of them had become copyholders, who could produce as title to their land a copy of the record of their admission on the court roll of the manor. They paid a fine to the lord on entering their farm and owed him a 'heriot' of their best beast on their death[1]. In everything that mattered they were free. Men who were styled 'gentlemen' were ready to take copyhold land[2], for there was now no taint of servitude about it. Copyholders could make wills and appoint executors to carry them out. But these wills, made by countrymen and women of the sixteenth century, reveal a culture and habit of mind which had changed little since the thirteenth century.

Some illustrations may be taken from the wills which have been pre-served among the records of the ancient minster of Southwell in Nottinghamshire. Southwell is still a small country town, as it was in the sixteenth century. The spiritual jurisdiction of the chapter covered more than twenty villages in which many farmers, both freeholders and copyholders, were prosperous enough to make wills. Copyhold tenure lasted there until it was ended by Act of Parliament in 1926. Inevitably there survive more wills made by men than by women, for it was not yet customary for country-women of modest position to make a will before widowhood. Most of the wills seem to be made when death was near. Nor was it yet customary for women to live unmarried. Nevertheless, the Southwell wills include two made by spinsters. Dorothy Kepeas of Beckingham made her will on 8 December 1534, and it was proved early in the next year. It is a brief document, perhaps made so that she might have the pleasure of reminding William Dawson of East Retford of £20, 'which he should have paid unto me the daye of my marriage'. That Dorothy never married is shown by her description when her will was proved, 'the late virgin'. She left the £20 'which is in the hands of the said William' to is three daughters. To every cottage house in Beckingham,

<hr/>

[1] See above, p. 22.
[2] *Court Rolls of Ingoldmells*, p. 293. William Craycrofte, gent., 1569.

Mattersey, and Mattersey Thorpe Dorothy left one penny[1]. The other unmarried woman's will was made on 14 June 1566 by Thomasina Whitehead of Farnsfield. She was a small farmer who owned four cows and a flock of sheep. She left her mother ten sheep, ewes and wethers, one cow, a red coverlet, a salt cellar, a pair of tongs, a turned chair, her best but one brass pot and a chest. She left her godson Brian Whitehead two ewes, two lambs, an iron bound chest, a bed hanging, a dish, a candlestick, a pair of cupboards, and her greatest brass pot of three. She also left him a pair of reckoners after her mother had need of them no longer. To her brother John's son she left two ewes, two lambs, a dish, a turned chair, and a pan; to John's daughter two ewes, two lambs, a dish, a salt cellar, a gown, a red petticoat, a kerchief, a coat, and an apron. She left to her brother William's son four lambs and a cow, and a dish, a porringer, and a kettle; to William's daughter, she left four lambs, a cow, a platter, a porringer, a salt cellar, and a brass pot. She also left one cow equally between her brother John and his children. To John Pawte she left a ewe and a lamb; to her sister Elizabeth her best hat and a ruff; to Agnes Bingham a russet petticoat; to Mistress Bingham three pounds of wool; to Joan May a kerchief; to Katherine, her brother's maid, a red petticoat; to James Fytton a ewe and a lamb; to John Longman a wether; to Thomas Hunt a hog sheep; to John Watson another hog sheep. To every one of her godchildren she left 6 pence and she made her mother her residuary legatee[2].

The widows whose wills were proved at Southwell in this period seem to have been rather better off than Thomasina Whitehead. There is no hint in her will that she had any arable, nor had she much ready money. Katherine Francis was able to leave a peck of barley to every poor house in Beckingham in 1558 as well as substantial sums, £10 or 20 marks, to each of her five children. She gave names to her best animals in the modern fashion. Her son John was to have the mare called Throstle, her son Robert the cow called Cherry, her son Richard the horse called Cutt and her son Robert the mare called Wynne. To her daughter she left a great pan and 20 marks. She left a petticoat each to several women and to Alice Harson a kerchief and a young goose[3]. Joan Atkinson of Halam in 1561

[1] The Southwell wills (Southwell MSS., vols. 8 and 9) were transcribed by the late W. A. James of South Muskham Prebend, Southwell, Hon. Librarian of Southwell Minster, who left his transcripts to my husband. Dorothy Kepeas's will is printed in *Visitations and Memorials of Southwell Minster*, ed. A. F. Leach, Camden Society, 1891, pp. 138–9.

[2] Southwell MSS., vol. 9, p. 479.   [3] *Ibid.*, pp. 393–5.

left to her daughter Alice 20 marks in money, a great pan, a great pot, two of her best kine, eight of her best pieces of pewter in the house, a pewter salt, a candlestick, a chafing dish, two of the best silver spoons, three pairs of linen sheets, a pair of hempen sheets, two pairs of harden sheets, two towels, three mattresses, three bolsters, three short pillows, three of the best coverings, three bedsteads with the hangings and painted cloths thereto belonging, her harnessed girdle, her best beads, her long table and best tablecloth, the best cupboard, the best chair, the best frying-pan, a long chest, an iron spit and fire-irons, a salting trough, a brazen mortar and a pestle, and a long form with trestles. Alice was perhaps dearest of all her children. Joan left to her son James 'one acre of wheat and one acre of barley and one acre of peas more than his fellows' and to her son Simon a silver ring. She left to her sister Fogge her best kerchief and a side saddle, to her sister Jane a russet gown and a black coat, and to her sister Sheppard a 'fresadowe' gown. All her grandchildren were to have 2 shillings and 4 pence. One grandson was to have a yearling foal called Sterre, and a granddaughter to have a black yearling calf, a ewe and a lamb. Her other bequests of articles of clothing, sheets, and oddments are punctuated with bequests to Alice which she had evidently overlooked before, a laundry iron, a basin, a green table and bench. She left her silk hat and her best cap to Margaret Kitchen. She left 3 shillings to the chapel, now the church, of Halam, 20 pence 'to the mending of the ways in Halam', and to every cottager one peck of malt. Her residuary legatees and executors were her three sons and three other men; perhaps one of them was to be the husband of Alice[1].

Many of the wills made by men show their trust in, and care for, their wives. Often the wife was made the sole executor. 'Also I will that Katherine my wife shall have my house, my close, and all my arable land with meadows and pastures and all kinds of ground within the town and fields of Upton for the term of her life. . . . The residue of all my goods, my debts and legacies paid and I honestly brought to ground, I give and bequeathe to Katherine my wife whom I ordeyne and make my sole executrix of this my last will and testament'. This will was made in April and proved in December 1559[2]. Thomas Kitchen of Westhorpe, Southwell, in 1561, left to his son John a young horse, a mare, a young foal, six sheep, an ironbound cart, a pair of iron gallows, a halbard, and a woodknife; 'and if my wife do marry she to have three quarters of barley and three

---

[1] Southwell MSS., vol. 9, pp. 416–18.   [2] Ibid., p. 502.

quarters of peas and if she do not marry she to occupy all together John
and she . . . and I bequeste to my brother Henry to be good to my wife and
my son 10 shillings and a pair of boots . . . to my brother Robert 10
shillings and my best hat to be good to my wife and my son. And I make
my wife and my son John my full executors of all my goods unbequest'[1].
Henry Pryde of Westhorpe in 1564 left to Joan his wife and Katherine his
daughter 'all my goods both quick and dead whom I make my full
executors, and also I will that my wife have all my land so long as she
doth live and after my wife be departed then I will that my land go to
Thomas my son'[2]. In 1566 Robert Frank of Southwell willed 'that my
wife have the oversight and order of my children and their partes until
they be at lawfull age, except she marrye. Then yf she marrye she to sett
forthe their partes to their owne proper uses. The residue of my goodes
not bequeathed I give and bequeath to Alice my wife whom I make my
fulle executrix of this my last wille and testament'[3].

    When these Southwell wills were made some three hundred years had
passed since Christina of Long Bennington distributed her goods and her
sheep among her dependants and between three and four hundred years
since the Lincolnshire farmers made their charters quoted earlier in this
chapter. The Reformation had broken the long dependence of the English
Church upon the Pope, the Renaissance was in full flood, and many changes
had been made in English law before these wills were made. Yet their
essential atmosphere is no different from that in which Christina of
Bennington and the free Saltfleetby farmers moved. The ancestors of most
of the people whose wills were proved at Southwell were far humbler
folk than Christina. They were more nearly on a level with the Lincolnshire farmers, but time had favoured their descendants. To them, as to all
farmers, life turned on the seasons of the agricultural year. Their wealth
was in their stock and crops. The implements in daily use in the house and
the cow-sheds can have changed little as the years passed. The general
increase in wealth had brought pewter dishes and silver spoons, but brass
pots, sheets, pillows, cushions and basins are still articles of value. A wider
range of materials and articles of dress are available for the country-woman
who could afford them, but her clothes are still important enough to be
bequeathed item by item to her kinsfolk and friends. The cap, an
indispensable article of dress to most ladies in Queen Victoria's reign, and
to the farmer's wife as late as the present century, has made its appearance

[1] Southwell MSS., vol. 9, p. 506.   [2] Ibid., p. 501.   [3] Ibid., p. 480.

to take the place of the Anglo-Saxon headband and of Christina of Bennington's wimple.

A hundred years before the earliest of these Southwell wills was written a family sprung from a similar environment in another part of England had begun to accumulate the vast body of correspondence which makes the Paston Letters a source of the first importance for English social history. The village of Paston in Norfolk lies about a mile from Bromholm Priory and the family had long been settled there. Enemies said that they were descended from an unfree husbandman, but Norfolk was, like Lincolnshire and Nottinghamshire, a land of free peasantry. The Pastons owed their rise to the fact that William Paston early in the fifteenth century took to the law and became a judge. Before his death in 1444 he had bought more land at Paston and had bought the manor of Oxnead for his wife's jointure. The manor of Gresham he purchased and left to his son. He left, too, a trail of lawsuits, the theme of many of the letters. The judge married Agnes, daughter of Sir Edmund Berry, head of a knightly Norfolk family. His son John married Margaret Mautby, daughter and heiress of John Mautby, of Mautby, Norfolk. This marriage was arranged by the parents of the young people, who had never seen each other before the 'young gentlewoman' was brought to her future husband's home. Agnes Paston wrote to tell her husband 'good tidings' of the occasion. 'And as for the first acquaintance between John Paston and the said gentlewoman, she made him gentle cheer in gentle wise and said he was verrily your son. And so I hope there shall need no great discussion between them. The parson of Stockton told me that if you would buy her a gown her mother will give thereto a goodly fur'. Agnes added that Margaret needed a gown and suggested that it should be a 'goodly blue or else a bright red'[1].

John Paston followed his father to the law, so that he spent the terms in London, and in 1460 was elected to represent the shire in Parliament. His mother and his wife remained in Norfolk, looking after the family interests there. Agnes Paston had much trouble over ways which her husband had stopped up. She had a wall built, but it was pulled down. Even in church a man came into her pew to tell her that 'the stopping of the way should cost her 20 nobles, yet it should down again'[2]. Margaret Paston, her son's wife, was a woman of strong will and great capacity, equal to more serious emergencies. She did not flinch at the prospect of

---

[1] *The Paston Letters*, ed. James Gairdner, vol. i, pp. 38–9.   [2] *Ibid.*, p. 219.

defending her husband's house against attack, but asked that he would send her some crossbows and 'wyndacs' to bind them with and bolts to shoot from them, 'for your house is so low that no man may shoot out with a long bow though we had never so much need'[1]. Lord Moleyns claimed the manor of Gresham against John Paston and in 1450 attacked his house with a great company while his wife was within with twelve people. They 'myned the wall of the chamber wherein Margaret Paston was and bare her out at the gates and cut asunder the posts of the houses and let them fall'[2]. Some fifteen years later Margaret Paston was again in a house threatened by her husband's enemies. Sir John Fastolf had made John Paston his executor and heir subject to certain conditions, but the Duke of Suffolk laid claim to Fastolf's manor of Drayton. Margaret Paston was living in the neighbouring manor of Hellesdon supported by her eldest son. They were prepared, with guns and ordnance and sixty men, to withstand an assault, so that although the duke's men came up three hundred strong they did not dare to attack. John Paston wrote to thank his wife for her 'labour and business with the unruly fellowship that came before you on Monday last past. And in good faith you acquitted you right well and discreetly and heartily to your worship and mine, and to the shame of your adversaries, and I am well content that you avowed that you kept possession at Drayton and so would do'[3]. Before the end of the year, however, the duke's men had plundered Hellesdon, destroying everything they could not carry away.

The letters which passed between husband and wife show complete trust, but their mutual affection is generally taken for granted. Margaret Paston was her husband's agent. Supported by a group of good servants, she was able to transact on his behalf any business that might arise. She knew the ordinary processes of the law and could interview the royal judges at Norwich and win them to her point of view. She could instruct counsel and report their advice to her husband. She reported also the local price of malt and told him when she thought of selling wool to raise ready money. The endless lawsuits in which John Paston was engaged were by no means unusual. Nor was it unusual for the head of a country family of some importance to find himself in prison. John Paston was in prison three times in the course of the actions resulting from Sir John Fastolf's will. Margaret Paston was an able woman, but there is no reason to doubt that many other women of her age were living similar lives and dealing

[1] *The Paston Letters*, vol. i, p. 82.   [2] *Ibid.*, p. 107.   [3] *Ibid.*, vol. ii, p. 209.

as competently with similar problems. The courts of justice were familiar to country folk throughout the Middle Ages, and it was important for women as well as men to know the elements of the processes of law. The medieval country-woman had much more to think about than the mere provision of food and comfort for her family and household.

Men and women alike were above all concerned with the increase of their 'livelihood', a word which recurs again and again in the correspondence. They wanted to be certain of a sure income and were unwilling that any member of the family should marry a man or woman who was not thus provided. Anxiety to provide well for daughters often made parents harsh to them. They were afraid that girls would entangle themselves with men without a livelihood or even with their fathers' servants. For this reason they sent them from home to be brought up in other men's houses. There, they would have duties which would keep them occupied. Elizabeth Paston, sister of John Paston, had a hard time at home with her mother Agnes Paston, according to a cousin who wrote before 1449 urging John Paston to find his sister a husband. 'She was never in so great sorrow as she is in nowadays, for she may speak with no man whosoever come. . . . And she hath since Easter been for the most part beaten once in a week or twice, and sometimes twice on a day and her head broken in two or three places. Wherefore, cousin, she hath sent to me in great counsell and prayeth me that I would send to you a letter of her heavyness and pray you to be her good brother, as her trust is in you'. The writer described how a widower had been to see Elizabeth, but that her mother hesitated about the marriage because she had not seen his daughter's marriage settlement. She feared that his lands might already be settled on his daughter and her children. The matter was urgent because the suitor would withdraw if it were not brought to a speedy conclusion. 'Wherefore, cousin, think on this matter, for sorrow often causeth women to beset them otherwise than they should do, and if she were in that case I wot well you would be sorry'[1]. Elizabeth Paston remained for some years yet unmarried and several husbands were canvassed for her. Meanwhile, she was put in the household of Lady Pole, and Agnes Paston noted among the errands she wished to have done for her in London: 'Tell Elizabeth Paston she must use herself to work readily as other gentlewomen do'[2].

It was not an easy matter to marry off a daughter, as the story of

---

[1] *The Paston Letters*, vol. i, pp. 89–91.   [2] *Ibid.*, p. 422.

Margery, daughter of John and Margaret Paston, showed. She was first mentioned in 1463 when her mother wrote to tell her father how a friend had come in and seen Margery and said that she was a goodly young woman. Agnes Paston, her grandmother, at once prayed the friend to get her a good marriage if he knew any, and he said he knew one which should be worth 300 marks a year[1]. Nothing came of that. In 1465 when Margaret Paston was visiting her husband in the Fleet prison her youngest son wrote to tell her how 'the garrison' at Hellesdon did and added a suggestion that she should take his sister Margery to shrines 'to pray that she may have a good husband ere she come home again'[2]. After the death of John Paston a certain J. Strange wrote to his son, now Sir John Paston, to ask for the hand of his sister Margery for a nephew, another J. Strange. He promised to make her sure of a jointure of £40 a year and an inheritance of 200 marks a year[3]. Nothing came of that either and in 1469 the family was shocked to learn that she wanted to marry Richard Calle and had, indeed, promised herself to him. He was the bailiff and manager of Sir John Paston's property and had served his father before him. Margery's brother, John, declared that Calle 'should never have my good will to make my sister sell candle and mustard in Framlingham'[4]. A moving letter written by Richard Calle to Margery in 1469 survives, although he asked her to burn it[5]. The affair had been going on for a long time, for he says that she has had no letter from him for the last two years. Richard Calle appealed to the Bishop of Norwich, who summoned Margery before him, spoke to her about the seriousness of marrying where her kin did not approve, and asked her solemnly what words she had said in pledging her faith to Richard Calle. She told him what she had said to Calle, and declared 'if those words made it not sure she said boldly she would make that surer before that she went thence'[6]. Her mother refused to receive her at home and the bishop had to find a lodging for her until he pronounced his sentence that she had indeed committed herself to marriage with Richard Calle. The Pastons could only acquiesce in the marriage, but they never accepted Margery's husband as a member of the family. He returned to the service of Sir John Paston, who could not do without him. Margaret Paston never forgave her daughter and did not remember her in her will. But she regarded herself as a just woman and therefore left £20 to Margery's sons.

---

[1] *The Paston Letters*, vol. ii, pp. 140–1.   [2] *Ibid.*, p. 233.
[3] *Ibid.*, p. 296.   [4] *Ibid.*, p. 347.   [5] *Ibid.*, pp. 350–3.
[6] *Ibid.*, p. 364.

Parents were not lacking in affection for their daughters when they sent them to the houses of other folk for training. It was expensive, for they often had to pay for their board, and always had to dress them better than they would have done at home. 'I would be right glad that she might be preferred either by marriage or by service', wrote Margaret Paston of one of her daughters to her younger son soon after he had himself entered the household of the Duke of Norfolk[1]. The suggestion that one of his sisters should enter the same household came to nothing. It was not always easy to find a place for a girl and parents often had to be content to put them with their own kin or friends. Anne Paston entered the household of a kinsman named Calthorpe and her mother was annoyed when in 1470 he wrote saying that he intended 'to lessen his household and to live the straitlier' and therefore wanted to send Anne home: 'she waxeth high and it were time to purvey her a marriage'. Her mother thought that Anne must have displeased him or been caught out in some way. She asked her son to enquire of a cousin in London if he would be willing to have Anne 'and send me word, for I shall be fain to send for her and with me she shall but lose her time. . . . Remember what labour I had with her sister, therefore do your part to help her forth'[2]. Anne was at last suitably married to William Yelverton, like herself the grandchild of a judge, but not before she had shown leanings towards a certain John Pamping, another of the Pastons' servants. Sir John wrote from London in 1473 saying that he heard that she had been sick, whereas he had thought that she was married. 'As for Yelverton, he said but late that he would have her if she had her money, and else not, wherefore me thinketh that they be not very sure. But among all other things, I pray you beware that the old love of Pamping renew not'[3]. The marriage with Yelverton took place at last in 1477.

The custom of sending boys and girls to serve in the household of some greater man than their father was a survival of the feudal practice which brought wards into their lord's charge and gave them wider opportunities than their home afforded. It lasted well into the seventeenth century. Girls found it more difficult than boys to adapt themselves to altered circumstances. They did not always succeed in pleasing their mistress. On 14 August 1616 the Lady Anne Clifford, then Countess of Dorset and living at Knole, noted in her diary that she 'fell out with Kate Burton and swore' that she 'would not keep her and caused her to send to her father'.

1 *The Paston Letters*, Introduction, p. 104.
2 *Ibid.*, vol. ii, pp. 418–19.   3 *Ibid.*, vol. iii, pp. 102–3.

Four days later Sir Edward Burton 'came hither and I told him that I was determined that I would not keep his daughter'. It was not, however, until 2 October that the Lady Anne recorded that 'Kate Burton went away from serving me to her father's home in Sussex'[1].

Hints of trouble and unhappiness can often be found in similar sources. In 1577 Lady Howard wrote to her nephew, Sir Edward Stradling of St. Donat's, Glamorgan, about his sister Wentlian: 'I sent for her upon the sight of your letter and dealt very friendly with her, and declared unto her that it grieved me, she being so near kin unto me, to see her go from service to service: she being so ill used, as she declared unto me, in the place where she was'. Lady Howard went on to say that she had arranged for Wentlian to come home to her brother, and that she, 'like a good and loving sister puts herself wholey to be governed by you'[2]. Lady Howard urged her brother to be kind to his sister, particularly since, unlike all her other sisters, she was contented to marry and be ruled by her friends. It is probable that Lady Howard was referring to one of Wentlian's sisters called Damasyn, who had gone off to Spain in the service of a lady and died there ten years before. Her mistress was Jane, daughter of Sir William Dormer of Eythrope in Buckinghamshire. While Jane Dormer was maid of honour to Queen Mary she married the Spanish ambassador, the Count, afterwards Duke, of Feria. Sir William Dormer proudly wrote to Sir Edward Stradling of 'my daughter the Dowchesse'[3]. Damasyn died in Spain in 1567 before the death of her father, Sir Thomas Stradling. The duchess wrote to him to break 'the dolefull news' and said that in the seven years Damasyn had served her 'I knew not what troubles meant; all my cares, all my business, all my lusts were discharged upon her back; she honoured me as her mother, and loved me as a sister, and served me with such fidelity and pains that not one woman living, I am sure, could vaunt themselves of so wise, noble, virtuous, loving, careful, nor able a servant as I'[4].

The daughters of knightly families like the Pastons and the Stradlings may have been unhappy in youth, but if they married and survived their husbands they often enjoyed, like the Lady Anne Clifford herself, an independence and importance which must have sweetened the sorrows of age. The Paston correspondence provides three examples of the long-lived

---

[1] *Diary*, ed. V. Sackville-West, pp. 106 and 107.
[2] *Stradling Correspondence*, ed. J. Montgomery Treherne, London, 1840, pp. 7–8.
[3] *Ibid.*, p. 1.   [4] *Ibid.*, pp. 342–3.

widow. Agnes Paston, the wife of the judge, lived as a widow from 1444 to 1479. She survived her eldest son by thirteen years and died in the same year as her grandson, his heir. Margaret Paston, whose husband died in 1466 and whose son died in 1479, lived until 1484. Both these ladies could hold their own with their sons and grandsons and did not hesitate to chide them. 'My cousin Clere', another widow, is frequently referred to by one or other of the letter-writers. Her opinions were respected and quoted and copies of her letters were forwarded to other correspondents. Messages were sent to her in letters written home. She was a widow when she first appears early in the Paston story and she remained a widow to the end. Her husband was Robert Clere of Ormsby, who must have died young. When Henry VI's queen visited Norwich in 1453 she summoned Elizabeth Clere to her presence. Margaret Paston wrote to tell her husband about it and said that the queen 'made right much of her and desired her to have a husband, the which you shall know of hereafter. But as for that he is never nearer than he was before. The queen was right well pleased with her answer and reported of her in the best wise and sayeth, by her truth, that she saw no gentlewoman since she came into Norfolk that she liked better than she doth her'[1]. The only occasion when Elizabeth Clere and the Pastons were at odds was when she claimed goods from a wrecked ship 'by title of the leet', that is, as the lord of the local court, and Sir John Paston claimed them as 'lord of the soil' on which they lay[2]. She last appears in the correspondence living with her son and his wife at Ormsby. Her will was proved in March 1493.

The more closely the Paston letters and other contemporary evidence is studied the more difficult is it to generalize about the position of the English country-woman in the Middle Ages. The law is clear enough and the Church's view is clear enough. But men and women are never ruled in their personal relationships by law alone or by the Church alone. No farmer could get along without a wife. It is probably not far from the truth to say that the nearer the household was to the land the stronger the tie between man and wife, the more nearly were they on equal terms. When man and wife stayed on their farm year in year out, going to market and the local courts of justice, but having no particular need to go much farther afield their lives were much what they had been for countless generations past; their thoughts those of their Saxon ancestors. When success followed on hard work new factors came into play. There were

---

[1] *Paston Correspondence*, vol. i, pp. 253–4.   [2] *Ibid.*, vol. iii, p. 211.

opportunities for the able man away from the farm as there were not for the woman. The men rose in the world, but women could only rise through them or through marriage. The law was the avenue by which families rose, as did the Pastons after one of the family became a judge. When the menfolk went to the law they were in the very forefront of the intellectual life of the country. The Paston boys were being sent to Eton before the end of the century. They either went on to Oxford, were placed in a noble household, or entered the Inns of Court. They bought books and were making enough money to invest largely in plate. The men in such a family ceased to be mainly interested in the seasons of the agricultural year. The women stayed at home.

CHAPTER IV

The Country-woman after 1600

There were innumerable rising families like the Pastons in the England of the sixteenth and seventeenth centuries, though none was so careful of its letters. Opportunities for able men in the law and in trade were seized daily and the new families of merchants and lawyers hardly gave a backward glance at the farms from which all ultimately came. They wished to be gentlemen, squires, and knights. If they lived in the country it was in a country house suited to their dignity rather than in a farm-house, though a home farm might serve to supply their table. The rhythm of country life went on with little change, dependent as ever on the uncertain English weather. The women of the ordinary farming house-hold found plenty to fill their days. If daughters did not marry they could be employed at home with profit. But the high death-rate in the Middle Ages and on almost to within living memory greatly reduced the number of unmarried and unoccupied women. Childbirth slew many women whose husbands needed another partner. Tuberculosis was an ever-present scourge. Described as 'a decline', it carried off girls and women of every class. Smallpox was endemic. Such manorial court rolls as have survived from the seventeenth century reveal a rural society in which women were playing their parts much as they had done four hundred years before.

The surviving court rolls of the manor of Sonning in Berkshire cover twenty-one years in the reigns of James I and Charles I[1]. The last entry was made in October 1636. When the first entry was made in October 1615 the manor was in the hands of the crown. James I had given it to his son Charles, Prince of Wales, before 20 April, 1619, when the first court was held in his name. In 1628 the crown sold the manor to two London merchants, Thomas Newman and Thomas Chamberlain, in whose names, as lords of the manor, the court was thenceforward held. The manor of

---

[1] Manuscript in private hands, unpaged.

Sonning in the seventeenth century still covered a large area in east Berkshire, stretching north across the Thames into Oxfordshire, to include what is now Sonning Eye and Dunsden. From Dunsden on the Chilterns to Sandhurst on the Bagshot Beds was a good fifteen-mile ride. The modern parishes of Dunsden, Sonning, Woodley and Sandford, Ruscombe, Arborfield, Wokingham (outside the town), and Sandhurst, as well as a number of little places not separate parishes, were within the jurisdiction of the manor court. It is worth looking at the rolls to see how women stood in this wide-stretching manor on the eve of the civil war.

In the manor of Sonning, as generally elsewhere, it was customary for the widow of a copyhold tenant to remain in occupation of his land until she married again or died. Her holding under these conditions was described as her 'widow's estate'. A new grant of a piece of copyhold land was normally made for the term of three lives. It often happened that the widow of the first of the three prospective tenants survived the other two persons named in the copy. The widow's estate must have caused bitterness among those who were kept out of tenancies by long-lived widows. When the crown sold the manor of Sonning a solemn entry was made on the court roll setting out the customs which had been agreed in the Exchequer chamber in Queen Elizabeth's day after differences of opinion between the queen and her customary tenants. Two of these customs deal with the problem of the widow's estate. 'The first wife of any customary tenant deceased is to enjoy her widow's estate and noe other'. If 'a widow not named in the copy' marry again 'though shee be licensed by the Lord to marry without the forfeiture of her estate if shee doe marry her estate is determined'—that is, ended—'any such licence by the lord to the contrary notwithstanding'. In the court held on 17 April 1619 it was reported that Anna Paine, widow, who held 'two messuages and one virgate and a half of land called Heathlands was lately married, since the last court, to Edric Baker, for which she has forfeited her widow's estate in the premises, and that Sara Hamlin daughter of John Hamlin is the next tenant of, and in, the premises'. The fact that remarriage meant the loss of her farm must have kept many widows from taking a second husband.

The position which widows held within this great manor appears on the surface of the rolls. On one court day in October 1631 widow Kent was ordered to scour the watercourse in Sheephouse lane sufficiently by All Saints' Day next so that the water may pass without stop, on pain of

5 shillings. It was reported that John Symonds, a copyhold tenant of the manor, had died since the last court seised of a yardland and a half and it was adjudged that Alice, his wife, shall have her widow's estate therein. Later in the proceedings Alice Symonds, widow, relict of John Symonds, came, did fealty, and was admitted tenant to the land her husband had held according to the custom of the manor. Another widow, Ruth Adams, relict of Thomas Adams, lately died, also came the same day and did fealty to hold the customary land of which Thomas, her husband, died seised. On the same day Elizabeth Breach, widow, was sued by William Buckeridge for a debt of 20 shillings. William was awarded damages of 6 shillings and 8 pence. There were few court-days which did not produce an entry of some sort about a widow. For example, she may want and be awarded, three loads of timber for necessary repairs, as was Elizabeth Chambers, widow, on 19 April 1619; or she may be instructed, as were 'widdowe Webbe and William Webbe her sonne', to remove wood from 'his Majesty's waste which straighteth his highnes way and passage of cattell'; or she may be ordered to remove undesirable tenants from her house as was widow Holton of Reading, who was charged in October 1631 to remove from her house in Winnersh widow Bassett and all her family. The last appearance of a widow upon the rolls was always the curt note of her death followed by the name of the next tenant who at last entered upon the land.

There is no doubt that women were often copyhold tenants in their own right. The changes made in the tenancies of farms and cottages in one court-day shows how often this could come about. On 20 April 1626 thirteen tenancies were before the court. It should be remembered that the tenants of customary land could dispose of it in no other way than by coming before the court and surrendering it into the hands of the lord, who thereupon gave it out to the new tenant. A 'heriot', consisting of his best beast, fell due to the lord from the retiring tenant and a fine, varying in amount with the value of the land, was paid to the lord from the new tenant. Apart from two tenants who were genuinely ending their connection with their former tenement, every one of these cases was a family arrangement, enabling the holder of the land, probably the last tenant of a former lease for three lives, to acquire a new copy in which two members of his family were joined with him in the tenancy. John Whitlock, gentleman, surrendered two acres of arable land in Wokingham and, with his daughters, Eleanor and Prudence Whitlock, received it back so that the three of them should hold it successively for the term of their lives and the life of the longest living of them. Henry Hellier resigned a messuage and half a virgate called Thedderings at Wokingham and, with Anne, his wife, and Henry, his son, received it back on the same terms. Richard Binte resigned a messuage and two virgates at Eye and Dunsden and, with Richard Binte, his son, and Anne Binte, his daughter, received it back on the same terms. William Button made two separate surrenders, one of a messuage and three-quarters of a virgate at Eye and Dunsden and the other of a cottage and two-and-a-half acres of arable land at Eye. With William Button, his son, and Jane Button, his daughter, he received both back on the same terms. The men who were thus surrendering their land and receiving it back were responsible for paying both the heriot and the fine.

When a man had the names of his wife and son put into his copy to be the holders of the land successively after him, as Henry Hellier did in 1626, he was making it possible for his widow to hold in her own right as a copyholder. Such an arrangement indicates a real equality between husband and wife. Since a wife could by ancient custom count on enjoying her widow's estate in the tenement of her husband it was not strictly necessary that her name should be in the copy. The land was, in any case, hers for life. The insertion of the name of Anne Hellier in the copy made it possible for her to continue to hold the land after her second marriage. Her second husband would have been bound by custom to do fealty for his wife's land. He could not exclude her son by Henry Hellier from entering the land on his mother's death, but until that happened the land would have remained in the possession of Anne Hellier and her second husband. Leases like this, complicated as they may seem, were by no means unusual in the manor of Sonning. The traditional outlook of the Anglo-Saxon peasant had changed little through the years. Farmers' wives were still holding their own in rural society despite the rigour of the common law.

Not all the women who appear on the rolls were copyhold tenants of the manor. At Sonning, as elsewhere, there were freeholders who formed a kind of rural aristocracy. They, like all others, were subject to the jurisdiction of the manorial court. In April 1631 a manorial jury presented that Anne Lewen, who was obviously a freeholder, 'hath sworne that her Ant Binfeld and her servant did fish and lay her ginns in the creek lying towards Paterlake strand and out of the Thames . . . and that she hath knowne it fortie yeeres and the said fishing as aforesaid for fifteene yeeres together'. Anne Lewen was claiming the right to fish as the heir of half her Aunt Binfield's land. Two of Anne Binfield's former servants came and testified that they had fished the water. Roger Breach 'had dwelt with the said Anne Binfield some halfe a yeare about fiftie years since when he had fished with Anne Binfield's brother with nettes, but never with any ginn or weeles'. Joseph Winter dwelt with Anne Binfield some twenty years together about fourteen years since in which time he did now and then fish the corner of the creek and sometimes people would rob his 'weeles' and sometimes he would rob theirs. He also said 'that sometyme he did take in his Dame's right some of the bulrushes growing upon the same rushbedd'.

Although the farmers' wives in the manor of Sonning were in a strong position this was due to customary law and the force of tradition rather than to any conscious thought about the proper relationship between man and woman. Since the Reformation and the establishment of the royal authority over the Church a real effort had been made by leading church-men to impress on the mass of the population the moral rules which should govern society. They brought fresh energy to the ancient courts through which the medieval Church had tried to control the morals of the laity. But it was through exhortation rather than judgments in court that they attacked the relationship between men and women in marriage. A set of twelve homilies, or sermons, was published by the authority of Edward VI in 1547 with instructions to all 'parsons, vicars, curates, and all others having spiritual care' to read and declare one every Sunday to their parishioners 'plainly and distinctly in such order as they stand in the book'. When the parsons had been once through the homilies they were to go back and read them through again in the same order[1]. In 1562 Queen Elizabeth reissued Edward VI's homilies, and repeated his instructions to ministers to begin at the beginning and go straight through the book. But she added a further twenty-one homilies which were preceded by an 'admonition to all ministers ecclesiastical' advising them 'prudently to choose out such homilies as be most meet for the time, and for the agreeable instruction of the people committed to your charge'. If the homily appeared too long for one reading the minister might divide it and read part in the forenoon and part in the afternoon[2]. The eighteenth

[1] *Certain Sermons or Homilies appointed to be read in Churches*, Oxford, 1844. 'The Preface as it was published in the year 1547', p. xii. [2] *Ibid.*, p. 141.

homily in this edition was a sermon 'Of the state of matrimony'[1]. Edward VI's advisers had come no nearer treating of matrimony than a long sermon in three parts against 'Whoredom and Adultery'[2].

In the minds of congregations starved of intellectual interests these homilies, written by masters of English rhetoric, must have brought new and vital interests. Many English villagers, who had never before been stimulated to thought, took to the new teaching with a fervour which created the dissenters of the seventeenth century. Such folk formed the backbone of Cromwell's New Model Army but they were also a problem to his Government. The homily on the state of matrimony forced even the people of remote villages to consider the relations between husband and wife. The homily begins by stating the divine purpose of matrimony, 'instituted of God to the intent that man and woman should live lawfully in a perpetual friendship, to bring forth fruit, and to avoid fornication'. After dwelling a little on the horrors of fornication, quoting from St. Paul 'Neither whoremongers, neither adulterers, shall inherit the kingdom of God', the author points out how the devil will try to sow discord between man and wife. 'How few matrimonies there be', he says, 'without chidings, brawlings, tauntings, repentings, bitter cursings, and fightings'. He points out that it is 'a miserable thing to behold, that yet they are of necessity compelled to live together, which yet cannot be in quiet together'. He adjures married folk to pray to God to govern their hearts and then turns to address the husband in the words of St. Peter. 'You husbands deal with your wives according to knowledge, giving honour to the wife, as unto the weaker vessel'. 'The husband', he says, 'should be the leader and author of love, in cherishing and increasing concord: which then shall take place, if he will use moderation, and not tyranny, and if he yield something to the woman. For the woman is a weak creature not endued with like strength and constancy of mind; therefore they be the sooner disquieted, and they be the more prone to all weak affections and dispositions of the mind, more than men be; and lighter they be, and more vain in their phantasies and opinions'. It is not a token of womanish cowardice for a man to remember these things, for 'a woman must be spared and borne with, the rather that she is the weaker vessel, of a frail heart, inconstant, and with a word soon stirred to wrath'.

[1] *Certain Sermons or Homilies appointed to be read in Churches*, pp. 446–58.
[2] *Ibid.*, pp. 108–23.

The author then turns to the woman: 'What shall become her? Shall she abuse the gentleness and humanity of her husband, and, at her pleasure, turn all things upside down? No, surely: for that is far repugnant against God's commandment: for thus doth St. Peter preach to them "Ye wives be in subjection to obey your own husbands". To obey is another thing to control or command, which yet they may do to their children and to their family: but as for their husbands, them they must obey, and cease from commanding, and perform subjection'. A woman should endeavour in all ways to content her husband, do him pleasure and avoid what may offend him. Even so, 'it can scantly be, but that some offences shall sometime chance betwixt them; for no man doth live without fault, specially, for that the woman is the more frail party'. Women should therefore readily acknowledge their fault 'not only to avoid strife and debate, but rather in respect of the commandment of God, as St. Paul expresseth it in this form of words: "Let women be subject to their husbands, as to the Lord: for the husband is the head of the woman, as Christ is the head of the church". Here you understand that ye should acknowledge the authority of the husband, and refer to him the honour of obedience'. Women must obey their husbands 'as Sarah obeyed Abraham, calling him lord'. The author admits that it is upon the women that the grief and pains of matrimony fall, for they 'relinquish the liberty of their own rule'. They have to bear children and bring them up. But the woman is again exhorted to obey her husband and take heed of his requests. She is reminded that the cap which she wears upon her head signifies that 'she is under covert or obedience of her husband'. The husband is again exhorted to bear with his wife even if 'she is a wrathful woman, a drunkard, and beastly, without wit and reason'. He is reminded that beating will only make her worse and that he will have a great reward if 'where thou mightest beat her, and yet for the respect and fear of God thou wilt abstain and bear patiently her great offences'.

A single reading of this homily from the pulpit of the village church would have assured every married man in the congregation of his right to demand obedience from his wife. Since ministers of religion were exhorted to choose the homily which fitted the occasion it is very likely that the homily on matrimony was often chosen for reading. It would certainly be suitable when any married couple in the village were known to be on bad terms or any wife was reported to be a scold. Men who had not ever considered the basis of the relationship between man and wife were now forced to think of it. Male authority was driven home with all the authority of the Church. Nor is the homily on the state of matrimony the only one which inculcates the husband's authority over his wife. In the sermon against excess of apparel wives are reminded of what Tertullian said, 'Let women be subject to their husbands and they are sufficiently attired'[1]. Nor were there lacking preachers in the succeeding generations to press home this teaching in the village churches.

A famous preacher of the early seventeenth century, William Whately, vicar of Banbury, wrote two tracts on marriage which were extremely popular in the lifetime of their author. The first, entitled *A Bride-Bush; or a direction for married persons; plainly describing the duties common to both, and peculiar to each of them, by performance of which, marriage shall prooue a great help to such, as now for want of performing them doe find it a little hell.* First printed in 1619[2], this tract was reprinted in 1623, at Bristol in 1768, at London in 1805, and translated into Welsh at Llanrwst in 1834. Such popularity may have been in part due to the belief forcibly expressed that marriage was dissolved and annihilated by the adultery or wilful desertion of either party, so that the innocent party could lawfully make another contract. These views caused the court of High Commission to summon Whately before it and he solemnly recanted in the 1623 edition. He again set out his former position and the grounds for his abandonment of it in the preface to his second tract on marriage, published in 1624, *A Care-cloth; or a TREATISE of the cumbers and troubles of marriage: intended to advise them that may, to shun them; that may not, well and patiently to bear them*'[3]. It might be suspected that Whately himself was unhappily married, but it was far otherwise: 'hee married the daughter of one Master George Hunt, the sonne of that tryed and prepared Martyr John Hunt . . . who was condemned to be burnt for Religion, but was saved from the execution thereof by the death of Queene Mary'[4]. Whately concluded the *Care-cloth* with a prayer to God to be made more obedient to Him than others 'because thou hast made my Matrimonie more easefull to me than many others'. He admits that such has been God's 'goodness to me that this

---

[1] *Certain Sermons or Homilies appointed to be read in Churches*, p. 279.   [2] London.
[3] Apparently not reprinted. My own copy was much read and corrected in ink. Religious verse was copied into blank spaces.
[4] *Prototypes, or The Primarie Precedent Presidents out of the Booke of Genesis*, London, 1640, sig. a2.

yoke hath been verie easy to mee, and my comforts have been as great, my crosses as few, as I could well expect in marriage'[1].

Behind each of these tracts there must have been sermons actually preached at Banbury. Indeed, Whately states in his preface to the *Bride-bush* that he brought together the ampler material he had collected because a sermon he had given on the subject had been printed without his authority. The fame of Whately as a preacher spread so far that 'great wits' and persons of many persuasions were drawn to cover the twenty-one miles from Oxford in order to hear him preach[2]. His sermons were so eloquent and so strongly delivered that he became known as the Roaring Boy of Banbury. Indeed, even today, the reader, far removed from the seventeenth-century habit of mind, can feel his sincerity and understand how his eloquent periods moved his hearers. 'Had it not grown out of fashion', he said, to preach without a text he would have taken none for his sermon, the *Bride-bush*, for the duties of married people have to be collected from many parts of the Bible but, since a text he must have, he chose St. Paul, Ephesians v. 23, 'The Husband is the wiues head'[3]. When he came to print this sermon he printed also the plan by which he had framed it. He dealt with his subject under the three main headings: the duties of both husband and wife; the duties of the husband; and the duties of the wife. They must both be chaste, show due benevolence to each other, and love each other. They must attain love by living together and praying together. The effects of love will be to make them please each other. They must be faithful to each other and helpful, both in health and in sickness. They must have a good opinion of each other and keep each other's secrets and do their duty by their family.

The duty of the husband is to 'govern his wife and maintain her'. 'Nature hath framed the lineaments of his body to superioritie and set the print of government in his very face, which is more sterne, and lesse delicate than the womans; he must not suffer this order of nature to be inuerted'. 'It is a sinne for a man to come lower than God hath set him. It is not humility, but basenesse, to be ruled by her, whom he should rule[4]. Since authority lies in the husband it is lawful for the husband to correct and punish his wife, though Whately doubted if he should beat her as he can his slave. But he finally came to the conclusion that 'only

---

1 *Care-cloth*, p. 85.
2 Wood, *Athenæ Oxonienses*, ed. P. Bliss, London, 1815, vol. ii, col. 640.
3 *Bride-bush*, 1619, p. 1.   4 *Ibid.*, pp. 97–8.

if she is intollerable' then 'he may launce his owne arme where it swelleth, and scrat his owne hand where it itcheth, though he make it smart after'. Nevertheless, he holds it to be 'intollerable' for a man to strike his wife in anger for ordinary weaknesses, 'but if she raile upon him with most reproachful termes, if she will affront him with bold and impudent resistances, if she will tell him to his teeth that she cares not for him, if she will flie in his face with violence and begin to strike him, or break into unwomanly words or behaviour, let him bear awhile', and admonish and exhort, and pray. If her father is still alive he suggests that the husband shall ask his aid. If all this is of no avail then he must at last use the authoritie bestowed upon him by God. 'But for blowes, for strokes with hand or fist, nothing should drive an husband to them, except the utmost extremities of unwifelike carriage'[1].

When it comes to the 'wiues peculiar duties' it is clear that obedience to her husband is considered the beginning and end of them. 'Firstly she must acknowledge her inferioritie'. 'Secondly she must carrie herself as an inferior'. 'Where the woman stands upon termes of equalitie with her husband (much more if she account herselfe his better) the very roote of all good carriage is quite withered, and the fountain thereof utterly dried up: out of place, out of peace; and woe to those miserable and aspiring shoulders, which will not content themselues to take their roome below the head'. He concludes with this advice. 'Whosoeuer hath the desire and purpose to be a good wife or to liue comfortably, let her set downe this conclusion within her soule: Mine husband is my superior, my better: he hath authoritie and rule ouer me'[2]. It may at least be gathered from all this rhetoric that the married folk around Banbury were sorely in need of advice, that husbands tended to beat their wives and that wives were ready to scold their husbands.

It is not easy to get into the minds of the country folk of the seventeenth century or to judge their reactions to the Church's teaching. Many men, conscious that their families depended on their strength for bread, may well have felt pleasure in authoritative statements of their right and duty to lead and control. Others may not have thought much about it, and simply continued on their brutish way. When a diary or autobiography sheds light on a country family, it is always worth reading carefully to see how the womenfolk are dealt with. From this standpoint, none of these private records is more revealing than the autobiography of Adam

[1] *Bride-bush*, pp. 107–9, 123.   *Ibid.*, pp. 189 ff.

Martindale (1623–86), a minister ejected from his living for nonconformity in 1662, who came from a yeoman family in south Lancashire[1].
While Adam was still a child, the whole family was shaken by the determination of his elder sister, Jane, to go off to London. A plague in London
in 1625 had driven many people far into the country, and when the
fugitives prepared to return home, Jane insisted on going with them.
She had 'her father's spirit and her mother's beauty' and could not bear
the restrictions of a yeoman's daughter in the north.

   The restrictions upon her dress are described in a passage to which
it is hard to find a parallel: 'Freeholders' daughters were then confined to
their felts, pettiecoates and waistcoates, crosse handkerchiefs about their
neckes, and white crosse-clothes upon their heads, with coifes under them
wrought with black silk or worsteed. 'Tis true the finest sort of them
wore gold or silver lace upon their waistcoates, good silk laces (and store
of them) about their pettiecoates, and bone laces or workes about their
linnens. But the proudest of them (below the gentry) durst not have
offered to wear an hood, or a scarfe (which now every beggar's brat
that can get them thinks not above her) noe, not so much as a gowne till
her wedding day'. Her family tried to prevent Jane from going to London,
arguing that 'she wanted nothing at home . . . and if she had a mind to
be married her father was then in a good ordinary capacity to preferre
her'. She said that she would get a place and 'serve a lady, being ingenious
at her needle'[2]. Although she went against her parents' will she was given
money to subsist on until she was settled, but unhappily she caught the
plague and her money grew low. The only hint she gave her family of
her straits was 'in a gentle way she writ for a goose-pie to make merry
with her friends; and a lusty one was immediately sent her, cased in
twig work'. They also sent 'money that the goose might swim without
her cost'. Unfortunately the carrier took three weeks in going and coming
and 'her money was so near at end that she had thoughts to sell her hair,
which was very lovely both for length and colour'. However, she was
rescued by a young gentleman who had gone up to London in her company
and had fallen in love with her. He was probably the reason for her
going, although this did not strike her brother. They married and took
the George and Half Moon outside Temple Bar. Her parents helped
them furnish the inn and often sent them country produce for their

---

[1] *The Life of Adam Martindale*, ed. R. Parkinson, Chetham Soc., 1845.
[2] *Ibid.*, pp. 6–7.

table[1]. Their happiness was short. When Jane heard in the early spring of
1632 that her mother was sick and like to die 'she bought an excellent
swift mare' and rode home as quickly as she could, but not in time to see
her mother alive. She and her husband then decided to leave London
and take an inn in Warrington. She went back, let the London house,
and sent down her goods, but on her way down again she caught smallpox from children at an inn where she stopped for a drink. She died and
was buried beside her mother in August 1632[2].

About this time Adam's father met with a great disappointment 'in
the matching of mine eldest brother'. He could easily have got a wife
with a fortune of £100 or £120 and indeed there was one that wanted
to marry him who had £140 to her fortune, 'was of very suitable years
and otherwise likely to make an excellent wife. But when things were
neare accomplishing, he on a sudden sleights her, and sets his affection
upon a wild airy girle, between fifteen and sixteen yeares of age: an
huge lover and frequenter of wakes, greenes, and merrie-nights, where
musick and dancing abounded. And as for her portion, it was only forty
pounds'. The whole family was against him, but 'have her he would'.
Adam has to admit that 'she proved above all just expectation not only
civill, but religious, and an exceeding good wife; whereas the other he
should have had proved (as I have heard) as much below it'. But 'the
smallnesse of her fortune was a great prejudice to our family'[3].

Of his own wife Adam Martindale says little directly, but it is clear
that she was a woman of spirit and a good wife through difficult times.
She was Elizabeth Hall, like her husband of a yeoman family and a Puritan.
Her father was a freehold farmer at Droylsden, Lancashire. When some
of her husband's congregation secretly put up a maypole upon 'a little
bank where in times past the Sabbath had beene wofully profaned' it
was Adam's wife who 'assisted with three young women, whipt it
downe in the night with a framing-saw, cutting it brest-high, so as the
bottom would serve well for a diall-post'[4]. It was his wife who, as he
says, 'wrangled' £10 out of the man who succeeded him in his living
after he had been dispossessed in 1662. She also made the same man buy
'a table, formes, and ceiling' for about £4 more[5]. What provision he
could make for his wife, Adam Martindale had made. He acquired
from the lord of the manor of High Leigh a lease of a house there for three

---

[1] *The Life of Adam Martindale*, p. 8.
[2] *Ibid.*, pp. 17–18.
[3] *Ibid.*, p. 16.
[4] *Ibid.*, p. 157.
[5] *Ibid.*, p. 172.

lives, those of his wife and his two eldest sons. Both boys died long before their mother. Writing in old age, Adam Martindale said: 'They are both dead long ago, their mother (blessed be God) being yet alive, (long may she so continue). . . . It'—that is the house and land at Leigh—'is but a little thing, yet I desire heartily to praise God for the helpe I have had from it in the time of my distresse,' and such sure, (though meane) provision for my poore faithfull wife, (that hath suffered so much with me,) if she overlive me, as I hope she may'[1]. Elizabeth Martindale outlived her husband, but no more is known of her.

All but two of Adam Martindale's children died before their father, some of them in infancy or childhood. Smallpox or a decline was generally the cause. Of the two daughters who survived him one was married to a tallow chandler. A disastrous fire destroyed his 'work-house' and Adam Martindale had to help the 'young people' as best he could[2]. His other surviving daughter, Hannah, had been seized with a painful fever at the age of ten which left her a cripple from the waist down[3]. His eldest daughter, Elizabeth, was 'bred up at home to her booke and pen, and in Warrington and Manchester to her needle and musick, though the latter she loved not, and after forgot it'. She entered the service of a Mrs. Fleetwood at Penwortham and went from her to 'young Mrs. Venables of Agden, who had too great an affection for her; for out of a loathnesse to part from her she concealed from us her falling in love with a fellow servant that was an unsuitable match for her, hoping that he only courted her as he had formerly others in the same place that kept the stores, for his owne ends'. Her parents took her away 'first home, and then to Manchester to her grandmother's . . . provided her a farre more lovely match, for persons, parts, goodnesse, and estate, and one that dearly loved her, but could not prevail'. She went into service in Staffordshire and on New Year's Day, 1672, the servants who had served for one year having gone and the new ones not yet come, Elizabeth cooked a 'great dinner' and stepping in thin shoes out into the snow to cool herself she caught a cold from which she died. She 'was so well beloved among the young women of the parish, that though she died almost a mile from the church, and the way very foule, they would not suffer any man to carrie her body a foote, but conveyed her on their owne shoulders to her grave'[4].

---

[1] *The Life of Adam Martindale*, p. 118.   [2] *Ibid.*, pp. 232–3.
[3] *Ibid.*, p. 214.   [4] *Ibid.*, pp. 206–9.

Adam Martindale's children, both girls and boys, were helped into the world rather than made to take a course laid down by their parents. No member of the family was forced into a distasteful marriage. Adam Martindale was an exceptionally able man, who taught himself mathematics at forty well enough to teach it to others and to write a textbook on surveying. But he was still very near to the land, and his wife's contribution to the family's needs in 1670 was to 'keep a little stock of kine as she had done formerly'[1]. Such a household, like countless others, was far too busy winning a livelihood to speculate on the relationship between man and woman. All their thoughts not directed to their daily problems went into religious meditation. The Puritan wife, well-versed in her Bible, would certainly have regarded her husband as the head of the house and have felt no resentment that the Church and the law held him to be her master.

Any woman might have been proud to serve Adam Martindale, whose attitude to wife and children is much that of a modern husband and father. But there was a grimmer side to the lives of many country-women though it is not often described by anyone who had seen it at first hand. The memoirs of her life, written by Mrs. Catharine Cappe (1744–1821)[2], offer a glimpse of the ordinary free farmer's wife in the middle of the eighteenth century. Mrs. Cappe was born at Long Preston in Craven, Yorkshire, where her father, the Reverend Jeremiah Harrison, had been the incumbent since about 1729. She describes the country-side as 'insulated from the rest of the kingdom; not so much by its high mountains, as by its almost impassable roads'. She says that the inhabitants were 'as uncivilized as their mountains were rude and uncultivated'. The free farmers at Long Preston were called 'statesmen'; if they held a large farm 'great statesmen', and if a little land only, 'little statesmen'[3]. Such people sent their daughters to a decayed gentlewoman in the village for instruction in reading and sewing, but they were much afraid that she might become a charge on the parish[4]. When visitors called on the wife of a great statesman they were invited to come in 'and make free'. The hostess then dusted the chairs with the corner of her apron and desired her guests to be seated. She next takes a brush to sweep the floor, apologizing all the time that it was not done before their arrival. She

[1] *The Life of Adam Martindale*, p. 190.   [2] See below, pp. 302–6.
[3] *Memoirs of the Life of the late Mrs. Catharine Cappe*, 2nd ed., London, 1823, pp. 5–6.
[4] *Ibid.*, p. 16.

then adjusts her own apparel, and not unfrequently goes through the whole ceremony of an entire change of upper garments, standing by her company with great unconcern, and relating the history of her family —when Thomas was born—where George goes to school—how fast he takes his learning, etc., etc. Her dress being finished she offers each of her visitors a glass of brandy, assuring them that "they are as welcome as if they were at home", this being done, she fetches a chair and seats herself beside them'[1].

This was a vivid childhood's memory, but Mrs. Cappe noted that she 'did not recollect a single instance in which any part of this ceremony was omitted, even so late as the year 1787'. Of the husbands of these hospitable ladies Mrs. Cappe has little that is good to say. In 1787 she, by this time married and living at York, went back again to Craven to sell some of the land at Preston which her father had acquired while he was vicar there. Her brother had died heavily in debt and it was necessary to raise money quickly. Fortunately Mr. Cappe went with her. 'When I saw more of the temper and disposition of the inhabitants of my native village, I was both grieved and disappointed', she writes. 'Far from finding these statesmen adorned with the simplicity and possessed of the integrity, which one might have expected in their retired situation, they appeared fraught with cunning and intrigue; and seemed to make it a common cause to keep me in profound ignorance. Had I gone alone, they would infallibly have imposed upon me exceedingly, for added to all the rest, they have a supreme contempt for women; but the appearance and manner of Mr. Cappe, the knowledge on agricultural subjects, which I did not previously imagine he had possessed,—the questions he put to them, and the further improvements he suggested, inspired them with so much respect, that seeing me thus assisted, they gave up their designs, and it became practicable for me to treat with them on equitable terms'[2]. The wheel has indeed come full circle in rural society; the homilies have brought forth their inevitable fruit. The countryman has at last 'a supreme contempt for women'.

Mrs. Cappe's description of a statesman's wife in her home relates to a distant part of the country where life was always hard and labour often unrewarding. The domestic setting of a wealthy farmer of the same date in a long-cultivated eastern county is depicted in the life of George Crabbe with which his son prefaced the complete edition of his works in 1834.

[1] *Memoirs of the Life of the late Mrs. Catharine Cappe*, pp. 13-14. [2] *Ibid.*, pp. 242-3.

In September 1791 Crabbe took his family to pay a visit to Parham in Suffolk, where his wife's uncle Mr. Tovell lived, whose 'establishment was that of a first-rate yeoman of that period'. He possessed 'an estate of some eight hundred pounds per annum, a portion of which he himself cultivated. Educated at a mercantile school he often said "Jack will never make a gentleman", yet he had a native dignity of mind and manners, which might have enabled him to pass muster in that character with any but very fastidious critics. His house was large, and the surrounding moat, the rookery, the ancient dovecot and well-stored fishponds, were such as might have suited a gentleman's seat of some consequence. . . . On entering the house, there was nothing at first sight to remind one of the farm: a spacious hall paved with black and white marble,—at one extremity a very handsome drawing-room, and at the other a fine old staircase of black oak, polished till it was as slippery as ice, and having a chime clock and a barrel-organ on its landing-places. But this drawing-room, a corresponding dining parlour, and a handsome sleeping apartment upstairs, were all *tabooed* ground, and made use of on great and solemn occasions only such as rent-days, and an occasional visit with which Mr. Tovell was honoured by a neighbouring peer. At all other times the family and their visitors lived in the kitchen along with the servants'. Mr. Tovell 'occupied an armchair, or when he had gout, a couch drawn up to one side of a large open chimney. Mrs. Tovell sat at a small table, on which, in the evening, stood one small candle in an iron candlestick, plying her needle by the feeble glimmer, surrounded by her maids, all busy with the same employment'. 'At a very early hour in the morning the alarum called the maids, and their mistress also; and if the former were tardy, a louder alarum, and more formidable, was heard chiding the delay—not that scolding was peculiar to any occasion, it regularly ran on through all the day, like bells on harness, inspiriting the work, whether it were done ill or well. After the important business of the dairy, and a hasty breakfast, their respective employments were again resumed; that which the mistress took for her especial privilege, being the scrubbing the floors of the state apartments. A new servant, ignorant of her presumption, was found one morning on her knees, hard at work at the floor of one of these preserves, and was thus addressed by her mistress: "*You* wash such floors as these? Give me the brush this instant, and troop to the scullery and wash that, madam! . . . As true as God's in heaven, here comes Lord Rochford, to call on Mr. Tovell.

Here take my mantle" (a blue woollen apron) "and I'll go to the door".[1]

The family, as a rule, ate in the kitchen, 'the heads seated at an old table; the farm men standing in the adjoining scullery, door open—the female servants at a side table, called a *bouter*'. Any chance visitors sat at the table with the family. After the meal was over, the fire made up and 'the kitchen sanded and lightly swept over in waves, mistress and maids, taking off their shoes, retired to their chambers for a nap of one hour to the minute'. The cats and dogs slept by the fire and Mr. Tovell dozed in his chair. When the hour was over Mr. Tovell's 'tea equipage', that is, the bottles, were placed on the table and all was ready for his boon companions to come in for an evening's carouse. Mrs. Tovell and Mr. and Mrs. Crabbe retired to Mrs. Tovell's own room when voices became raised in the pleasant talk over the bottles. The little boy, George Crabbe, thought too young to understand the talk of the ribald old men, stayed in the kitchen, as the servants did, and enjoyed the excitement of the evening. Looking back on those days he describes the household at Parham as 'a primitive set'[2], but to anyone who can remember the farm households of the end of the last century, or the beginning of the present one, there is nothing very remote in the Tovell establishment. By the end of the nineteenth century the best rooms were no longer unused by the farmer and his family. Nor were they so splendid as the heightened imagination of a child painted the rooms at Parham. But the head of the house still sat with his grog beside him and welcomed the arrival of a friend to share his drink and talk. His wife, in her afternoon cap, with his daughters about her were still plying their needles as Mrs. Tovell had done, but by the light of an oil lamp with a duplex burner. Servants were fewer, for daughters lived to grow up and could do the work of the house. Many farmers' wives were still as little interested in literature as Mrs. Tovell, but like her they knew all too well who was the head of the house.

When all allowance has been made for the rise and fall of families and for the movement of country people into the towns, there remained in the country-side countless families which had gone on from century to century in much the same walk of life. They had often gone through the years on the same farm. Centuries of Bible teaching had driven home the

---

[1] *Life and Poems of the Reverend George Crabbe*, London, 1834, vol. i, pp. 142–4.
[2] *Ibid.*, p. 146.

wife's subjection to her husband. Centuries of inherited practice had taught many a farmer's wife how to get her own way. Yet until Parliament had been forced to take action and the full married women's Property Act was passed in 1882 a man could use as his own any money inherited by his wife. Many families preserve the tradition of a little money inherited by a grandmother or great-grandmother and thrown away on horse-racing by her husband. It was not only the big race-meetings which attracted countrymen to risk their cash. 'Cock fighting and trotting horses', the temptation to which my own great-grandfather fell, could be enjoyed all over the country near at home. At the end of the nineteenth century a good wife was as essential to the farmer's prosperity as she was in the Middle Ages. She played as important a part in the life of the farm community. The farmers' wives in the manor of Sonning in those days always spoke of their husbands as 'the Master', or more often as 'Master'. In one household the husband walked in from the fields and, as a matter of course, put his feet up one after the other into his wife's lap for her to take his boots off. But in that same household it was the wife who had the last word in any question of policy.

Paradoxically enough it was the unmarried woman who suffered most through the teaching of the Scriptures about the subjection of the wife, for a good wife who loves a good husband is always willing to let him take the lead. Such rhetoric as William Whately and others of his kind poured forth from the pulpit inevitably had its effect on the attitude of all men to all women. The homily of the state of matrimony of 1562 hints at the independence which women must give up for the trials of marriage, but no teaching was directed to the praise or encouragement of independence in a woman, even in an unmarried woman. The only real hope of the farmer's daughter was marriage. The unmarried woman was a burden on her family, a failure, since she had not caught a man to keep her. Farmers' daughters were never well enough educated to get a living at anything else but farming. By the end of the nineteenth century it had long gone out of fashion for them to go into service as their predecessors had been anxious to do. Farmers despised the new profession of school-teaching and resented it because it was paid for out of the rates. One of my own great-aunts who ultimately became the head mistress of an infants' school in London and is now many years in her grave, was helped by kind friends to learn enough to become one of the first students in a Church training college, but it was in spite of her parents rather than with their help. She had to do her share of the milking before she slipped away for lessons, and it was hard to get permission to go to college. Independence in a woman was only becoming when she had survived matrimony and graduated into a prosperous widowhood. All through the centuries the comfortably-off widow enjoyed the respect of all her neighbours.

The wives and daughters of farm labourers lived in the same atmosphere as the wives and daughters of their employers, but even at the end of the last century no labourer's wife could look beyond the needs of the passing day. In past centuries their state had been far worse. In the remotest times to which our knowledge goes back women, married as well as unmarried, had taken a full part in the agricultural work of their village. Their wages—not much lower than those of men employed on the same tasks—are set down in wage assessments put out by Quarter Sessions. But women's work was continually interrupted by the birth of children, of whom many in the labouring class, as indeed in every other class, died before maturity. No farm labourer's wife can ever have felt well. The women were old long before their time. Even within living memory younger women and children were glad to earn a little money by stone-picking. Potato picking has always been and still is work for women or children.

Fifty years ago in the villages which had grown up in the ancient manor of Sonning the earnings of the labourer's wife still formed an essential part of the family income. The work she did was generally washing, sewing, and cleaning for women better off than herself. The weekly wage of a farm labourer was generally 11 shillings with a house and garden; a gardener would get 12 shillings. If no house were provided 15 shillings remained the labourer's wage up to the outbreak of war in 1914. House-rent was at most 4 shillings. Gardens had no fruit trees because the lady of the manor held that potatoes should be grown instead. Daughters were sent out to service at the earliest possible moment in order to get them properly fed. Well into the twentieth century many parents pleaded that girls should be allowed to leave school for service long before the statutory school-leaving age. An examination with a modest standard was devised to justify this. Church-going familes could expect presents of coal and blankets at Christmas and help in times of sickness and dire necessity. Many families in every village were brought up under such conditions. That the husband was provided with enough food to keep him at work, that children were often decently clothed, and that many of them lived to grow up was entirely due to the quality of the labourers' wives.

Some of these women are still living today and their spirit is as indomitable in extreme old age as it was in what one of them persistently describes as 'the good old days'. Her husband worked first on a farm and then on the roads. He never earned more than 15 shillings a week and she paid 4 shillings rent for her cottage which she still lives in today at the same rent. 'Then I had a pig in the sty, and vegetables in the garden. Tea and sugar were cheap and we never wanted'. Women whose early years had been spent in 'good service' never forgot the lessons they learned in the homes of their employers. Nevertheless, in most villages there was at least one family which had sunk under the intolerable burden of life. Large families in cottages too small for decency often resulted in consumption and sometimes in incest and the appearance of more unwanted children. That incest was rare was due entirely to the good sense and courage of the farm labourers' wives in thousands of indifferent cottages up and down the land. Every woman old enough to remember a village of the beginning of the present century can only rejoice that those days are gone for ever.

CHAPTER V

The Renaissance and Reformation
and their consequences, 1400–1642

Signs of a coming change in the position of women can be seen in many European countries at the end of the Middle Ages. They were part of the enrichment of life which is commonly called the Renaissance. This movement came to England rather later than to other European countries, for it needed the establishment of the strong Tudor monarchy to free men from the fear of civil war. But already before the Wars of the Roses had begun in England the first of many female autobiographies had been written down for its author by a man. Whatever view of the *Book of Margery Kempe* is taken it remains a portent[1]. Written in English, it sets out the efforts of Margery, 'this creature', to live a life of chastity and Christ's service. She herself thought that she was a true mystic whose virtues would be known all over the world. But it would not be unfair to conclude that she was a victim of hysteria whose sanity had been imperilled by too much child-bearing. It was not difficult to find celebate priests and anchorites eager to enter into the imaginings of such a woman. It is fortunate that two of them were ready to write them down. She travelled about England with her husband trying to persuade him to continence and at last succeeded in June 1413[2]. She visited many parts of England and saw the Archbishops both of York and Canterbury. She and her husband went to the Bishop of Lincoln to take their vow of chastity and were affronted that the bishop would not give her 'the mantle and the ring'[3]. She travelled to the Holy Land and visited Rome on her return. She went to St. James of Compostella in Spain, to Danzig, blown on to the coast of Norway as she went, and returned by way of Aachen and Calais. Her tears were continuous and called attention to her holiness. When she could not weep she was unhappy. Although she

---

[1] *The Book of Margery Kempe*, ed. S. Brown Meech with Prefatory note by Hope Emily Allen, E.E.T.S., London, 1940.   [2] *Ibid.*, p. 24 and *n.*   [3] *Ibid.*, p. 35.

was more than once put in prison and she never hesitated to speak to the people, she had no serious trouble with those who feared and disliked the Lollards.

Margery Kempe was about a generation younger than the anchoress Juliana of Norwich, a Benedictine nun from Carrow, who went to live in the churchyard of St. Julian in Norwich as an anchoress and wrote meditations on divine love. Margery visited her and 'much was the holy dalliance that the anchoress and this creature had communing in the love of our Lord Jesus Christ many days they were together'[1]. It is perhaps a sign of a coming change that these women could express themselves and arouse the respectful attention of their contemporaries. Margery Kempe came of burgess stock. She was proud of her father's distinction in the town of Lynn, 'mayor five times of that worshipful borough and alderman also many years'[2]. Her husband was also a burgess of Lynn, although Margery did not regard him as of so good birth as herself. All through the Middle Ages the women in the towns retained a strong tradition of independence. Although the inhabitants of towns were, like all other people, subject to the common law which developed in the twelfth and thirteenth centuries they preserved an attitude of mind alien to the feudal outlook of barons and knights and their ladies. Women took a prominent part in the business life of the community. As in country villages the trade of brewing was in their hands. When Margery Kempe wanted to make a show she set up as a brewer and 'was one of the greatest brewers in the town for three or four years', but she gave it up because something always went wrong with the ale however good her servants were. Then she acquired a horse-mill and a couple of good horses with a man to grind corn, but her horses would not work[3]. It is significant that the first woman to leave behind her an account of her life, her thoughts, and her dreams was a member of the urban aristocracy in an East Anglian town.

Margery Kempe was an individualist who would have seemed an isolated figure in any historical setting. In her own age, she stood apart from each of the two intellectual movements which agitated the fifteenth century, Lollardry and the scholarship of the early humanists. In the next century many women were to feel the excitement of the new learning in religion which accompanied the new learning in scholarship. But the

---

[1] *The Book of Margery Kempe*, p. 43.
[2] *Ibid.*, p. 111.   [3] *Ibid.*, pp. 9–10.

change came slowly, and the woman of the fifteenth century who was most influential as a patroness of scholars belonged in spirit to the medieval world. The portrait of Margaret, Countess of Richmond, drawn by Bishop Fisher in her funeral sermon would have served in most of its features for any devout lady of the Middle Ages[1]. It is in her consciousness that she had missed much through her ignorance of Latin, in the spirit which made her translate devotional books from French into English, above all, in the lamentation of 'the students of both Universities to whom she was as a mother, all the learned men of England to whom she was a very patroness', that the signs of a coming age appear[2]. The accession of her grandson Henry VIII in 1509 brought to the throne a king responsive to the new learning and a queen imbued with the Renaissance spirit. Queen Katherine of Aragon was the daughter of Queen Isabella of Castile, who had learned Latin and taken care that all her daughters were educated to read and speak it.

The scholars of Renaissance Europe moved freely from country to country in search of patrons and kept up a close correspondence in the artificial Latin which was their common tongue. All were drawn to Italy to study for a time in one or other of the Italian universities, but they were ready to go where their scholarship could win them bread. Queen Katherine invited a Spanish scholar named Luis Vives to come to England to supervise the education of her daughter Mary, for whom he wrote *A Plan of Studies for a Girl*[3]. An English scholar, Thomas Linacre, who had studied in Italy, wrote a Latin grammar for the young princess. Already before Mary was born Sir Thomas More was bringing up his daughters in the new learning, providing them with the best teachers he could find. Margaret Roper, his eldest daughter, born in 1505, was the first of the learned English ladies of the sixteenth century. More was a friend of Vives, and of Erasmus, who had visited England for the first time as early as 1497. Erasmus thought that Vives was too hard on married women in his work *The Instruction of a Christian Woman*, and hoped that he was kinder to his own wife[4]. Sir Thomas More's home life at Chelsea

---

[1] *The Funeral Sermon of Margaret countess of Richmond and Derby*, reprint in black-letter facsimile. London, 1708; the text of the sermon was *Dixit Martha ad Jhesum*.

[2] *Ibid.*, pp. 13 and 22.

[3] Foster Watson, *Vives: on Education*, Cambridge, 1913, p. lxxiv.

[4] *Ibid.*, p. lxxxviii. Vives's books were written in Latin. This work was translated by Richard Hyrde, London, 1557, under the title *A very fruitful and pleasant book called the Instruction of a Christian Woman*.

was a living proof that women could profit from a liberal education as had the ladies of the ancient classical world.

In England, the influence of such men as Erasmus, More, and Vives was far-reaching, and the example of the court was followed by aristocratic parents all over the country. Anne Boleyn (born in 1507) in Norfolk and Katherine Parr (born in 1512) in Westmorland were brought up to the new learning. Young women of high birth whose fathers employed one or more learned chaplains could be taught Greek, Latin, and even Hebrew, with their brothers. The skill and enthusiasm of their teachers contrasted favourably with their parents' severity. Lady Jane Grey, whom Ascham found reading Greek while her parents were hunting in Bradgate Park, told him that she was thankful to have been blessed by God with 'so sharp and severe Parents and so gentle a Schoolmaster'. Her parents 'so sharply taunted, so cruelly threatened, yea presently sometimes with Pinches, Nips, and Bobs, and other ways (which I will not name for the Honour I bear them) so without Measure misorder'd, that I think myself in Hell, till Time come that I must go to Mr. Elmer; who teacheth me so gently . . . that I think all the Time nothing, while I am with him'[1]. Nevertheless firm parental control must have been necessary to enforce the long hours of study which alone could have produced young people as precocious as Edward VI, Lady Jane Grey, and even the Princess Elizabeth herself. The elegant Italianate handwriting of the day cannot have been easily achieved, but as a girl Queen Elizabeth wrote an amazingly beautiful and precise hand. Anne Boleyn, her mother, wrote almost as well, but in a somewhat earlier form of script[2]. She had entered the household of Mary, sister of Henry VIII, at the age of seven in 1514. Lady Jane Grey entered Queen Katherine Parr's household in 1546 when she was nine years old, the youngest of the queen's maids.

Proficiency in the mannered hands of the day was an accomplishment worth recording on a woman's tombstone in this generation. Among the additions made to John Stow's *Survey of London* in the first edition published after his death were many inscriptions from city churches, among them that put up to Elizabeth Lucar, who died on 29 October 1537, 'of yeares not fully 27', by her husband Emmanuel Lucar, merchant taylor of London in the church of St. Lawrence Pountney in Candlewick ward.

[1] *The Schoolmaster by Roger Ascham*, ed. James Upton, London, 1711, pp. 34–5.
[2] W. J. Hardy, *The Handwriting of the Kings and Queens of England*, 1893, opposite p. 62.

'Every Christian heart seeketh to extoll
The glory of the Lord, our onely Redeemer:
Wherefore Dame Fame must needs enroll
Paul Withypoll his child, by loue and nature,
Elizabeth, the wife of Emanuel Lucar,
In whom was declared the goodnesse of the Lord,
With many high vertues, which truely I will record.

She wrote all Needle-workes that women exercise,
With Pen, Frame, or Stoole, all Pictures artificiall.
Curious Knots, or Trailes, what fancie could devise,
Beasts, Birds, or Flowers, even as things natural:
Three manner Hands could she write them faire all.
To speake of Algorisme, or accounts in euery fashion,
Of women, few like (I thinke) in all this Nation.

Dame Cunning[1] her gave a gift right excellent,
The goodly practice of her Science Musicall,
In diuers Tongues to sing, and play with Instrument,
Both Viall and Lute, and also Virginall;
Not onely one, but excellent in all.
For all other vertues belonging to Nature
God her appointed a very perfect creature.

Latine and Spanish, and also Italian,
She spake, writ, and read, with perfect vtterance;
And for the English, she the Garland wan,
In Dame Prudence Schoole, by Graces purueyance,
Which cloathed her with Vertues, from naked Ignorance;
Reading the Scriptures, to judge Light from Darke,
Directing her faith to Christ, the onely Marke'[2].

Elizabeth Lucar died before the difficult years when Henry VIII was

[1] The reference to Dame Cunning has been taken to imply a Dame's School for the children of London citizens, but the writer was certainly using Dame in an allegorical sense. He speaks also of 'Dame Fame' and 'Dame Prudence'.

[2] *The Survey of London*, written in the yeare 1598, by John Stow, Citizen of London. Since then continued, corrected, and much enlarged. London, 1618, pp. 415–16. Quoted by George Ballard, *Memoirs of several Ladies of Great Britain who have been celebrated for their writings, or skill in the learned languages or arts and sciences*, Oxford, 1752, pp. 36–7, from the 1633 ed. of Stow. Ballard assigned the monument to the wrong church.

forcing his subjects to acknowledge as Head of the Church in England a king who insisted on their conformity in doctrine with the Church of Rome. In those years, the queen herself, who was thought to be in sympathy with persons of advanced opinions about the court, only preserved her influence with the king by ostentatious deference to his authority as her husband. It was during this time that the Lincolnshire girl Anne Askew suffered martyrdom as a heretic. Her main interest seems to have lain in searching out the exact meaning of the Biblical text. Under the compulsion of his confessor, her husband, a member of the old Lincolnshire family of Kyme, turned her out of his house. She sought a divorce, basing her claim on the words of St. Paul: 'But if the unbelieving depart, let him depart. A brother or sister is not under bondage in such cases'. Many Puritans in the next century, and even some members of the Church of England, would have allowed divorce to either party for wilful desertion, as for adultery. Anne Askew went to London, perhaps to further her plea for divorce, but was soon arrested and charged with heresy. She was brought before the council, repeatedly examined, and tortured in the hope of extorting evidence against other persons suspected of religious disaffection. Refusing to betray any confidences, she was burned as a heretic on 16 July 1546, at the age of twenty-five. Many other women suffered for their faith during the next thirteen years; one in the reign of Edward VI and sixty under Queen Mary[1].

In his reflections on the state of learning written late in the seventeenth century William Wotton, then chaplain to the Earl of Nottingham, remarked on the zeal for learning which marked the sixteenth century: 'men fancied that everything could be done by it, and they were charmed by the Eloquence of its Professors. . . . It was so very modish that the Fair Sex seemed to believe that *Greek* and *Latin* added to their charms; and *Plato* and *Aristotle* untranslated, were frequent ornaments of their closets. One would think by the Effects that it was a proper Way of Educating them, since there are no Accounts in History of so many truly great Women in any one Age, as there are to be found between the years MD and MDC'[2]. It is more than a coincidence that in an age when women were enjoying an education equal in quality to that of men individual women held dominating positions in many European countries.

[1] J. D. Mackie, *The Earlier Tudors*, Oxford, 1952, pp. 520, 524, and 553.
[2] William Wotton, *Reflections upon Ancient and Modern Learning*, 2nd ed., London, 1697, p. 412.

From the accession of Queen Mary in 1553 England was ruled by a woman for half a century, save for a few years between Mary's marriage to Philip of Spain in 1554 and her death in November 1558, during which the face of Philip appeared with that of Mary on some issues of English coins. But no one in this country or in Europe can have regarded Philip of Spain as in any true sense the ruler of England. To Protestants exiled in Queen Mary's reign from England and Scotland to Geneva, Frankfurt and other German cities the present and future of each country seemed to lie in a woman's hands. In England Mary Tudor was intent on restoring the Catholic faith, and her heir was a woman. Mary of Guise was the Regent of Scotland for her daughter, Mary Stuart. Early in 1558 John Knox published anonymously at Geneva *The First Blast of the Trumpet against the monstrous Regiment of Women*, announcing in his preface that he intended 'thrise to blow the trumpet in the same matter, if God so permitte: twise I intend to do it without name, but at the last blast to take the blame upon myself'[1]. The blast of the trumpet was in particular directed against 'that horrible monstre Jesabal of England', 'the cursed Jesabel of England', 'that cruell monstre Marie (unworthie by reason of her bloudy tyranny, of the name of woman)'[2]. Mary died soon after the issue of the book and Queen Elizabeth was bitterly enraged at the author.

The opinion of exiled English Protestants about this tract was forcibly expressed by John Aylmer, the kindly teacher of Lady Jane Grey, in a treatise of some length which he called *An Harborowe for Faithfull and Trewe Subjects agaynst the late blowne blast, concerninge the Government of Wemen, wherein be confuted all such reasons as a straunger of late made in that behalfe, with a breife exhortation to obedience*[3]. Aylmer dated his book on the title-page 'at Strasborowe 26 April 1559', but it seems to have been published in England. By this time Mary had been succeeded by Elizabeth and it was again politic to speak with respect of Anne Boleyn, the queen's mother. 'Was not', he wrote, 'Quene Anne, the mother of the blessed woman, the chief, first, and only cause of banyshing the beast of Rome with all his beggarly baggage'. Aylmer disposed decisively of all objections to a woman's rule. Even the suggestion that a woman 'is not mete to go

---

[1] The English Scholar's Library of Old and Modern Works, Old Series, Limited Library Edition, No. 2. *John Knox, The First Blast of the Trumpet, etc.*, 1558 (1880), p. 10.

[2] *Ibid.*, pp. 52 and 45.

[3] This book is unpaged. I have consulted the copy in the British Museum.

to the warres' was met by 'some women have gone and sped well'. That a woman 'is not of so sound judgment' was countered by 'peradventure better . . . as it happeneth at this tyme, that you can never shewe in al Englande synce the Conquest, so learned a Kyng as we have now a Quene'. John Aylmer was aggressively patriotic and went out of his way to point out how little impression the Norman Conquest had made upon England: 'We have a few hunting termes and pedlars French in the lousye lawe brought in by the Normans, yet remayning: But the language and customs bee Englyshe and Saxonyshe'.

To all leading European Protestants Knox's blast seemed untimely. They had looked for the accession of Queen Elizabeth in hope and deprecated anything that might anger her against them. John Calvin wrote to Sir William Cecil that 'Two years ago [i.e. in 1557] John Knox asked of me in private conversation, what I thought about the Government of Women. I candidly replied that, as it was a deviation from the original and proper order of nature, it was to be ranked, no less than slavery, among the punishments consequent upon the fall of man; but that there were occasionally women so endowed' that it was evident that they were 'raised up by Divine authority'. 'I brought forth', he said, 'Huldah and Deborah; and added that God did not vainly promise by the mouth of Isaiah that "Queens should be nursing mothers of the Church"; by which prerogative it is very evident that they are distinguished from females in private life'[1]. Such half-hearted acceptance of a woman's rule contrasts sharply both with the warm welcome that her own subjects had given to the new queen and with the new attitude towards women's place in society which individual scholars had recently expressed.

Fifty years before the accession of Queen Elizabeth the first modern treatise designed to prove the excellence of the female sex was foreshadowed in an oration in honour of the Princess Margaret of Austria, sister of the Emperor Charles V, by Henry Cornelius Agrippa on his appointment to the chair of Hebrew at the university of Dol. Cornelius Agrippa, a scholar, a soldier, and a magician, was a native of Cologne who taught, lectured, and practised in many cities and countries, London among them. At almost every place he became involved in quarrels and he stayed nowhere long. A quarrel prevented him from publishing

---

[1] *John Knox, The First Blast,* quoted in Introduction from David Laing's Preface, pp. xvi–xvii.

his full treatise on the nobility of women until 1529. It was written in Latin, but an English translation was published in London in 1542 and again three times during the seventeenth century[1]. His work became a classic quoted by seventeenth-century English writers on behalf of women in the same sentence with Anna Comnena and the seventeenth-century Dutch scholar, Anna Maria à Schurman[2]. Agrippa's treatise has been described as 'a monument of varied learning'[3]. Already by 1547 an Italian, Lodivico Domenichi, librarian in the Medici court at Florence, had expanded Agrippa's taut argument into a dialogue which was supposed to have taken place on successive evenings during a week of wedding festivities. Domenichi deserves mention only because an Englishman, William Bercher or Barker, who does not seem to have seen either the original or the English translation of Agrippa's work, used his book in writing a treatise on *The Nobylyttye of Wymen* which he dedicated to Queen Elizabeth in 1559[4].

Bercher's work was not published in his own lifetime. It remained in manuscript until 1904 when, edited by R. Warwick Bond, it was presented to the Roxburghe Club. But Bercher must have hoped to print it himself, for he set out the title, wrote a Preface and a letter of dedication to the queen, which he signed and dated. He reminded Queen Elizabeth that her mother 'Quene of most worthy memorye earnestly myndinge the advauncement of learnenge' had supported a number of students at Cambridge, of whom Bercher himself had been one. Some of them gave up their studies and left Cambridge 'after that crewell deathe had beraft us her most desyred lyffe', but Bercher stayed on for a time and then travelled abroad. Later he returned to England to enter the service of the Duke of Norfolk. His book purported to be an account of a discussion about the nobility of women held at the baths of Siena one evening for the entertainment of a countess who had gone there for her health. The particular importance of Bercher's work lies in his own additions to the matter he derived from Domenichi,

---

[1] *William Bercher's Nobility of Women*, ed. by R. Warwick Bond for the Roxburghe Club, 1904, pp. 51 and 81.

[2] E.g. Hannah Woolley, *The Gentlewoman's Companion; or a Guide to the Female Sex*, London, 1675, p. 29.   [3] *Nobility of Women*, p. 47.

[4] Domenichi had also plagiarized another work in praise of women published by Galazzo Flavio Capella in 1525 which Warwick Bond, who owned a copy of the book, was convinced Bercher did not use. I am indebted for my knowledge of all these works to R. Warwick Bond's learned introduction to Bercher's tract.

setting out the learned English ladies of the sixteenth century who could be quoted in support of women's claims.

Bercher wrote his treatise while Edward VI was still alive, for he made an Italian gentleman, Mr. Orlando, who spoke on behalf of women, mention Mary, the king's eldest, and Elizabeth, his youngest sister. Of Mary he said that he had heard that 'she hath shewed marvelous examples of wisdom and constantness and by her godly and sincere life hath put to silence all her enemies and adversaries'. He described Elizabeth as 'young of years', but as one who had already 'shewed such great and wonderful proof of royal heart in troubles that she of late have had as all men do honour her virtues and think she shall become a most noble princess'. Mr. Orlando said that he had heard of these two ladies when he was ambassador in Flanders, and added that one of the Englishmen present could tell the company more of them[1]. When towards the end of the talk an Englishman set out to tell of the learned ladies of England, he described Mary as 'excellent and passing in all kind of learning and language as few have been the like'. He described Elizabeth as one 'in whose tender years is seen so wonderful towardness of ancient virtue as is great comfort to all her country her learning is so notable in which she hath most delight; her other qualities be correspondent'. Another Italian gentleman in the company, Mr. Flaminio, added the three daughters of Sir Thomas More, a Knight of England, to his own list of learned ladies, for they could 'speak well Latin, Greek, and Hebrew'.

Since Mr. Flaminio had mentioned Sir Thomas More the Englishman began his own speech by recalling that Magaret Roper had 'proved so notable not only in learning but all other virtues that she may compare with any notable man'. After describing the merits of the two princesses the Englishman went on to speak of 'a most noble house most unjustly afflicted, I mean the house of Howard whereof an ympe hath been so cruelly cut off and the old stock so rigourously dealt withall that it would make a stoney heart to rewe'. The 'ympe' or scion of the family who had been 'cut off' was the poet Henry, Earl of Surrey, executed by Henry VIII in 1547. The 'old stock' was his father, the third Duke of Norfolk, who, saved from execution by the king's death, remained in prison throughout the reign of Edward VI. The Englishman's excuse for mentioning this tragedy was that 'of this family be three sisters, whereof one Lady Jane Howard, who is of such marvellous towardness in learning

[1] *Nobility of Women*, pp. 100–1.

as few men may compare with her, both Greek and Latin is vulgar unto her; her composition in verses is so notable, that all the world doth acknowledge her a worthy daughter of a most worthy father'. The three Howard sisters, Jane, Catherine, and Margaret, were daughters of Henry, Earl of Surrey, and sisters of Bercher's later patron and employer, the fourth Duke of Norfolk. They all made marriages suitable to their rank. The Lady Jane Howard, who married Charles Neville, Earl of Westmorland, was one of 'the ladyes of Honour now being with the court and about London' in the first years of Queen Elizabeth's reign[1].

The Englishman next mentioned 'the daughters of the Duke of Somerset uncle to the king by the mother's side and late Protector of the realm which be well trained in learning; of whom one named Jane likewise doth prosper very much both in Latin and in other languages'. It is probable that Bercher wrote his treatise before 22 January 1552, for on that day the Duke of Somerset was executed. His three daughters, Anne, Margaret, and Jane Seymour are known for the Latin poems they wrote on the death of Margaret of Valois, Queen of Navarre and grandmother of Henry IV of France. Their poems were translated into French, Greek, and Italian by French poets and scholars and published in France in 1551. The book was dedicated to another Margaret de Valois, niece of the lady in whose memory the verses were written[2]. An ode in honour of the three sisters was included in the book. The Lady Jane Seymour, who was specially praised by Bercher, was a maid of honour to Queen Elizabeth at the beginning of her reign 'and in great favour with her royal mistress'. She died unmarried on 20 March 1561 and was buried in Westminster Abbey six days later[3].

The next lady who earned mention in this company was the Lady Jane Grey. 'A marquis we have also', said the Englishman, 'whose daughters be brought up in learning and one of them as I hear, called Jane, proveth very notable in Greek and Latin and of very good conditions as may be requisite in so worthy a person'. To a contemporary, writing under Edward VI, the Lady Jane Grey is simply one of a number of young women of high birth who were educated as scholars. Her unhappy fate has singled her out from the rest to be remembered where they are now

[1] J. Nichols, *The Progresses and Public Processions of Queen Elizabeth*, London, 1823, vol. i, p. 37; hereafter cited as *Progresses*.
[2] *Le Tombeau de Marguerite de Valois Royne de Navarre*, Paris, 1551.
[3] *Progresses*, vol. I, p. 88.

forgotten[1]. From the Lady Jane Grey the Englishman passed on to speak
of the two daughters of the Earl of Arundel 'Lady Jane and Lady Mary
which be brought up in knowledge and do so prosper in it as the one
already hath shewn great testimony of her profit therein and the other
goeth forward in the study of good letters as they both be like to match
with any of the other that have purchased fame thereby and be of so
good qualities besides in any manner of virtue as they augment the honour
of their most honourable house'. The Lady Jane married Lord Lumley
and the Lady Mary was the first wife of the Duke of Norfolk, later
Bercher's patron. The duchess died in childbirth in 1557. The learned
exercises of these two young scholars have reached the British Museum
through their preservation in Lord Lumley's library. Lady Lumley was
one of the 'Ladies of Honour' at Queen Elizabeth's court in the early
years of the reign[2].

'Divers other lords and gentlemen there be', went on the Englishman,
'whose daughters prove well learned, in especially the daughters of Sir
Anthony Cooke a knight, which for Greek and Latin be not inferior to
any that we have named'[3]. The learning of the daughters of Sir Anthony
Cooke, of Giddy Hall in Essex, was as famous in the middle years of the
century as that of Sir Thomas More's daughters half a generation earlier.
In recording the death of their father in 1576 William Camden described
him as 'a man of severe Gravity and great Learning, having been Schoolmaster to King Edward the sixth in his childhood'. He was, says Camden,
'happy in his daughters, whom having brought up in Learning, both
Greek and Latine, above their Sex, he married to men of good Account;
namely to Sir William Cecyl, who was Treasurer of England, to Sir
Anthony Bacon, Lord Keeper, and Sir Thomas Hobey, who died Embas-
sadour in France, Sir Rolf Roulet, and Sir Henry Killegrew'[4].

Sir Anthony's second daughter, Anne Bacon, was the most learned
of the sisters and is said to have been associated with her father in teaching
the young king, Edward VI. As early as 1550, when only twenty-two,

[1] The Englishman made no reference to Lady Jane's two sisters, Catherine and Mary,
who survived to become maids of honour to Queen Elizabeth: Catherine was well educated; Mary was almost a dwarf. They both suffered for their connection with the royal
line, see *D.N.B*, Seymour, Lady Catherine, Countess of Hertford, and Keys, Lady Mary.

[2] *Progresses*, vol. i, p. 37.

[3] *Nobility of Women*, pp. 153–5, contain the whole section on English women.

[4] William Camden, *The History of the most Renowned and Victorious Princess Elizabeth, late
Queen of England*, 3rd. ed., London, 1675, p. 218.

she published a translation of twenty-five sermons on predestination. Later, she translated into English Bishop Jewel's Apology for the Church of England. Both Matthew Parker and Jewel himself read her translation before it was published, but did not alter a single word. This work was published in 1564 and reissued in 1600[1]. A few of her letters have survived and are printed in the life of Sir Francis Bacon, by James Spedding. One long letter written to Burleigh in 1584 reveals her intervening in the quarrel between the bishops and preachers, as the Protestant Nonconformists were at that time called. She declared how she herself had profited by the public exercises of the preachers and besought Burghley to 'choose two or three of them, which it likes best, and licence them before your own self, or other at your pleasure, to declare and prove the truth of the cause, with a quiet and attentive ear'[2]. Anne Bacon remained, as she had been bred, a Protestant against anything that savoured of Popery. She was deeply troubled by her son Anthony's long residence in Roman Catholic France, and by his employment of servants suspected of Roman Catholicism. Her letters to both her sons are full of anxious affection, advice, and warning about untrustworthy servants. 'Be not speedy of speech nor talk suddenly, but where discretion requireth, and that soberly then. For the property of our world is to sound out at first coming and after to contain. Courtesy is necessary, but too common familiarity in talking and words is very unprofitable, and not without hurt taking, *ut nunc sunt tempora*. Remember you have no father', wrote Anne Bacon to her son Anthony in February 1592 when he was thirty-four[3]. She survived until 1610, but her mind gave way before the end.

The marriage of Mildred Cooke and Sir William Cecil lasted forty-two years and was a happy one, save for the early deaths of many of their children. When she died in 1589 her husband, then Lord Burleigh, sought consolation in writing what he called a *Meditation*. He gave thanks to Almighty God for His favour in permitting her to live so many years with him and he set out her merits and good deeds. Many of them he did not know until after she was dead. They were not the haphazard charities of the unthinking, but imaginatively conceived by a clever woman. Among them were books for the libraries of learned institutions, fires in the hall of St. John's College, Cambridge, in the depth of winter,

---

[1] G. Ballard, *Memoirs of British Ladies . . .*, pp. 188–93.
[2] Spedding, *The Letters and The Life of Francis Bacon*, London, 1861, vol. i, p. 41.
[3] *Ibid.*, pp. 112–13.

and wool and flax distributed 'to poor women of Cheshunt parish to work into yarn and bring it to her to see their manner of working; and for the most part she gave them the stuff by way of alms. Sometyme she caused the same to be wrought into cloth and gave it to the poore, paying first for the spynning more than it was worth'[1].

If Sir Anthony Cooke was 'happy in his daughters' they were no less happy in their father, for unlike most parents, he did not marry them off as children. Anne must have been nearly thirty when she married Sir Anthony Bacon. Mildred, the eldest sister, was close on twenty when she married Sir William Cecil in 1546. Since Katherine Cooke married Sir Henry Killigrew in 1565, she must have been at least thirty when she married. The marriage between Elizabeth and Sir Thomas Hoby was certainly arranged by Cecil, for the first hint of it in Sir Thomas Hoby's commonplace book is a notice of a visit paid to the Hobys at Bisham by 'Sir William Cecill, my Lady Bourne, my Lady Cecill, and her sister Elizabeth Cooke' at Midsummer 1557. In 1558 he recorded that he went to London on 11 May and 'retourned again the xiij, taking my way by Wimblton, where I communed with Mrs. Elizabeth Cook in the way of marriage'. Since she was twenty-eight or nine and Hoby himself twenty-eight there was no reason for delay and the bridegroom records that 'Monday the xxvij June, the marriage was made and solemnised betweene me and Elizabeth Cooke, daughter of Sir Anthony Cooke, knight. The same day also was her sister Margaret, the Quene's maide, maried to Sir Rauf Rowlet, knight, who shortlie after departed out of this lief'. Margaret died within a year of her marriage. 'The rest of the sommer', added Sir Thomas, 'my wief and I passed at Burleighe, in Northamptonshire'[2].

Sir Thomas and his wife had similar tastes, for he had already published a translation of Martin Bucer's *Gratulation . . . unto the churche of Englande for the restitution of Christes religion*. In 1561 he published an even more popular translation, *The Courtyer*, by Count Baldesar Castiglione, which passed through several editions. It first appeared in 1528 and is one of the first of the many books of the sixteenth century which deal with the relations between men and women[3]. Sir Thomas died in Paris where he was ambassador to France in 1566. Elizabeth Hoby brought his body home to Bisham, where she erected a splendid monument to his memory and

[1] Ballard, pp. 184–7.
[2] *The Camden Miscellany*, vol. x, Camden Soc., 3rd series, vol. iv (1902), where 'A Booke of Travaile and the Life of one Thomas Hoby' is printed in full, pp. 1–130. The passages quoted are on pp. 126 and 127.   [3] *Nobility of Women*, p. 77.

that of his elder brother, Sir Philip Hoby, with epitaphs in Latin and Greek verse written by herself. She had given birth to a son and two daughters before her husband's death. Thomas Posthumus Hoby, unborn when his father died, may perhaps have found his mother's upbringing somewhat harsh. She wrote to Burleigh that she had wanted to put him 'in the Innes of Court for his better instruction', but 'the boy sayth that by no meanes he can frame himself to lyke or to take that course to his own good and my comfort'. He wanted to travel, but she would not let him: 'The danger most great, I have but two sons. The profit uncertain, frivolous; the language to be learned with the sight of countries, [can be acquired] here at home by books with less danger than in these dayes by journey. The certain fruits daily found of young mens travel nowadays nothing but pride, charge, and vanity'[1]. Lady Hoby had married again in 1574 and in this letter to Burleigh she prided herself on not allowing her second husband to have the wardship of her sons. He was Lord John Russell, heir to the earldom of Bedford, who died in 1584 before his father. Lady Russell herself wrote the inscriptions in Greek, Latin, and English on her second husband's tomb in Westminster Abbey. She died in 1609.

The daughters of Sir Anthony Cooke were perhaps more austerely learned than most of their contemporaries, but during the reign of such a queen as Elizabeth no man of position whose daughters might go to court could fail to pay some attention to their early education. An uneducated girl would have cut a poor figure at the court of a queen whose teacher, writing between 1563 and 1568, could say that 'she readeth here now at Windsor more Greek every day than some Prebendary of this Church doth read Latin in a whole Week. And that which is most praiseworthy of all, within the Walls of her privy Chamber, she hath obtained that Excellency of Learning to understand, speak and write both wittily with Head, and fair with Hand as scarce one or two rare Wits in both the Universities have in many years reached unto'[2]. It was customary for girls of good birth to enter the queen's service so young that their education was completed under the eyes of their mistress and the mistress of the queen's maids. If they did not marry they stayed in her service until death.

[1] Ballard, pp. 195-7 n.
[2] Roger Ascham, *The Schoolmaster*, London, 1711, pp. 62-3. This book was first published in 1570 after Ascham's death and dedicated to Sir William Cecil.

The inscription on the monument of Blanche Parry in Bacton Church in her native county of Hereford reveals something about the outlook of one of the queen's women who passed her whole life at court. Blanche Parry's name appears regularly from the beginning of Elizabeth's reign among those who gave the queen new year's presents and received presents from her[1].

'I lived always as handmaide to a Queen,
In chamber chiefe my tyme did overpasse,
Uncarefull of my welthe there was I sene,
Whylst I abode the rynnynge of my glasse,
Not doubtyng wante whylst that my mystresse lyvde,
In woman's state whose cradell saw I rockte,
Her servant then, as when she her crown atcheeved,
And so remayned till death he my doore had knockte:
Preferrynge still the causes of each wyghte,
As far as I doorste move her grace's eare
For to reward decerts by course of ryghte
As needs resyte of sarvys done eache wheare.
So that my tyme I thus did passe awaye
A maed in court, and never no man's wyfe,
Sworne of Queene Ellsbeths hedd chamber allwaye,
With Maeden Queene a mayde did end my lyfe'[2].

Blanche Parry died on 12 February 1589, in her eighty-second year. Her monument at Bacton shows her kneeling before Elizabeth, who is sitting in majesty. Blanche Parry is dressed in a full gown with tight-fitting bodice and sleeves. She has ruffs round her wrists and her dress has a high collar with a small ruff. On her head she is wearing a flat cap with a veil flowing down her back[3].

The queen was fortunate that at least one of the ladies who had been with her almost from the beginning of her reign was with her to its end. Anne, Countess of Warwick, the eldest daughter of the Earl of Bedford, was with the queen as maid, wife and widow and was 'more beloved and in greater favour with the queen than any other woman in the kingdom'.

[1] *Progresses*, vol. i, pp. 116, 125; vol. ii, pp. 87, 270.
[2] Quoted by Ballard, *Memoirs of British Ladies. . . .*, pp. 178–9.
[3] A photograph of the tomb appears in *Royal Commission on Historical Monuments, Herefordshire*, vol. i, plate 82, and a description on p. 19.

Both Lady Warwick and her sister, Margaret, Countess of Cumberland, were praised by Henry Constable, a contemporary poet, for their learning and virtue. The Lady Anne Clifford was named after her aunt, Lady Warwick, and always wrote of her with the warmest affection, describing her as 'a great friend to virtue and a helper to many petitioners and others in distress'[1]. The present writer possesses a little vellum-covered book, printed in 1609, which is dedicated to Anne, Countess of Warwick. It contains a translation of *The markes of the Children of God, and of their comforts in Afflictions*, which was written in French by John Taffin and addressed by him to 'the faithfull of the Low Countrie'. The translator was named Anne Prowse, of whom nothing seems to be known. Her work was done between 1588 and 1603, for in her dedicatory letter the writer speaks of the 'Halcion daies' which were then in England and of Queen Elizabeth as alive[2]. Lady Warwick herself died in 1604. 'And because your honour hath bin of long time, not onely a professour, but also a louer of the truth, whom the Lord (exalting to an higher place of dignitie than many other) hath set up, as it were a light upon an high candlesticke to give light unto many, I have especially dedicated unto your Honour This my poore travaile', wrote Anne Prowse. She explained that she had undertaken the work because 'everyone in his calling is bound to doe somewhat to the furtherance of the holy building; but because great things by reason of my sexe I may not doe, and that which I may, I ought to doe, I have according to my duetie brought my poor basket of stones to the strengthening of the wals of that Jerusalem, whereof (by Grace) we are all both Citizens and members'. Anne Prowse was in more than her Christian name at one with Anne Bacon.

The work of Anne Prowse is but one illustration of the fact that the daughters of noble families were not the only women who could acquire a good education in the sixteenth century. The desire to read the words of Christ in the language in which the words were spoken was a powerful motive driving the women of Puritan stock to take every opportunity of learning which their circumstances offered. The mother of Edward Rainbowe, who was born in 1608 and died as Bishop of Carlisle in 1684,

[1] George C. Williamson, *Lady Anne Clifford*, p. 37. The first mention of Lady Warwick in *Progresses* is the account of the tourney held at Westminster 'for the honour and celebration' of her marriage, vol. i, p. 199. It took place on 11 November 1565.

[2] Overseene Againe, and augmented by The Author, and translated out of French by Anne Prowse, London, 1609. The 'Epistle Dedicatorie' is unpaged. It is signed 'Your Honors in the Lord, most humbly. A. P.' First printed 1591, *B. M. Catalogue*.

was Rachel, daughter of David Allen, Rector of Ludborough, Lincoln-shire. She was learned in Latin, Greek, and Hebrew, and doubtless acquired her knowledge from her father. His name appears in the records at Lincoln early in James I's reign as one of the nonconforming ministers of religion in the diocese[1]. He was still the incumbent of Ludborough in 1614[2]. Sir Simonds d'Ewes, himself a man of strong Puritan tendencies, describes how early in 1615 he went to school in St. Mary Axe at the house of Mr. Reynolds, who 'had a daughter named Bathshua, being his eldest, that had an exact knowledge in the Greek, Latin, and French tongues, with some insight also into the Hebrew and Syriac; much more learning she had doubtless than her father, who was a mere pretender to it; and by the fame of her abilities which she had acquired from others, he got many scholars which else would never have repaired to him'[3].

Learning in women was not confined to those of Puritan stock. It even led a daughter of the Church of England back to the Roman Catholic Church. Elizabeth, daughter and heiress of Lawrence Tanfield, Lord Chief Baron of the Exchequer, was born in 1585 and early applied herself to learning both ancient and modern languages. She mastered the French, Spanish, Italian, Latin, Hebrew, and Transylvanian tongues and applied herself to a study of the fathers of the Church. When she was sixteen she married the first Viscount Falkland and three years later was received into the Roman Catholic Church. She concealed this change of religion from her husband for twenty years, but in 1625 it became known and he would no longer live with her. She died in 1639. Lord Clarendon, looking back over the history of the Great Rebellion, remembered Lady Falkland as 'a woman of a most masculine understanding, allayed with the passions and infirmities of her sex'[4]. All her four daughters eventually became nuns in the convent of Cambrai. The life of Lady Falkland may well have seemed to many a sound argument against encouraging women to be learned.

It was perhaps natural that the classical learning of the Elizabethan Age should fall out of fashion in the next generations, but women were moved by the outbreak of romantic poetry which marked the age.

[1] *The State of the Church*, ed. C. W. Foster, Lincoln Record Society, vol. xxiii (1926), p. 365.   [2] *Ibid.*, p. 367 *n.*
[3] *The Autobiography and Correspondence of Sir Simonds d'Ewes*, ed. F. O. Halliwell, London (1845), vol. i, p. 63.
[4] Clarendon, *History of the Great Rebellion*, Book VII, par. 221.

Lady Carey, a kinswoman of Spenser, is one of the patrons he commemorates in an introductory sonnet to the *Faery Queene*. Her daughter, another Elizabeth Carey, was a patron of Nash and herself the author of *The Tragedie of Marian the faire Queene of Iewry*, published in 1613, a work which is deservedly forgotten. Here and there women were appearing who could think and write about those matters which all regarded as their particular concern. The first of a vast library of books written, and still being written, by women on the upbringing of children appeared early in the seventeenth century. Mistress Dorothy Leigh, whose name does not figure in the *Dictionary of National Biography*, wrote *The Mother's Blessing*, which had reached its seventh edition by 1621. She addressed her work to her 'beloved sonnes, George, John, and William Leigh, saying that she was moved to write it because God had 'taken their father out of this vale of teares'. The book contains much wisdom. The author dedicated it to the Princess Elizabeth, daughter of James I and wife of the Elector Palatine. Her work is worth remembering because, despite the harsh treatment children often received in her day, she pointed out that 'What disposition so ever they bee of, gentlenesse will soonest bring them to virtue'[1].

It is not easy to judge how much influence such a writer had in her own day, but in 1651 a certain Charles Gerbier wrote a little book in praise of women and, in his chapter on 'Pious and religious Women', named Dorothy Leigh, whom he described, perhaps taking his description from her own title-page, as 'not long deceased' and 'a pious and religious gentlewoman'. Her book was, he said, 'godly counsel, containing many good exhortations and admonitions'[2]. When George Ballard, in the early eighteenth century, wrote his book about learned British ladies he could find out very little about her[3]. Another lady of this period whose affection for her children prompted her to write was Elizabeth, Countess of Lincoln, one of the daughters and coheiresses of Sir Henry Knevet, of Charlton, Wiltshire. In 1628 she published what Ballard describes as 'a small, but valuable treatise', which was already 'very scarce'. It consisted of twenty-one pages 'full of fine arguments' and was addressed to her

---

[1] *The Mother's Blessing or Godly Counsaile of a Gentlewoman not long deceased, left behind her for her Children*, by Mistress Dorothy Leigh, 7th ed., London, 1621. The pages of the British Museum copy are in the wrong order.

[2] *Elogium Heroinum, or The Praise of Worthy Women*, by C. G. Gent, London, 1651, p. 144. This book was kindly lent me by Mr. Edwards, antiquarian bookseller of Ashmore Green, near Newbury.   [3] Ballard, p. vii.

daughter-in-law, Bridget, Countess of Lincoln, setting out the 'necessity and advantages of mothers nursing their own children'[1].

The attitude of an uncompromising idealist of this period towards the education of women is brought out in the life of James Harrington, published by John Toland in 1700. Toland was helped in the preparation of this life by the survivor of Harrington's two sisters, Dorothy, widow of Alan Bellingham, of Levens, Westmorland. Toland obtained from her the 'collections and observations' about Harrington which had been recorded by the other sister, Elizabeth, wife of Sir Ralf Ashton. According to these reminiscences, Harrington took 'all the care of a parent in the education of his sisters, and would himself make large discourses to 'em concerning the reverence that was due to Almighty God; the benevolence they were obliged to shew to all mankind; how they ought to furnish their minds with knowledge by reading of useful books, and to shew the goodness of their disposition by a constant practice of virtue: in a word he taught 'em the true rules of humanity and decency, always inculcating to 'em that good manners did not so much consist in a fashionable carriage (which ought not to be neglected) as in becoming words and actions, an obliging address and a modest behaviour'[2]. It sounds a formidable pro- gramme, but it seems to have been successful. Toland describes Lady Ashton as 'a woman of extraordinary parts and accomplishments'[3].

Two more famous women, associated in tragedy, owed much of their distinction to their upbringing. Each of them had fond and careful parents and each of them married happily. Their husbands were close friends who fell together at the first battle of Newbury in 1643. Dorothy Sidney, daughter of the Earl of Leicester, was immortalized by Edmund Waller under the name Sacharissa. In 1639 she married Henry, Lord Spenser, who was created Earl of Sunderland in 1643. After his death Lady Sunderland and her children lived with her parents for a time at Penshurst, but moved to her husband's house at Althorpe in 1650. To many of those who suffered for their loyalty to the king 'her house was a sanctuary, her interests a protection, her estate a maintenance, and the livings in her gift a preferment'[4]. She married again in 1652, but as she

[1] Ballard, pp. 265–6.
[2] *The Oceana and other works of James Harrington with an account of his Life by John Toland*, London, 1771, p. xiii.   [3] *Ibid.*, p. xi.
[4] Quoted in the introduction to *Diary of the Times of Charles the Second by the Honourable Henry Sidney*, ed. R. W. Blencowe, London, 1843, vol. i, p. xii from Lloyd's *Memoirs of the Loyalists*.

married a man of lower rank than her own she continued to be referred to as 'the Lady Sunderland'. Her husband, Robert Smith or Smythe, was an old admirer and, according to Dorothy Osborne, 'a very fine gentleman'[1]. Lady Sunderland outlived her second husband and died in 1684.

Lettice Cary, Lady Falkland, survived her husband by only four years, but she had been his wife since 1630 or 1631. She was thirty-five when she died in 1647. Her father was Sir Richard Morrison of Tooley Park, Leicestershire, and her marriage was a love-match, opposed by Lucius Cary's father, Lord Falkland, because she had no portion. According to her biographer she 'set out early in the ways of God in the dawn or morning of her age' and 'these riches, of her piety, wisdom, quickness of wit, discretion, judgment, sobriety, and gravity of behaviour being perceived by Sir Lucius Cary seemed portion enough to him'[2]. Lucius Cary was independent of his father, for his grandfather, Sir Lawrence Tanfield, had made him his heir, passing over his daughter and her husband, perhaps because he knew of her tendency to Roman Catholicism. At Great Tew, which was part of this inheritance, Falkland passed the years before the war, making his home a centre of hospitality for learned men from Oxford and poets and wits from London. After his death in battle his widow lived on at Great Tew giving herself to works of piety and charity. An account of her many good deeds was written by her chaplain, John Duncon, who described himself as 'parson (sequestered)'[3], in the form of a letter addressed to her mother, Lady Morrison, at Great Tew. 'Neither', he wrote, 'was her care of improving others confined to the present age; designs and projects she had also for posterity; of setting up schools, and manufacture trades in the Parish; to shut out (by those engines) for ever, ignorance, idleness, and want. But that magnificent, and most religious contrivement, that there might be places of education for Gentlewomen, and for the retirement of widows, (as Colleges and the Inns of Court and Chancery are for men) in several parts of the Kingdom, this was much in her thoughts, hoping thereby that learning and religion might flourish more in her own sex, than heretofor having such opportunities to serve the Lord without distraction; A project this, adequate to

[1] The Love Letters of Dorothy Osborne to Sir William Temple, ed. I. Gollancz, London, 1903, p. 30.

[2] The Returnes of Spiritual comfort and grief in a Devout Soul. . . ., London, 1648, p. 189.

[3] On the title-page of the 3rd ed., 1653. The 1st ed. bears no author's name on the title-page.

the wisdom and piety, of this Mother in Israel; and not beyond the power and interest she had with great ones, to have effected it'[1]. The writer dated this letter 15 April 1647.

The mere existence of the highly educated ladies of the Elizabethan age and their highly intelligent successors of the early seventeenth century forced men to reflect on the social and legal position of all women. Such a woman as Mary, Countess of Pembroke—Sidney's sister, Pembroke's mother—could no more be ignored than Queen Elizabeth herself. Even John Aubrey, writing his brief lives of seventeenth-century characters between the years 1669 and 1696, was constrained to record what gossip he could collect about her[2]. It was natural that in a note-book of the sort he was compiling he should include something about the famous harlots and beauties of the age. That he thought it worth while to include such women of distinction as the Countess of Pembroke, Elizabeth Danvers[3] and Katherine Philips[4]—'the matchless Orinda'—shows that even a gossip writer was conscious of a new quality in women. Women were as yet making no open challenge to male authority, but an unconscious reaction by men can be discerned to the intelligence which the Renaissance and the Reformation had called out in women.

It was not long before this male reaction was expressed brutally in print. In 1615 a writer under the unlikely name of Joseph Swetnam put out a pamphlet which was a general attack on women. The title was *The arraignment of Lewde, idle, froward, and unconstant women: or the vanitie of them, choose you whether, with a Commendation of wise, vertuous and honest women. Pleasant for married men, profitable for young men, and hurtfull to none*[5]. 'There is', he said, 'no woman so good but hath one idle part or other in her which may be amended'. He could find little to say in favour of any woman. Widows he regarded with especial dislike: 'Woe be unto that unfortunate man that matcheth himself unto a widowe, for a widowe will be the cause of a thousand woes'[6]. Two years later a reply to this tract was issued by someone who hid behind the pseudonym of Ester Sowernam, 'neither maide, wife nor widdowe, yet really all, and therefore

---

[1] *The Returnes of Spiritual comfort and grief in a Devout Soul. . . .*, 1st ed., pp. 190–1.

[2] *Brief Lives, chiefly of contemporaries, set down by John Aubrey, between the years 1669 and 1696*, ed. A. Clark, Oxford, 1898, vol. i, pp. 310–13.

[3] Elizabeth Danvers had 'prodigious parts for a woman'. She knew Italian and 'had Chaucer at her fingers' ends'. *Ibid.*, vol. i, p. 193.

[4] *Ibid.*, vol. ii, pp. 152–5; see below, p. 167.

[5] London. Printed by Edw: Allde for Thomas Archer, 1615.   [6] *Ibid.*, p. 89.

experienced to defend all'[1]. She, or perhaps he, called the reply *Ester hath hanged Haman: or an answer to a lewd Pamphlet, entitled, The Arraignment of Women. With the arraignment of lewd, idle, froward and unconstant men, and Husbands.* From this time at latest it is clear that the position of women, the education of daughters, the relations between husband and wife were not only in the forefront of men's thoughts, but had become a theme for journalistic by-play.

In 1599, while he was still King of Scotland only, King James I had written a book, full of wisdom, for the training of his eldest son, Prince Henry. It was published in England in his collected works in 1616[2]. He reminded his son that 'marriage is one of the greatest actions that a man doeth in all his time, especially in the taking of his first wife'. She should belong to the same Church as her husband. She should not be 'beneath his rank'. She should come 'of a whole and cleane race, not subject to the hereditary sicknesses either of the soule or the body'. The Scripture, says the king, 'can give best counsell' on how to treat a wife. 'Treat her as your owne flesh, command her as her Lord, cherish her as your helper, rule her as your pupill, and please her in all things reasonable; but teach her not to be curious in things that belong her not: Ye are the head, shee is your body: It is your office to command, and hers to obey; but yet with such a sweet harmonye, as she should be as ready to obey, as ye to command; as willing to follow, as ye to go before'. Three rules in regard to a wife the king lays down: She must never be allowed to meddle in the government, but kept to 'the oeconomicke rule of the house; and yet all to be under your direction'. Secondly, 'good and chaste company' must be kept about her, 'for women are the frailest sex'. Thirdly, a husband should never allow himself and his wife to be angry at the same time; 'when ye see her in a passion, ye should with reason danton yours: for both when yee are settled, ye are meetest to judge her errours; and when she is come to herselfe, she may be best made to apprehend her offence, and reverence your rebuke'[3].

Here in the calm prose of royal, and indeed, Divine authority the king sets out the attitude of a reasonable man towards his wife. Already before the publication of the complete edition of King James's works this advice had attracted attention. *A Discourse on Marriage and Wiving and of the*

---

[1] London, for Nicholas Browne, 1617.
[2] Ed. James, Bishop of Winchester and Deane of His Majesty's Chappell Royall, London.
[3] *Ibid.*, pp. 172–3.

Mystery contained therein[1], published as a tract in 1615, quotes with approbation the king's words on choosing a healthy wife. The author condemns early marriage, saying that 'forward Virgins of our Age', asked what is the best age to marry, will say that 'fourteen is the best time of their Age, if Thirteen be not better, and they for the most Part have the Example of their Mothers before them'. But, he points out, the results of so early marriage are 'dangerous Births, Diminution of Stature, Brevity of Life and such like'[2]. The author of this tract describes himself as 'Alex Niccholes, Batchelor of the Art he never yet put in practice'. He advises the prospective husband to make sure of a competency and 'prevent Indigence and Want, two Great Allayers of Affection'; to plant religion in his wife, 'for so she cannot love God, but, withal, she must honour thee'; and to give her 'Assurance and Testimony of thy love'. These things 'discretely put in practice' will, he assures his reader, preserve a wife's loyalty far better than spying upon her, showing jealousy, or putting her under restraint[3]. There is much sense in this tract, for the author has realized that no husband will get much profit by insisting on his authority, a lesson which the Church was slow to learn.

Women in town and country alike heard the authority of the male sex preached from the pulpit on texts drawn from St. Paul. The Homilies had long been driving home the same lesson in those parishes where incumbents were not presumptuous enough to make up their own sermons[4]. The reading public was offered treatises on the relations between men and women which were often expanded versions of the author's sermons. What William Whately's country parishioners heard at Banbury was offered in print to a larger public and found eager buyers[5]. The congregation at the church of St. Anne, Blackfriars, were the first to hear the sermons which Dr. William Gouge afterwards published in a volume of over seven hundred pages under the title *Of Domesticall Duties, Eight Treatises*[6]. He prefaced his book with a dedicatory letter to 'the Right Honourable, Right Worshipfull, and other of my beloved parishioners' and in it dealt with criticisms which had been made of his general statements. He had been censured by some of his congregation when he first preached on the subject of his book because he set out very clearly the

---

[1] *The Harleian Miscellany*, London, 1744, vol. ii, pp. 141–67.
[2] *Ibid.*, pp. 147–8.   [3] *Ibid.*, p. 158.   [4] See pp. 105–6 above.   [5] See pp. 107–9 above.
[6] William Gouge, *Of Domesticall Duties, Eight Treatises*, 1st ed., London, 1622.

duties of the wife and her subjection to her husband. He had said from the pulpit that a wife could not dispose of the common goods of the family without or against her husband's consent[1]. In saying this he was stating the law of the land. It is revealing to find that the womenfolk of Black-friars were clearly independent enough to think and act for themselves.

Gouge goes on to say that 'other exceptions were made against some other particular duties of wives. For many that can patiently enough heare their duties declared in generall tearmes cannot endure to heare those generals exemplified in their particular branches'. All that Gouge could say in justification was that he had set out first the wives' duties 'according to the Apostles method' and 'taught (as must have been taught, except the truth should have been betrayed) what a wife, in the uttermost extent of that subjection under which God hath put her, is bound unto, in case her husband will stand upon the uttermost of his authority; which was so taken, as if I had taught that an husband might and ought to exact the uttermost, and that a wife was bound in that uttermost extent to doe all that was delivered as dutie, whether her husband exact it or no. But when I came to the Husbands duties, I shewed that he ought not to exact whatsoever his wife was bound unto (in case it were exacted by him) but that he ought to make her a joynt Governour of the family with himself, and deferre the ordering of many things to her discretion, and with all honourable and kinde respect to carrie himself towards her'[2]. Gouge himself was a gentle, kindly scholar, happily married, and the father of seven sons and six daughters[3]. 'This just apologie' which he 'had been forced to make that I might not ever be judged (as some have censured me) an hater of women[4]' perhaps expresses his true nature and that of the best of his contemporaries, but no woman can have listened to him with much enjoyment.

One London lady of the generation which was affronted by Gouge's preaching caused a young curate to write a book of devotions especially for women. 'Mistress Elizabeth Keate, wife of Mr. Gilbert Keate, a grave and eminent citizen of London much complained' to John Featley, then his uncle's curate at Lambeth, 'that her sex was so much neglected by Divines that they had not penned Devotions, for all their several suffer-ances that are common to many: only here and there she found a few small gleanings proper for some occasions of grief'. Featley set about

---

[1] *Domesticall Duties,* p. 3d.   [2] *Ibid.,* pp. 3d–4.
[3] *D.N.B.*   [4] *Domesticall Duties,* p. 4.

repairing this deficiency and after about five years completed his book, but Mrs. Keate's 'house was visited by the pestilence, and shut up by her own appointment: one of her sweet and tender children and a gracious Matron cosin unto her, died of that uncomfortable disease: And her weak self was moulting and crumbling away in a Consumption'. This book was published some years afterwards as *A Fountain of Tears emptying itself into three rivolets, viz. of 1. Compunction. 2. Compassion. 3. Devotion, or Sobs of Nature sanctified by Grace*[1]. It aimed at providing tears for twenty-seven different occasions of life ending with tears in the distressed time of civil wars, which 'could not chuse but put her in mind of the Almighty, who in Psal. 89, 10. is said to have scattered his enemies with his strong arm. . . . For her dear sake, these Soliloquies and Prayers were fitted for Females, and taught to speak in the persons of the weaker Vessels: 1. Peter 3, 7. I hope no Man will blame me for it'.

Women unlikely to be moved by the argument of William Gouge or the lacrimosity of John Featley were approached for their improvement with compliment by the learned north-country layman, Richard Brathwaite. In 1631 he published *The English Gentlewoman*[2], a companion piece to his book *The English Gentleman* of 1630[3]. Nothing could be more virtuous, restrained, or, indeed, dull than the English lady described by Richard Brathwaite. The title-page has a full-length picture of the perfect English lady surrounded by eight little pictures portraying her qualities discussed in the book[4]. It is not for her to be a scholar. No 'tutoresses' are more suitable to educate a young lady than her mother and the young lady herself must in her turn grow up and educate her own children[5]. The possibility that she might be instructed by a man is not considered. 'She desires not to have the esteeme of any *She-clarke*; shee had rather be approved by her living than *learning*. . . . Some bookes she reads, and those powerfull to stirre up devotion and fervour to prayer; others she reads, and those usefull for the direction of her household affaires. Herbals she peruseth, which she seconds with conference'[6]. A gentlewoman must

---

[1] At Amsterdam, 1646. Featley wrote the preface from his home at Flushing. My copy was printed at London in 1683.

[2] *The English Gentlewoman, drawne out to the full Body*, London, 1631.

[3] In 1641 the two books were issued in one volume: *The Gentleman* dedicated to the Earl of Pembroke and *The Gentlewoman* to the countess. In the dedication to the Countess of Pembroke Brathwaite reminds her that his father held his land of her 'noble and heroick' father.   [4] See plate opposite p. 160.   [5] *The Gentlewoman*, pp. 182–3.

[6] *Ibid*. The end of the book, unpaged. The character of a Gentlewoman.

beware of the company she keeps. She can hardly go into company without 'a maiden blush, a modest tincture'[1]. She should not 'enter into much discourse or familiarity with strangers', for it argues 'lightness or indiscretion: what is spoken of Maids, may be properly applied by an usefull consequence to all women: They should be seen and not heard: A Traveller sets himself out best by his discourse, whereas their best setting is silence'[2]. Her 'carriage should be neither too precise, nor too loose. . . . Modesty and mildnesse hold sweetest correspondence'[3].

Modesty, piety, and skill to keep her husband's love and to care for her family in health and sickness were the chief characteristics of the perfect English gentlewoman conceived in the mind of Richard Brathwaite. This is, indeed, the reactionary's ideal woman of whom her friends could say with Charles Kingsley 'Be good, sweet maid, and let who will be clever'. It is a little surprising to meet this Victorian conception of womanhood so clearly portrayed in the first half of the seventeenth century. In view of other writings by the same author his English gentlewoman becomes even more unreal. Richard Brathwaite is best known today as the author of *Drunken Barnaby's Four Journeys to the North of England*, lighthearted verses, in Latin on the left-hand and in English on the right-hand page, setting out the adventures of the author on the roads and in the inns of contemporary England. The writer was skilled in the technique of writing Latin verse and had few inhibitions in describing the drunken and amorous progresses of his Barnaby. The verses were very popular in the eighteenth century and can be read with entertainment today[4]. Perhaps it was natural that one who could describe with such relish the unseemly pleasures of the road should glorify the modest flower of English womanhood.

He expressed an ideal which long retained its power and was accepted by many women without question. But among Drunken Barnaby's contemporaries were men who delighted in seeing women develop their full capacity. Thomas Heywood was one of the most laborious writers of his day. He was an actor and playwright, a translator and writer of epitaphs. Many of his plays have been lost, for they were written on odd scraps of paper in eating houses, but he published two considerable books in praise of women, 'intimating', he says, 'to myself that it is a kind of duty in all that have had mothers, as far as they can to dignifie the

---

[1] *The Gentlewoman*, p. 41.   [2] *Loc. cit.*   [3] *Ibid.*, p. 42.
[4] A new edition printed from the edition of 1778, London, 1822.

sex'. The first was published in 1624, *Nine Books of Various history concerninge Women*[1]. It was reissued after his death in 1657 as *The General History of Women*. The work was thought of, begun and printed in seventeen weeks, as he records in a concluding sentence[2]. Heywood dedicated it to the Earl of Worcester, saying 'To whom more pertinently may I recommend the patronage of good women, than to your Honor, who hath been the Happy Husband and fortunate father of such'[3].

To Heywood, a true Elizabethan, although he lived until about the middle of the seventeenth century, all sorts of women were worthy of description. 'Here thou mayest reade of all degrees, from the Scepter in the Court to the Sheepehooke in the Cottage: of all Times from the first Rainbow to the last blazing Starre'[4]. Each of the nine books was given the name of one of the Muses, and history and legend were searched for stories which might entertain his readers. His fifth book deals with 'Amazons, and other women famous for valour or beauty'. His three English 'viragos' are Æthelflæd, King Alfred's daughter, the Empress Maud, daughter of Henry I, and King Stephen's wife. He gives an English rendering of the Latin verses which Henry of Huntingdon had devoted to Æthelflæd in the twelfth century. It begins:

> 'Oh Elphlede, mighty both in strength and mind,
> The dread of men and victresse of thy kind'

and ends:

> 'Great Cæsar's acts thy noble deeds excell,
> So sleepe in peace, Virago maide farewell'[5].

Heywood's second book appeared in 1640 under the title *The Exemplary Lives and memorable acts of nine of the most famous women of the world*. They are prefaced by dedications which show him the friend and admirer of contemporary women of distinction and charm. The first dedication is a poem to 'the Lady Theophilia, the learned consort of the Right Worshipfull Sir Robert Cooke, knight'. She excelled in the 'Greek, Roman, French, Castillian, and Teutonic' tongues, and her 'learning morall and Divine' could lift her 'to a tenth muse among the nine'. The second dedication is a letter addressing 'Mistress Elizabeth the vertuous consort of Clovill Tanfield of Copt-Fold Hall in Essex (Esquire)', as 'Excellent Creature'.

[1] By Thomas Heywoode, London, 1624.
[2] In capitals: OPUS EXCOGITATUM, INCHOATUM, EXPLICITUM, ET A TYPOGRAPHO EXCUSUM, INTER SEPTEMDECEM SEPTIMANAS. LAUS DEO. p. 466.
[3] *Ibid.*, Dedication unpaged, A3 *d.*   [4] *Ibid.*, A4.   [5] *Ibid.*, p. 237.

Beauty and charm seem to be her attributes rather than learning. Neither of these ladies has earned a place in the *Dictionary of National Biography*, nor are they mentioned by George Ballard among his famous women. But the learning of Lady Cooke deserves notice for she was carrying the Elizabethan tradition into a later age[1].

Heywood's books in praise of women had several imitators in the generations immediately following him. Charles Gerbier's *Elogium Heroinum, or The Praise of Worthy Women*, was largely derived from it. Gerbier introduced his little book with three separate dedications. The first commended it to 'the most excellent, most illustrious, and high-born Princess Elizabeth of Bohemia', whom he described as 'a Minerva in the Temple of Virtue'. Her 'marvellous wisdom and profound knowledge in the Arts, Sciences, and Languages, is', he said, 'admired by all men'. The second dedication was to 'the most honourable the Countess Dowager of Claire, The Patroness of all Vertue and Learning'. To her 'knowing judgement', he said, 'all learned men have recourse'. She was the wife of the first Earl of Clare and died on 26 November 1651[2]. The third dedication was to 'the vertuous accomplish't lady, Anne Hudson', whose modesty, the mildness of her discourse and her 'gracious humility' he described as 'precious jewels which do atchieve your renown'[3].

Heywood wrote to entertain his contemporaries, but the anonymous author of *The Lawes Resolutions of Womens Rights* had a more serious purpose. His book has been discussed in a previous chapter, but deserves mention here because it marks an important stage in the development of a new attitude towards women. Both the I. J. who wrote the book and the T. E. who 'in the compasse of a Lent Vacation' revised it and added further 'reasons, opinions, cases and resolutions of cases to the Author's store' were men with an extensive knowledge of the common law. They were conscious that the law dealt hardly with women and took care to point out for their benefit the pitfalls which they must avoid. It is remarkable to find a writer of this date suggesting, about one particular instance

---

[1] It is remarkable how many women in the seventeenth century earned a mention by some writer or other for qualities which women of that age are not much credited with. Nothing is known of some of them. Occasionally they even published books, now almost forgotten; e.g. Lady Mary Wroath, *The Countess of Mountgomeries Urania*, London, 1621; and Anna Weamys, *A Continuation of Arcadia*, by Mrs. A. W., London, 1651. Dorothy Gardiner, *English Girlhood at School*, Oxford, 1921, p. 233.   [2] *Complete Peerage*.

[3] The book was published in London by William Nott. Its preliminary pages, including the dedications and commendatory poems, are unnumbered.

of legal inequality between husband and wife, that women should 'have patience' and 'move for redress by Parliament'[1]. This book was published in 1632, the year following the appearance of Richard Brathwaite's *English Gentlewoman*.

The Lawes Resolutions of Womens Rights makes grim reading, for over and over again the point is driven home that against her husband a wife is almost rightless. But the fact that even lawyers could be concerned at the legal inequality between the sexes is at any rate a sign of changing times. It would seem that two schools of thought were taking shape. One, to which Richard Brathwaite belonged, would keep women where feudal law had placed them and would have them simply submissive, devout, unselfish, obedient wives and good housekeepers. The other point of view is expressed in no uncertain terms by William Austin in his little tract *Haec Homo wherein the Excellency of the Creation of Women is described by way of an Essaie*[2]. Austin was born in 1587. His reputation was high for his name was on the list of members proposed for the abortive Royal Academy of Letters. None of his writings was published in his lifetime, but they circulated among his friends in manuscript. He died in 1634 and in the next year a volume of his meditations was published with a portrait of the author on the title-page. The work was 'set forth after his decease by his deare wife and executrix, Mrs. Anne Austin'. A second edition was issued in 1637 and *Haec Homo* in 1638. *Haec Homo* has been described as 'a dreary scholastic disquisition' and today it seems almost unreadable. But its argument, that *homo* stands equally for man and woman, and that each have souls, which are equal before God, is incontrovertible. 'What', says Austin, 'should make man so proud, as to *Despise*, and, with so many sought for words to contemn woman (his other self)? Doubtles, it proceeds from his ignorance or forgetfulnesse: in That he knowes not, or will not remember his lowe beginnings, (even out of Dust)'. The first edition of this book was quickly exhausted and another was published in the next year[3].

The Puritan view of the right relations of husband and wife is set out

---

[1] P. 146. See above, p. 63.   [2] London, 1637.
[3] Each of the four copies of *Haec Homo* which I have seen has been well read and much worn by contemporaries.

William Austin's line of argument was carried further in 1686 by John Shirley in his *Illustrious History of Women*. He devoted a section of the book to 'Reasons and Arguments for the capacities of the Soul of Women, etc.; in relation to learning, Arts, and Sciences etc.', *The Illustrious History of Women*, pp. 123–31.

again at considerable length in a book published at the end of the period covered by this chapter. The author of *Matrimonial Honour*[1] was Daniel Rogers, a Puritan minister of Wethersfield, Essex, who was born in 1573 and died in 1652 at the age of eighty. He came of a family strongly Puritan in traditions. His father, who was also 'preacher' at Wethersfield, had been suspended for not conforming with the Elizabethan settlement[2]. No Puritan minister could ignore the Scriptural texts which stress the wife's subordination to her husband. The three special duties of the wife to the husband are, he considered, subjection, 'which is the first and maine comprehending all the rest'; the second is helpfulness and the third gracefulness[3]. But Rogers had grown away from the violent rhetoric of William Whately[4] and the uneasy firmness of William Gouge. He was a scholar, who could hold his own in a debate with Archbishop Laud. He was clearly far from happy about the absolute subjection of the wife to her husband which the Scriptures might seem to demand. To women who said that 'ordinary husbands' do not deserve the subjection of their wives, he replied that God 'puts this burden of subjection on no woman, who takes not the yoke of marriage upon herselfe; which the Lord doth force upon none, but allowes each woman to be her own Refuser'. Moreover, Rogers could conceive of circumstances which might be exceptions and modifications to the wife's subjection. If a husband orders his wife to do unlawful things she must rather obey God than him. Also every woman is allowed 'such a libertie in Gods matters with her husband, as to prompt and occasion him unto Christian speech, good counsell, with modestie and in season: for the subjection we treat of is not slavish, but equall and royall in a sort'. Nor should a woman be forced to obey her husband if he wishes to enter upon a course of action which might imperil her and her home, such as 'removall from present dwelling, upon great charge and losse, or, to places of ill health, ill neighbours, with losse of Gospell, long voyages by sea to remote Plantations, or in the sudden change of Trades, or venturing a stock in some new project, lending out or borrowing of great sums'[5].

A woman, said Rogers, must be subject to her husband 'in matters of God's worship'. He recalled the words of the Apostle: 'I suffer not the

---

[1] *Matrimonial Honour*, London, 1642.
[2] T. W. David, *Annals of Evangelical Nonconformity in Essex*, London, 1863, p. 108.
[3] *Matrimonial Honour*, p. 253.
[4] See above, pp. 107–9.   [5] *Matrimonial Honour*, pp. 260–4.

woman to teach, or usurp authority over the man, but to be in silence'[1].
'I would not', he wrote, 'be taken to patronage the pride and licentious
impudency of women, who having shaken off the bridle of all subjection
to their husbands, take upon them to expound the Scriptures, in private
assemblyes, and to be the mouth of God to both Sexes. Not blushing one
whit to undertake by the 4. or 5. houres together, yea whole dayes (if
their vainglorious humor masked under the colours of humility be suffred)
to interpret the word: applying it according to their way by Reproofe,
Comfort, Admonition and the like, as if Shee-preachers were come
abroad into the world'. But before giving vent to this denunciation,
this seventeenth-century minister had felt bound to set out the occasions
when a woman 'may undertake the service of God in her family'. She
can pray with and teach her maids and her family in the absence of her
husband. Her servants are her inferiors and she 'has the duty of a Governor
to them'. Rogers also concludes that, under certain conditions, she may
even conduct the service of God in her household when her husband is
present. 'First, she may attempt it, in case of utter insufficiency of parts
in her husband, I meane knowledge and understanding. 2. In case of
invincible defects of expression and utterance in the husband. 3. And
much more when there is an utter looseness and carelessness in him to
look after it, much more a vicious contempt, so that (so far as lieth in him)
the worke were like to be quite cashierd out of the family. 4. If her husband
do allow her with all cheerfulnesse, or request her to undertake it. . . . 5. If
she (beside, her ablenesse to performe it) bee also, qualified with singular
modesty and humility, awe and reverence'[2]. Rogers was even prepared
to admit that 'the Lord hath gifted and graced many women above some
men, especially with holy affections'. The sureness of touch with which
William Whately and the writers of the homilies had put women in their
place has gone. They are still in subjection, both in law and theory, but
in fact they are confounding those who would keep them there.

---

[1] *Matrimonial Honour*, p. 266.   [2] *Ibid.*, pp. 268–9, 284.

CHAPTER VI

Women in the English Revolution

Since the end of the Middle Ages, freedom from invasion and civil war had made possible the ideal woman of Richard Brathwaite, one who cultivates the graces of life and ignores its harsher side. But the outbreak of the troubles in 1640 was followed by twenty years in which many women, particularly those of royalist families, found themselves charged with unforeseen responsibilities. Charlotte Stanley, Countess of Derby, proved herself a competent commander in war by her successful defence of Lathom House in 1644 against a Parliamentarian army[1]. Her little daughters were with her, and in after years were angry when they found that the two sieges of Lathom House were confused in the most popular history of the war. The second siege had ended in a surrender, but by that time the defence was in other hands. Lady Dorchester, one of the girls who had been besieged with their mother, tried to get the error put right in later editions of this history[2].

Many women, like Lady Verney or Lady Hatton, were tireless in travelling between England and France and in soliciting Parliament on their husbands' behalf. Mrs. Heylin, wife of Dr. Peter Heylin, subdean of Westminster, earned honourable mention in the contemporary life of her husband. He was able to continue his studies because 'his good wife, a discreet and active lady, looked both after her Housewifery within doors, and the Husbandry without; thereby freeing him from that care and trouble which otherwise would have hindered his laborious Pen'[3]. As a result of this happy arrangement, he was also able to aid many royal-

---

[1] *Tracts relating to military proceedings in Lancashire during the Great Civil War*, ed. G. Ormerod, Chetham Soc., 1844, pp. 161 ff.

[2] Sir Maurice Powicke, 'Notes on Hastings Manuscripts', *The Huntington Library Quarterly*, vol. i, 1938, pp. 264–6.

[3] *The Historical and Miscellaneous Tracts of the Reverend and Learned Peter Heylin, D.D.*, London, 1681, p. xix.

ists less fortunate than himself. But when Cromwell tried the experiment of governing through major-generals, Dr. Heylin was again in trouble. 'One Captain Allen, formerly a Tinker, and his Wife a poor Tripe-wife, took upon him to reprove the Doctor for maintaining his Wife so highly, like a Lady; to whom the Doctor roundly replied, that he had married a Gentlewoman, and did maintain her according to her quality, and so might he his Tripe-wife: adding withall, that this rule he always observed, For his Wife to go above his Estate, his Children according to his Estate, and himself below his Estate, so that at the years end he could make all even'[1].

Of all the ladies of the seventeenth century none has left a more intimate and appealing picture of herself, her husband, and their world than Ann Harrison, who married Richard Fanshawe in 1644. In her widowhood she wrote for her infant son an artless account of her husband and their life together. She was nineteen and he thirty-five when they married and the marriage lasted 'but twenty-three years and twenty-nine days'[2]. Anne had been educated 'with all the advantage that time afforded, both for working all sorts of fine works with my needle, and learning French, singing, [the] lute, the virginals, and dancing; and notwithstanding I learned as well as most did, yet was I wild to that degree, that the hours of my beloved recreation took up too much of my time; for I loved riding in the first place, and running, and all other active pastimes; and in fine I was that which we graver people call a hoyting girl. But to be just to myself, I never did mischief to myself or [other] people, nor one immodest action or word in my life; but skipping and activity was my delight'[3]. It was fortunate for her that she was brought up so freely. Twenty-one births in twenty-three years were enough to weaken the strongest frame. Only four daughters and one son survived their mother. Her narrative is punctuated by the births and deaths of her children and the record of where their bodies lay.

Both the Harrison and Fanshawe families paid heavily for their loyalty to the crown. But throughout her married life Ann Fanshawe was blessed in the love and trust of her husband. 'Glory be to God', she says, 'we never had but one mind throughout our lives, our souls were wrapped up in each other, our aims and designs were one, our loves one, and our resent-

---

[1] *The Historical and Miscellaneous Tracts of the Reverend and Learned Peter Heylin, D.D.*, p. xxi.
[2] *The Memoirs of Ann, Lady Fanshawe*, London, 1907, p. 13.　　　[3] *Ibid.*, p. 22.

ments one. We so studied one the other that we knew each other's mind by our looks; whatever was real happiness, God gave it me in him'[1]. Again and again Lady Fanshawe crossed the Channel with only servants to attend her; sometimes to raise money in England; sometimes to carry it to her husband in France. She was proud to say that wherever they were forced to go, France, Ireland, or Spain they left no debts behind them. This was largely due to her management of their affairs, for Sir Edward Hyde, afterwards Lord Clarendon, who was with them in Spain in 1650, wrote home saying that he himself knew not how to get 'either bread or money'[2]. During her husband's life her spirit never failed her. The hoyting girl, repressed behind the façade of the graver person, still lived within her. When her husband, captured after the battle of Worcester in 1651, was in prison at Whitehall, she was lodging in Chancery Lane. Every morning she started out at four o'clock 'with a dark lantern in my hand, all alone and on foot' to stand 'beneath his window and softly call him'[3]. At her first call he put his head out and they talked together. Sometimes she was so wet with rain that the water ran in at her neck and out at her heels. She obtained a medical certificate from her husband's doctor, took it herself to the council chamber, and secured his liberation upon bail.

After Cromwell's death Fanshawe was released from his bail through the kind offices of his friend, the Earl of Pembroke, and crossed to France to put himself at the service of King Charles II. When he had received his instructions from the king he wrote to his wife to come to France with their children. Without a pass she could not leave the country and her application for one was refused. The hoyting girl again took control, and 'leaving my maid at the gate, who was a much finer gentlewoman than myself, with as ill mien and tone as I could express, I told a fellow I found in the office that I desired a pass for Paris to go to my husband. "Woman", says he, "what is your husband and your name?" "Sir", said I, with many courtesies, "he is a young merchant, and my name is Ann Harrison". "Well", says he, "it will cost you a crown". Said I "That is a great sum for me; but pray put in a man, my maid and three children"—all which he immediately did, telling me that a Malignant would give him five pounds for such a pass. She describes how she altered the name Harrison into Fanshawe 'so completely that none could find out the change'. Without delay she set out by barge to Gravesend and thence by coach to

---

[1] *The Memoirs of Ann, Lady Fanshawe*, p. 5.   [2] *Ibid.*, p. 409.   [3] *Ibid.*, p. 80.

Dover. One of the 'searchers', on seeing her pass, said that he little thought that they would give a pass 'to so great a Malignant, especially in such a troublesome time as this'[1].

The restoration of King Charles II seemed to promise a happy future for the Fanshawes, but Sir Richard never played a great part in affairs. Lady Fanshawe blamed Clarendon for this, but there is no evidence that Fanshawe had any aptitude for statecraft. He served as ambassador in Portugal in 1662–3 and afterwards in Spain. In 1666 he was recalled because he had overstepped his authority in making a treaty between Spain and England. Before he could return to England he died at the age of fifty-eight. Broken by grief Lady Fanshawe brought his body home and survived him for fourteen years, but she felt that her life was over with his death. She could never recover from the crown all the money due to Sir Richard despite the king's fair words. Like her venerable contemporary Lady Anne Clifford, Lady Fanshawe had no sympathy with the loose morals of the Restoration court. She belonged to the hard world of the civil war in which her youth and her best years were passed. There were many women who felt as she did in the 'sixties and 'seventies of the seventeenth century. She died in 1680 at the age of fifty-five.

The war and the troubles which followed it had called out qualities in Lady Fanshawe which might have lain dormant in happier times. She would have been well content to emulate Richard Brathwaite's ideal, enjoying the simple pleasures of a peaceful life. Margaret, Duchess of Newcastle, was a far more complex character. She was born in 1617, daughter of Sir Thomas Lucas, of St. John's near Colchester. Her father died in her infancy and she was brought up by her mother, who gave her much the same sort of education which Lady Fanshawe had received. Margaret Lucas was always, as she said herself, 'bashful' and 'given to contemplation'[2]. At her own request she was allowed in 1643 to enter the service of the queen, though she had such difficulty in overcoming her shyness that she wanted to go home again. She went with the queen to Paris and in 1645 met the Marquis of Newcastle, who fell in love with her and married her in the same year. He was born in 1592, so that there were twenty-five years between their ages. Whatever may have been Newcastle's defects as a general, his character and loyalty were beyond question and his political sense was far greater than his master's. When

[1] *The Memoirs of Ann Lady Fanshawe*, pp. 89–90.
[2] *Memoirs of the Life of William Cavendish, Duke of Newcastle*, ed. C. H. Firth, p. 161.

forced into exile the Newcastles settled at Rotterdam, where 'my Lord pleaseth himself with the management of some few horses, and exercises himself with the use of the sword. . . . Also he recreates himself with his pen, writing what his wit dictates to him, but I pass my time rather with scribbling than writing, with words than wit'[1].

There is a modern touch in the autobiography of the duchess when she says that she was always more addicted to write with her pen than to work with her needle. She was an unwearied writer of poems, essays on philosophy, orations for diverse occasions, and plays. She wrote an account of her husband's life and kept a record of his sayings. In practical affairs she seems to have had little success. When she and her husband were reduced to desperate straits for money he sent her to England with his brother, Sir Charles Cavendish, to apply for the subsistence allowed to the wives of royalists from their husband's estates. Her brother, Lord Lucas, accompained her to the Goldsmiths' Hall to state her case, 'but they told him that by reason I was married since my Lord was made a delinquent I could have nothing, nor should have anything, he being the greatest traitor to the State, which was to be the most loyal subject to his king and country'[2]. She was in England eighteen months and solaced herself by writing 'a book of poems and a little book called my *Philosophical Fancies*'[3]. When King Charles II was restored to his throne he rewarded the Marquis of Newcastle with a dukedom, but his estates were greatly impoverished and he retired to the country to restore them. The duchess had no taste for society: 'and for revelling, I am of too dull a nature to make one in a merry society'. Nevertheless, she sometimes visited the town. 'I hold necessary sometimes to appear abroad, besides I do find that several objects do bring new material for my thoughts and fancies to build upon'[4].

Lady Lucas had taught her daughter to love fine clothes, and she never lost her pleasure in 'attiring, fine dressing, and fashions, especially such fashions as I did invent myself, not taking that pleasure in such fashions as was invented by others. Also I did dislike that any should follow my fashions, for I always took a delight in a singularity, even in accoutrements of habits'. In the writings of Restoration diarists the duchess appears as an eccentric figure in fantastic dress. Pepys speaks of meeting her 'going with her coaches and footmen all in velvet; herself (whom I never saw before) . . . with her velvet cap, her hair about her ears, many black

1 *Memoirs of the Duke of Newcastle*, pp. 171–2.   2 *Ibid.*, pp. 56 and 167.
3 *Ibid.*, p. 170.   4 *Ibid.*, p. 173.

patches because of pimples about her mouth, naked necked, without anything about it, and a black just-au-corps. She seemed to me a very comely woman'. On May Day 1667 Pepys went to the park like many others simply to see her 'which we could not, she being followed and crowded upon by coaches all the way she went, that nobody could come near her only I could see she was in a large black coach, adorned in silver instead of gold, and so white curtains, and every thing else black and white, herself in her cap'[1]. Evelyn records his pleasure 'with the extraordinary fanciful habit, garb, and discourse of the Duchess'. In a preface to her first book she asks readers 'Be not too severe in your censures, for first I have no children to employ my care and attendance on. Next, my Lord's estate being taken away in those times when I writ this book, I had nothing for housewifery or thrifty industry to employ myself in, having no stock to work upon'[2]. Older women even today can sympathize with her slight sense of guilt for neglecting what was popularly supposed to be women's work in favour of writing.

The duchess soon overcame her original diffidence. A duchess could safely play the eccentric and express her opinions, even on matters of philosophy and science. Her husband praised her works and letters and poems were written in her honour. The Royal Society even held a reception for her in 1667. She became ambitious and desirous of praise. 'It will satisfy me', she says, 'if my writing please the readers, though not the learned; for I had rather be praised in this by the most, although not the best; for all I desire is fame, and fame is nothing but a great noise, and noise lives most in a multitude'. Her success increased her desire for fame. 'I confess', she wrote, 'that my ambition is restless, and not ordinary, because it would have an extraordinary fame; and since all heroic actions, public employments, powerful governments, and eloquent pleadings, are denied our sex in this age, or at least be condemned for want of custom, is the cause I write so much'[3].

In 1662 she published a volume of *Orations of Divers Persons accommodated to Divers Places*[4] of which one section contained Female Orations supposedly made by women who were deliberating on the possibility of

---

[1] These references from Pepys and Evelyn are quoted by Sir Charles Firth, *Memoirs of the Duke of Newcastle*, p. 175 *n*.

[2] Quoted by Sir Charles Firth, *ibid.*, p. xxx.   [3] *Ibid.*, pp. xxxi–xxxii.

[4] London, 1662. I owe a sight of this book to Professor Dickins, who allowed me to examine the copy presented by the duchess to Corpus Christi College, Cambridge.

combining to make themselves as 'free, happy and famous as men'[1]. She made one of her speakers declare that 'the truth is, we live like Bats or Owls, Labour like Beasts, and Dye like Worms'. But after all the company had said their say the conclusion that the duchess came to was set out: 'Wherefore, women have no reason to complain against Nature, or the God of Nature, for though the gifts are not the same they have given to Men. Yet those Gifts they have given to Women, are much Better; for we Women are much more favour'd by Nature than Men, in giving us such Beauties, Features, Shapes, Graceful Demeanour, and such Insinuating and Inticing Attractives, as Men are forc'd to Admire us, Love us, and be Desirous of us, in so much as rather than not Have and Injoy us, they will deliver to our Disposals, their Power, Persons, and Lives, Inslaving themselves to our Will and Pleasures, also we are their Saints whom they Adore and Worship, and what can we Desire, more, than to be Men's Tyrants, Destines, and Goddesses?'

This vital creature died in 1673 at the age of fifty-seven, three years before her aged husband. He assuaged his grief by erecting a monument to her memory above the tomb where he also was to lie. 'Here lyes the loyall Duke of Newcastle, and his Dutches, his second wife, by whom he had noe issue: Her name was Margaret Lucas, yongest sister to the Lord Lucas of Colchester, a noble family; for all the Brothers were Valiant and all the Sisters virtuous. This Dutchess was a wise, wittie, and learned Lady, as her many Bookes do well testifie; and she was a most virtuous and a Loveing and carefull wife, and was with her Lord all the time of his banishment and miseries, and when he came home, never parted with him in his solitary retirements'[2].

Each of these three royalist ladies, Mrs. Peter Heylin, Lady Fanshawe, and the Duchess of Newcastle, were wives involved in contemporary troubles through their husbands. The career of the royalist Anne Murray shows that the civil war made it possible for a single woman to take an unconventional part in public affairs. She was born in 1622 and in 1656 married Sir James Halket. She lived happily with him for fourteen years, bearing four children, of whom only one survived. She lived as a widow for twenty-three years, dying in 1699. During her widowhood she indulged in devotional meditation and left many volumes of manuscript behind her. The most notable of her writings is an autobiography of which

[1] Pp. 225–32.
[2] *Memoirs of the Duke of Newcastle*, p. xxxii.

the end and several isolated pages are lost[1]. It has nothing of the artless simplicity of Lady Fanshawe or the inconsequent eccentricity of the duchess. Anne Halket was an extremely able and attractive woman, who was unfortunate in her early love affairs and wanted to justify her behaviour in her own eyes. She had no false modesty and knew her own worth. Her education was superintended by her mother, 'who paid masters for teaching my sister and me to write, speak French, play on the lute and virginalls, and dance, and kept a gentlewoman to teach us all kinds of needleworke'[2]. Anne Murray's father had been tutor to the future Charles I and her mother was twice entrusted with the office of governess to the Duke of Gloucester and the Princess Elizabeth. Anne was born and brought up in England and spoke and thought of herself as English, but she came of good Scots families on both sides.

Of her childhood and youth Anne Murray says little, save that she was 'seldom or never absent from divine service at five a'clocke in the summer and six a'clocke in the winter till the usurped power put a restraint to that publicke worship so long owned and continued in the Church of England'[3]. She enjoyed plays and was the first to suggest that several girls should go together with a manservant to pay for them rather than depend on a gentleman to attend them. In the year 1644 she was, she says, 'guilty of an act of disobedience, for I gave way to the adrese of a person whom my mother, att the first time that ever hee had occation to be conversantt with me, had absolutely discharged mee ever to allow of'[4]. The young gentleman was the brother of her dearest friend and came of a very good family, for he was the eldest son of Edward, Lord Howard of Escrick. Since it was essential that Mr. Howard should marry a wife with a good portion Anne's mother would not allow the young people to consider marriage. Such were the merits of Anne herself that Lord Howard would have been glad to see her married to his son, if her mother's pride would have let her agree to the match. The story of this love affair which had no happy ending is told in full, including a stolen meeting in the cellar, at which Anne kept the letter of her mother's command never to see her lover again, by blindfolding herself before they met[5]. Mr. Howard was sent off abroad and Anne remained at home, unhappy, for her mother was so angry at her persistent refusal to give

---

[1] *The Autobiography of Anne, Lady Halket*, ed. J. Gough Nichols, Camden Soc., 1875. This had also been used by the writer of *The Life of Lady Halket*, published in 1701.

[2] *Autobiography*, p. 2.   [3] *Ibid.*, p. 3.   [4] *Loc. cit.*   [5] *Ibid.*, p. 13.

up her lover while he was loyal to her, that she never gave her her blessing for fourteen months. Anne was moved to write to a kinsman in Holland to ask him about the conditions of entry to a Protestant nunnery there. Instead of answering her letter he wrote to her mother to persuade her to be kinder to her daughter, and thereafter her mother used her more like a friend than a daughter. In July 1646 Mr. Howard married the Lady Elizabeth Mordaunt, daughter of the Earl of Peterborough, and the way was clear for Anne to interest herself in someone else.

Anne's story of her mother's death is lost, but it happened not long after Mr. Howard's marriage. She then, at the invitation of her brother, Charles, took an apartment in his house for herself and her maid. She was living there when she met Colonel Bampfield, a royalist agent, who 'came to see me sometimes in company of ladys who had been my mother's neighbours in St. Martin's Lane, and sometimes alone, butt when ever he came his discourse was serious, handsome, and tending to impress the advantage of piety, loyalty, and virtue'[1]. Anne was evidently taken with the charms of this Irish adventurer, whose apparent loyalty to the crown was to her sufficient guarantee of his virtue. When an acquaintance told her that the colonel had not seen his wife for a year she took it upon herself to reproach him about it. His answer satisfied her for he said that his business on behalf of the king kept him in London, and that his wife lived among friends in the country who were loyal to the Parliament. Anne's acquaintance with the colonel drew her into a dangerous adventure for which historians have given her too little credit. In the spring of 1648, Colonel Bampfield was charged by Charles I with the duty of smuggling his second son, James Duke of York, to France. Anne Murray caused her own tailor to make a girl's dress to the duke's measurement. The tailor said that he had never made a gown to such measurements in his life. The dress was 'mixed mohaire of a light haire couler and blacke, and the under-petti-coate was scarlet'[2]. Anne awaited the duke's coming in a private house near London Bridge which the Colonel had hired, She was told to 'shift for herself' if they did not bring the duke by ten o'clock. They were late, but she waited. At last they came, the duke calling 'Quickely quickely dress me'. He looked very pretty in his woman's habit and was sent down the Thames in a barge with a Wood Street cake, which he loved[3].

---

[1] *Autobiography*, p. 19.   [2] *Ibid.*, p. 21.   [3] *Ibid.*, p. 22.

When Lord Clarendon came to write his history of the great rebellion he did not record, and perhaps did not know, the part a woman played in the duke's escape[1].

No one was taken for the escape, although the authorities knew pretty well who had been involved. The colonel returned secretly to England and summoned Anne to come to see him. Through the last months of Charles I's life she was collecting information and carrying it to Bampfield in his lodgings. 'The earnest desire I had to serve the King made me omitt noe opertunity wherein I could bee usefull, and the zeale I had for his Majesty made me nott see what inconveniencys I exposed myselfe to'[2]. Frequent private visits to the colonel led to warmer feelings on both sides. One day she found him 'lying upon his bed, and asking him if he were nott well, hee told me he was well enough', but he had learned that morning that his wife was dead[3]. Soon after this he suggested that now that he was free they might get married, pointing out that it would be a reasonable thing to do since if the king were restored to his throne they would certainly have a joint income of about eight hundred pounds a year. Whenever she was with him he pressed her to agree and at last she did so, but they put off the marriage until they could see how the king's affairs went. It was as well that they had delayed for soon after the execution of Charles I the colonel told her that he had news that his wife was not dead after all. He had, he said, sent off a servant to find out the truth[4]. Anne's own affairs were driven from her mind by the return from France of her brother William, whom she nursed through his last illness. She then accompanied Sir Charles Howard and his lady to Naworth Castle, fearing that if she stayed in London she might be put in prison for her share in the duke's escape. The colonel had intended to escape to the north also, but was taken and imprisoned.

News of the colonel's imprisonment was followed almost at once by letters from Anne's brother and sister, denouncing him as 'the most unworthy person living; that he had abused mee in pretending that his wife was dead, for she was alive'[5]. All this threw Anne into an illness from which she almost died. She was saved by the housekeeper pointing out that if anyone else were equally ill Anne herself would have known how to cure her. With this stimulus she told her maid what remedy to prepare and in due course recovered her health. The egregious colonel

---

[1] Clarendon, *History of the Great Rebellion*, Bk. XI, par. 20. [2] *Autobiography*, p. 24.
[3] *Ibid.*, pp. 24–5. [4] *Ibid.*, p. 27. [5] *Ibid.*, p. 32.

escaped from prison to Flanders, but Anne's brother-in-law was a passenger on the same boat and challenged him to a duel. Unfortunately the colonel wounded his opponent severely in the hand. This news was distressing but Anne was cheered by the fact that her sister's husband was prepared to fight a duel on her behalf, 'which hee would never have done (I was assured) if he had believed mee vicious'[1]. In Flanders the colonel met the Earl of Dunfermline, who had gone abroad to invite King Charles II to Scotland. He persuaded the earl to invite Anne to Scotland to be presented to the king, and wrote to her himself urging her to come. She left for Edinburgh on 6 June 1650. After the battle of Dunbar on 3 September she went north to Fyvie with Lady Dunfermline. Her skill in the dressing of wounds enabled her to help many of the men fleeing north after the battle; 'for I had provided myself very well of things necessary for that imploymentt, expecting that they might be usefull'[2]. The king gave her fifty pieces of gold for her services to the wounded.

At Fyvie Castle, where Anne stayed for almost two years, the colonel reappeared to plead that he was a much maligned man. When the English army had reduced all Scotland the household of Fyvie broke up and Anne returned to Edinburgh, hoping to straighten out her financial affairs. Her lodgings in Edinburgh became a centre for royalist plotters. Early in her stay there she met Sir James Halket, a widower, who seems from her account to have fallen in love at first sight. He made excuses to visit her frequently, so that she had to tell him about the colonel. Instead of withdrawing his attentions Sir James was as attentive as ever and even did all he could to help his rival. In March 1653 she learned that the colonel's wife was indeed alive and had gone up to London to prove her existence. Unfortunately a leaf of the autobiography is lost on which her reaction to this news was recorded. Sir James Halket urged her to marry him and when she refused he persuaded her to undertake the charge of his two daughters. She set up house with them in Edinburgh and after a time agreed to marry Sir James as soon as she had settled her affairs. For that reason she went to London, where for the last time she saw the colonel. He came to her lodgings and asked her if she were Sir James Halket's wife, because if she were he would trouble her no more. 'I am', she said out loud, adding to herself 'not'. The colonel 'immediately rose up and said "I wish you and him much happiness together" and, taking his leave, from that time to this I never saw him or heard from him'[3]. After she had

---

[1] *Autobiography*, p. 53.   [2] *Ibid.*, p. 63.   [3] *Ibid.*, p. 99.

raised a little money there was nothing to delay her marriage, which took place on 1 March 1656. She returned to Scotland with her husband, but her autobiography breaks off before they had lived long together.

Someone who signed his dedication S. C. published an account of Lady Halket within two years of her death in 1699[1]. The author says that he has based his work on Lady Halket's own diary, even using her own words. Although he went in great detail into her financial affairs, he passed lightly over her relations with the colonel and her part in the Duke of York's escape. These passages in the life of a spirited young woman may well have seemed remote from the elderly lady filling a long widowhood with works of piety. Sir James had died in 1670, and Lady Halket always rejoiced that while he was alive her creditors had left her in peace. Like many other royalists, she carried a burden of debt which could only be reduced by further borrowing. In 1683 she even thought of giving up her home in Scotland and returning to England, but instead, she opened her house to children of noble families whose mothers had died. At one time, she was entrusted with 'the Heirs and Children of eight several Families; all of them Motherless, save one, who was Fatherless'[2]. One of her religious works is a guide to a virtuous life called *Instructions for Youth* 'for the use of those young Noblemen and Gentlemen, whose Education was committed to her care'. It is to the credit of James II that when he became king he gave her a pension of £100 a year for life.

Lady Halket was evidently a woman of charm with whom it was easy to fall in love. She was a good friend, afraid of nothing in the king's service. She faced a hostile band of soldiers at Fyvie Castle, though not until she was quite sure that Lady Dunfermline would not regard her action as presumptuous[3]. They were immediately reduced to politeness by her dignity. She was concerned lest the world should misjudge her, for she was conscious that from 1644 until her marriage she had often behaved unconventionally. She might never have troubled to write about

---

[1] *The Life of Lady Halket*, Edinburgh, 1701. A list of her writings is appended to the book, six pages unnumbered. Several of them were printed in the course of 1701 and 1702. *Meditations on the Twentieth and Fifth Psalm*, 1701. This was written at Fyvie and finished 1 January 1652. *Instructions for Youth*, 1701. *Meditations and Prayers upon the First Week with observations on each days creation*, 1701. *Meditations upon the seven gifts of the Holy Spirit*, 1702. *Meditations upon Jabes his Request*, and other papers, 1702. All these are collected into one volume which was kindly lent to me by Mr. Arnold Muirhead of St. Albans. His copy had belonged to the Halket family, for on the front page is written 'Charles Andrew Hacket. July 13th, 1842. Received from Aberdeen among the effects of his Cousin C. H.'

[2] *Ibid.*, p. 45.   [3] *Autobiography*, pp. 68–9.

her life if it had been the placid married existence of a peaceful age. As it is she has left a record of two lives to which there is no parallel even among all the copious memorials of the seventeenth century.

Like King James II, his brother King Charles had once escaped from England with a woman's help. Unfortunately Jane Lane, the heroine of King Charles's flight after the battle of Worcester, never wrote her autobiography. She was the daughter of Thomas Lane, of Bentley near Walsall, and at the time of the battle was living at Bentley with her brother, Colonel John Lane. She had a sister married to a Mr. Norton, who lived about three miles from Bristol, which gave her 'a fair pretence' of going there[1]. She obtained a pass for herself, a manservant and her cousin, Henry Lascelles. The king was dressed in a servant's clothes and took the name of William Jackson, one of her brother's men. Jane rode pillion behind him. Too many people knew Charles II's strong features for the journey to be anything but extremely hazardous. After various adventures, the party reached Trent, near Sherborne, where the king stayed at Frank Windham's house while his friends looked for a boat for France. Jane Lane went home and the king rode to Lyme Regis before Mrs. Judith Coningsby, a cousin of Windham's[2]. After the king had gone Jane Lane and her brother escaped to France in disguise, knowing that their story would become known. Charles II welcomed her there as his 'life'. After the Restoration she married a Warwickshire country gentleman and enjoyed a life pension from the crown. Nothing intimate is recorded of her later years, but a hint that she remained a woman of spirit to the end is given by her justification for living up to her income; her hands, she said, should be her executors[3].

None of the picturesque royalist heroines was so widely known and praised in the nineteenth century as Mrs. Lucy Hutchinson, the Puritan wife of Colonel Hutchinson. She was born in 1620, daughter of Sir Allen Apsley, Lieutenant of the Tower of London. Her mother had lived for some time in Jersey, where she learned French from a minister who had fled from religious persecution in France. From him, too, she learned 'their Geneva discipline', which she imparted to her daughter[4]. Lady Apsley's dream when she was awaiting the birth of Lucy that a

---

[1] *An Account of the Preservation of King Charles II after the Battle of Worcester drawn up by himself*, Edinburgh, 1801, pp. 28–9.   [2] *Ibid.*, p. 47.   [3] *D.N.B.*
[4] *Memoirs of the Life of Colonel Hutchinson by his widow Lucy*, ed. the Rev. Julius Hutchinson, revised by C. H. Firth, London, 1906, p. 9.

star came down from heaven to her hand, may have been the reason for the extraordinary care taken over the child's education. Her father felt that the dream signified that the infant about to be born would be of 'some extraordinary eminency'. She was carefully instructed by many tutors and was even taught Latin by her father's chaplain, 'a pitiful dull fellow', as she ungratefully describes him. Despite his dullness she out-stripped her brothers who were at school[1]. Her writings show that she had acquired a knowledge of Greek and Hebrew and read much classical and theological literature. Like the Duchess of Newcastle, Mrs. Hutchinson never loved her needle. 'My genius', she says, 'was quite averse from all but my book'. In her youth, although religious, she thought it 'no sin to learn or hear witty songs and amorous sonnets or poems'. She even trans-lated the six books of Lucretius into English verse. She gave her trans-lation to the Earl of Anglesea at his own request in 1675, asking him to 'conceal it as a shame'[2]. She became touched with anabaptist doctrines and in 1647 would not have one of her children baptized. Many of her own kinsfolk were royalists, but she became an ardent republican, as hostile before the end to Cromwell as she had been to Charles I.

Like Lady Fanshawe, Mrs. Hutchinson wrote her memoirs in order that her children might be instructed in their father's virtues. Her own qualities of mind, carefully tended by her education and reading, enabled her to write a book which has become a classic. Her *Life of John Hutchinson of Owthorpe, in the county of Nottingham, Esquire*, was written between 1664, when her husband died, and 1671. He was not a great man, nor did he play a great part in events. He was a Nottinghamshire squire of secondary rank who held Nottingham Castle and town for the Parliament and he was one of those who signed the king's death-warrant. The book has no particular value for the general history of the time, but it preserves an accurate story of the war in Nottinghamshire. Its unique value lies in its picture of a Puritan family in the middle seventeenth century. There is real charm in the story of Mr. Hutchinson's courtship and early married life. Very naturally Mrs. Hutchinson left out anything which might tend to detract from her husband's character, and sometimes suggests he did kind actions when he certainly did not. The fact that Hutchinson had not held with Cromwell's 'tyranny' helped him to escape the fate of other regicides on the restoration of Charles II. The royalist friends and kinsfolk on both sides of the family united to testify that he had worked in the

[1] *Memoirs of Colonel Hutchinson*, pp. 13–14.   [2] *Ibid.*, p. xviii.

interest of Charles II. This kindly misrepresentation, supported by a letter to Parliament humbly petitioning for his life, secured him for a time. Mrs. Hutchinson says that she herself wrote the letter, signed it with her husband's name and sent it to the Speaker. Hutchinson's old fellow-soldiers felt that he had betrayed them and he himself was conscious of denying the cause for which he had fought. It may have been a relief when in October 1663 he was arrested on suspicion of treason. He died in prison in 1664.

Even those who have least sympathy with the stern religious creed professed by Mrs. Hutchinson cannot but admire the skill and power of her description of her husband and the relationship between them. She must have been by far the stronger character, but she had no desire to rise above the accepted woman's place. 'Never man', she says, 'had a greater passion for a woman, nor a more honourable esteem of a wife; yet he was not uxorious, nor remitted not that just rule which it was her honour to obey, but managed the reins of government with such prudence and affection that she who would not delight in such an honourable and advantageable subjection, must have wanted a reasonable soul. He governed by persuasion which he never employed but to things honourable and profitable for herself. . . . So liberal was he to her and of so generous a temper, that he hated the mention of several purses; his estate being so much at her disposal, that he would never receive an account of anything she expended'[1]. In her last writings she expressed her acceptance of the Apostle's attitude to women: 'but as our sex, through ignorance and weakness of judgment, which in the most knowing women is inferior to the masculine understanding of men, are apt to entertain fancies and be pertinacious in them, so we ought to watch over ourselves in such a day as this, and embrace nothing rashly'[1]. The writings of the half-educated royalist ladies rouse in the reader's mind feelings of real affection for their authors. Respectful admiration is the warmest emotion it is possible to have for one so sure of herself and her rightness as the learned Mrs. Hutchinson.

Nevertheless, there is a quality in Mrs. Hutchinson's writing, derived from thought and wide reading, which is absent from the work of the royalist ladies. The Puritan zeal for learning which had flourished under Queen Elizabeth was by no means dead a hundred years later. In the sixteenth century it had encouraged noble families to educate their

---

[1] *Memoirs of Colonel Hutchinson*, p. 26.   [2] *Ibid.*, p. xix.

daughters; in the seventeenth century it can be found exercising its beneficent influence among the growing professional and merchant classes. Schools were being set up for their children, particularly in the neighbourhood of London. It was to Mrs. Salmon's school at Hackney that Katherine Fowler—known to her friends and admirers as 'the matchless Orinda'—was sent at the age of eight. She was the daughter of a London merchant of Presbyterian leanings and was born in 1631. She is said to have read the Bible through 'before she was full four years old'. She could 'take sermons *verbatim*, when she was but ten years old'[1]. This remarkable capacity seems to have been due as much to her early religious zeal as to the skill of her teachers.

The 'matchless Orinda' had left the Presbyterians for the Church of England and become a royalist long before she died. The change probably resulted from her mother's second marriage to Hector Philips, of Porteynon, in Glamorgan, and her own marriage at the age of sixteen to her stepfather's eldest son, James Philips, of the Priory, Cardigan. Katherine Philips was not a scholar, but a poet whose verses, handed about in manuscript, or prefixed to the books of others, gave her a considerable reputation. She was one of a group of friends who gave each other fanciful, pseudo-classical names. She was Orinda and her husband Antenor. Jeremy Taylor, whom she must have met when he was in retirement at Golden Grove in the Towy valley, was Palæmon and Sir Edward Dering was Silvander. Katherine Philips's reputation as a poet did not long outlive her, but she deserves to be remembered as the lady, 'eminent in friendships', to whom Jeremy Taylor addressed *A Discourse of the nature, offices and measures of friendship, with Rules conducting it. In a Letter to Mrs. K. P.*[2] He described marriage as 'the Queen of friendships, in which there is a communication of all that can be communicated by friendship'[3]. 'You may see', he wrote, 'how much I differ from the morosity of those Cynicks who would not admit your sex into the communities of a noble friendship. I believe some Wives have been the best friends in the world'[4]. Katherine Philips replied in a poem addressed 'To the noble Palæmon, on his Incomparable Discourse on Friendship'[5]. Her poems

---

[1] Ballard, pp. 287–8.
[2] Written by Jer. Taylor, D.D., London, 1671. Mrs. Philips's name is written in full in the short title on p. 1.   [3] *Ibid.*, p. 73.   [4] *Ibid.*, p. 87.
[5] *Poems by the most deservedly admired Mrs. Katherine Philips*, London, 1710, pp. 19–21.

'To my dearest Antenor, on his Parting', 'To Antenor', and 'To my Antenor' show that her marriage was happy[1]. She died of smallpox in London in 1664 at the age of thirty-one.

The exaggerated reputation of Katherine Philips implies that not many ladies, whether Puritan or royalist, could compete with her. It is probable that some girls were educated beyond their capacities, and that the scepticism which their elders sometimes expressed may have been justified. The royalist Dr. Denton, a fashionable doctor who remained in his London practice all through the Commonwealth, had educational ambitions for his daughter. She was a god-daughter of Sir Ralf Verney, of Claydon, and in July 1652 wrote to him in France that although she knew that he could 'outreach' her in French she hoped that she would 'outreach' him in 'ebri, grek, and laten'[2]. Her father added an apologetic postscript, saying that he expected Sir Ralf, who could see that the letter was her own work, to be as pleased with it as if 'Nat Hobart or Selden' had written it for her. Sir Ralf answered affectionately but firmly, pointing out that 'a Bible (with the common prayer) and a good plaine cattichisme in your Mother tongue well read and practised, is well worth all the rest and much more sutable to your sex; I know your Father thinks this false doctrine, but bee confident your husband will bee of my oppinion'. On the other hand he told her that she could not know French too well and promised to send her some French books—plays, novels, and cookery books—to start her library. To her father he wrote urging him not to let Anne learn either Latin or shorthand; 'the difficulty of the first may keep her from that Vice, for soe I must esteem it in a woeman'. The danger of shorthand was that she might want to take down sermons in it and St. Paul would certainly have disliked women writing in church as much as he disliked them speaking there. His own daughter, Peg, Sir Ralf described as 'very backward', but 'I doubt not that she will be scholar enough for a woman'[3]. Sir Ralf Verney was in full agreement on this subject with Richard Brathwaite.

If the women of position in the middle years of the century were as a rule not highly educated, they could nevertheless write good love-letters. Seventy-seven letters written by Dorothy Osborne to her future husband, Sir William Temple, have passed into the body of seventeenth-century

---

[1] *Poems by Mrs. Katherine Philips*, pp. 60, 97, 180.
[2] *Memoirs of the Verney Family*, ed. M. M. Verney, 2nd ed., vol. i, p. 501.
[3] *Ibid.*, pp. 500–1.

literature[1]. The lovers first met in 1648 when Dorothy was twenty-one and Temple was twenty. It was not until December 1654 that they were married. Dorothy's letters reveal something of the slow, quiet country life that most royalist ladies lived under 'the Commonwealth. Other suitors courted her with the good will of her family, and Temple's father wanted him to look elsewhere for a wife. The one letter of Temple's which survives reveals him a passionate and masterful lover[2]. Dorothy's letters show her gradually coming to trust him with all her thoughts. The same quality is present in an isolated letter of the seventeen-year-old Mary Whichcote to her future husband, Dr. John Worthington, Master of Jesus College, Cambridge. 'I cannot', she writes, 'but acknowledge the moving of my heart to you, that of all the men that ever I saw, if I were to chuse of ten thousand, my heart would not close with any as with yourself'[3]. The touch of austerity in the phrasing is appropriate in a letter from a girl who, like Mary Whichcote, had lived among the most intelligent scholars of her time.

Until the victory of the Parliamentary forces in the civil war the Puritans had been in opposition to the Church and Government throughout the century. Their insecurity as the opponents of the established order in the Church tended to make them aggressive and argumentative. Their womenfolk shared these qualities. Although many of them had much the same sort of education as the daughters of the Church of England they tended to take a more vigorous part in theological argument. Some of them had been educated in Holland, like Lady Fairfax and Brilliana, Lady Harley. According to Clarendon it was this breeding in Holland which had deprived Lady Fairfax of 'that reverence for the Church of England, which she ought to have had' and made her concur in her husband's joining the rebels. Of this she repented when King Charles was brought to trial, and she found sufficient courage to protest in court. Lord Fairfax, although commander-in-chief of the Parliamentary army, was not present, and when his name was called 'there was a voice heard that said, that he had more wit than to be there; which put the court into some disorder, and somebody asking who it was, there was no answer

---

[1] *The Love Letters of Dorothy Osborne to Sir William Temple*, ed. Israel Gollancz, The King's Classics, 1903.   [2] *Ibid.*, pp. 269–72.

[3] *The Diary and Correspondence of Dr. John Worthington*, ed. James Crossley, Chetham Society, vol. xiii, 1847, p. 88. Mary's uncle, Dr. Benjamin Whichcote, was a leader among the Cambridge Platonists.

but a little murmuring. But presently, when the impeachment was read, and that expression used, of "all the good people of England", the same voice in a louder tone answered, "No, nor the hundredth part of them!" . . . it was quickly discerned that it was the general's wife, the Lady Fairfax, who had uttered both those sharp sayings; who was presently persuaded or forced to leave her place, to prevent any new disorder'[1].

Her cousin, Lady Harley, was the daughter of Sir Edward Conway, commander of the fortress of the Brill in Holland. From her birth there (in 1600) she was given the name of Brilliana. In 1623 she became the third wife of Sir Robert Harley, of Brampton Bryan Castle, Hereford-shire, an ardent Puritan. The incumbent of Brampton Bryan from 1612 to 1633 was Thomas Pierson, of Emmanuel College, 'a profound scholar and theologian'[2]. He was succeeded by Stanley Gower, another man of similar quality. Brampton Bryan in the civil war was an island of Puri-tanism in a county mainly royalist. A large number of the letters written by Brilliana Harley have survived. Most of the earlier ones, between 1625 and 1633, were sent to her husband, and most of the rest to her son, Edward, who in October 1638 went up to Oxford as an undergraduate. Her letters show that she kept well in touch with affairs through news letters and letters from kinsfolk in other shires[3]. She often spoke of books she had read or wished to read and on one occasion suggested that Ned should send her the French version since she preferred to read that lan-guage. Parcels of foodstuff were sent constantly from home to Ned at Oxford, a 'loyn of veale', apples, a turkey pie sometimes made from two turkeys, a kid pie with a different flavouring in each half of it, bacon, violet cakes, eight bottles of cider. Always his mother sent her love or remembrances to his 'worthy tutor'. The Puritan sympathies of the Harleys at Brampton Bryan brought upon them the suspicion of the royalists, who on 25 July 1643 laid siege to the castle. Both her husband and son were away, but Lady Harley had laid in powder and shot and muskets. The siege lasted six weeks. On 25 August Lady Harley wrote to tell her son 'the gentillmen of this county have effected their desires in bringing an army against me. . . . The Lord in mercy preserve me that I fall not into their hands'[4]. Her last letter, dated 9 October 1643, told Ned that she had 'taken a great cold'. She died of it before the end of the month.

---

[1] Clarendon, *History of the Great Rebellion*, Bk. XI, par. 235.

[2] *The Letters of the Lady Brilliana Harley*, ed. T. T. Lewis, Camden Society, 1853, p. xv.

[3] *Ibid.*, pp. 72, 81.   [4] *Ibid.*, p. 207.

Lady Harley came of an aristocratic family, but the Puritan women of the professional classes shared the same qualities of zeal and courage. Oliver Heywood, one of the outstanding Nonconformist ministers ejected from their livings in 1662, described his own mother as 'very kind to her poor neighbours', and one who 'paid for the schooling of many poor children'. She was 'a great lover of peace; when people quarrelled she used to fall upon them with plain, downright, homely rhetoric and scripture grounds, that few had power to deny her request'. She was 'the centre of news for knowing the time of weekday sermons; kept conferences and private fasts'. She was 'an irreconcilable enemy' to bishops' government and rejoiced at their downfall during the Commonwealth. She 'showed her forwardness in demolishing relics of superstition', which must mean that she encouraged the breaking of stained glass windows and other medieval works of scriptural art. Nevertheless, 'she did recount and cause to be written fair over', a great number of the 'national mercies and admirable deliverances, to excite a present thankfulness and to be a memorial to succeeding ages'. When the chapels in the neighbourhood were vacant, she used every means in her power to procure the settlement of pious ministers in them. 'The very last day she spent at Bolton, and the very last work she did in Lancashire, was to exert herself to bring such a minister to the chapel at Ainsworth, having succeeded in getting together a meeting of ministers and some of the people to consult about it, which was the only means to accomplish the end'[1].

Mrs. Heywood is here seen through the mind of her son. It is possible to come into closer touch with one of the women who shared the dreams of the more advanced enthusiasts of the Commonwealth. Two tracts written by 'M. Cary a servant of Jesus Christ' were published together in 1651[2]. The first is entitled *The Little Hornes Doom and Downfall* and the second *A New and more exact Mappe or Description of New Jerusalems Glory*. At the end of her book the author added three deplorable poems: one addressed

> 'Unto the Court of Parliament, who are
> Supreme, in England, Ireland, and elsewhere';

[1] Joseph Hunter, *The Rise of The Old Dissent exemplified in the life of Oliver Heywood*, London, 1842, pp. 25–6.

[2] At London. Printed by W. H., and are to be sold at the sign of the Black-spread-Eagle at the West End of Pauls.

the second addressed

> 'Unto the Armies Faithful Leaders, and
> Unto the Faithful under their command';

the third addressed

> 'Unto those people of the Lord that do
> In Babylon abide unto their wo'[1].

In her preface the author explained that since in her former book[2], published in April 1648, she had subscribed her name Cary, she has thought it best to put the same name upon her title-page although she is now known as Mary Rande.

She is not remembered under either name today but in her own time famous people were interested in her work[3]. She was a believer in the Fifth Monarchy, basing her beliefs on her interpretation of Scriptural prophesies. She held that the four beasts seen by the prophet Daniel were the four great monarchies, which in turn had dominated the world, the Babylonian, the Persian, the Grecian, and 'the fourth, which was the most dreadfull, and terrible, and the last of the foure, was the Roman which succeeded the Grecian'[4]. The Roman monarchy was the worst because the Pope had succeeded to the power of the Emperor and controlled the kings of Europe, the ten horns, of which the prophet spoke. The little horn, whose doom and downfall had been foretold, was Charles I, upon whom Parliament had executed 'THE JUDGEMENT WRITTEN'[5]. The Fifth Monarchy, which would be the rule of Christ and the saints, was about to come upon the world. By Mary Cary's calculations Christ had begun to enter into His kingdom in 1645. The Jews would be converted in 1656. The millennium, or the Fifth Monarchy, would come in 1701, 'or neer this year'[6].

Mary Cary's book was prefaced by letters from Hugh Peters, Henry Jessey, and Christopher Feake. Hugh Peters, best remembered today as

---

[1] Unpaged.

[2] *The Resurrection of The Witnesses.* In a postscript to her 1651 book she added a number of corrections to her former work.

[3] She was presumably identical with the 'Mistris Carew' whose prophesies were mentioned by Sir William Sanderson, *The Life and Reign of King Charles,* 1658, p. 126.

[4] *The Little Hornes Doom and Downfall,* p. 4.   [5] *Ibid.,* p. 41.

[6] *New Jerusalems Glory,* pp. 119 and 209.

an uncompromising republican who suffered death as a regicide in 1660, was a leader among the religious enthusiasts whose undisciplined passion both inspired the Cromwellian armies and embarrassed their commanders. His preface was obviously regarded as of particular value, for it is printed in the largest and heaviest type that was available. But it was 'respect to the author' rather than concurrence in her views which moved him to write his preface, and the militant Puritan's ideal of the place of a woman in religion gives it exceptional interest. What he found himself able to say about the book is arranged under three headings: 'First, that she hath taught her sexe that there are more ways than one to avoid idleness (the devils cushion) on which so many sit and sleep their last. They that will not use the Distaff, may improve a Pen.

'Secondly, A holy, modest and painfull spirit, runs through her endeavours, which I desire not to be slighted by any, nor thrown by: for good wine may be found in this Cluster: in this dress you shall see neither naked Brests, black Patches, nor long Trains; but an heart breathing after the *coming of Christ*, and the *comfort of Saints*.

'Thirdly, Scriptures cleerly opened, and properly applied; yea so well, that thou might easily think she plow'd with anothers Heifer, were not the contrary well known. . . .

'Two of this sexe I have met with, very famous for more than their mother-tongue, and for what we call Learning, yet living. The one an unhappie branch of that Tree which is cut off, and pulling up by the roots; of whom I could say much, to whom I owe much. The other of deserved note in Utrecht, the glory of her sexe in Holland[1]. But this my Country-woman speaks the best language: yea. I will adde: Other daughters have done vertuously, but thou surmountest them, Prov. 31. 29. . . .'

The Judgement of H. Jessey follows the cool praise of Hugh Peters and is printed in rather smaller type. Jessey was a Baptist divine who raised £300 in 1657 and sent it to the distressed Jews in Jerusalem with his good wishes for their conversion. After 1660 he was for a time in custody; he was released and died in 1663. Although his interpretation of the Scriptures might differ in detail from Mary Cary's he was in essential agreement with her views. He seems to have felt some resentment that she had put them in print before his own work had appeared. He says that 'before

---

[1] The Dutch lady is Anna Maria à Schurman, whom Peters must have met when he was in Holland.

1650' he had 'made a collection from the Book of the Revelation, and from Daniel, and other Scriptures' about 'these Great Changes in the World now at hand; of the pouring out of four Vials; and of the slaying and rising of the Witnesses, and of the conversion of the Jews, probably before 1658, and of the Scriptures order in these proceedings, before the conversion of the Jews, and thence until the thousand yeers of Christs reign begin'. The commendation by Christopher Feake is printed in the type used for the rest of the book. He himself was a believer in the Fifth Monarchy and in 1650 had preached a sermon about it before the Lord Mayor of London, Sir Thomas Foote. The Fifth Monarchy men disliked the Protectorate and tried to persuade the army to overthrow it. Feake was imprisoned in 1654 for his attacks on Cromwell. That Mary Cary was not the only woman who interested herself in explaining scriptural prophecies is shown by Feake's reference to the offence felt by many that 'a company of illiterate men and silly women should pretend to any skill in dark prophecies and to a foresight of future events'.

Mary Cary dedicated her book to 'The Vertuous, Heroicall, and Honourable Ladies, The Lady Elizabeth Cromwel, The Lady Bridget Ireton, and The Lady Margaret Role'. 'I have chosen', she wrote, '(being of your own sex) to dedicate these Treatises to your Ladiships, (whom I honour because God hath honoured) and under your favourable aspects to publish them to the world'. She observed 'how that among the many pious, precious, prudent, and sage Matrons, and holy women, with which this Commonwealth is adorned; as with so many precious jewels, and choice gemmes (which God having here and there placed in it doe set out the glory and lustre of the Nation) God hath selected and chosen out your Ladiships, and placed you in some of the highest places of honour'. The Lady Elizabeth Cromwell was the general's wife, who appears little in history. Her acceptance of this dedication is one of the few pieces of evidence which may indicate her personal sympathies. Mrs. Hutchinson called Cromwell's daughters 'insolent fools', but she excepted Bridget Ireton from her condemnation[1]. When Mary Cary was writing, Henry Ireton, Bridget's husband, was in command in Ireland. He died, worn out by over-work before the year was over. Of the Lady Margaret Role little is known, but she was the daughter of Sir Thomas Foote, Lord Mayor of London, before whom Feake had preached in the previous year, and the wife of Henry Rolle, Chief Justice of the Upper Bench.

[1] *Memoirs of Colonel Hutchinson*, p. 298.

Mary Cary's writing is noteworthy because she looked forward to women's future achievements in the reign of the saints. She commented on the prophecy of Joel ii. 28, 'And it shall come to pass, that I shall pour out my spirit upon all flesh; and your sons and your daughters shall prophesie: your old men shall dream dreams and your young men shall see visions: and also upon the servants, and upon the handmaids, in those days, will I pour out my spirit'. She regarded this as a prophecy for the present time, but one that was not yet fulfilled, for few of the saints have the spirit of prophecy: 'witness the complaints of many Country towns and Parishes, which they make for want of faithful able men to preach the Gospel among them. And if there be very few men that are thus furnished with the gift of the Spirit; how few are the women! Not but that there are many godly women, many who have indeed received the Spirit: but in how small a measure is it? how weak are they? and how unable to prophesie? for it is that that I am speaking of, which this text says they shall do; which yet we see not fulfilled. Indeed, they have tasted of the sweetness of the Spirit; and having tasted, are longing for more, and are ready to receive from those few that are in any manner furnished with the gifts of the Spirit for prophesying; but they are generally very unable to communicate to others, though they would do it many times in their own families, among their children and servants: and when they would be communicating to others into whose company they come, though sometimes some sprinklings come from them, yet at other times they finde themselves dry and barren. But the time is coming when this promise shall be fulfilled, and the Saints shall be abundantly filled with the spirit; and not only men, but women shall prophesie; not only aged men, but young men; not only superiours, but inferiours; not only those that have University learning, but those that have it not; even servants and hand-maids'[1]. The Quaker discipline, which gave women equality with men, was a natural product of an age when a woman could write like this[2].

The movement began when in 1644 George Fox left his home in Leicestershire, although it was not until 1646 that he realized that learning alone was not enough to make a man a minister of God. He took the logical step of preaching in 1647 and began his travels, which lasted to the end of his life. During the Commonwealth period religious meetings of the various Protestant sects could be freely held, and humble folk, as

---

[1] *The New Jerusalems Glory*, pp. 136–238. The pages are wrongly numbered in my copy: p. 238 follows p. 137.   [2] See below, p. 179.

well women as men, rejoiced to take part in them. But for a stranger to enter a church in service time and testify to the people was a disturbance of ordered services. In 1649 George Fox was imprisoned for brawling in church, the first of many such imprisonments. He urged men and women to trust in the knowledge of God within them, the 'inner light', to abandon forms and ceremonies, and to speak the truth without swearing to it[1]. In such a faith there could be no distinction between men and women, for both could testify to the light within them. The first name of this new society was 'The Children of Light', but this soon gave way to 'The Friends of Truth' or 'Truth's Friends', and so 'Friends' by which the community is known today. The name 'Quakers' was first given them by a member of the Derby bench of Justices in 1650, after Fox had enjoined him and his companions to 'tremble at the name of the Lord'[2].

The new preaching attracted followers from all the Protestant sects, and in early years its future was in danger from visionaries and enthusiasts. The ranting preaching of early converts attracted others, but needed curbing and repressing. In establishing a form of Quaker government George Fox was greatly helped by an able woman, Margaret Fell, who later became his wife. She was born in 1614 and married at the age of eighteen to Thomas Fell of Swarthmore Hall, near Ulverston, Lancashire. Her husband appears in George Fox's autobiography as Judge Fell. In the winter of 1652 George Fox was received at Swarthmore, while the judge was holding the Assizes, and Margaret Fell and her household were converted[3]. Fell himself was never converted, but helped and protected the Quakers until his death in 1658[4]. Even during Judge Fell's life Swarthmore Hall had become the Quaker headquarters and Margaret Fell was already writing letters of exhortation and encouragement to Friends both in England and abroad[5]. By the Restoration the Quakers had become an orderly and organized religious body. Fox introduced the discipline of silence into meetings, which reduced the ranting element to submission. A system of regular meetings, visitations by travelling preachers, the

---

[1] *The First Minute Book of the Gainsborough Monthly Meeting of the Society of Friends*, vol. i, ed. Harold Brace, Lincoln Record Society, vol. xxxviii, 1948. The editor, clerk of Lincolnshire Monthly Meeting, sets out briefly but clearly the modern Quaker's attitude to the history of Friends in his Introduction, pp. ix ff. Hereafter referred to as *Quaker Minutes*.

[2] *Autobiography of George Fox*, ed. H. S. Newman, London, 1886, p. 22.

[3] *Ibid.*, p. 51. *A Brief Collection of Remarkable Passages and Occurrences Relating to . . . Margaret Fell*, London, 1710, p. 3.   [4] *Loc. cit.*

[5] *A Brief Collection*, pp. 47–196. All this was written by her between 1653 and 1657.

registration of births, deaths, and marriages had given coherence to the society before the full burden of persecution fell upon it after 1662.

Margaret Fell in her remote home at Swarthmore Hall was the heart of the movement. Her 'general epistles to friends' are written with authority[1]. To her, the travelling preachers reported, and to Swarthmore Hall George Fox returned between journeys or imprisonments. It was Margaret Fell who wrote and signed the appeal to Charles II on behalf of 'the People of God called Quakers' which she delivered to him on 22 June 1660, within a month of his return to England[2]. In the name of all Quakers the appeal was witnessed by the thirteen chief members of the community. In the eleven years between the death of her first husband and her marriage to George Fox in 1669, Margaret Fell was incessantly occupied in the business of the society, visiting meetings in many parts of England, holding meetings at Swarthmore, lying in prison at Lancaster, and, in the months immediately before her marriage, visiting all prisons in which Quakers were held. Persecution tightened and strengthened the Quaker organization. It eliminated weaklings and toughened the strong. The earliest surviving records of Quaker meetings reveal the close-knit organization of a religious society which was already strong enough to insist on a stricter control of marriage than the negative banns of the Church of England. Quakers were not expected to marry outside the society and enquiries were always made as to the suitability of the contracting parties[3].

From the account book kept by Sarah Fell, daughter of Margaret Fell, between 1673 and 1678, a sidelight is thrown both on the Society of Friends and the home life of their founder. The accounts are complicated, for although the Swarthmore estate was still in Margaret Fell's possession each of her three daughters living at home had an individual income. They engaged in various business ventures which are reflected in the accounts, iron smelting, trading by boat with west coast ports as distant as Cornwall[4]. Sarah Fell indicated on whose account the various items of expenditure ought to go[5]. George Fox appears in the account book as 'father'. On 7 December 1677 'father gave Tho: Benson, bayliffe of ye Liberties, for his civillity to mee being A Prisoner, 2s. 6d'[6]. Payments for

---

[1] *A Brief Collection*, pp. 196–201.   [2] Reprinted in *A Brief Collection*, pp. 202–10.
[3] E.g. *Quaker Minutes*, p. 2.   [4] Isobel Ross, *Margaret Fell*, London, 1948, pp. 266–75.
[5] *The Household Account Book of Sarah Fell of Swarthmoor Hall*, ed. Norman Penney, Cambridge, 1920, see p. 281.   [6] *Ibid.*, p. 337.

letters to father frequently occur. On 17 June 1676 'glue and tobacco pipes for father' cost 3 pence[1]. On 25 January 1677 the carrier was paid 2 pence for bringing some writing paper for father from Lancaster[2]. On 11 February 1678 a quarter of a pound of tobacco was bought for $2\frac{1}{2}$d. 'to wash father's horse with, he being troubled with an Itch'[3]. On 22 March 1677 'a pair of Stockens for father' cost 1 shilling and 4 pence[4]. Women's meetings were established by this time and Sarah Fell herself was closely concerned with the organization of those in the neighbourhood of Swarthmore. On 10 May 1674 she records 'Received at weomens Meettinge here being a Collection for ye weomens Stocke 14s. 2d.' 'Received of 5 weomen of our Meeting that were not at weomens Meettinge for said collection 2s. 2d.'[5] On 15 July 1674 she records the expenditure of 5s. 6d. 'by Mother and my selfe when wee went to ye weomens Meettinge at Hugh Tickells'[6].

The Society of Friends had established a system of poor relief long before their founder's death. Money collected by the meetings became a stock from which sums could be dispensed in charity to poor Friends. On 6 February 1677 Jane Cowell was entrusted with 3 shillings 'to bee given to Jane Colton, who is sicke, and at want for supply'[7]. On 4 December 1677 4 shillings of the women's meeting's stock was paid by their order to 'Isabell Strickland of Cartmell meetting, being Sickly'[8]. On 7 January 1674 Sarah noted 'paid of ye weomens Meettinge stocke to ffriends of the Hawxheade Meettinge yt gave it to a woman for lookeinge to Tomasin Sawrey when she was sicke, 3s.', and again, 'paid more of said money, to friends of the Cartmell Meettinge, for some in Necessity at their Meettinge, 2s'[9]. On 8 May 1677 the 2 shillings which Anne Birkett was behind in her house rent were found from the women's meeting stock[10]. As much as 10 shillings was contributed on 6 June 1676 towards buying a cow for Ellin Braithwait of the Cartmell meeting[11]. The women's meeting stock provided 2 shillings on 1 September 1674 towards the 'Necessity of Christofer Harrison of Cartmell Meettinge, hee being poore'[12]. It is possible that the Swarthmore Friends had organized their stock earlier than Friends in other parts. Their women's meeting was in full working some years before the Friends in north-west Lincolnshire

[1] *Household Account Book*, p. 283.
[2] *Ibid.*, p. 349.
[3] *Ibid.*, p. 459.
[4] *Ibid.*, p. 369.
[5] *Ibid.*, p. 68.
[6] *Ibid.*, p. 101.
[7] *Ibid.*, p. 353.
[8] *Ibid.*, p. 439.
[9] *Ibid.*, p. 29.
[10] *Ibid.*, p. 387.
[11] *Ibid.*, p. 281.
[12] *Ibid.*, p. 129.

had succeeded in establishing one. Although the necessity of setting up a women's meeting was discussed there in 1675 and again in 1689 the women's monthly meeting was not set up until 1690[1]. Margaret Fell and her daughters from time to time can be seen contributing small sums to the stock of meetings in other parts[2].

In remembering the achievements of Margaret Fell there is a danger of forgetting that she alone could have secured nothing. George Fox was not only the founder of the society, but its inspirer and leader until he died in 1691. Nor was Margaret Fell the only woman in the Quaker ministry in the early history of the society. Two women, Elizabeth Hooton and Elizabeth Miers, were members of the mission to Barbados in 1671, and Elizabeth Hooton, 'who had travelled much in the truth's service, and suffered much for it', died in Jamaica at a great age[3]. Most of the early converts were humble folk. Their women, though capable of bearing testimony and preaching, had little education. Margaret Fell was not only an able, but a cultivated woman, who could express herself on paper and was not afraid of print. She wrote easily, but her sentences are long and involved. She occasionally hits off a phrase that is memorable— 'Now let any honest hearted People judge, whether these be sound principled men, that can turn, conform, and transform to every change, according to the Times?'[4] In 1666 she wrote a tract to justify the ministry of women entitled *Women's Speaking Justified, Proved, and Allowed of by the Scriptures*, introducing into her title the words: 'how Women were the first that preached the tidings of the Resurrection of Jesus and were sent by Christ's own Command, before he Ascended to the Father, John, 20. 17'[5].

The ministry of women in the Quaker community continued through the many generations during which the ordinary women of other beliefs remained content under male authority. Not until the end of the eighteenth century did another woman appear among the Friends who displayed a power comparable with that of Margaret Fell. But contemporary lives of Quaker women reveal an independence of character which marks them out as strongly as did their way of life. Sarah Stephenson, for

[1] *Quaker Minutes*, pp. xvii, 40–2, 47, 130–3; women Friends were asked to come to the men's meeting, pp. 49, 52, 62.

[2] *Household Account Book*, pp. 237, 285, 349.   [3] *Autobiography*, pp. 284, 293.

[4] Margaret Fell, *A Declaration and an Information from us the People of God called Quakers*, London, 1660, p. 5. Reprinted in *A Brief Collection*, p. 208.

[5] *A Brief Collection*, pp. 331–50.

example (1738–1802), travelled about England, Wales and Ireland, commissioned by her own meeting as a public minister and visitor of the families of Friends[1]. In 1801, when she felt her health to be failing, her yearly meeting authorized her to visit families of Friends in America, where she died in the next year. Her brief notes of her journeys show many obscure women of her community engaged, like herself, in preaching and visiting[2]. In 1794 there appeared the life of another woman who, like Sarah Stephenson, had given herself to the Quaker ministry of women. Sarah Tuke was born at York in 1756, and married an Irish Quaker, Robert Grubb, who had lived there for many years. She died when she was only thirty-four, but she had travelled in her ministry over much of England, and into Scotland, Ireland, and parts of the Continent[3].

But the outstanding woman in the later succession of English Quakers is Elizabeth Fry (1780–1845). She was one of the seven daughters of John Gurney of Earlham, Norfolk, and Gurney's bank in Norwich. Although the Gurneys were a Quaker family Elizabeth and her brothers and sisters enjoyed a gay youth, for their father's position drew him into a wide acquaintance outside the Society of Friends. Elizabeth was stirred to religious zeal by the preaching of an American Quaker, William Savery, who visited Norwich in 1798. The seven Gurney sisters sat in a row under the gallery at the meeting and one of them remembered her amusement at Elizabeth's 'very smart boots'[4]. They were purple laced with scarlet. After this, Elizabeth adopted the dress and speech of Friends. Her marriage at the age of twenty to Joseph Fry brought her into a family which, like her own, had been Quakers from the early days of the society, but the Frys strictly observed Quaker speech and dress and their friends were like-minded with them. Elizabeth Fry and her husband lived in London, and notwithstanding the births of many children she maintained an active interest in work for the poor. In 1810, after long uncertainty, she became a minister among the Friends. Her calling as a minister was formally recognized by the meeting of which she was a member early in the following year. Her eminent contemporary, Mary Somerville, who had heard her preach, wrote 'her voice was fine, her delivery admirable,

---

[1] *Memoirs of the Life and Travels in the service of the Gospel of Sarah Stephenson*, London, 1807.   [2] *Ibid.*, pp. 33, 35, 43.
[3] *Some Account of the Life and Religious Labours of Sarah Grubb*, 2nd ed., London, 1794.
[4] Susanna Corder, *Life of Elizabeth Fry*, London, 1853, p. 19.

and her prayer sublime'[1]. Her life's work lay among the women in English prisons and she took it up when in 1813 she began to visit female prisoners in Newgate.

When Elizabeth Fry first went to Newgate, she was accompanied by a cousin, Anne Buxton, and other Quaker ladies came forward to support and help. Their first visits to Newgate were followed by three years in which Elizabeth Fry could do little outside her home. She herself fell ill; her ninth child was born, and her seventh daughter died. But at the end of 1816 she took up her work again. With the wife of a London clergyman and ten ladies of the Society of Friends she formed 'an association for the improvement of the female prisoners in Newgate'. Its object was 'to provide for the clothing, the instruction, and the employment of the women; to introduce them to a knowledge of the Holy Scriptures, and to form in them as much as possible, those habits of order, sobriety, and industry, which may render them docile, and peaceable whilst in prison, and respectable when they leave it'[2]. Other women than Quakers were moved to share in this work, and its scope became greatly enlarged. But its inspiration and direction came from Elizabeth Fry.

When reflecting on the permanence of the movement in which Margaret Fell was an original leader, it should not be forgotten that the great mass of English women were at no time capable of reaching the heights of religious exaltation. Even amid the austerities of the Puritan revolution the age-long arts of feminine adornment were not forgotten. In 1656 there appeared a curious little book called *A Discourse of Auxiliary Beauty or Artificial Handsomenesse In point of conscience between two Ladies*[3]. The treatise is anonymous, and it has been variously attributed to John Gauden, Bishop of Worcester, to Jeremy Taylor, and to Obadiah Walker. In this uncertainty, there seems no reason to doubt the word of Richard Royston, one of the most respectable publishers of the century, who prefaced the first edition with a letter addressed by 'The Publisher to the Ingenuous Reader'. He was, he said, 'certainly informed' that 'a Woman was not only the chiefe occasion, but the Author and writer'. When the discourse came into his hands he was about to destroy it because he disliked women improving their looks 'beyond that portion which God and Nature had given them', but being secretly ashamed to condemn it unread, he not only read it himself, but tested it by persuading 'two

[1] *Personal Recollections of Mary Somerville*, by her daughter, Martha Somerville, London, 1874, p. 145.   [2] Susanna Corder, *Life*, p. 225.   [3] London, 1656.

or three severe censors' to read it, 'persons of Socratick browes, and Catonian lookes, wholly bred up in Academicall shades, and in no way partiall to the delights of women'. With their opinion behind him he concluded that the book ought to be published for three reasons: firstly, because it is 'a very necessary debate, in a case so much (they say) practised by women of unspotted worth and honour: And yet so much censured as sinful and abominable by others of a very warm and commendable piety': secondly, it was only civil to let ladies know the issue of the debate: and thirdly it might be profitable to the publisher[1].

The book takes the form of thirteen objections to women painting their faces put forward in turn by a lady who is addressed as 'Your Ladyship' and disposed of by a lady who is addressed as 'Madam'. The discourse was probably written some little time before it was printed, for it treats as an authority a divine who was writing in the reign of Charles I. The defender of women who used some form of artificial beauty asked 'Whom did her Ladyship ever blame (if in other things unblameable) for using a Glasse eye? . . . When was your Ladyship scandalized with any grave and sober matron, because she laid out the combings or cuttings of her own or others more youthfull haire, when her own (now more withered and autumnall) seemed lesse becoming her? How many both mens and womens warmer heats in religion, do not now admit not onely borders of forain haire, but full and fair peruques, on their heads, without sindging one haire by their disputative and scrupulous zeal, which in these things of fashion, is now grown much out of fashion. Your Ladyship's charity doth not reprove, but pity those poor Vulcanists, who ballance the inequality of their heels, or badger leggs, by the help of the shoemaker; . . . Who fears to set straight, or hide the unhandsome warpings of bow leggs and baker feet?'[2] After all her arguments had been met, her ladyship thanked her opponent for the generous freedom of her discourse, more particularly since she was not so much pleading her own cause as 'civilly affording a charitable relief and protection to others, whose infirmity may require or use such helps'. The text with which the dialogue is drawn to its conclusion is Tit. i. 15. 'To the pure all things are pure, but to the defiled and unbelievers nothing is pure, but even their mind and conscience is defiled'[3]. It is not surprising that this tract, for all its outmoded language, was reprinted in 1662 and again in 1690.

---

[1] The Publisher to the Reader is unpaged.
[2] *A Discourse of Auxiliary Beauty*, pp. 59–60.   [3] *Ibid.*, pp. 199–200.

CHAPTER VII

The Beginnings of English Feminism

A tradition of the learned lady was carried through the Commonwealth period in England to the Restoration by women of Puritan birth and upbringing. In matters of learning England was not isolated and the most famous woman scholar in Europe, Anna Maria à Schurman, was in correspondence with Englishmen and women of similar tastes to her own. Of German extraction, she had settled in Holland, where she was a zealous member of the reformed Church[1]. In 1645 she wrote to Sir Simonds D'Ewes from Utrecht in reply to a letter from him. She was, she said, 'not a little encouraged' to write to him by his 'most equitable sentence concerning our sexe'. Sir Simonds had desired to meet her because her 'industry in the sublimer studies' had been so highly commended by 'the most learned matron, Madam Bathshua Makin'. Anna Maria asked to be informed about 'what is achieved by your most honourable assembly —that is, the Long Parliament—either in peace or war' and concluded 'Farewell, *Great Patron of learning*, with your most generous Wife, whom I entreat you most humbly to salute in my name'.

This letter was added by Clement Barksdale to his translation of the best known of Anna Maria à Schurman's writings, *The Learned Maid or Whether a Maid may be a Scholar?*' which he published in 1659, with the sub-title, *A logick exercise*[2]. It had first appeared in Latin in 1641. The author concludes that 'maids may and ought to be excited and encouraged by the best and strongest reasons, by the testimonies of wise men: and lastly by the examples of illustrious women, to the embracing of this kind of life, especially those who are above others provided of leisure, and other means and aides for their studies. And because it is best that the

---

[1] Her autobiography, written in Latin, was published at Altona in 1673.
[2] Written in Latin by that incomparable Virgin Anna Maria à Schurman of Utrecht.

mind be seasoned with Learning from Infancy: therefore the Parents themselves are chiefly to be stirred up, as we suppose, and to be admonished of their Duty'[1]. An engraving, purporting to be a picture of the author at the age of fifty-two, forms the frontispiece to the book. Clement Barksdale prefixed to his translation a letter of dedication to 'the honourable lady A. H.' 'This strange maid', he wrote, 'being now for the second time dressed up in her English Habit, cometh to kiss your hand. She hopes you will admit her to your closet, and speak a good word for her to your worthy friends, and endear her to them also. Her company will be the more delightful because her discourse is very rational and much tending to the perfection of that Sexe, whereof you, Excellent Lady, by your Noble Virtues are so great an ornament and Example. The honourer of your Piety, more then of your Fortune. C. B.'[2] It is a pity that the honourable lady A. H. cannot be identified.

Clement Barksdale was a true friend to women's education, who deserves better treatment than history has given him. Anthony Wood described him as 'a writer and translator of several little tracts most of which are mere scribbles'[3]. He was certainly indefatigable in writing, translating, and publishing. He was born in 1609 at Winchcombe and educated at Abingdon Grammar School. At Oxford he was ordained; in 1637 went to Hereford to be master of the free school and a vicar choral. In 1646 he retreated from Hereford before the Parliamentary army to Sudeley Castle, where for a time he acted as chaplain. Then he went to Hawling in the Cotswolds and set up a school. At the Restoration he was presented to the livings of Naunton, near Hawling, and Stow-on-the-Wold. He died in 1687, aged seventy-eight, leaving behind him 'the character of a frequent and edifying preacher and a good neighbour'[4].

It may be supposed that, like Dr. Denton, Barksdale was more of a royalist than a Parliamentarian, but both men were less interested in politics than in following their professions. Barksdale was a schoolmaster who believed in teaching girls properly as well as boys. One of his numerous tracts deals with the possibility of setting up what he described as a college of maids or a virgin-society. He was not alone in feeling that women had lost something by the destruction of the nunnery schools

[1] *The Learned Maid or Whether a Maid may be a Scholar?*, p. 32.
[2] Unpaged, 4A and dorse.
[3] *Athenæ Oxonienses*, ed. P. Bliss, London, 1820, vol. iv, col. 221.
[4] *Ibid.*, col. 227.

PLATE IV

The title-page of Richard Brathwaite's *The English Gentlewoman.*
(See pp. 145–6.)

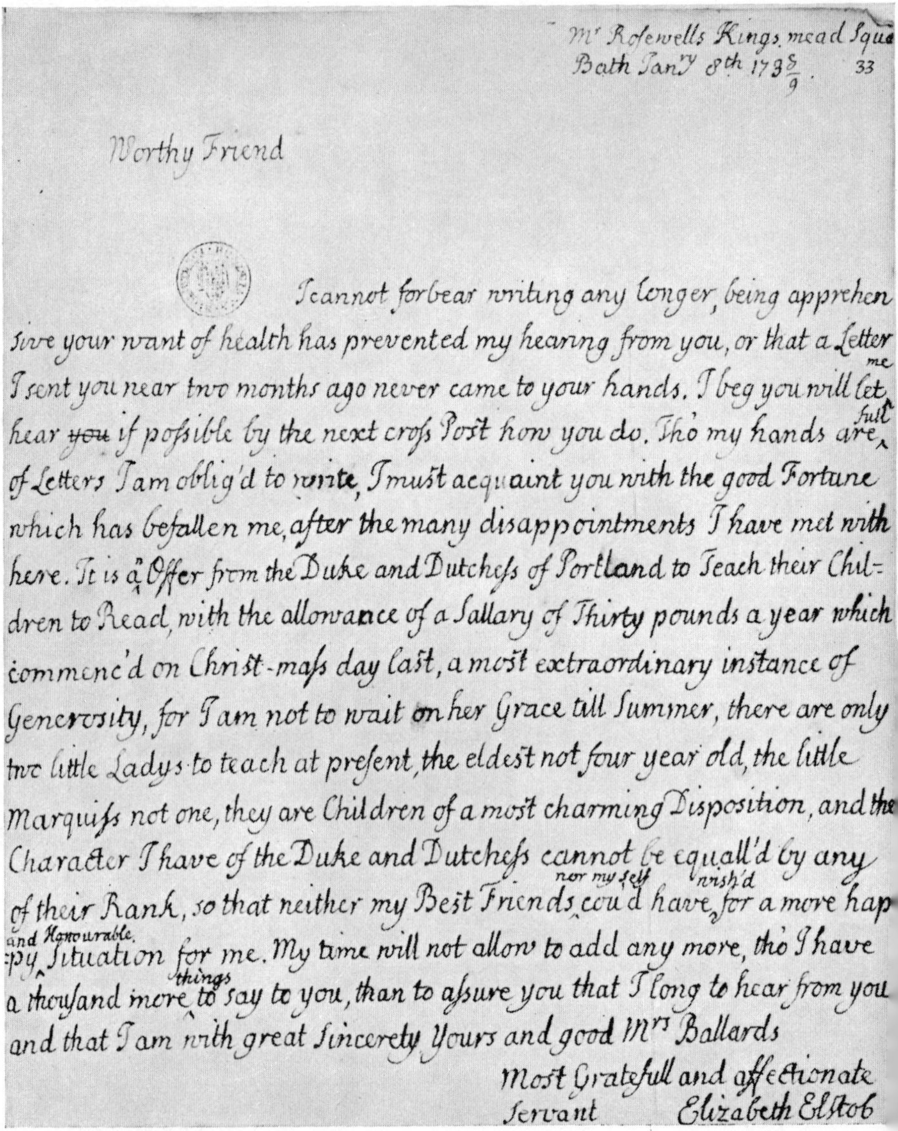

Worthy Friend

I cannot forbear writing any longer, being apprehen
sive your want of health has prevented my hearing from you, or that a Letter
I sent you near two months ago never came to your hands. I beg you will let me
hear you if possible by the next cross Post how you do. Tho' my hands are full
of Letters I am oblig'd to write, I must acquaint you with the good Fortune
which has befallen me, after the many disappointments I have met with
here. It is a Offer from the Duke and Dutchess of Portland to Teach their Children to Read, with the allowance of a Sallary of Thirty pounds a year which
commenc'd on Christ-mass day last, a most extraordinary instance of
Generosity, for I am not to wait on her Grace till Summer, there are only
two little Ladys to teach at present, the eldest not four year old, the little
Marquiss not one, they are Children of a most charming Disposition, and the
Character I have of the Duke and Dutchess cannot be equall'd by any
nor my self   finish'd
of their Rank, so that neither my Best Friends cou'd have, for a more hap
and Honourable.
-py Situation for me. My time will not allow to add any more, tho' I have
things
a thousand more to say to you, than to assure you that I long to hear from you
and that I am with great Sincerety Yours and good Mrs Ballards
Most Gratefull and affectionate
Servant   Elizabeth Elstob

PLATE V

Letter from Elizabeth Elstob to George Ballard.

(See page 242.)

which the seventeenth-century schools had not replaced. The nuns' schools were by no means efficient, but in the retrospect their defects were forgotten and imaginary virtues attributed to them. In later years girls belonging to Roman Catholic families were sometimes sent to France for education, and religious houses for English Catholics were in time established abroad. But for members of the Church of England this was of no help. In the early seventeenth century it had been dangerous to send a girl to a foreign nunnery and in 1612 a Lady Parkins forfeited her estate for doing this[1]. The author of *The Ladies Calling*, published in 1673, went so far as to say 'As for the religious orders of Virgins in the present Roman Church, tho some and those very great abuses have crept in; yet I think 'twere to be wished that those who suppress them in this nation, had confin'd themselves within the bounds of a reformation, by choosing rather to rectify and regulate, then abolish them'[2].

The Ladies Calling is one of a group of devotional works attributed to the author of *The Whole Duty of Man*[3]. With this famous book they set out the orthodox Church of England view and may perhaps be regarded as the Church's answer to the extreme religious reformers of the day. All these books were published anonymously, but their authorship, or at least that of *The Whole Duty*, has been several times claimed for a woman, the royalist Lady Pakington, who died in 1679. She was the daughter of Thomas, Lord Coventry, who became guardian of Sir John Pakington when, at the age of five, he inherited his title and the estate of Westwood, Worcestershire. The year when Sir John married his guardian's daughter is unknown, like the year of her birth. But from 1649 until his death in 1660 the royalist divine, Dr. Hammond, made his home at Westwood with Sir John and Lady Pakington[4]. Eminent royalist clergymen, Dr. Fell and Richard Allestree among them, frequently visited their friend

---

[1] *D.N.B.* under Perkins or Parkins, Sir Christopher, quoting *Cal. State Papers*, 1611–18, p. 107.   [2] Fifth impression, 1677, p. 157.

[3] *The Practice of Christian Graces or the Whole Duty of Man*, for T. Garthwaite, 1659. *The Gentleman's Calling*, for T. Garthwaite, 1660. *The Causes of The Decay of Christian Piety*, 1667. *The Ladies Calling*, Oxford, 1673. *The Government of the Tongue*, Oxford, 1674. *The Art of Contentment*, Oxford, 1677. *The Lively Oracles given to us*, Oxford, 1678. Each of these books is said on the title-page to be '*by the Author of the Whole Duty of Man, etc.*' A paper by Michael Lort on the authorship of *The Whole Duty* and the kindred works is printed in Nichols, *Literary Anecdotes*, vol. ii, pp. 597–604. The many tastefully bound copies of these works in existence, most of them in decorated calf and fully gilt-edged, suggest that they were popular as presents for many years.

[4] John Fell, *The Life of the most Learned, Reverend and Pious Dr. H. Hammond*, 1661, pp. 65 and 163.

Hammond there. Lady Pakington was not only the generous hostess but the understanding friend of these men. She was well educated and could write unusually clear and well-turned prose. She was deeply interested in religion. The first suggestion that she had any part in writing *The Whole Duty of Man* came from Dr. George Hickes, the nonjuror and founder of Anglo-Saxon studies in England. In dedicating his *Thesaurus* to Lady Pakington's grandson he recalled that 'her practical piety, talents, and the excellence of her composition entitles her to be called and esteemed the author of the Whole Duty'[1]. Richard Allestree, who at the Restoration became a canon of Christchurch, Oxford, in 1663 Regius Professor of Divinity, and in 1665 Provost of Eton, is now generally regarded as the author, perhaps in association with Dr. Fell, of all seven books in question. But the evidence which Hickes acquired, as he himself records, from divines who were friends of Hammond and Lady Pakington, is enough to suggest that she not only gave shelter to the author, but discussed the work with him and helped to refashion his sentences into a smoother style.

Clement Barksdale cast his tract about a women's college into the form of a letter dated 12 August 1675 and beginning 'Noble Sir, You may expect I should give you some account of our design mentioned yesterday at our Venison (where we had half a dozen fair young ladies, rich and virtuous) concerning the Colledge of Maids, or the Virgin-Society'[2]. The end of the plan was, he explained, 'to improve ingenuous Maids in such qualities as best become their Sex, and may fit them both for a happy life in this and much more in the next world'. 'The meanes' to secure this was by separating them from 'the contagion of common Conversation' in a convenient house where they could find employment and exercise, and live and eat together, 'somewhat like the Halls of Commoners at Oxford'. On entering the society each should put caution money into the hands of the Steward, 'an aged, grave Gentleman, of known integrity', five pounds or more or less according to her quality. In the common dining-room those of higher quality should sit at the higher table, presided over by the chief governess and those of lower at the lower table presided over by the pro-governess. Maids of meaner birth and estate whose friends cannot at all or cannot fully maintain them

---

[1] *D.N.B.* The translation of Hickes's difficult Latin given by W. D. Macray.

[2] *A Letter concerning a Colledge of Maids, or a Virgin-Society*, written 12 August 1675. The letter is printed on a single folded sheet and is signed B. C.

shall wait upon the two tables. An 'ancient Divine, of competent Gravity and learning, should be appointed by the Lord Bishop of the Diocese' 'to attend at the Chappel or Dining-room once or twice a day for prayers; and he also preacheth once or twice a week'. The two governesses, chosen yearly, would 'appoint the ladies a method of private reading and Devotion'. The virgins' fathers, or two among them, were to be visitors. They could 'when they please, take their daughters home for a few days; and dispose of them in marriage when they please, taking a fair farewell of the Society'. The ladies would learn the use and virtue of the herbs in the 'fair garden'.

This letter sets out the first considered plan for a women's college on the lines of those to which their brothers went. It is possible that in putting forward this design Clement Barksdale was remembering how Lady Falkland had wished to establish such colleges in various parts of England[1]. His inclusion of an account of Lady Falkland, the only woman thus honoured, in his *Memorials of Worthy Persons* is significant[2]. In drawing up the plans for the college Clement Barksdale considered also the work to be done in it. The students' library, kept in the dining-room, was to contain 'authors of History, Poetry, and especially Practical Divinity and Devotion: Not only English, but of learned and Modern languages, Wherein divers of the Society are skilled and willing to teach the rest, as many as are inclined and apt to learn'. There will also be among them those who can teach 'music and dancing (besides needlework and drawing), so far as, at least (which is enough) as concerneth decent motion and gesture of body, and may serve for recreation or for the service of God, I mean music of voice or instrument'. 'Some of them', he continues, 'are capable and well-affected to studies of Philosophy, especially Natural and Moral; and are delighted with making some of the easier experiments in natural things'. The 'chambers and liberty of going abroad' can be regulated by their parents and their governesses. Their apparel should

---

[1] See above, p. 140. In 1638 Drunken Barnaby described (1822 ed., p. 95) Little Gidding as a 'new founded college' and when John Evelyn read Mary Astell's *Proposal* (see below, p. 225) he remembered how under Mrs. Ferrer a household devoted to religion had lived at Little Gidding. But members of the Ferrer household were bound by no vows. In his visitation Bishop Williams of Lincoln refused to allow two of the daughters to take vows of chastity. (John Hackett, *Scrinia Reserata*, London, 1693, Part II, pp. 50-2.) Several of the girls brought up at Little Gidding married. Something of the way of life there can be discerned from *The Story Books of Little Gidding*, London, 1899.

[2] *Memorials of Worthy Persons*, London, 1661, pp. 201-4.

be modest and suitable, 'a loose gown girt about them and a large Hood, the gentlewomen wear silk of some sad colour, their maids fine serge. But when with their friends they go in any becoming habit, not showing any part naked, except their face and hands'. Finally they should go to their parish church on holy days. Barksdale added a postscript about a house which had evidently been considered as suitable for the venture, saying that it would contain twenty gentlewomen and their ten maids, two for the kitchen, two for the buttery and six for the dining-room. 'The Persons', he thought, 'may be found within seven miles compass'.

Nothing came of this suggestion, the day-dream of a happy company of friends, but Clement Barksdale felt strongly enough about it to put his letter into print and circulate it. The idea of a college for girls was mooted again nine years later. In his sermon upon almsgiving preached on Easter Tuesday, 1 April 1684, before the Lord Mayor and aldermen of London, Dr. George Hickes, then Dean of Worcester, suggested various suitable objects of charity to the congregation. Among them he suggested the 'building of schools or colleges for the Education of young Women, much like unto those in the universities for the Education of Young Men, but with some Alteration in the Discipline Oeconomy, as the nature of such an Institution would require'. He argued that not only would daughters be safer in such colleges than in private schools but they would be bred up in the religion now established in the land. Women were, he thought, in danger of being led into enthusiasm and schism 'for want of Ingenious and Orthodox Education, and not for want of Parts'[1]. There are many indications that in the 'seventies and 'eighties of the seventeenth century much thought was put into the problems of educating girls. The author of *The Ladies Calling*, whose third paragraph of his section 'Of Virgins' Clement Barksdale quoted at the end of his *Letter*, was more concerned with manners, morals, and general behaviour than the subjects which girls should study. But he fully realized that the folly of many girls and women was the result of bad upbringing.

Between 1670 and 1675 two professional teachers, Mrs. Hannah Woolley and Mrs. Bathshua Makin, separately published their views on the education and upbringing of women. All that is known of Hannah Woolley's family and youth is what she tells in one or other of her own books. Thrown on the world at fourteen, she was the sole mistress of a

[1] *A Collection of Sermons, formerly preached by the Reverend George Hickes*, D.D., London, 1713, vol. i, pp. 397–8.

little school by the time she was fifteen. She owed her advancement in life to a lady who employed her to teach her daughter[1]. From her mother and elder sisters Hannah Woolley had learned something of the art of healing[2]. She could even treat wounds 'not desperately dangerous'[3]. Since she was born in 1623 she may well have found her skill useful in the civil war. From her first employer she learned much about the management of a great house and the way to behave at court. After this lady died, Hannah entered the service of another as governess, rising during the next seven years to be her mistress's 'Stewardess, and her Scribe and Secretary'. Hannah continued her education, reading all the collections of published letters which she was able to consult[4]. In the supplement to her book *The Queen-like Closet*, published in 1675, she printed examples of bad and good letter-writing as a guide to her readers, saying that she did so because 'in writing most Women are to seek'[5]. Hannah Woolley improved her knowledge of 'Physick and Chyrurgery' both by practice as her mistress's almoner, and by reading and instruction. When she was twenty-four she married Mr. Woolley, the master of the free school at Newport, Essex. She had four sons of her own and a large number of boarders both at Newport and afterwards at Hackney, the fashionable suburb for schools[6].

Hannah Woolley's first cookery book was published in 1661, perhaps in the hope of making money to maintain her family after her husband's death. She married again in 1666, but again was widowed[7]. By 1674, when the second edition of *The Queen-like Closet* was issued, she was living 'at Mr. Richard Wolley's house in the Old Bailey in Golden Cup Court'. He was probably her son. 'He is', wrote Hannah Woolley proudly, 'Master of Arts, and Reader at St. Martin's Ludgate'. There she sold remedies 'at reasonable Rates'. She was prepared to train gentle-women who wished to enter service and to recommend them to her friends[8]. Her best known book is *The Gentlewoman's Companion*, published in 1675 with a preface signed by Hannah Woolley and dated 1672. Her publisher kept the copy by him and at last issued it with some

---

[1] Hannah Woolley, *The Gentlewoman's Companion*, London, 1675, p. 11.

[2] Hannah Woolley, *The Queen-like Closet*, London, 1675, Supplement, p. 10. This book was first published in 1670 by Richard Lowndes, Ada Wallas, *Before the Bluestockings*, p. 31.   [3] *The Gentlewoman's Companion*, p. 10.   [4] *Ibid.*, p. 11 ff.

[5] *The Queen-like Closet*, Supplement, p. 148.   [6] *Ibid.*, pp. 11–15.

[7] Ada Wallas, *Before the Bluestockings*, pp. 28 and 29.

[8] *The Queen-like Closet*, Advertisement to Supplement (1675), unpaged.

additions by another hand. Hannah Woolley therefore produced an enlarged edition of *The Queen-like Closet*, first published in 1670[1]. Both books were popular and ran through many editions. There was nothing of the scholar about Hannah Woolley. She was a practical woman, who always supported herself by hard work. It had taught her to admire learning and to resent the limitations of every woman's life.

'The right education of the female sex', she wrote in the Introduction to *The Gentlewoman's Companion*, 'as it is in a manner everywhere neglected, so it ought to be generally lamented. Most in this depraved later Age think a woman learned enough if she can distinguish her Husband's bed from anothers. Certainly Mans soul cannot boast of a more sublime original than ours; they had equally their effulux from the same eternal immensity, and are therefore capable of the same improvement by good Education. Vain man is apt to think we were meerly intended for the world's propagation and to keep its inhabitants sweet and clean; but by their leaves had we the same Literature, he would find our brains as fruitful as our bodies. Hence I am induced to believe that we are debarred from the knowledge of humane learning lest our pregnant wits should rival the touring conceit of our insulting Lords and Masters.

'Pardon the severity of this expression since I intend not thereby to infuse the spirit of Rebellion into the sweet blood of females; for know I would all such as are entered into the honourable estate of matrimony to be loyal and loving Subjects to their lawful (though lording) Husbands. I cannot but complain of, and must condemn the great negligence of Parents, in letting the fertile ground of their daughters lie fallow, yet send the barren Noddles of their sons to the University, where they stay for no purpose than to fill their empty sconces with idle notions'[2].

Hannah Woolley's experience as a writer of cookery books and guides to housekeeping had taught her that more attention is paid to an exaggerated advertisement than to a sober statement. She felt bitter about the casual way girls were educated and envious for them of their brothers' chances at the universities. She had sensible views about the qualities which should be looked for in a governess. 'Those who undertake the difficult employ of being an instructress of children should be persons of no mean birth and breeding, civil in deportment, and of an extraordinary winning and pleasing conversation'[3]. When she discussed the

---

[1] *The Queen-like Closet*, Supplement, pp. 131–3.
[2] *The Gentlewoman's Companion*, 1675, pp. 1–2.   [3] *Ibid.*, p. 4.

qualities which become a gentlewoman she again reverted to the relation between the sexes saying 'I have already endeavoured to prove that though Nature hath differed mankind into sexes, yet she never intended any great difference in the intellect'[1]. In proof of this statement she cited the treatise in vindication of the female sex by Cornelius Agrippa[2], and 'the many learned and incomparable Writings of Famous Women' such as Anna Comnena and Anna Maria à Schurman[3]. That Hannah Woolley was serious in her advice to young girls to become scholars is shown by her recommendation of Latin as a subject for their serious study. 'Apply yourselves to your Grammar by time', she says, 'and let your endeavours be indefatigable, and not to be tired in apprehending the first principles of the Latin tongue. Your understanding of the Latin tongue will enable you to write and speak true and good English, next it will accommodate you with an eloquent style in speaking, and afford you matter for any discourse'. French and Italian should also be learned 'by reason of our Gentries travelling into foreign parts occasioned by our late unhappy and inhumane home-bred distractions'[4].

Bathshua Makin's *An Essay to revive the Ancient Education of Gentle-women in Religion, Manners, Arts, and Tongues* was published in 1673 and, as well as a treatise on education, it was a prospectus of Mrs. Makin's own school where this education could be acquired at reasonable charges[5]. Here again the author's wares were cried up and shown to more advantage by stressing the evils of the time. In her dedication addressed 'To all ingenious and virtuous ladies and especially to her highness the Lady Mary, eldest daughter to his royal highness the Duke of York'—the future Queen Mary II—Mrs. Makin said 'The barbarous custom to breed Women low is grown general amongst us, and hath prevailed so far, that it is verily believed (especially amongst a sort of debauched Sots) that Women are not endoued with such Reason as Men; nor capable of improvement by Education, as they are. It is lookt upon as a monstrous thing, to pretend the contrary. A learned Woman is thought to be a Comet, that bodes Mischief, whenever it appears. To offer to the World the liberal Education for Women is to deface the Image of God in Man, it will make Women so high, and men so low, like Fire in the House-top it will set the whole world in a Flame'[6]. The tract is prefaced by

---

[1] *The Gentlewoman's Companion*, p. 29.   [2] See above, p. 128.
[3] *The Gentlewoman's Companion*, p. 29.   [4] *Ibid.*, pp. 30–2.
[5] London. The prospectus is headed 'Postscript', pp. 42–3.   [6] *Essay*, p. 3.

two letters, one purporting to come from a supporter and the other from an opposer of the proposals set out by Mrs. Makin. The man who opposes female education states roundly 'Women do not much desire Knowledge; they are of low parts, soft fickle natures, they have other things to do they will not mind if they be once Bookish; The end of learning is to fit one for publick Employment, which Women are not capable of. Women must not speak in the Church, its against custom. Solomon's good House-wife is not commended for Arts and Tongues, but for looking after her Servants; And that which is worst of all, they are of such ill natures, they will abuse their Education, and be so intolerably Proud, there will be no living with them: If all these things can be answered, they would not have leisure'[1].

The treatise took up and answered, point by point, all the objections contained in this letter. Mrs. Makin pointed out that women have in the past been educated in the Arts and Tongues and been eminent in those studies. Like all who wrote of education in the sixteenth century she went to the classical period for examples, but Lady Jane Grey could not be overlooked. Also the 'present Duchess of New-Castle, by her own Genius, rather than any timely Instruction, over-tops many grave Gown-men'. She went on to quote her own pupil, the Princess Elizabeth, daughter of Charles I, 'who at nine years old could write, read, and in some measure understand, Latin, Greek, Hebrew, French, and Italian. Had she lived, what a miracle would She have been of her Sex!' She cited also Mrs. Thorold, daughter of Lady Carr in Lincolnshire, Lady Mildmay, and Dr. Love's daughters, all of whom were, presumably, her pupils also[2]. Queen Elizabeth was, of course, mentioned as pre-eminent in languages and oratory. Women who have understood Logic, have been profound philosophers, mathematicians, and poets are named to confound her opponent. Finally in a postscript enquirers are informed that this education can be acquired at 'a school lately opened at Tottenham-high-Cross within four miles of London, in the road to Ware, where Mrs. Makin is Governess, who was sometimes Tutoress to Princess Elizabeth, Daughter to King Charles the First'. The fees were £20 per annum, but if 'a competent improvement be made in the Tongues, and other things aforementioned . . . something more will be expected'. Further 'information could be obtained every Tuesday at Mr. Mason's Coffee-House in Cornhil, near the Royal Exchange; and on Thursdayes at the Bolt and Tun

---

[1] *Essay*, p. 6.   [2] *Ibid.*, p. 10.

in Fleetstreet, between the hours of three and six in the Afternoon, by some person whom Mris. Makin shall appoint'[1].

Bathshua Makin was a more fashionable teacher than Hannah Woolley. As the woman chosen to teach the king's daughter her position in the world was secure. Her father had been the rector of Southwick, Sussex, and her brother was Dr. John Pell, an eminent mathematician. Her friendship with Anna Maria à Schurman and with Sir Simonds D'Ewes indicates, as does her name, that she leaned to the Puritan side of religion. She claimed to have taught Lucy, Countess of Huntingdon[2], who must have been of about the same age as Bathshua herself. Probably they read classical authors together when Bathshua Makin was governess to the countess's daughter, Lady Elizabeth Hastings, who married Sir James Langham of Cottesbrook, Northamptonshire, and died in 1664, little more than a year after her marriage. Her funeral sermon, preached by Simon Ford of Northampton, was printed in the next year together with a number of poems written in her honour[3]. Among the poems is one by Bathshua Makin, who in it mentions how the Lady Elizabeth

'in Latine, French, Italian, happilie
Advanced in with pleasure'[4].

One story told by the preacher suggests that learning had not always come easily to the Lady Elizabeth. 'She was known once in her younger years to address herself to her Governess with tears, intreating her pardon for that in her very child-hood she was conscious that she had been defective in affection to her, for she thought, that she did not love her'[5].

Both Hannah Woolley and Bathshua Makin were trying to make a living in a hard world. Each was advertising her wares with all the eloquence at her command. It would be grossly unfair to their contemporaries to take their strictures on the education of women at their face value. Yet this has often been done. The implication that the heads of sons were 'barren noddles' while the brains of daughters were sharper than swords was as far from the truth as the suggestion that there was no desire to educate daughters. The fact that these women of the middle class were making a living by writing and teaching indicates that the education of daughters has become a matter of general concern. The

---

[1] *Essay*, pp. 42–3.   [2] *Ibid.*, p. 10.
[3] Simon Ford, *A Christian's Acquiescence in all the Products of Divine Providence*, London, 1665.   [4] *Ibid.*, pp. 162–3.   [5] *Ibid.*, p. 111.

question that troubled many minds was not how much education women should be given but what schools or tutors were available.

It should not be forgotten that one woman who survived through nineteen years of Charles II's reign was respected for her intellectual power by the leading Cambridge philosopher of the day, the learned Dr. Henry More. Anne Finch, later Viscountess Conway, was the sister of one of More's Cambridge pupils, John Finch. Their father, Sir Heneage Finch, recorder of London and Speaker of the House of Commons, died in 1631. Richard Ward, a younger contemporary of Henry More, wrote an account of his life and in it described Lady Conway as his 'Heroine pupil' of 'Incomparable Parts and Endowments.[1] Between 'this *Excellent* Person and the *Doctor* there was', writes Ward, 'from first to last a very High Friendship. . . . And I have heard him say: That he scarce ever met with any Person, Man or Woman, of better Natural Parts than the Lady Conway'[2]. Nearly every summer for many years More stayed with Lady Conway at Ragley Castle, in Warwickshire. Ward records that 'some of his learned Treatises are expressly owing to her own Desire or Instigation' and that 'we have peculiar obligations to Ragley, and its Woods, as the place of his composing divers of them'[3]. Lady Conway was tormented by headaches, which even the most rigorous remedies did nothing to alleviate, but 'notwithstanding these great Impediments, and hard Batterie laid against her intellectuals, her Understanding continued quick and sound, and had the greatest facility imaginable for any, either Physical, Metaphysical, or Mathematical Speculations'. She had learned Latin and read in that language the ancient philosophers. When a proposal to print 'some remains of this Excellent Lady' was made More wrote a Preface for them in which he described them as 'Writings abruptly and scatterdly, I may say also obscurely, written in a Paper-Book, with a Black-lead Pen, towards the latter end of her long and tedious Pain and Sickness; which She never had opportunity to revise correct or perfect. But so sincere and Pious a Spirit breathing in them it was thought fit by some to make them public'[4]. The relationship between Lady Conway and Henry More is a classic example of platonic friendship[5]. For nearly thirty years they

[1] Richard Ward, *The Life of the Learned and Pious Dr. Henry More*, London, 1710, p. 192.
[2] *Ibid.*, p. 193.   [3] *Ibid.*, p. 202.   [4] *Ibid.*, p. 203–5.
[5] Many of the letters which passed between them were edited by M. H. Nicolson, *Conway Letters*, London, 1930. Ward, *op. cit.*, in 1710 was in possession of some of Lady Conway's letters to More and printed part of one of them in his book, pp. 289–90.

kept up a close correspondence, only failing when More was spending the summer months at Ragley. They wrote to each other as friends together engaged in the endless search for truth[1].

In another social sphere and a different mental environment an unregarded contemporary of Lady Conway was giving perhaps a more effective proof of the education available to women in her day. In 1672 there appeared an account of the life of Joseph Alleine who had been an assistant to the incumbent of Taunton, Mr. Newton, and with him was ejected in 1662. The book was 'drawn up by several of his most worthy and judicious friends', each chapter being the work of a different hand[2]. His widow, Theodosia Alleine, wrote the account of the last years of his life, from his ejection in 1662 to his death in 1668 at the early age of thirty-four. She added also something of their life together and her husband's devoted work at Taunton[3]. For a woman to share in such a publication was unheard of. Hence the publisher inserted a note at the end of the table of contents desiring the reader to take notice that Mrs. Theodosia Alleine sent her account to the editor 'to be published in his own Stile, she not imagining that it should be put forth in her own words. But that worthy Person, and divers others, upon perusal, saw no reason to alter it, but caused it to be printed as it is'. The Puritan tendency to encourage women to use their intellects which was strong in the sixteenth century had not weakened in the generations between the Reformation and the Restoration.

Theodosia Alleine was the daughter of Richard Alleine, rector of Batcombe, Somerset, who, like his son-in-law, was ejected in 1662. Joseph and Theodosia Alleine were married young, for he was only twenty-one. They had intended 'to have lived much longer single', but Mr. Newton, whose curate Joseph Alleine was at Taunton, 'seeing him restless in his Spirit and putting himself to many tedious Journeys to visit me, (as he did once a Fortnight 25 miles) he persuaded him to marry'. She describes how they lived for nearly two years with Mr. Newton. Then 'hoping to be more useful in our Station we took a house, and I having been always bred to work, undertook to teach a School, and

---

[1] It is a striking testimony to the quality of thought which shaped the beliefs of the early Quakers that Lady Conway, despite the protests of Henry More, joined the society and adhered to it until her death in 1679, Ward, pp. 195 ff.

[2] *The Life and Death of that most excellent minister of Christ Mr. Joseph Alleine, Late Teacher of the Church of Taunton in Somerset shire; Assistant to Mr. Newton.* London, 1672, p. 25.

[3] *Ibid.*, pp. 62–70 and 79–100.

had many Tablers' (i.e. boarders) 'and Scholars, our Family being seldom less than Twenty, and many times Thirty; my School generally [had] fifty or sixty of the Town and other places'[1]. Theodosia Alleine's account of her husband's ministry at Taunton and the day-by-day story of his last years is moving in its simplicity and candour. She was still a young woman when Joseph Alleine died, but of her life after his death she says nothing.

The new interest in educating women and the occasional appearance of a woman who could write something more than a good letter serves but to throw into sharper relief the greedy and lascivious society of which the Restoration court was the centre. No statesman could expect to keep office if he ignored the reigning mistress of the king. No great lady could refuse to meet and entertain her. Royal mistresses were flattered and royal bastards considered eligible to marry into the best families in the land. John Evelyn was distressed to see the only daughter and heiress of the first Earl of Arlington married at the age of twelve to the Duke of Grafton, then sixteen, although he was 'exceeding handsome, by far surpassing any of the King's other naturall Issue'. All the bride's mother could reply when Evelyn said that he could not wish her joy of the marriage was 'the King would have it so, & there was no going back'[2].

Though every man of position expected his own wife to be chaste, he had no scruples about taking mistresses himself. One of the most handsome men about the court was Henry Sidney, the best-loved brother of Dorothy, Countess of Sunderland. He was one of the seven men who invited William, Prince of Orange, to England in 1688, and was rewarded with the Earldom of Romney. He never married, but lived for many years with a mistress, Grace Worthley, some of whose pathetic letters to him have survived. His reduction of her allowance from £80 to £50 a year made her appeal to Charles II for help in 1682, telling him that she had become acquainted with Mr. Sidney after her husband had been killed in the Dutch war in the pestilence year. Grace Worthley came of a good Cheshire family and in 1694 wrote to Sidney 'How I wish I were to accompany King William in his progress into Cheshire that I might once before I die make a visit to the good old wooden house at Stoak, within three miles of Nantwich, where I was born and bred'[3].

[1] The Life and Death of that most excellent minister of Christ Mr. Joseph Alleine, Late Teacher of the Church of Taunton in Somersetshire; assistant to Mr. Newton, p. 95.

[2] The Diary of John Evelyn, ed. E. G. de Beer, Oxford, 1955, vol. iv, pp. 184–5.

[3] Diary of the Times of Charles II, ed. R. W. Blencowe, London, 1843, vol. i, p. xxxii.

The notorious immorality of courtiers and the irresponsible pens of some contemporary literary men have perhaps made people too ready to assume that women were little better than their husbands. It has, for example, often been implied that Anne, Countess of Sunderland, was Sidney's mistress, but her letters to him give no colour to this tale. The Earl of Sunderland was Sidney's nephew and close friend. There was only a year between their ages. Lady Sunderland was a lively woman, keenly interested in the uneasy politics of the day. Her letters to Sidney are affectionate, but there is no hint of any warmer feeling than that which a close kinsman and friend might expect. She constantly refers to her 'Lord', who sends political news to Sidney by his wife's pen. Princess Anne disliked both Lord and Lady Sunderland: 'Sure there was never a couple so well matched as she and her good husband, for as she is throughout in all her actions the greatest jade that ever was, so he is the subtillest workinest villain that is on the face of the earth'[1]. John Evelyn was another of Lady Sunderland's correspondents, but no one has ever suggested that they were more than friends.

By long tradition the chastity of maids of honour, who often entered the queen's service as children, was protected. Queen Elizabeth had imprisoned Sir Walter Raleigh for his intrigue with Elizabeth Throckmorton, a maid of honour, who subsequently became his wife[2]. Evelyn's affection for the maid of honour, Margaret Blagge, later Mrs. Godolphin, moved him to write an account of her life. She had entered the household of the Duchess of York when she had 'scarcely yet attained the twelfth year of her age'[3]. Her father had been a royalist colonel and her mother 'a woeman soe eminent in all the vertues and perfections of her sex, that it were hard to say whether were superior her Beauty, Witt, or

---

[1] *Diary of the Times of Charles II*, vol. ii, p. 265.

[2] Edmund Lodge, *Illustrations of British History*, vol. iii, p. 67.

[3] *The Life of Mrs. Godolphin by John Evelyn of Wootton, Eng.*, ed. Samuel Wilberforce, Bishop of Oxford, London, 1848, p. 9. Too much stress has been laid by Mr. Hiscock (*John Evelyn and Mrs. Godolphin*, 1951, and *John Evelyn and his Family Circle*, 1955) on his own highly imaginative interpretation of Evelyn's relations with Margaret Blagge, derived from reading their correspondence and Evelyn's religious writings. It would have been extremely unlikely and, indeed, unnatural, that some carnal love for a charming and devout young woman should not have arisen in the middle-aged Evelyn's heart. That he tried to sublimate it is to his credit. That Margaret Blagge should have become restive under it is natural. It seems to this reader of Mr. Hiscock's pages that neither party was left with anything to be ashamed of. It is greatly to be hoped that Mr. Hiscock will print in full the important material which he has exploited.

Piety'[1]. She was left in difficult circumstances but lived to provide 'an honourable competency' for her three daughters. All three became maids of honour to the Duchess of York. The eldest, Henrietta Maria, married Sir Thomas Yarburgh of Snaith Hall, Yorkshire, and their daughter became a maid of honour to Queen Catherine of Braganza and Queen Mary. The second of the three sisters, Mary, was still unmarried in 1678[2]. Margaret, the youngest, was born in 1652. As a child of six she was sent to France and put into the charge of the Countess of Guilford, groom of the stole to the queen mother. Lady Guilford tried hard to persuade the child to become a Papist, but without success. She did not stay long in France, but returned to her mother with whom she lived until she became a maid of honour. She attended the death-bed of the Duchess of York and passed into the service of the queen. John Evelyn owed his introduction to Margaret Blagge to Anne Howard, one of the two daughters of the second Earl of Berkshire, who were also maids of honour. To Anne Howard, who became Lady Sylvius, Evelyn addressed his account of their friend. It is worth remembering that Anne's sister Dorothy, who married Colonel John Grahme of Levens, Westmorland, was one of the ladies whose virtues are commemorated by Dr. George Hickes in the preface to his Thesaurus[3]. Although he already knew the two Howard sisters Evelyn was still slow to believe that young women at court could preserve their innocence, virtue and love of religion. He expected to find Margaret Blagge 'some airy thing that had more Witt than Discretion'[4]. He 'was not a little pleased' to find 'that soe young, soe elegant, soe charming a Witt and Beauty should preserve soe much Virtue in a place where it neither naturally grew nor much was cultivated'[5].

The friendship between Evelyn and Margaret Blagge became so close that he looked upon her as a daughter and she confided in him all her difficulties[6]. She had early fallen in love with Sidney Godolphin, later Lord Godolphin and a Whig politician. There were difficulties in the way of their marriage. She wanted to serve God in a life of retirement and found 'in him none of that tormenting passion to which I need sacrifice myself'. He was perpetually engaged in business and had to 'follow the court and live always in the world'[7]. She determined to leave the court and live with

---

[1] Mrs. Godolphin, p. 6.

[2] C. B. Robinson, History of the Priory and Peculiar of Snaith, London, 1861, pp. 69–70. The author records that when he wrote 'My Lady Yarburgh's Book of Meditations, made by herself when she lived at Snaith Hall' still survived.   [3] See below, p. 235.

[4] Mrs. Godolphin, p. 29.   [5] Ibid., p. 32.   [6] Ibid., p. 42.   [7] Ibid., p. 53.

Lady Berkeley. Evelyn was at court when she asked permission from the king and queen to go. She took leave in seemly fashion of the mother of the maids, but she wept on parting with Dorothy Howard, and left to the Howard sisters 'her pretty Oratorye, soe often consecrated with her prayers and devotions'[1]. For a time Margaret Blagge even thought of leaving the world of fashion and retiring to Hereford to live under the direction of her 'spiritual father', the dean. But she was still sufficiently worldly to be anxious to secure her maid of honour's marriage portion and in 1674 she returned to court to take part in a play in which the princesses, Mary and Anne, and Sarah Jennings, later Duchess of Marlborough, took part. Margaret was Diana, the goddess of chastity, and is said to have worn jewels worth twenty thousand pounds[2]. The marriage of Margaret Blagge and Sidney Godolphin at last took place privately on 16 May 1675. She did not tell Evelyn about it for some time, although she had previously promised him that he should give her away. He had forgiven her long before she died on 9 September 1678 after giving birth to a son six days before. Evelyn wrote of her as a saint and her husband, who lived until 1712, did not take a second wife.

John Evelyn dedicated his treatise on medals to Margaret Godolphin's only son, Francis. A chapter in this book deals with the possibility of striking medals bearing the heads of men who deserve to be remembered. But Evelyn also considered the possibility of commemorating 'some instances of the Learned, Virtuous and Fair Sex'. He listed the women whom he thought worthy of the honour, beginning by saying 'How should one sufficiently value a Medal of the Famous Heroina Boadicia Queen of the Iceni! The British Lady Cardelia; the Chast Queen Emma, Elfreda, Abbess Hilda were it possible to meet with them, or at least their true Pourtraits, with that of Julian Barnes who wrote a Poem on Hunting'. His list differs little from that which lies behind this book[3]. When he drew nearer his own time he mentioned the names of

---

[1] *Mrs. Godolphin*, p. 60.   [2] *Ibid.*, p. 97.

[3] Evelyn included among his learned ladies 'Mrs. Weston, who besides other things, writ a Latin poem in praise of Typography', p. 264. She was Elizabeth Jane Weston (1582–1612), who came of a Surrey family and was herself born in London. Her parents had settled in Bohemia some years before her father's death in 1597, so that it is not clear whether Elizabeth acquired her learning in England or Bohemia. She corresponded with scholars and wrote verses in Latin, which were collected and published at his own expense by a Silesian nobleman at Frankfurt in 1602. She married in Prague and bore four sons, who predeceased her, and three daughters. *D.N.B.*

Margaret, Duchess of Newcastle, famous for her learning and her love
of learning, 'Mrs. Philips, and our Sappho Mrs. Behn; Mrs. Makins,
the Learned Sister of the Learned Dr. Pell'[1]. The success of Aphra Behn,
who earned her living by writing plays and novels, is a sign of the increasing opportunities opening for women. Her tomb lies in Westminster
Abbey, but she remains a romantic and elusive creature. The authority
for the main facts of her life is 'The Life and Memoirs of Mrs. Behn,
Written by one of the Fair Sex' and prefixed to the collected edition of
her novels, first published in 1698[2]. Fortunately this lady's statement
that Aphra was the daughter of a man called Johnson is born out by an
entry in the parish register of Wye, Kent, which records the birth in
1640 of Ayfara to John and Amy Johnson. Her father obtained an appointment in the West Indies, at Surinam, then in English hands, and left
England with his family when Aphra was still a child. She could already
write 'the prettiest soft engaging Verses in the World'[3]. Her father died
before the party reached 'that land flowing with milk and honey, that
Paradise'[4], but her stay there gave Aphra material for her novel *Oroonoko
or The Royal Slave*. The author of her memoirs wrote in a high-flown
style which gives a sense of unreality to her story. She included a number
of letters, mostly love-letters, written to, or by Aphra, who signed them,
in the fashion of the day, with a poetical name, Astrea, and concealed her
lover's identity under the name Lycidas'[5]. Her biographer's reference to
the 'unjust aspersions' which were circulating about the relations between
Astrea and the Prince Oroonoko illustrates the intellectual level of the
first generation of English novel-readers. The writer assured 'the World
that there was no affair between the Prince and Astrea'. 'I knew her
intimately well, and I believe that she would not have concealed any
Love-Affair from me, being one of her own Sex, whose Friendship and
Secrecy she had experienced'[6].

In 1658 Surinam was handed to the Dutch and Aphra returned home.
She 'gave King Charles II so pleasant and rational an Account of his
Affairs there, and particularly of the misfortunes of Oroonoko, that he
desired her to deliver them publicly to the world'[7]. After she had married
Mr. Behn, a city merchant of Dutch extraction, her biographer says that
the king 'committed to her Secrecy and Conduct, Affairs of the highest

[1] J. Evelyn, *Numismata. A discourse of Medals*, London, 1697, pp. 264–5.
[2] The copy which I possess is the 6th ed., 1718.   [3] *Ibid.*, p. 2.
[4] *Loc. cit.*   [5] *Ibid.*, pp. 38–50.   [6] *Ibid.*, p. 3.   [7] *Loc. cit*

importance in the Dutch War'[1]. Astrea thus became in her own person
the prototype of the beautiful secret service agent. She herself knew very
well that simple people reading stories like to think that they are true,
hence her story of the noble savage purports to be an account, put out
with royal encouragement, of a prince she knew in Surinam. 'Her stay
at Antwerp, presented her with the story of Prince Tarquin and his false
wicked Fair-one Miranda. The full account of which you will find
admirably writ in the following volume'[2]. After her husband's death Astrea
chose to go to Amsterdam because there she expected to meet with a
former lover through whom she hoped to get news for the king. From him
she obtained intelligence 'which might have saved the Nation a great
deal of Money and Disgrace, had credit been given to it'[3], for she learned
of the projected Dutch raid on Chatham in 1667. No notice was taken
of her information, so that Astrea 'gave over all sollicitous Thought of
Business'[4] and turned to her own affairs. She agreed to marry the man
who had given her news of the raid, but he died of fever at Amsterdam.
Astrea returned to England and 'the rest of her life was entirely dedicated
to Pleasure and Poetry'.

This phrase is a flowery way of saying that Aphra Behn thenceforward
made her living by writing for the amusement of the town. She felt,
as other women have felt since her day, that her wares would be more
readily accepted if it were thought that a man had produced them. Her
first plays were therefore anonymous, but in 1681 she brought out the
second part of an early play with her name on the title-page. She enjoyed
a few years of great prosperity, although 'the envious of our sex and the
malicious of the other' put it about that a man was the author of most
of her work. A successful dramatist of the Restoration period was bound
to write freely of love. Hence her biographer felt it necessary to explain
that 'she was a Woman of Sense, and by consequence a Lover of Pleasure,
as indeed all both Men and Women are; but only some wou'd be thought
to be above Conditions of Humanity, and place their chief Pleasure in a
proud vain Hypocrisy. For my part, I knew her intimately, and never
saw ought unbecoming the just Modesty of our Sex, tho more gay and
free than the Folly of the Precise will allow. She was, I'm satisfied, a
greater Honour to our Sex than all the Canting Tribe of Dissemblers,
that die with the false Reputation of Saints[5]. Aphra Behn's death occurred

[1] 'The Life and Memoirs of Mrs. Behn', p. 4.   [2] *Loc. cit.*
[3] *Ibid.*, p. 5.   [4] *Ibid.*, p. 7.   [5] *Ibid.*, pp. 28, 50-1.

on 16 April 1689 'occasion'd by an unskilful Physician'. As an offset to the follies and immoralities of the Restoration period it is worth remembering that it at least allowed a woman writer to make a great reputation by her pen[1].

Restoration society also permitted women to earn their livings on the stage. Although the court of Charles I entertained itself with amateur theatricals in which the queen took part, women's parts on the professional stage were played by boys until the victory of the army over the king resulted in the closure of theatres. Before Cromwell died Sir William Davenant had been permitted in 1656 to produce an entertainment in the style of opera. Mrs. Coleman, wife of Dr. Coleman, a successful teacher of music and singing, took part with her husband in *The Siege of Rhodes*. She thus has the distinction of being the first woman to appear professionally upon the English stage. The Colemans were friends of Pepys and often spent an evening and sang in his house. Pepys records that he himself first saw women acting on the stage on 3 January 1661. When in 1663 Davenant revived and enlivened *The Siege of Rhodes* Mrs. Coleman did not appear in it, but four women, whom Davenant lodged in his house, were in the cast. One of them was Mrs. Saunderson, who soon married Thomas Betterton, an actor and dramatist who died in 1710. Mrs. Betterton was a good actress and a woman of high character, but few of her immediate successors withstood the temptations lavishly spread before youth and beauty in the late seventeenth century. Mrs. Barry was trained to speak and act by the Earl of Rochester and bore him a son. Mrs. Bracegirdle was thought to be either Congreve's wife or his mistress. Mrs. Oldfield had at least one illegitimate son. Nell Gwyn, who began life as an orange seller in Drury Lane, is the best remembered of them all[2].

In the two hundred years which had passed since the first Tudor prince

---

[1] Aphra Behn soon had many imitators of whom the best known is Mrs. Susannah Centlivre, wife of Mr. Joseph Centlivre, chief cook to Queen Anne and George I. She wrote a number of successful plays between 1700 and 1722 and died in 1723. The most successful woman novelist of the period was Mrs. Manley, who wrote about current political and society figures in the form of romance. Her most popular work was *Secret Memoirs and Manners of Several Persons of Quality of both Sexes. From the New Atalantis*, 1709. Two further volumes appeared in 1710. She died in 1724. In the 1720 edition of this work is inserted an advertisement of seven volumes of novels by the same author on the subject of *The Power of Love*.

[2] *The Story of Nell Gwyn and the sayings of Charles II*, related and collected by Peter Cunningham, London, 1852.

was king much had happened which was of good omen for women. No one had forgotten that a woman had ruled England when the Spanish Armada was defeated. Nor had it been forgotten that Queen Elizabeth was a scholar as well as a great queen. Some men, though a small minority, were conscious of the unfair treatment the law gave to women. Others desired to give women an education more nearly equivalent to that of men. The shrill insistence of other men on the superior qualities of men over women is, perhaps, equally significant. Individual women in ever-increasing numbers had displayed qualities of mind and character which have carried them into history. By the end of the Restoration period the movement which at long last was to carry women to freedom and independence had begun.

Nevertheless, the famous tract written by Lord Halifax as a new year's gift for his youngest daughter shows that in the last decade of this period there were men of position who had hardly moved from their medieval attitude to women. The child for whose guidance *Advice to a Daughter* was written was married in 1692, so that her father, who felt that her understanding had not yet grown up to all he wished to say, probably wrote his tract a little time before it was first printed in 1688. It is significant that he hardly expected his daughter to be happy in the world, but hoped that, aided by his advice, she might live with dignity and not 'make an ill figure'. He set out his discourse under the headings Religion; Husband; House, Family, and Children; Behaviour and Conversation; Friendships; Censure; Vanity and Affectation; Pride; Diversions. His love for his daughter and his fears for her inform his words with such sincerity that his tract was again and again reprinted through the eighteenth century[1]. Much of what he says is timeless, particularly his discussion of religion, the relations between parents and children and between mistress and maids. It is still good advice to tell a woman to grow old gracefully and not to ape youth. But Lord Halifax was particularly concerned to teach his daughter as best he could how to live as happily as might be with her husband. That section of his tract is longer by far than any other. It was not for women 'to make their own choice' of husbands. 'Their Friends' Care and Experience are thought safer Guides to them, than their own Fancies; and their Modesty often forbiddeth them to refuse

---

[1] 1688, 1692, 1696, 1699, 1700, 1701, 1704, 1707, 1717, 1734, 1741, 1765, 1784, 1791, 1794, and more than once in French. H. C. Foxcroft, *Life and Works of the Marquis of Halifax*, vol. ii, pp. 379–88.

when their Parents recommend, though their inward Consent may not entirely go along with it. In this case there remaineth nothing for them to do, but to endeavour to make that easie which falleth to their lot, and by a wise use of every thing they may dislike in a Husband, turn that by degrees to be very supportable, which if neglected, might in time beget an aversion'.

Lord Halifax was too wise to say openly that his daughter might be forced to marry a man she disliked for reasons of family interest, but the reality of such coercion underlies all he says. He advises his daughter to accept the fact of the 'inequality of the sexes', since men have 'the larger share of reason and women are the better prepared for the compliance that is necessary for the better performance of their duties'. He agrees that 'the Laws of Marriage run in a harsher stile towards your Sex. Obey is an ungenteel word and less easy to be digested, by making such an unkind distinction in the Words of Contract, and so very unsuitable to the excess of Good Manners, which generally goes before it'. The 'institution of marriage is too sacred to admit a liberty of objecting to it' and a wife must learn how to live with her husband. Men may claim 'grains of allowance' for frailty which would be criminal in women since 'the honour of families' is in their keeping. It is wise to ignore a husband's infidelities. If a drunken husband should fall to his daughter's lot he urges her to be 'wise and patient' and then 'his wine shall be of your side'. A husband may be choleric and ill-humoured, covetous or 'a close-handed wretch'. He may be weak and incompetent. The best husband to be hoped for is a 'wise husband, one that by knowing how to be master for that very reason will not let you feel the weight of it'.

Lord Halifax describes the position of married women from the stand-point of a humane and intelligent man of the world. The cruder side of contemporary opinion may be gathered from a wedding sermon preached by John Sprint, a Nonconformist, at Sherborne, Dorset, and published in 1700 under the title *The Bride-Woman's Counsellor*[1]. It at once elicited rejoinders in print from two intelligent women of quality. Sprint took for his text 'But she that is Married careth for the things of the World, how she may please her Husband' and prefixed his sermon by an 'Epistle to the Reader' saying that he was forced to print his sermon because 'the Doctrine therein contained is so unhappily represented to the World by some ill-natured Females'. He hoped to show 'that I am not

[1] London, price 6d.

such an impudent Villain as my waspish Accusers have reported me to be'. He assures his readers that 'I have not met with one Woman amongst all my Accusers whose Husband is able to give her the Character of a Dutiful and Obedient Wife'[1]. The sermon was short, no more than forty-four small pages of large wide-set type, setting out a crude commentary on the wife's duty to love, honour, and obey her husband. The fact that at least two women are known to have protested in print against this sermon is an indication both of the movement of opinion against the subjection of women and of the increasing number of women sufficiently well educated to follow an argument.

The present writer's edition of John Sprint's sermon is bound up with a little tract entitled *The Female Advocate; or A plea for the just Liberty of the Tender Sex, and particularly of Married Women. Being Reflections on a late Rude and Disingenuous Discourse delivered by Mr. John Sprint, in a Sermon at a Wedding, May 11th, at Sherburn in Dorsetshire, 1699.* By a Lady of Quality[2]. The anonymous author dedicated her work 'To the Honourable Lady W – – – ley, assuring her that' it is 'not because You have any occasion of a Discourse of this kind that I lay these Reflections at your Ladyship's feet; but because you are a perfect Example how little need there is of an unsociable Majesty on the one hand, or a vile Submission on the other, where Virtue and Goodness, Noble and Generous Souls, Tender and Sublime Affections are mutually contemplated and enjoyed'.

The author signed her dedication Eugenia and informed her readers that 'I am one that never came yet within the clutches of a *Husband*'. Nor could she 'boast of any great Beauty, or a vast Fortune, two things (especially the latter) which are able to make us Conquerors thro' the World. But I have endeavoured to furnish myself with something more valuable: I shall not brag that I understand a little Greek and Latin (Languages being only the effect of Confusion) having made some attempt to look into the more solid parts of Learning, and having adventur'd a little abroad into the World, and endeavoured to understand Men and Manners. And having seen something of the Italian and Spanish Humors, I solemnly profess I never observ'd in Italy, nor Spain itself, a Slavery so abject as this Author would fain persuade us to'. Eugenia informed her readers that the sermon was so ill thought of that 'Mr. L – –, the minister who is resident at Sherborn, looked on himself as obliged to tell the World in the public News, that he was not the Author of that Discourse,

[1] The 'Epistle to the Reader' is unpaged.   [2] London.

lest it being preach'd where he lives, they who knew not his name might impute it to him'. She concluded her preface by recommending women 'to furnish their Minds with true Knowledg, that (as an Ingenious Lady tells us) you may know something more than a well-chosen Petticoat, or a fashionable Commode. Learning becomes us as well as the Men. Several of the French Ladies, and with us the late incomparable Mrs. Baynard, and the lady that is Mr. Norris's Correspondent, and many more, are Witnesses of this. Hereby we shall be far enough from being charmed with a great Estate, or mov'd with the flowing Nonsense and Romantic Bombast of every foppish Beau; and shall learn (if we choose Companions for our Lives) to select the Great, the Generous, the Brave and Deserving Souls, Men who will as much hate to see us uneasy, as this Gentleman is afraid of coming under the discipline of the Apron'[1].

Eugenia took up every point which Sprint had made and answered it, pouring ridicule upon the author, who indeed had laid himself open to attack on every side. It was unwise of him to declare that 'Subjection and Obedience unto Husbands is required as peremptorily as unto Christ himself, P. 40'. Eugenia could remark 'I thought the Authority of Husbands had been at least one degree inferior to the Authority of Christ'[2]. He commended Sarah for calling her husband Lord and remarked that it was 'a custom more common than comely, for Women to call their Husbands by their Christian Names'. Eugenia cannot refrain from remarking that 'it would look a little odd for a Man of low degree to be greeted, My Lord, Your Lordship's most obedient Servant, etc., by his Lady in a blew Apron, or a high-crowned Hat'[3].

In disposing of Sprint's argument, Eugenia concealed her own identity. The second woman who protested against his abuse was well known as an author in her own day. Lady Chudleigh was born at Winslade, Devon, in 1656 and married Sir George Chudleigh, of Ashton, Devon, where she died in 1710. She wrote a poetical dialogue, called *The Ladies Defence*, in 1700 in answer to John Sprint and was persuaded by her friends to publish it anonymously. Her printer afterwards included it in a second edition of her poems without her consent and caused her some distress. Her first volume of poems had appeared under her own name in 1703 and was dedicated to Queen Anne. She published a volume of essays in 1710 dedicated to the Electress Sophia. She took the opportunity of explaining in the Preface to her essays that in her poetical dialogue she had

---

[1] *The Female Advocate*, pp. v–viii.   [2] *Ibid.*, p. 46.   [3] *Ibid.*, p. 42.

made no aspersions against anyone except John Sprint, the author of the offensive sermon. 'Him I only blame', she added, 'for his being too angry, for his not telling us our Duty in a softer, more engaging way'[1]. When she wrote these words in 1710 her anger at Sprint's infelicitous remarks had faded, but in all her writings she shows as much concern as Eugenia about the welfare of women. She wrote both her poems and essays for women in particular to read. She hoped that they would be persuaded 'to cultivate their Minds, to brighten and refine their Reason, and to render their Passions subservient to its dictates'. That Lady Chudleigh and Eugenia were friends is proved by the poem addressed 'To Eugenia' in the first edition of Lady Chudleigh's poems[2].

Her poetry was, as she herself says, 'the innocent Amusement of a solitary Life'. When her mother died and, again, when her daughter died she found relief in writing a poem[3]. She herself declared that in her poetry her readers would find 'a Picture of my Mind, my Sentiments all laid open to their view'[4]. It is therefore not unfair to regard her poem addressed 'To the Ladies' as a revelation of her own unhappiness and resentment at the inevitable subjection of a woman in a loveless marriage:

> Wife and Servant are the same,
> But only differ in the Name:
> For when that fatal Knot is ty'd,
> Which nothing, nothing can divide:
> When she the word *obey* has said,
> And Man by Law supreme has made,
> Then all that's kind is laid aside,
> And nothing left but State and Pride:
> Fierce as an Eastern Prince he grows,
> And all his innate Rigor shows:
> Then but to look, to laugh, or speak,
> Will the Nuptial Contract break.
> Like Mutes she Signs alone must make,
> And never any Freedom take:
> But still be govern'd by a Nod,
> And fear her Husband as her God:

---

[1] *Essays upon Several Occasions*, written by the Lady Chudleigh, London, 1710, 'To The Reader', unpaged.

[2] *Poems on Several Occasions*, by the Lady Chudleigh, London, 1703, p. 29.

[3] *Ibid.*, pp. 88 and 94.   [4] *Ibid.*, Preface, unpaged.

Him still must serve, Him still obey,
And nothing act, and nothing say,
But what her haughty Lord thinks fit,
Who with the Pow'r, has all the Wit.
Then shun, oh! shun that wretched State,
And all the fawning Flatt'rers hate:
Value yourselves, and Men despise,
You must be proud, if you'll be wise[1].

Here is real bitterness.

[1] *Poems on Several Occasions,* p. 40.

CHAPTER VIII

Women and the new Scholarship

The revolution of 1688 which removed James II from the throne placed on it his daughter, Mary, with her husband William, Prince of Orange. Until her death from smallpox on 28 December 1694 Queen Mary and her husband ruled England together. Her face, although almost masked by his, appears on the English coinage in those years. To many of her contemporaries the lightness of heart induced by a bloodless revolution was increased by the fact that a woman again sat on the English throne. The queen was a religious and kindly woman, interested in architecture and gardening. Many years after her death the Duchess of Marlborough wrote 'that she wanted bowels', because she showed no feelings natural in a daughter when she and her husband took her father's place'[1]. But to Gilbert Burnet, Bishop of Salisbury, she was 'our late Blessed Queen', who 'was incessantly employed, in possessing her Mind with the best Schemes, that were either laid before her by others, or suggested by her own Royal Heart, for Correcting every Thing that was amiss, and Improving everything that wanted finishing among us. . . . She had arrived at such a superior degree of Knowledge, and had such a Sweetness of Temper, that if our Sins had not provoked God to blast all those Hopes, by her early admission to a better Crown, we might have seen a glorious face put on our Church'[2]. These words were written in 1713, when Queen Mary had been dead for nineteen years. The bishop had written a full account of the queen's tastes and virtues in an essay which appeared in the year following her death[3].

Inevitably, the queen's subjects looked back to the glorious days of

---

[1] *An account of the conduct of the Dowager Duchess of Marlborough from her first coming to court to the year 1710, in a letter to my Lord ——*, London, 1742, p. 25.

[2] *The New Preface to the Third edition of the Pastoral Care*, London, 1713, p. 18.

[3] *An Essay on the memory of the late Queen*, London, 1695.

Queen Elizabeth. All women had gained by the skill and courage with which she led her people through a dangerous age. There were in Queen Mary's lifetime signs that women were again to profit by the mere fact that one of their sex was the ruler. Two anonymous publications, one issued in 1691 and the other in 1692, are symptomatic of the feeling of the age. Since each was anonymous neither author can have expected personal advantage from flattery of the queen. *A Dialogue concerning Women, being a defence of the Sex. Written to Eugenia*, was the work of William Walsh[1], a man of fashion, a critic and a poet, who himself declared that he had 'an amorous heart'[2]. He wrote in prose and verse of love and lovers[3]. It has been supposed without evidence that the Eugenia to whom his *Dialogue* was addressed was his mistress. It is more satisfactory to identify her with the Eugenia who in 1700 trounced John Sprint for his contemptuous address directed against married women[4]. The style of Walsh's Preface is that of a man about town addressing a lady of position. She is 'your Ladyship' or 'Madam'. 'I little thought', he writes, 'when I talk'd with Your Ladyship of the Vertues of your Sex, that you would have commanded me to have given my Sentiments upon that Subject in Writing'[5]. To help him to express his belief in the ability of women he used the conceit of two men discussing the sex, Mysogynes, the disbeliever in female capacity and virtue, and Phylogynes, the lover and upholder of women. All the arguments of Mysogynes were answered and his criticisms disposed of by Phylogynes. Like others who wished women well Phylogynes compared the long time spent on a man's education with the little thought given to that of women. 'Consider what time and charge is spent to make Men fit for somewhat; Eight or Nine Years at School; Six or Seven at the University; Four or Five Years in Travel; and after this are they not almost all Fops, Clowns, Dunces or Pedants? I know not what you think of the Women; but if they are Fools, they are Fools I am sure with less pains and less expense than we are'[6]. Many learned women of ancient times and modern were cited by Phylogynes, who declared that 'granting the equal capacities of both sexes, 'tis a greater Wonder to find one Learned Woman, than a hundred Learned Men, considering the difference of their Educations'[7].

[1] London, 1691.
[2] *The Works of the English Poets with Prefaces*, ed. S. Johnson, London, 1779, vol. xii, p. 309.   [3] See for example his Preface, *Ibid.*, pp. 301–8.
[4] See above, p. 205.   [5] *Dialogue*, pp. 1–2.
[6] *Ibid.*, p. 101.   [7] *Ibid.*, p. 100.

The conclusion and final proof of the argument for women was their capacity to rule. 'But it is generally agreed that all Vertues are requisite for those who Govern well; and since there are some Countries where Women are Excluded from the Throne, and no Countrey where they are not postponed, it would be convenient methinks to see what they do when by accident they are placed upon it'. Ignoring all women of the ancient world the author confines himself 'within the bounds of our own Countrey'[1]. There he finds that 'at a time when the Britains groaned under the Servitude of the Romans . . . Boadicia arose'. He is obliged to admit that the end of her enterprise 'was not answerable to the Successes of the Beginning'. Nevertheless 'as one of the greatest attempts the Britains made for their Liberty was whilst they were led by a Woman; so we must own the Greatest Glory our Nation could ever boast was under the Government of one of the same Sex. It was in the time of Queen Elizabeth that this island arrived at a pitch of greatness, to which it had been ascending for several Ages, and from which it has been declining 'till very lately ever since'[2]. His final example of the reigning queen was Queen Mary. 'Yes, Sir, without going to foreign Countries, without searching the Histories of our own; we have even in our own Time and our own Countrey, a Princess who has governed to their general satisfaction, a People the most curious, to pry into the faults of their Governours, of any People under the Sun. A Princess, who though she never shew'd any fondness of Vainglory, or Authority, yet when the necessity of the Kingdom called her to the Helm, Managed Affairs with that dexterity which is rarely found in those who are the most ambitious of Command'[3]. The virtues of the queen seemed all the greater since she very readily yielded up 'that Authority which she owed to the absence of a Husband whom she loved so much better than that. Does it not put you in mind of the old *Roman* Generals, who quitted their plow to command an Army, and when the Victory was gained returned to their Plow again?'[4] William Walsh tried to ensure the success of his book by persuading John Dryden to write a Preface for him. In it the poet declared that he would rather see some women 'praised extraordinarily, than any of them suffer by detraction: and that in this Age, and at this time particularly, wherein I find more Heroines than Heroes'[5].

To Nahum Tate, whom Dryden befriended, is attributed *A Present for*

[1] *Dialogue*, pp. 126–7.   [2] *Ibid.*, pp. 127–8.   [3] *Ibid.*, pp. 129–30.
[4] *Ibid.*, pp. 132–3.   [5] *Ibid.*, last page of Preface, unpaged.

the Ladies, being an Historical Vindication of the Female Sex[1]. After a rapid survey of the famous women of the ancient and modern world the author states that 'All nations have had experience of the excellent Rule and Administration of their Princesses . . . the Britons their Boadicia of ancient times, and of late their illustrious Elizabeth. What was wanting to accomplish this Princess? She was endu'd with great spirit: to discharge the Duties of Government, she levied Armies, she presided in the Councils, she managed her Subjects with Clemency, her Enemies with Terrour: She did everything in an extraordinary manner. . . . But after all, if Queen Elizabeth had never bless'd the World, if yet no Age or Country had seen a Princess sitting at the Helm of Government and skilfully steering through all Extremities of State, . . . if the times past, I say, had never shown such a Phoenix, yet to the eternal Glory of the Sex, it must be confess'd, that the present season is happy in an Example: All Europe have lately turn'd their eyes upon Great Britain, and there beheld upon the Throne, a Female Regent administering in the absence of her Royal Heroe, and every day affording just occasions for admiration and astonishment'. The writer concludes that 'the inference to be naturally drawn from the Illustrious Instances we have produced, is, that we should at last render this NOBLE SEX their just respect and honour. That we should no longer look upon them as the Entertainments of idle Hours, but place them in the venerable Estimation which is due to their Merit. Let us bear in mind the Obligations wherein we stand indebted to them from our Birth and Infancy even through the whole Course of our Lives'[2]. Neither of these two anonymous works gives the impression of mere bookmaking. William Walsh, at least, was a man of position with an estate in Worcestershire, who could afford to write what he chose. His poems suggest that he both admired and liked women and enjoyed their company, though he never married. The sincerity of both writers is evident.

Nevertheless some ladies, at least, did not think well of Walsh's attempt to do them justice. The anonymous female author of *An Essay in the Defence of the Female Sex*, published in 1696[3], wrote despiteously of 'Mr. W.'s laboured Common Place Book'. The romantic days, she thought, were over when a man of wit might arise 'to be the champion of our sex against the injuries and oppressions of his own'. She called Walsh's book 'a feint of something of this nature' in which 'he has taken more care to

---

[1] London, 1692.
[2] *A Present, etc.*, pp. 98–101.   [3] London. My copy is the 4th ed., 1701.

give an edge to his satyr, than force to his Apology: he has played a sham Prize, and receives more Thrusts than he makes'. She seemed to resent his method of argument: 'He levels scandal at the whole Sex, and thinks us sufficiently fortify'd, if out of the story of Two Thousand Years he has been able to pick up a few Examples of Women illustrious for their Wit, Learning, or Vertue, and Men infamous for the contrary'[1]. It is refreshing and new to find a defender of the female sex who declares that she will 'leave Pedants and School-Boys to rake and tumble the Rubbish of Antiquity, and muster all the Heroes and Heroins they can find to furnish Matter for some wretched Harangue, or stuff a miserable Declamation with instead of Sense or Argument'[2]. Her purpose was, indeed, a contemporary one, for she aimed at showing that men could improve and divert their minds in the company and conversation of women: that women are 'qualified for the Conversation of ingenious Men, or to go yet farther, their Friendship'[3].

Whoever wrote this book was certainly a lively and intelligent woman, who looked on the world about her and saw with a clear eye the follies and stupidities of men. She had no mercy on any of them. Scholars are pedants, 'superstitious, bigotted Idolators of times past' and 'children in their Understanding all their lives'[4]. The country squire gets off no better. 'He wearies you in the Morning with his sport, in the Afternoon with the noisie Repetition and Drink, and the whole day with Fatigue and Confusion. His Entertainment is stale Beer, and the History of his Dogs and Horses, in which he gives you the Pedigree of every one with all the exactness of a Herald; and if you be very much in his good Graces, 'tis odds, but he makes you the Compliment of a Puppy of one of his favourite Bitches, which you must take with abundance of Acknowledgments of his Civility, or else he takes you for a stupid, as well as an ill bred Fellow'[5]. She pokes gentle fun at the scientists and members of the Royal Society, whom she stiles 'Virtuosos'[6] and pours scorn on the 'beaus' and 'bullies' of the town, the 'fop-poets', the 'coffee-house politicians', and the 'scowrers', that is, 'men of nice honour that love fighting for the sake of blows'[7]. Her satire is good reading and her book was popular. It was already in its third edition in 1697[8].

[1] *Defence*, pp. 4–5.   [2] *Ibid.*, p. 5.   [3] *Ibid.*, p. 8.   [4] *Ibid.*, p. 26.
[5] *Ibid.*, pp. 28–9.   [6] *Ibid.*, pp. 86–91.   [7] *Ibid.*, pp. 55 ff.
[8] One sign of its success was the appearance of *A farther Essay relating to the Female Sex* in the same year, 1696, in which this work appeared. The dedication to Elizabeth, Countess of Kildare, is signed 'Ez. Symson'. The whole tenor of this book suggests a masculine

She is refreshing after the earnest propaganda of Hannah Woolley and Bathshua Makin, for unlike them she made no apology for the contemporary state of women's education. Women, unlike men, do not have to waste years learning the classical languages, a labour she regarded as completely unnecessary for them, since all the best writers of antiquity can be read in translation. For the only purpose of learning foreign languages 'is to arrive at the Sense, Wit, or Arts, that have been communicated to the world in 'em'[1]. She cites a large number of translations of classical authors and points out that 'Assisted by these Helps 'tis impossible for any woman to be ignorant that is but desirous to be otherwise, though she know no Part of Speech out of her Mother-Tongue'[2]. Moreover, she argued, there are so many excellent works written in English— verse, prose, plays, history and philosophy—that 'Women want not the means of being wise and prudent without more Tongues than one; nay, learned too if they have any Ambition to be so'[3]. Idleness keeps women from acquiring knowledge, but so it does many men. This, she thinks, must be the reason why women 'who are commonly charged with talking too much, are guilty of writing so little. I wish they would shake off this lazy Despondence, and let the noble Examples of the deservedly celebrated Mrs. Philips, and the incomparable Mrs. Behn, rouze their Courages, and shew Mankind the great Injustice of their Contempt'[4]. They would not, she thinks, need foreign tongues to follow these examples. In fact ignorance of Latin and Greek is a great advantage to women, for they spend their time reading romances, novels, plays and poems, which give them command of words. They go visiting with their mothers which gives them 'the Opportunity of imitating, conversing with, and knowing the Manner, and Address of elder Persons'[5].

Ballard was not able to come by a copy of this tract or he would never have attributed it to Mary Astell. It is far too light-hearted for that serious and religious lady. The author was a woman of the world, at home both in the town and the country. Her tract was seen through the press by James Drake, a doctor, who wrote many pamphlets in the Tory interest and was a young man of twenty-nine when this essay appeared. He wrote a long poem in praise of the author, a much better poem than was often

author. In the Preface addressed to 'the fair sex' the author states that the object of the book is to draw characters which would help women to correct their faults; this suggests an answer to the author of the *Defence*.

[1] *Defence*, p. 37.   [2] *Ibid.*, p. 39.   [3] *Ibid.*, p. 47.
[4] *Ibid.*, p. 50.   [5] *Ibid.*, p. 51,

written to commend books to their readers in the seventeenth century. It has been suggested that the essay was written by his sister, but without evidence[1]. The dedication of this book to the Princess Anne is a good illustration of the assurance women drew from the realization that William III would be succeeded by a queen. 'I have only endeavoured to reduce the Sexes to a level', wrote the author in her Preface, 'and by arguments to raise ours to an Equality at most with the men: but your Highness by illustrious example daily convinces the world of our Superiority'[2]. There is in this essay none of the humourless sense of mission that in the writings of her predecessors and many of her successors breeds weariness with their cause.

There is other evidence of a genuinely popular nature which implies that opinion was moving in favour of women in the last decade of the century. Between March 1690 and February 1696 an eccentric publisher, John Dunton, was issuing a weekly or bi-weekly paper called *The Athenian Gazette*[3], a title soon changed to *The Athenian Mercury*. Each issue was a single sheet of questions and answers. The first number was presumably composed, both as to questions and answers, by Dunton himself, but in it he announced that 'All Persons whatever may be resolved gratis in any Question that their own satisfaction or Curiosity shall prompt 'em to if they send their questions by a penny post letter to Mr. Smith at his Coffee house at Stocks Market in the Poultry'[4]. This early type of *Answers*, or 'Twenty Questions', was popular at once and in the fourth number publication twice a week was announced. From time to time the papers were made up into a volume with a list of the questions answered therein. Dunton was insistent that questions from persons of either sex were welcomed. In the part issued on 5 May 1691 he inserted

---

[1] Despite the author's jibes at Walsh's book and 'his Eugenia' it is tempting to wonder whether Eugenia was not herself the author. If so this book might be that referred to by Lady Chudleigh in her poem 'To Eugenia':

> 'Yet of this wretched Place so well you've Writ,
> That I admire your Goodness and your Wit,
> And must confess your excellent Design
> To make it with its native lustre shine:
> To hide its faults and to expose to view,
> Nought but its Beauties, is becoming you.'—*Poems*, p. 31.

[2] Unpaged.

[3] *The Athenian Gazette: or Casuistical Mercury, Resolving all the most Nice and Curious Questions proposed by the Ingenious*, vol. i, for John Dunton, at the Raven in the Poultry, 1691.   [4] *Ibid.*, at the end of the first number.

an advertisement: 'We have received this week a very ingenuous letter from a lady in the country, who desires to know whether her Sex might not send us questions as well as men, to which we answer, Yes, they may, our design being to answer all manner of Questions sent us by either Sex, that may be either useful to the publick or to particular persons'. But the publishers were already overwhelmed with questions and asked their readers to send no more until they had dealt with arrears.

Dunton came of a family which for several generations had provided clergymen for the Church of England. He married a daughter of Samuel Annesley, one of the band of eminent Nonconformist ministers who were ejected from their livings in 1662. Another of Annesley's daughters married Samuel Wesley, who became rector of South Ormsby, Lincolnshire, in 1690 and moved to the rectory of Epworth in 1695, where his illustrious son, John Wesley, was born and bred. When the answering of questions became more than one man could manage Dunton enlisted the help of Samuel Wesley and Richard Sault, a mathematician. Occasional help from other scholars was sought and queries came both from Oxford and Cambridge. In his Lincolnshire rectory Samuel Wesley wrote a poem on the Life of Christ which he dedicated to Queen Mary[1], and dealt with the many questions on religious subjects propounded to the *Athenian Mercury*. He brought sound learning and good sense to the answering of such questions as 'What is the meaning of the present union between the Presbyterians and the Independents?', 'Whether a universal accommodation amongst Protestants may ever be expected?' and 'What is the soul of man, and whether Eternal?' The questions posed by the public covered the whole range of human interests and many people obtained free medical and legal advice. The pages of *The Athenian Mercury* are well worth turning over today for the light the questions and answers throw on England at the end of the seventeenth century. In the first number the question 'Whether 'tis lawful for a man to beat his wife?' was posed[2]. The answer admits that the legality of beating is unquestionable, but 'the time and measure are generally too critical for a Calculation'. The writer suggests that a 'sympathetick Remedy, as the Rebuke of a Kiss' is more likely to be efficacious than beating.

This answer provoked the question whether a woman having a sot to her husband might not beat him, but the editor clearly regarded this as frivolous and replied that the power was vested in man without any

[1] W. O. Massingberd, *History of Ormsby*, p. 344.   [2] Question 6.

distinction or limitation, a view that might be expected from an authority so well versed in the Scriptures as Samuel Wesley[1]. In the fourth number a question about the right of divorced persons to marry was disposed of by reference to 'the 5th St. Matth. 32'[2]. 'In general the answers show sympathy with women. The question 'Why is it supposed by some that women have no souls?' received short shrift: 'They are a parcel of Jews for their pains; if any be so foolish and barbarous to make such a supposition: And the Reason why they think Women have no souls is because they have none themselves'. To the enquiry how a man may restrain a headstrong or unruly wife the editor replied 'Give her rope enough, Our meaning is, e'en let her alone, for she's not to be made civil by anything but the worms'. He concluded his answer, however, by saying that 'the surest way' of improving her 'is being a good Husband yourself, for 'tis bad Husbands are very often the cause that the Wives are no better than they should be'. On 23 May 1691 the question whether it be proper for women to be learned was faced and the decision reached that 'on the whole since they have as noble Souls as we, a finer Genius, and generally quicker Apprehensions, we see no reason why women should not be learned now, as well as Madam Philips, Van Schurman and others have formerly been'.

Questions relating to love and marriage were put in considerable numbers by both sexes. The answers are revealing, for they reflect the professional and middle-class attitude to marriage which was very different from that set out in the lucid prose of Lord Halifax. *The Athenian Mercury* issued on 5 May 1691 was devoted to answering a number of questions relating to love and marriage 'proposed by a Gentleman at different times'[3]. The first question was 'Whether it is lawful to make addresses to young ladies without a prior acquainting their parents and relatives therewith?' The advice given was that it was first necessary to find out if the young lady were deserving of love before any approach was made to her parents. When assured on that point it was perhaps best to make application to both the lady and her parents at as nearly as possible the same time, so 'that neither might conceive umbrage of the other'. The second question was 'Whether it is lawful to marry a person one cannot Love, only in compliance to Relations and to get an estate?' 'Such a practice', said the answer, 'would be the most

---

[1] The writer of the law-book for women discussed in an earlier chapter thought otherwise. See above, p. 62.   [2] Question 2.   [3] No. 13, vol. i.

cruel and imprudent thing in the world—society is the main end of marriage, Love is the bond of society, without which there can be neither found in that State Pleasure, or Profit, or Honour'. The thirteenth question was 'Whether 'tis convenient for a lady to marry one she has an aversion for, in Obedience to her Parents?' The answer is 'Undoubtedly 'tis not convenient, but the Querist intends [to say is it] necessary? We answer that it is by no means so. Parents are not to dispose of their children like cattel, not to make 'em miserable because they happened to give 'em Being; they are indeed generally granted a negative voice, nor am I sure that will always hold if they are signally unreasonable, if they have given permission or connivance before, and after engagements too deep to be broken would endeavour to retract it: But that they have an irresistable despotical, positive Vote, none but a Spaniard will pretend, but I'm sure our English ladies will very unwillingly grant'.

The men who answered the questions often encouraged their readers by giving a semi-humorous turn to their answers, but they gave good practical advice when it was needed. One question posed by an apprentice throws a little light on women who appear as the heads of businesses in the seventeenth century. It was 'Whether an apprentice, being bound to the Husband, (the Husband dying) may be forced to serve out his time with the Widow, she keeping up her Husband's trade?'[1] The answer was that 'the Widow is bound to teach him his trade, either by taking someone of the same Profession into her house, or by turning him over to another master'. This answer agrees very well with the large amount of information which has been collected by Miss Clark about the part played by women in trade and business in the seventeenth century[2]. The wives of members of the city companies were, like the wives of medieval guildsmen, members of the company to which their husbands belonged. Widows often carried on their husband's business, taking in someone to manage it for them. In some trades a widow lost the freedom of the company when she married again, unless she married a man already a member of it. But the widows of printers were in a much stronger position for they kept their freedom of the Stationers' Company even after remarriage. The eccentric York printer, Thomas Gent, wrote his autobiography in 1746 and in it has preserved a characteristic picture of a London printer's wife, Mrs. Midwinter. Gent was apprenticed to her

[1] Question 11, no. 5, vol. ii.
[2] Alice Clark, *The Working life of Women in the Seventeenth Century*, London, 1919.

husband and in 1717 became a freeman of the Stationers' Company. He wanted to leave his master, who when he heard this insultingly asked if Gent had any of the firm's copies in his trunk. 'At which Madame Midwinter said "My dear, don't be too hard, neither, upon the young man, since he will go; . . . don't spoil what you have done for him, nor hinder him getting a living in the best manner he is able".'[1] Gent experienced so much kindness from Mrs. Midwinter that in an autobiographical poem he likened her to the Empress Maud[2]. She did her best to persuade him to return, but he was afraid of the 'awful reverence' he would be 'obliged to submit to'[3]. Nevertheless, he walked ten miles to attend her funeral[4]. For a time he was employed by a Quaker widow, Mrs. Bradford, who carried on a printer's business in Fetter Lane[5]. When he entered the employment of the York printer Mr. White it was Mrs. White who wrote to engage him[6].

The questions posed to *The Athenian Mercury* by apprentices generally turned on the conditions of their employment and were easily answered. Questions on abstruse philosophical points were more difficult. Here the publishers received considerable help from John Norris, the scholarly incumbent of Bemerton, Wilts, who would take no pay for the hints he was able to give, despite the fact that his large family meant that he was always in need of money. He was their link with the learned ladies of the age, for he addressed a treatise on love to Damaris, Lady Masham, in 1688[7], and corresponded with Mary Astell on the nature of the love of God. Damaris Masham (1658–1708) was the daughter of the Cambridge scholar, Ralf Cudworth, and is best remembered for her friendship with John Locke. From 1691 to his death in 1704 Locke lived at Oates, in Essex, as a paying guest of Sir Francis and Lady Masham. John Norris wrote *Reflections upon the Conduct of Human Life with reference to the Study of Learning and Knowledge, in a letter to an excellent Lady, the Lady Masham*, in 1690. The second edition appeared in 1691 still addressed to her. Norris wrote on the assumption that she had lost her sight and consoled her for the loss of opportunities of study by assuring her of the worthlessness of human knowledge. But Lady Masham had not lost her sight. In 1696 she wrote a *Discourse concerning the Love of God*, which appeared in a French translation in 1705. In the latter year she published

---

[1] *The Life of Mr. Thomas Gent, printer, of York, written by himself*, London, 1832, p. 72.
[2] *Ibid.*, pp. 30–2.   [3] *Ibid.*, p. 90.   [4] *Ibid.*, p. 93.   [5] *Ibid.*, pp. 14, 17.
[6] *Ibid.*, p. 18.   [7] *The Theory and Regulation of Love*, London, 1688; 2nd ed., 1694.

Occasional Thoughts in reference to a Vertuous or Christian Life, written some years since. Both books were anonymous. Women, felt Lady Masham, were generally so ill brought up that they could not reason for themselves. Their religion was acquired 'when their Nurses, or Maids Taught them their Catechisms; that is to say, Certain Answers to a Train of Questions adapted to some approved System of Divinity'[1]. Locke published his *Thoughts concerning Education* while he was living at Oates. He was Lady Masham's guide in the education of her son. She agreed with him that women should be so educated that they could teach their own young children: 'young ladies cannot better employ so much of their time as is requisite hereto than' in acquiring enough knowledge to teach their children 'what is fit for them to learn in the first eight or ten years of their lives. As to Read English perfectly; to understand ordinary Latin and Arithmetick; with some general knowledge of Geography, Chronology, and History'[2]. She knew that 'Parents sometimes do purposely omit' to have their daughters instructed 'from an apprehension that should Daughters be perceived to understand any learned Language, or be conversant in Books, they might be in danger of not finding Husbands; so few men, as do, relishing these accomplishments in a Lady'[3].

Damaris Masham had been fortunate in her home life at Cambridge and doubly so in her friendship with such a man as John Locke. Mary Astell was less fortunate, for she was without the secure background of the happily married woman. Nor, so far as can be known, had she any close friendship with able men. Surprisingly little is known of her family position or her way of life in Chelsea, particularly in her early years there. She was born in Newcastle in 1666 and removed to Chelsea after her mother's death in 1684. She lived there until her death in 1731. Her writings, although published anonymously, were soon known to have come from her pen and she became famous before she died. She enjoyed the friendship of women of position younger than herself, who perhaps owed something of their own outlook to the writings of the older woman. Ballard, writing in the decade after her death, found it difficult to acquire authentic.information about her and even to see all her books. It was on hearsay alone that he excused the 'warmth of temper' discovered in her *Reflections upon Marriage* on the grounds of 'her disappointment in

---

[1] *Occasional Thoughts in reference to a Vertuous or Christian Life,* London, 1705, p. 18. This rare book was kindly lent me by Mr. Arnold Muirhead, of St. Albans.

[2] *Ibid.,* pp. 195–6.   [3] *Ibid.,* p. 197.

a marriage contract with an eminent clergyman'[1]. There is no shadow of evidence for this suggestion. She herself said that her pamphlet was occasioned by reading the *Duke and Duchess of Mazarin's Case*[2]. It seemed to her that 'Had Madame Mazarine's Education made a right Improvement of her Wit and Sense, we should not have found her seeking relief by such imprudent, not to say scandalous Methods, as running away in disguise with a spruce Cavalier, and rambling into so many Courts and Places, nor diverting herself with such Childish, Ridiculous, or Ill-natured Amusements, as the greatest part of the Adventures in her Memoirs are made up of'[3]. Mary Astell, like Damaris Masham, saw around her many unhappy marriages, particularly unhappy from the woman's point of view. The only remedy seemed to them both that women should be properly educated. They would then, said Mary Astell, 'marry more discreetly and demean themselves better in the Married state than some people say they do. The foundation indeed ought to be laid deep and strong. She should be made a good Christian and understand why she is so, and then she will be everything else that is good'[4].

This tract was written with passion. There was no indication of the sex of the author in the first edition, published in 1700, but to the third edition which appeared in 1706, Mary Astell added a long Preface, in which she spoke as a woman, mocking at 'the ingenious gentleman' who 'had the good nature to own these Reflections, so far as to affirm that he had the original MS. in his closet'[5]. She denied that her tract had tried to stir up sedition or undermine the 'Masculine Empire' and argued at length against the supposition that the subjection of women to men was divinely ordered. It was difficult for so true a daughter of the Church of England to dispose of Scriptural texts which place women in clear subordination to men. The task had been attempted a generation earlier by a French author whose tract *The Woman as Good as Man or the Equality of Both Sexes* was published in English translation in 1677 by someone who hid behind the initials A. L.[6] He had argued that the objections drawn from Scripture 'are but Sophisms of Prejudice; whereby sometimes Men understand (of all women) Passages which only agree to some few in Particular: sometime they refer to Nature, that which only flows from

---

[1] Ballard, pp. 449–50.
[2] *Reflections upon Marriage*, 3rd ed., London, 1706, p. 1. An excellent note (9) on the duchess was written by Mary Berry in her edition of some of Lady Russell's letters, *Some Account of the Life of Rachel Wriothesley, Lady Russell*, p. 10.
[3] *Reflections*, p. 4.   [4] *Ibid.*, p. 80.   [5] *Ibid.*, Preface, unpaged, f. 1d.   [6] London.

Education or Custom, and that which sacred authors have spoken with relation to their own time'[1]. There is no evidence that Mary Astell had read this tract. Her argument was that the relationship between the male and female sex was a matter which concerned human nature in general and was not particular to those to whom the Word of God had been revealed. Therefore it was a question which should be decided by natural reason only. The design of the Scriptures was to make men good Christians and not great philosophers. They were written 'for the Vulgar as well as the Learned and therefore are accommodated to the common way of speech and the usage of the world'. She set out a long list of eminent women who appear in the Scriptures to show that men ought not to justify from that source their habit of 'despising Women and keeping them in ignorance and slavery'. 'The Bible is for, not against us and cannot without great violence done to it, be urg'd to our Prejudice'[2]. A fourth edition of the tract, revised, appeared in 1730.

Mary Astell's most famous book is *A Serious Proposal to the Ladies for the advancement of their true and greatest interest*[3], of which the first part, containing a proposal for a women's college, was published in 1694 and the second in 1697. Both were anonymous, but Mary Astell wrote as a woman and made no attempt to conceal her authorship. Her identity seems to have been an open secret from the first. She advocated the establishment of what she described as 'a *Monastery*, or, if you will (to avoid giving offence to the scrupulous and injudicious, by names which tho' innocent in themselves, have been abused by superstitious practices), a *Religious Retirement*'[4], which should be so conducted 'as not to exclude the good Works of an *Active*, from the pleasure and serenity of a Contemplative life'[5]. She saw it as a 'Seminary to stock the Kingdom with pious and prudent Ladies, whose good Example it is to be hoped, will so influence the rest of their Sex, that Women may no longer pass for those useless impertinent Animals, which the ill conduct of so many has caused 'em to be mistaken for'[6].

As a strong High Church woman[7], Mary Astell would have had the

---

[1] Advertisement at the end of the book, unpaged.   [2] *Reflections*, f. 11.
[3] In two parts. By a Lover of her SEX, London, 1697.
[4] *A Serious Proposal*, p. 36.   [5] *Ibid.*, p. 43.   [6] *Ibid.*, pp. 43-4.
[7] In addition to the work in which she set out her faith, *The Christian Religion as Profess'd by a Daughter of the Church of England*, London, 1704, Mary Astell intervened in the current pamphlet war about dissent. She wrote, e.g., *A Fair way with Dissenters and their Patrons*, London, 1704, as an answer to Defoe's satire *The shortest way with Dissenters*.

members of her college 'observe all the Fasts of the Church, *viz. Lent, Ember* and *Rogation-days, Fridays* and *Vigils*'[1]. Her own nature was deeply religious. In 1695 John Norris published, with her consent, the correspondence which had passed between them on the nature of the love of God. The unfortunate influence of the tract which John Norris had addressed to Lady Masham is apparent when Mary Astell discusses what subjects shall be studied in her retreat. 'It is not intended', she writes, 'that our *Religious* should waste their time, and trouble their heads about such unconcerning matters, as the vogue of the world has turn'd up for Learning, the impertinency of which has been excellently expos'd by an ingenious Pen' (*Mr. Norris Conduct of Human Life*, is inset in the text here) 'but busy themselves in a serious enquiry after *necessary* and *perfective* truths'. She argues that such study 'will not be out of the reach of a Female Virtuoso, for it is not intended that she shou'd spend her hours in learning *words* but *things*'[2]. The most concrete suggestion for the ladies' study was that, since most ladies understand the French tongue, they shall study the French philosophers rather than romances[3]. It was necessary for them 'to redeem their Time'. 'For a stated portion of it being daily paid to GOD in Prayers and Praises, the rest shall be imploy'd in innocent, charitable, and useful Business, either in study in learning themselves and instructing others, . . . or else in spiritual and corporal Works of Mercy, relieving the Poor, healing the Sick, mingling Charity to the Soul with that they express to the Body, instructing the Ignorant, counselling the Doubtful, comforting the Afflicted, and correcting those that err and do amiss'[4].

That there were temporal as well as spiritual advantages in this retreat Mary Astell was careful to point out. 'Heiresses and Persons of Fortune may be kept secure from the rude attempts of designing Men; and She who has more Money than Discretion need not curse her Stars for being expos'd a prey to bold importunate and rapacious Vultures. She will not here be inveigled nor impos'd on, will neither be bought nor sold, nor be forc'd to marry for her own quiet, when she has no inclination to it'[5]. Men, she argues, will be much better off if they marry educated women. 'Piety is often offensive when it is accompanied with indiscretion; but she who is as Wise as Good possesses such Charms as can hardly fail of prevailing. Doubtless her Husband is a much happier Man and more likely

[1] *A Serious Proposal to the Ladies*, p. 55.   [2] *Ibid.*, pp. 45–6.
[3] *Ibid.*, p. 51.   [4] *Ibid.*, pp. 53–4.   [5] *Ibid.*, p. 90.

to abandon his ill Courses than he who has none to come home to but an ignorant, froward, and fantastick Creature'[1]. Mary Astell was not appealing on behalf of all women. Those whom she addressed were 'Persons of Quality who are overstock'd with children'[2]. Five or six hundred pounds, she thought, 'may be easily spar'd with a daughter, when so many thousands would go deep; yet as the world goes be a very inconsiderable Fortune for Ladies of their birth, neither maintain them in that *Port* which Custom makes almost necessary, or procure them an equal Match'[3]. But this sum would establish her in this retreat and might well save her from making some dishonourable match in order to avoid 'the dreadful name of *Old Maid*'[4].

The 1697 edition of the work was dedicated to the Princess Anne. She was thought to have been the noble lady who promised £10,000 towards establishing the college. The offer was withdrawn, on the advice, as was supposed, of Gilbert Burnet[5]. The daughters of James II had been carefully educated in the doctrines of the Church of England. Although in her second part Mary Astell stressed the fact that 'our Institution is rather Academical than Monastic'[6] the thoughts of many of her readers undoubtedly turned to the Roman Catholic nunneries. Burnet himself was certainly not opposed to women's education, nor even to the idea of a women's college, as his own words show: 'The ill methods of schools and colleges give the chief rise to the irregularities of the gentry; as the breeding of young women to vanity, dressing, and a false appearance of wit and behaviour, without proper work or a due measure of knowledge and a serious sense of religion, is the source of the corruption of that sex. Something like monasteries without vows would be a glorious design, and might be so set on foot, as to be the honour of a Queen on the throne'[7]. Mary Astell's proposal was widely read and discussed, but there could be no easy way of securing a good education for all women until an adequate supply of well-trained teachers was secured and that was far in the future. The proposal and its author were held up to ridicule in several numbers of the *Tatler*, but the interest which her book aroused had carried it into a fourth edition by 1701.

Mary Astell's project was in tune with her times. The new societies for the Reformation of Manners, the Promotion of Christian Knowledge,

[1] *A Serious Proposal to the Ladies*, pp. 97–8.   [2] *Ibid.*, p. 100.
[3] *Loc. cit.*   [4] *Ibid.*, p. 102.   [5] Ballard MSS. XLIII, 29.
[6] *A Serious Proposal to the Ladies*, 2nd part, p. 286.
[7] Gilbert Burnet's *History of his Own Time*, vol. iv, p. 437.

and the Propagation of the Gospel all derived from the spirit which moved Mary Astell, and encouraged the establishment of charity schools and the provision of parochial libraries. Robert Nelson, a supporter of all these efforts, pointed out in his survey of *Ways and Methods of Doing Good* that 'We have not Houses for the Reception of Ladies and Gentlewomen, beyond Boarding-Schools, in order to their Improvement both in Knowledge and Piety; though there was some Years ago a *Proposal to Ladies* for this End, made by a very Ingenious Gentlewoman; which was then well approved of by several Ladies and others'[1]. Mary Astell's book reminded John Evelyn of Mrs. Ferrar's household at Little Gidding. Like others before and after him, 'he wished that at the first Reformation in this Kingdom, some of those demolished Religious Foundations had been spared both for Men and Women: where single Persons devoutly inclined might have retired and lived without Reproach or insnaring Vows'[2].

The diffusion of knowledge controlled by religion for which Mary Astell had laboured gave an overriding purpose to the energies of her younger contemporary, Lady Elizabeth Hastings. Early in the eighteenth century she figures as a paragon of beauty and learned innocence in the polite journalism of the time. The phrase 'To love her is a liberal education' survives among these faded compliments[3]. But the satisfactions of her life were found in austerer circles and in a distant part of England. Lady Elizabeth was the daughter of the seventh Earl of Huntingdon by his first wife, daughter and heiress of Sir John Lewis, of Ledstone Hall, Yorkshire. In 1705 Lady Elizabeth inherited her grandfather's estates and soon afterwards took her four half-sisters to live with her at Ledstone Hall. This household of five women formed what Mary Astell would have recognized as a genuine religious society[4]. Lady Elizabeth was firm in her adherence to the Church of England, but she was sympathetic to the movement within the Church from which Methodism arose, and her first biographer thought it necessary to defend her from the charge of being herself a Methodist[5]. She might well have subsided into the leader-

---

[1] Robert Nelson, *An Address to Persons of Quality and Estate*, London, 1715, p. 213.

[2] *Numismata*, p. 265.   [3] *Tatler*, no. 49.

[4] *The Diary of Ralf Thoresby, F.R.S.*, ed. Joseph Hunter, London, 1830, vol. ii, pp. 302, 313, 314.

[5] Thomas Barnard, M.A., Master of the Free-School in Leedes, *An Historical Character relating to the holy and exemplary Life of the Right Honourable the Lady Elizabeth Hastings*, Leeds, 1742, pp. xxiii–xxvi.

ship of a small community of dedicated women had it not been for the influence of Robert Nelson and like-minded friends of her earlier years. Under their advice she used her great fortune in a way which placed her in the front rank of benefactors to the cause of English education. As a foundress of schools she insisted that the institutions which she endowed should be governed by regulations which she herself had planned. She felt a personal responsibility for the educational condition of the North of England, and the scholarships which she founded at Queen's College, Oxford, still preserve her memory.

The idea of an academy for women was one of many suggestions put forward by the Nonconformist Defoe in a volume of 336 pages entitled *An Essay upon Projects*, published in 1697[1]. He had read Mary Astell's book, but feared that her scheme 'would be found impracticable. For saving my Respect to the Sex, the Levity, which perhaps is a little peculiar to them, at least in their Youth, will not bear the Restraint; and I am satisfied that nothing but the heighth of Bigotry can keep up a Nunnery'. Although his plan differed 'from what is proposed by that Ingenious Lady' he confessed to a great esteem for her proposal and a great opinion of her wit. He would have an academy for ladies 'differ but little from Public Schools, wherein such Ladies as were willing to study, should have all the advantages of Learning suitable to their Genius'[2]. Their academy was to be a plainly built house with a moat all round and but one entrance. No men were to be admitted. 'No Guards, no Eyes, no Spies' should be set over the ladies who were 'to be try'd by the Principles of Honour and strict virtue'[3]. The ladies were to be 'taught all sorts of Breeding suitable to both their Genius and their Quality; in particular Music and Dancing'. They were to be taught languages, 'particularly French and Italian; and I would venture the injury of giving a Woman more Tongues than one'. They were to be taught 'all the Graces of Speech and all the Necessary Air[4] of Conversation which our common Education is so defective in'[5]. They were to be brought to read books, and especially history. 'To such whose genius would lead them to it' Defoe would 'deny no sort of learning, but the chief thing is to cultivate the Understandings of the Sex'.

The plan outlined by Defoe was eminently sensible and the demand for such academies as that which he described might well have been as

---

[1] London, pp. 282–304. [2] *An Essay upon Projects*, pp. 285–7.
[3] *Ibid.*, p. 288. [4] *sic*, ? for 'Art'. [5] *Ibid.*, p. 292.

large as he expected. He thought that there should be at least one in every county and about ten in the city of London, but he made no estimate of the initial cost of such establishments. His practical suggestion about finance was that the ladies should pay the expenses of the house and that each lady should pay for the whole year although she might withdraw before the year was ended. That such a sound plan should be put forward by a man of Nonconformist origin is in keeping with the evidence for a continuous succession of well-educated women in the families of Nonconformist clergymen from Puritan days. It is possible that Defoe was speaking from experience when he said that 'a Woman well bred and well taught, furnished with the additional accomplishments of Knowledge and Behaviour, is a Creature beyond comparison'[1]. He strongly believed that 'all the world are mistaken in their practice about Women; for I cannot think that God Almighty ever made them so delicate, so glorious Creatures, and furnished them with such charms, so Agreeable and so delightful to Mankind, with Souls capable of the same Accomplishments with Men, and all to be only Stewards of our houses, *Cooks and Slaves*'[2]. Defoe was thinking of the women of the middle classes from which he had sprung rather than of the ladies of position for whom Mary Astell was writing.

There is a real danger that the modern student, reading the works of Mary Astell or Defoe and skimming through the pages of the *Tatler* and *Spectator*, may come to the conclusion that, with the exception of Mary Astell and Lady Elizabeth Hastings, all women of the end of the seventeenth century were idle, empty-headed, ignorant creatures seeking only pleasure to fill their days. But the fact that the High Church Mary Astell and the Nonconformist Defoe agreed in urging upon their contemporaries the value of education for women is only one sign of a genuine intellectual ferment distinguishing that age. English society was moving towards a time when the cultivated woman who could hold her own in conversation with the best brains of the age was to be an object of admiration. But it was moving reluctantly, with outcries against illiterate, pleasure-loving idlers and jibes at 'the female Virtuoso'. Even in the later part of the eighteenth century, the age of the female wits and the blue-stockings, there were plenty of coarse jeers at learned women from the foolish of both sexes. They have been heard even in our own time. There have always been those who urge educated women to hide their learning if

---

[1] *An Essay upon Projects*, p. 294.   [2] *Ibid.*, p. 302.

they want to find husbands. Nevertheless, when George Ballard undertook the necessary research he was able to find out something about a
surprising number of learned women who flourished at the end of the
seventeenth century.

George Ballard is a remarkable example of the learned amateurs who
are characteristic of English historical scholarship. He was born in 1706
and earned his living as a habit-maker or ladies' tailor at Chipping Camden, where he lived with his mother, a midwife. He was described by a
younger contemporary as 'a mantua-maker, a person studious in English
antiquities, laborious in his pursuits, a Saxonist, and after quitting external
adornments of the sex a contemplator of their internal qualifications'.
He continued his trade by day and his studies by night until 1750 when he
was enabled to go to Oxford through the generosity of Lord Chedworth
and other gentlemen who usually spent a month in the neighbourhood of
Campden every year for the hunting. Ballard had visited Oxford on
several occasions before he went there at the age of forty-four to be one
of the eight clerks at Magdalen, where he received free rooms and commons. The only book he published was *Memoirs of British Ladies who have
been celebrated for their Writings or skill in the Learned Languages, Arts, or
Sciences*, which appeared in 1752. He died in 1755 'owing, it was thought,
to too intense application to his studies'[1]. Women, in particular women
scholars, should remember George Ballard with gratitude for his selfless
work to preserve the memory of their predecessors[2].

The limitation which Ballard placed upon his work means that nothing
can be found in his pages about some able women of the last decades of
the seventeenth century whose names are better known today than those
of his learned ladies. The letters of Rachel, Lady Russell, were unknown to
Ballard, for they were first published in 1773. They were popular at
once and had reached their fourth edition in 1792[3]. They reveal a woman
of high principles, deep religious feeling and strong affections struggling
against overwhelming grief. Rachel Wriothesley was a daughter of the
Earl of Southampton and his Huguenot wife and married as her second
husband Mr. William Russell, who on his elder brother's death became

---

[1] J. Nichols, *Literary Anecdotes of the Eighteenth Century*, London, 1812, vol. ii, pp. 466–70.

[2] Mrs. Delany, see below, pp. 251 ff., was annoyed that Ballard wished to dedicate part of
his book to her and would have refused had not Dr. Delany said that 'it would be using
the man ill'. Her reason was that she feared too fulsome compliments. *Life and Correspondence of Mrs. Delany*, ed. Lady Llanover, London, 1861, vol. ii, pp. 595–6.

[3] *Letters of Lady Rachel Russell*, 4th ed., London, 1792.

by courtesy Lord Russell and heir to the earldom of Bedford. From opposition to the Government, natural enough in a man of his rank, he passed to activities sufficient to support a charge of high treason. He was convicted on this charge and executed in 1683. During his trial his wife 'appeared in open court, attending at her Lord's side, she took notes, and made observations on all that past, in his behalf'[1]. After sentence, she vainly endeavoured to obtain a pardon from the king, reminding him of her dead father's services. The account of Lord Russell's preparation for death and his execution, written by his friend Gilbert Burnet, shows Lady Russell bravely encouraging her husband and helping him to prepare his apologia: 'she had command of herself so much that at parting she gave him no disturbance'[2].

Lady Russell lived a widow until September 1723, when she was in her eighty-seventh year. The letters published in 1773 provide ample evidence of the regard in which she was held by men in high position. It was through her influence that the future Lord Chancellor Cowper became a king's counsel at the age of twenty-four[3]. Dean Tillotson, who had been a close friend of Lord Russell and was with him on the scaffold, consulted her about his own future and was encouraged by her to accept King William's offer of the See of Canterbury. Her letter, he said, 'helped very much to settle and determine my wavering mind'[4]. Many of Lady Russell's letters were written to Dr. Fitzwilliam, who had been her father's chaplain and had taught Lady Russell and her sisters. He was Rector of Cottenham and Canon of Windsor. His 'good letter and excellent prayer' stirred Lady Russell in her grief to write to him on 30 September 1683, not quite two months after her husband's execution: 'I know I have deserved my punishment, and will be silent under it, but yet secretly my heart mourns, too sadly, I fear, and cannot be comforted, because I have not the dear companion and sharer of all my joys and sorrows. I want him to talk with, to walk with, to eat and sleep with; all these things are irksome to me now; the day unwelcome and the night so too; all company and meals I would avoid, if it might be; yet all this is, that I enjoy not the world in my own way, and this sure hinders my comfort'[5]. In 1689, like George Hickes, Dr. Fitzwilliam became a nonjuror. In a long letter to Lady Russell he set out his scruples and asked her

---

[1] *Letters of Lady Rachel Russell*, p. cxciv.
[2] Gilbert Burnet's *History of his own Time*, vol. ii, p. 219.
[3] *Letters*, pp. 433-9.   [4] *Ibid.*, p. 501.   [5] *Ibid.*, pp. 244-5.

three things: first, that she would keep her good opinion of his integrity and his zeal to serve her; second, that she would allow him to make over his property to her; and third, that he might have some room in her house for his books[1]. Lady Russell tried to persuade him to take the oath of allegiance, but in vain.

The wisdom and integrity of Lady Russell were remembered through the eighteenth century before her letters were published to rouse interest again in her story. When the Duchess of Marlborough in 1742 published her account of her life at court she recorded that before advising her mistress, the Princess Anne, to acquiesce in the revolution of 1688 she 'consulted with several persons of undisputed wisdom and integrity, and particularly with the Lady Russell at Southampton House, and Dr. Tillotson, afterwards Archbishop of Canterbury'[2]. At York in 1754 the ten-year-old Catharine Harrison, later Mrs. Cappe, was entertained by her grandmother's tales of 'the fortitude of lady Rachel Russell, of the disinterested patriotism of her virtuous lord, and of the piety of Archbishop Tillotson'[3]. The publication in 1819 by Miss Mary Berry of a series of letters from Lady Russell to her husband written between 1672 and 1682 offered a glimpse of the happy wife instead of the sorrowing widow of the later letters[4]. There is in them, here and there, a hint that Lord Russell might with advantage have taken his wife's advice. 'My sister being here tells me she overheard you tell her Lord last night, that you would take notice of the business (you know what I mean) in the House: this alarms me, and I do earnestly beg of you to tell me truly if you have or mean to do it. If you do, I am most assured you will repent it. I beg once more to know the truth. It is more pain to be in doubt, and to your sister too; and if I have any interest, I use it to beg your silence in this case, at least today'[5]. This note was brought to Lord Russell 'while the House was sitting' in March 1678. Again in November 1681 Lady Russell concluded a letter from the country to her husband in London: 'One remembrance more, my best life: be wise as a serpent, harmless as a dove. So farewell, for this time'[6]. Lord Russell has been held in great posthumous honour as a political martyr, but it is his wife who deserves the regard of posterity.

[1] *Letters*, p. 461.   [2] *Conduct of the Duchess of Marlborough*, p. 22.
[3] *Memoirs of the life of the late Mrs. Catharine Cappe*, written by herself, London, 1823, p. 40.
[4] *Some Account of the life of Rachel Wriothesley, Lady Russell . . . followed by a series of letters*, London, 1819.   [5] *Ibid.*, p. 21.   [6] *Ibid.*, p. 64.

Another woman of strong personality of whom Ballard can have known nothing is Celia Fiennes, daughter of Colonel Nathaniel Fiennes, second son of the first Viscount Saye and Sele. Between 1687 and 1702 she undertook a series of journeys through England and into Scotland and Wales, of which she made a careful record. She arranged her material in the form of a published work, but she never sent it to press and made no reference to it in the detailed will she signed in 1738 and revised three times before her death in 1741. In her preface addressed 'to the reader' she disclaimed any intention of publishing her work, but at the same time she took care to explain how she came to take her journeys and declares that 'if all persons, both Ladies, and much more Gentlemen, would spend some of their tyme in Journeys to visit their native Land, and be curious to inform themselves and make observations of the pleasant prospects, good buildings, different produces and manufactures of each place, with the variety of sports and recreations they are adapt to, would be a sovereign remedy' . . . for 'the vapours, should I say Laziness? It would also form such an idea of England, add much to its Glory and Esteem in our minds and cure the evil itch of overvalueing foreign parts'. She concludes by promising to add corrections where she is proved wrong and recommending 'to all, but especially my own Sex, the studdy of those things which tends to improve the mind and makes our Lives pleasant and comfortable as well as proffitable in all Stages and Stations of our Lives, and render Suffering and Age supportable and Death less formidable and a future State more happy'. This lengthy apology for her travels is really beside the point, for her narrative makes it plain that she rode about the country in a spirit of pure curiosity, delighting in what she could learn of the lie of the land, and mercilessly investigating the habits of the people and the houses of the great folk of her own class. In this way she produced a book which is both interesting to read and highly important as a first-hand description of England at the end of the seventeenth century'[1].

The omission from Ballard's book of any account of Catharine Cockburn is less easily explained. She was well known as a playwright, a poet and a philosophical writer in the early years of the century, and in 1751 Thomas Birch published in two volumes an account of her life, an edition of her writings, and a number of letters to and from her[2]. Her portrait in

[1] *The Journeys of Celia Fiennes*, ed. Christopher Morris, London, The Cresset Press, 1947.

[2] Thomas Birch, *The Works of Mrs. Catharine Cockburn, with an account of the Life of the Author*, London, 1751.

the first volume shows a woman with a long oval face, a long thin nose, and a large forehead on which the hair grew far back. The eyes are set far apart and the lips faintly smile. She was 'short in stature', but with 'a remarkable liveliness in her eye and delicacy of complexion which continued to her death'[1]. She was born in London in 1679. Her father, David Trotter, was a Scottish naval commander who died when she was an infant. Charles II gave his widow a pension, which ended at his death. It was renewed in Queen Anne's reign, when £20 a year was paid by the Duchess of Marlborough to Bishop Burnet for the use of Mrs. Trotter. Catharine was brought up in the Church of England, but owing to early friendship with Roman Catholic families of position she entered that Church and remained in it until 1707. She began her career as a playwright when she was only sixteen with a tragedy based on the story of Agnes de Castro which Aphra Behn had translated from the French. The play was printed anonymously in 1696, but Catharine made no attempt to conceal her authorship from her friends. In 1697 she addressed a poem to Congreve on his *Mourning Bride*, and in the next year produced another tragedy, *Fatal Friendship*, which she dedicated to the Princess Anne. Catharine was one of nine ladies who wrote poems on Dryden's death in 1700 and she produced both a tragedy, *The Unhappy Penitent*, and a comedy, *Love at a Loss*, in 1701.

Despite this early effervescence Catharine Trotter was essentially a scholar. She read Locke's *Essay of Human Understanding* with delight and ventured to write a defence of it from anonymous attacks. To her friend Gilbert Burnet, of Kemnay, near Aberdeen, she wrote on 9 December saying that she had finished the work and was determined to publish it, 'though I am conscious that so noble a cause deserves a better advocate'. 'I am more afraid of appearing before him I defend than of public censure; and chiefly for the honour I bear to him, resolve to conceal myself. A woman's name would give a prejudice against a work of this nature'[2]. Her correspondent evidently felt some doubt about the wisdom of publishing anything 'upon such a nice and important subject, especially from one of your sex and years, and in defence of such an aged philosopher, and whose notions have not been thought by many to have done the best service to religion'[3]. But Catharine Trotter was not to be put off and her *Defence* appeared in May 1702. The name of the author was

---

[1] *The Works of Mrs. Catharine Cockburn, with an account of the Life of the Author*, p. xlvi.
[2] *Ibid.*, vol. ii, p. 153.   [3] *Ibid.*, p. 160.

revealed by Mrs. Burnet, wife of the Bishop of Salisbury, when she realized that the book was approved by her own husband, by 'several others of great judgment in such matters', and by Mr. Locke himself. After this Locke was moved to write to his defender and send her a present of books[1].

Catharine Trotter was a good letter-writer and could offer a spirited challenge to those who would belittle the natural abilities of women. In 1705 she protested strongly against a friend's suggestion that Damaris Masham, Locke's friend, was incapable of a piece of writing attributed to her: 'It is not to be doubted that women are as capable of penetrating into the grounds of things, and reasoning justly, as men are, who certainly have no advantage of us, but in their opportunities of knowledge. And as Lady Masham is allowed by everybody to have great natural endowments, she has taken pains to improve them; and no doubt profited much by a long intimate society with so extraordinary a man as Mr. Locke. So that I see no reason to suspect a woman of her character would pretend to write anything, that was not entirely her own. I pray be more equitable to her sex than the generality of yours are; who, when anything is written by a woman, that they cannot deny their approbation to, are sure to rob us of the glory of it, by concluding 'tis not her own; or, at least, that she has some assistance, which has been said in many instances to my knowledge unjustly'[2]. The perennial complaint of able women here appears in an eighteenth-century idiom.

The letters written by Catharine Trotter during 1705 show that she was moving away from the Church of Rome, and in 1707 she published *A Discourse concerning a Guide to Controversies: Written to one of the Church of Rome, by a person lately converted from that communion*, with a Preface by Gilbert Burnet, Bishop of Salisbury. Much of her correspondence survives from that year, which was the turning-point of her life. In 1708 she married a learned young clergyman of Scottish birth and education, Patrick Cockburn, whose preferment was long delayed by an unwillingness to abjure the Stuart dynasty. In the end he was presented to the vicarage of Long Horsley, in Northumberland, where Catharine Cockburn died in 1749. Marriage put an end to her writing for many years, but in 1726 she again came forward in defence of Locke and her letters show that she had never allowed her brain to rust.

---

[1] *The Works of Mrs. Catharine Cockburn, with an account of the Life of the Author*, vol. ii, pp. 166–7.   [2] *Ibid.*, p. 190.

Catharine Cockburn has been long forgotten, but in her own day she was widely held in respect. The long list of subscribers to Birch's two volumes shows that although she had in her later years fallen out of the public view, interest in her life and work could quickly be revived. Many of the nobility, many ecclesiastical dignitaries, many fellows of Oxford and Cambridge colleges subscribed. Addresses in Scotland and the North of England suggest a personal concern for a neighbour and a friend. Many people subscribed for large paper copies, some for more than one copy and two men gave considerable sums to help print the work. The most noteworthy feature of the list is the large number of women's names which it contains. The presence of a woman's name may not mean that she could read and understand Locke, but it certainly points to a willingness to support a member of her own sex.

But even without Lady Russell, Celia Fiennes, and Catharine Cockburn, Ballard's work showed that, despite the hard words written about women's education in this age, an able woman of whom her contemporaries could be justly proud could appear in any part of England. Two only of the women he described were born in or near London and only two belonged to a noble family. They were all gentlewomen whom Mary Astell would have regarded as worthy of entering her women's college. Two of them, Frances, Lady Norton, and her daughter Grace, Lady Gethin, hardly deserve their places in his book. Lady Norton, who was still living in 1720, owed her reputation to two volumes of religious meditation which she was moved to write after the death of her daughter Grace. She cannot have been a woman of wide reading for she was a party to the curious publication on which her daughter's fame rests. Lady Gethin died at the age of twenty and was buried in Westminster Abbey. After her death her relatives were impressed to find among her papers a number of essays, which, since they were in her handwriting, they assumed that she had herself composed. They published them in 1699 with a title-page headed *Misery's Virtues Whet-stone* and ended *Let her own works praise her in the Gates, Prov. xxxi, 31*. The full title of the work, *Reliquiæ Gethinianiæ or some remains of the most Ingenious and Excellent Lady Grace Gethin, Lately Deceased, being a collection of Choice Discourses, Pleasant Apothegmes, and Witty Sentences, written by her for the most part by way of an essay and at spare hours*[1], conceals the fact that Lady Gethin had simply copied out a number of Bacon's essays which none of her admiring relatives was able

[1] With an Epistle Dedicatory signed J. M.

to recognize. The work ran into more than one edition, without anyone recognizing the unconscious plagiarism. Ballard was deceived and, after him, Edmund Gosse[1].

Three more distinguished ladies of this period received the signal honour of mention by the great Dr. George Hickes in his Preface to the *Thesaurus* published in 1705. Having set out in his stately Latin his obligations to his male friends and fellow scholars, Hickes continued in the same tongue and style 'Here also come three distinguished and most elegant ladies; our books, indeed, have no one to whom they owe more than to them. The very noble matron, Dorothy Grahme, dearest wife of James Grahme of Levins in the county of Westmorland Esq., having already acquired immortality among those above, outstanding in her virtues, is worthy of eternal memory. The noble matron, worthy of veneration, Susanna Hopton of Kington in the county of Hereford, an outstanding example of Christian piety and a great glory to the Church of England, who having acquired no common knowledge of the sacred Scriptures, has put forth not a few anonymous books which are worn to pieces in the hands of pious men and women. That she had put them forth she refused to make plain because of her unshakable modesty, as one who prefers to be instructed and to be good, rather than to seek recognition. The most eminent and most honourable matron, Catherine Bovey of Flaxley in Gloucestershire, the Christian Hypatia of our England, of whom there is no praise so moderate that it does not greatly offend her extreme modesty; nor is it possible to speak of her in such an exalted or magnificent fashion that her virtues will not equal, or even exceed it'[2]. Such words are praise indeed.

A writer, less august but now more famous than George Hickes, has recorded an incident from Dorothy Grahme's virtuous youth as a maid of honour to Charles II's queen. John Evelyn on 8 July 1675 rode from Oxford to Northampton with Mrs. Howard, Dorothy's mother, and her two daughters to be present at the assizes. Under the date 11 July he records that 'in this journey, went part of the way Mr. James Grahame [since Privy Purse to the Duke], a young Gent: exceedingly in love with Mrs. Dorothy Howard, one of the Mayds of honor in our Company. I

---

[1] In his life of Congreve (1888), who had likewise been deceived and wrote a poem in honour of Lady Gethin published in her *Remains*. Leslie Stephen called Gosse's attention to the error. 'I wonder neither you nor Congreve spotted "reading makes a full man"!' Evan Charteris, *The Life and Letters of Edmund Gosse*, London, 1931, p. 207.

[2] *Linguarum Vetterum Septentrionalium Thesaurus*, Oxford, 1705, p. XLVII.

could not but pitty them both; the Mother not much favouring it. This Lady was not only a greate beauty, but a most virtuous & excellent Creature, and worthy to have been the Wife of the best of men: My advice was required, & I spake to the advantage of the young gent: more out of pitty than that she deserv'd no better; for, though he was a gent: of good family, yet there was great inequality, etc.'[1] Evelyn's success in this negotiation appears from a letter written in the same year by Lady Russell, who told her husband that 'Mr Grimes [sic] that was at Wickham, was married yesterday to Dol. Howard, the maid-of-honour'[2].

When Hickes published his *Thesaurus* in 1705 Susanna Hopton was drawing near to the end of a long life. She died in 1709 at the age of eighty-two. During the civil war she had been converted by the Catholic apologist, Henry Turberville, but returned to the Church of England after making herself 'as perfect in the controversie as English writers could make her'[3]. She wrote to Father Turberville setting out her reasons for returning to the Church of England, and Hickes after her death printed her letter in the second volume of his *Controversial Letters*. Her first book of devotions was published as early as 1673 as the work of 'an Humble Penitent'. Hickes himself revised and published her second book in 1701, with an Introduction by himself in which he said that the author 'hath already given the world one book of devotion, which hath been very well received in four or five editions, and will leave it another for which posterity will bless the author's name; one, whose house is a temple, and whose family is a church, or *Religious Society*, and whose hands are daily lifted up unto Heaven with alms as well as prayers'[4]. Hickes is said to have written the inscription on her tomb at Bishop's Frome.

Catharine Bovey, the third lady to whom Hickes expressed his grati-tude, earned great praise from her contemporaries not only for her charity but for her learning and beauty. She died in 1726 at the age of fifty-seven having been a widow for thirty-five years. Even Mrs. Manley, the scurrilous author of *The New Atalantis*, could find only praise for Mrs. Bovey, whom she called Portia. 'She is one of those lofty, black, and lasting Beauties, that strikes with Reverence and yet Delight; there is no Feature in her Face nor any Thing in her Person, her Air and Manner,

---

1 *The Diary of John Evelyn*, ed. E. S. de Beer, Oxford, 1955, vol. iv, p. 69.
2 *Some Account of the Life, etc.*, p. 10.
3 Quoted by Ballard, p. 390, from the Preface to *Controversial Letters*, vol. ii.
4 Ballard, p. 393.

that could be exchanged for any others, and she not prove a Loser'[1]. Sir Richard Steele dedicated to her the second volume of *The Ladies Library*. 'With the Charms of the fairest of your own Sex', he wrote, 'and Knowledge not inferior to the more Learned of ·Ours, a Closet, a Bower, or some Beauteous Scene of rural Nature, has constantly robbed the World of a Lady's Appearance, who never was beheld but with Gladness to her Visitants, nor ever admired but with Pain to Herself'[2]. That a beautiful young woman of twenty-two should prefer to remain unmarried and devote her life to study and good works surprised her contemporaries. But her short married life had been unhappy. She was the heiress of both her father's and her husband's wealth.

The zeal of George Hickes for the cause of education made him willing to write a Preface or dedication to any serious work which had the improvement of the mind and manners as its end[3]. He was equally concerned with the education of men and women. He revised a translation of the treatise on the education of daughters written by François S. de la Motte Fénélon, Archbishop of Cambrai. Hickes wrote a dedication of the book to the Duchess of Ormonde, mother of five daughters[4]. Fénélon understood and sympathized with women. He wrote mainly for women of position, to encourage them to educate their daughters at home, rather than in religious houses. In France the work was immediately popular and in England the translation was widely read. Steele pillaged it for *The Ladies Library*, though without acknowledgment. A second edition was issued in 1708. The publishers of the 1750 edition felt it necessary to say that they were 'sensible that this translation is far from that elegance, that might have been expected in one revised by a person of Dr. Hickes' learning'. Nevertheless a comparison of the French and English versions shows that Hickes took trouble to see that the words suited an English audience.

George Hickes was the leading figure among those interested in the new scholarship. It is remarkable how far his influence penetrated. It was

[1] *Secret Memoirs and Manners of Several Persons of Quality of both sexes from the New Atalantis*, London, 1720, vol. iii, pp. 245–6.

[2] *The Ladies Library*, vol. ii. 'Written by a Lady'. 'Published by Mr. Steele', London, 1714 Dedication, unpaged.

[3] Hicks wrote a dedication to Lord Cornbury, the son and heir apparent to the Earl of Clarendon, for a treatise on the proper behaviour of young men entitled *The Gentleman Instructed in the Conduct of a Virtuous and Happy Life*. My copy is the 6th ed., London, 1726.

[4] *Instructions for the Education of a daughter by the author of Telemachus*. Done into English, and Revised by Dr. George Hickes, 4th ed., London, 1721.

felt in remote country houses up and down England as well as in the universities and the city of London. In his writings on the religious controversies of his time he showed respect for women's capacities and appreciation of their achievements without a trace of condescension[1]. In the studies for which he is now chiefly remembered he gave valuable encouragement to Elizabeth Elstob, the first woman to study the Anglo-Saxon tongue. She was born at Newcastle in 1683, so that she was still a child when Mary Astell left Newcastle for Chelsea. Elizabeth's father died when she was five and her mother three years later, but before she died Mrs. Elstob did all she could to encourage her daughter to become a scholar, for she was herself an admirer of learning, 'especially in her own sex'[2]. At eight years old Elizabeth had gone some way towards mastering her Latin grammar. After her parents' death she lived with her aunt and uncle at Canterbury, but her uncle, the Reverend Charles Elstob, had no belief in the education of women. She could not pursue her classical studies, although her aunt enabled her to learn French. Her real education was acquired from her brother William, who had been a fellow of University College, Oxford. In 1702 he became the incumbent of two City churches and Elizabeth came to look after his house. She lived with him, 'the delightful and tireless companion of my studies'[3], until his death in 1715. In dedicating his sermons to the Dean and Chapter of Durham in 1713 Hickes recorded his pleasure in seeing some of the work which he had been forced to abandon 'for want of Help and Supply' being 'attempted with so much Success, by two private and very modest persons, I mean the Reverend Mr. William Elstob, Rector of St. Swithin's, London, and his sister Mrs. Elizabeth Elstob; . . . the latter with incredible Industry hath finished a Saxon HOMILARIUM, or a collection of the English Saxon Homilies of Alfric archbishop of Canterbury, which she hath translated and adorned with learned and useful Notes, and for the printing of which she hath published proposals; and I cannot but wish, that for her own sake as well as for the advancement of Septentrional Learning,

---

[1] *Two Treatises: one of the Christian Priesthood and the other of the Episcopal Order*, 2nd ed., London, 1707. Preface, pp. i–iii.

[2] Bodleian Library: Ballard MSS. XLIII, 59, which is an account of her life written by herself for George Ballard, quoted by Ada Wallas in her chapter on Elizabeth Elstob in *Before the Bluestockings*, London, 1929, p. 133.

[3] *dulcis et indefessa studiorum meorum comes*, from William Elstob's Latin letter to his sister, printed as an Introduction to his Latin version of the homily, *An English-Saxon Homily on the Birthday of St. Gregory*, ed. Eliz. Elstob, London, 1709, unpaged.

for the Honour of our English Saxon Ancestors, and the service of
the Church of England, and the Credit of the Country, and the honour
of her Sex, that Learned and most Studious Gentlewoman may find such
encouragement as she and her great Undertaking deserve'[1].

Elizabeth Elstob's edition of Alfric's *Homilies* was never published, for
after her brother died she had to earn her living. She entrusted her papers
to a woman friend who went to the West Indies and the papers were
lost[2]. But before Hickes wrote the dedication to his sermons in 1713 she
had already published enough to establish her reputation as a precise
scholar. She dedicated her edition of the *Homily on the birthday of St.
Gregory*, which appeared in 1709, to Queen Anne, reminding her that
a woman had secured the acceptance of Christianity by the Roman
Empire, that the conversion of the English owed much to the first Christian
English queen, Bertha, and that the Christian faith in England had been
restored from corruption by Queen Elizabeth. In her long Preface Elizabeth
Elstob set out to answer the question 'What has a woman to do with
Learning?' and further to explain how she came to study Anglo-Saxon.
'For my part', she says, 'I could never think any part of Learning either
useless, or contemptible, because I knew not the Advantages of it; I have
rather thought my self obliged to reverence those who are skilful in any
Art or Profession, and can gladly subscribe to the Praise of any liberal
Accomplishment, be it in any Person, of any Sex'. There speaks the
truly magnanimous scholar. It is not surprising after reading those words
to find that both William and Elizabeth Elstob subscribed to *The History
and Antiquities of the Exchequer* by Thomas Madox in 1711, despite their
narrow means and despite the fact that they lived together. The young
Elizabeth Elstob is not only the first woman to study Anglo-Saxon but
the first woman scholar who would be at home in the learned world
today.

In a book dedicated to Queen Anne it was to be expected that the
name of the nonjuring Hickes would not appear. Elizabeth Elstob,

---

[1] *A collection of Sermons formerly preached by the Rev. George Hickes*, D.D., London, 1713,
vol. i, The Dedication, pp. 3–4.

[2] Ballard MSS. XLIII, 59. No other woman devoted herself to Anglo-Saxon for a hundred years. Anna Gurney (1795–1857) was the next, but her work was that of a good
amateur of scholarship rather than a scholar. She translated the Anglo-Saxon Chronicle
from printed sources and printed it for private circulation among her friends, see G. N.
Garmonsway, 'Anna Gurney: Learned Saxonist', in *Essays and Studies 1955*, published by
the English Association, pp. 40–57.

however, speaks of him under the description of 'the great Instaurator of Northern Literature' and 'this great Patron of Septentrional Studies'. He had, she said, urged her to publish something in Saxon so that she might 'invite the Ladies to be acquainted with the language of their Predecessors and the original of their Mother Tongue'. She called attention to Hickes's translation of Fénélon as proof of his belief in the importance of educating women properly. Elizabeth Elstob also wrote an Anglo-Saxon *Grammar*, which she dedicated to the brilliant Princess of Wales, Caroline of Anspach'[1]. Her Preface took the form of a letter addressed to Hickes. In it she explained her purpose in writing an Anglo-Saxon *Grammar* in English. It was in order that women, who were not able to read Latin, could study Anglo-Saxon. She told Hickes that after she had published the *Homily of St. Gregory* she took a holiday in Canterbury on the invitation of her friends. She was there 'more particularly gratified, with the new Friendship and Conversation, of a young Lady, whose Ingenuity and Love of Learning, is well known and esteemed, not only in that Place, but by yourself: and which so far indear'd itself to me, by her promise that she would learn the Saxon tongue, and do me the Honour to be my scholar, as to make me think of composing an English Grammar in that language for her use'. Unfortunately 'that Ladies Fortune' had separated them so far that they could no longer 'treat on this Matter by Discourse or by Correspondence'[2].

Although Elizabeth Elstob's uncle might feel and say that one tongue was enough for a woman, she received ample encouragement during the years she lived with her brother not only from George Hickes but also from most eminent scholars and antiquaries of the day. To Ralf Thoresby of Leeds she was 'the Saxon nymph' and 'the ingenious sister' of Parson Elstob, whom he visited when he was in London[3]. Chief Justice Parker, later Lord Macclesfield, paid for the Saxon type used for Elizabeth Elstob's *Grammar*[4]. Robert Nelson, a 'learned and pious layman'[5], son of a wealthy London citizen, wrote in 1714 to thank Lord Oxford for procuring 'the Royal Bounty for Mrs. Elstob: she wants only that to set the press to work'[6]. A learned woman might well have felt that she lived in a fortunate age in the early eighteenth century. Queen Anne

[1] *The Rudiments of Grammar for the English-Saxon Tongue*, London, W. Bowyer, 1715.
[2] *Ibid.*, p. ii.
[3] *The Diary of Ralf Thoresby, F.R.S.*, ed. Joseph Hunter, London, 1830, vol. ii, p. 131.
[4] Nichols, *Literary Anecdotes*, vol. ii, pp. 354–5.
[5] *Ibid.*, vol. iv, p. 188.   [6] *Ibid.*, vol. iv, p. 199.

was sympathetic to learned women. The Electress Sophia of Hanover, whose death prevented her succession to the English throne, was the most highly educated woman of rank in Europe. In the dedication of her *Grammar* to the Princess of Wales, later Queen Caroline, the author stated that she had hoped 'to have had the Honour of dedicating it to her Royal Highness the Princess Sophia, a lady endowed with all Princely Accomplishments, and particularly a most Bounteous Patroness of Letters'. The list of subscribers to Elizabeth Elstob's first book shows that a woman's work could receive support from a large number of women as well as from men. The list is particularly interesting, for it contains not only the names of many noble ladies, such as the Duchesses of Beaufort, Bolton, and Somerset, several countesses and many other ladies of title, but also the names of obscure women, some of whom it would be difficult to identify today. In all, one hundred and twenty-one women subscribed to a book in which few of them could have felt much interest. Well might the authoress speak of 'the many Compliments and kind Expressions, which their favourable Acceptance of my first Attempt in Saxon, had obtained for me from the Ladies'[1].

It was hard enough for a man to make a living by his pen if he had not taken orders. To make a living entirely by works of scholarship would have been as impossible for a man as it was for Elizabeth Elstob. In 1718 she gave up the struggle to publish her work on the homilies and retired to Worcestershire. How she lived during the next few years cannot be known with certainty. When her name next appears in contemporary correspondence she was keeping a little school at Evesham. The Cotswold country had a tradition of cultivated society. Clement Barksdale had spent his life there a generation earlier. In 1715 Colonel Granville, a younger brother of Lord Lansdowne, had come with his family to live at Buckland, near Campden. His daughter Mary, born in 1700, became the close friend of a lively and intelligent girl, Sarah Kirkman, daughter of the incumbent of Stanton. The girls met in the fields between their fathers' houses since Colonel Granville regarded Sarah as 'too free and masculine' for a woman[2]. Mary Granville called her Sappho and the friendship thus formed lasted through their joint lives. Mary Granville, better known by her second married name, Mrs. Delany, belonged to

---

[1] *Grammar*, p. ii.
[2] *The Autobiography and Correspondence of Mary Granville, Mrs. Delany*, ed. Lady Llanover, London, 1861, vol. i, pp. 15–16.

a great family and was drawn into the fashionable world. Sarah married a poor parson, named Capon or Chapone, who kept a school at Stanton. How she came into contact with Elizabeth Elstob is unknown, but once she had met her she did not rest until she had tried to improve her situation.

During 1730 she wrote a letter about Elizabeth Elstob which Mary Granville, now Mrs. Pendarves, could put into the hands of people about the queen. In October 1730 Mrs. Pendarves wrote to her sister describing how the matter had gone. Queen Caroline 'was so touched with the letter' that she 'ordered immediately an hundred pounds for Mrs. Elstob, and said she need never fear a necessitous old age whilst she lived'[1]. The queen promised to give Elizabeth Elstob a hundred pounds every five years. It was probably through the kind offices of Mrs. Chapone that Elizabeth Elstob met George Ballard. It gave Elizabeth Elstob great pleasure to enjoy again the friendship of an antiquary. He was engaged in collecting material for his book on learned British ladies and was evidently delighted to meet one. He carefully preserved her letters, written in her beautiful script-like hand, and they have passed with his papers into the Bodleian Library. Their friendship began in August 1735, when she explained that she was unwilling to give up her school at Evesham for a better post because of the friendship she had received from the good ladies there. Ballard obtained first-hand information from her about Mary Astell, whom she had known in London. He persuaded her to write an account of her own life for him. This, too, is preserved among her letters[2]. She does not figure in his book for she was still alive when he brought it out in 1752.

Elizabeth Elstob's letters to George Ballard show how much pleasure she derived from the friendship of this sensitive and intelligent man. He visited her at Evesham and on one occasion she rode the five miles to Campden to spend a day with him and his mother. He made her such gifts as he could and interested his antiquarian friends in her. One of them brought her three guineas collected for her use, a gift she found embarrassing. Apart from failing health these years at Evesham were not unhappy. She had no desire to become the mistress of Lady Elizabeth Hastings's charity school, where she would have to teach spinning and knitting. The death of Queen Caroline in 1737 renewed her fears for the future. But Mrs. Chapone was still her friend. Through the good offices of Mrs. Pendarves, Elizabeth Elstob was at last established in the

[1] Mrs. Delany, vol. i, pp. 263–4.   [2] Ballard MSS. XLIII, 59.

household of the Duchess of Portland in 1739. 'When I see the Duchess of Portland', wrote Mrs. Pendarves to her sister, 'I shall have Sally's historical epistle'[1], that is, the letter which had so much impressed the queen. The duchess was the daughter of Lord Oxford, the founder of the Harleian Library, who had procured the queen's bounty towards publishing Elizabeth Elstob's *Homilies* many years before. Until her death in 1756 Elizabeth Elstob remained in the household of the duchess.

The position of a dependant in a great household cannot always be easy, but it is foolish to pity Elizabeth Elstob for her fate. She was honoured for her learning to the end of her life. Her letters show that she loved her pupils and that they profited by her teaching. As her hands contracted with rheumatism one of them wrote her letters for her. She would have liked, but failed to get, permission for Ballard to dedicate his book to the duchess, but at least five copies of it were subscribed for by members of the household at Bulstrode. The duchess took a copy, as did her son, the Marquis of Titchfield[2], and her three daughters. For Elizabeth Elstob there was no lonely old age with no one to look after her. She had her own apartment where her friends could visit her. Mary Granville, now Mrs. Delany, wrote to her sister on 24 May 1756 that 'Mrs. Elstob is gradually drawing towards that happy repose which we may suppose so good a woman may obtain. I have made her many visits during my constant attendance at Whitehall, and urged her, as the Duchess desired me, to have some physician: she said she had a better opinion of Mr. Groat than any of them, and would have none. She did not at first know me the last visit I made her, and Mr. Groat tells me today her memory is rather worse'. The duchess was alarmed at the constant visits of one of Elizabeth Elstob's cousins, who was a Roman Catholic. 'She brings her presents of chocolate, and seems to pay great court to her'[3]. Early in June Elizabeth Elstob died, and seventy guineas were found among her belongings.

Her story has often been used to illustrate the unhappy position of women, and particularly women scholars, in the eighteenth century.

---

[1] *Mrs. Delany*, vol. ii, p. 31.

[2] Two phases of Anglo-Saxon scholarship were brought together for a moment in 1807 when the Rev. James Ingram, in his inaugural lecture as professor of Anglo-Saxon at Oxford, observed that Mrs. Elizabeth Elstob had been 'the first preceptress to his Grace the present Chancellor of Oxford', that is, the third Duke of Portland, known to Elizabeth Elstob as the Marquis of Titchfield. *An Inaugural Lecture on the Utility of Anglo-Saxon Literature*, Oxford, 1807.   [3] *Mrs. Delany*, vol. iii, pp. 428–9.

But if her career is looked at as a whole and in perspective it appears in a very different light. She was extraordinarily fortunate in youth beyond other women who may have felt the impulse towards scholarship but had no learned brothers to make them the companions of their studies. Above all she was fortunate in the friendship of Hickes, whose magnanimous spirit rejoiced to find a woman interested in learning. Throughout her life she had memories of days when she talked familiarly with the leading scholars of their generation. Even in her darkest moments after her brother's death and the death of Hickes one eminent man, George Smalridge, Bishop of Bristol, endeavoured to supply her necessities. His was the poorest see in the country and Elizabeth Elstob would not allow him to impoverish himself on her behalf[1]. He, too, died in 1719, but she had then been for a year in Worcestershire. She was not a great scholar, though perhaps she might have become one had things fallen out differently. She was not much more than thirty when her brother died. Her two slender books were given their full measure of admiration by her contemporaries, even in the fashionable world. She herself might, in moments of depression, feel 'that the prospect of the next age is a melancholy one to me who wish Learning might flourish to the end of the World, both in Men and Women'. In such a mood she wrote to Ballard that 'the choice you have made for the Honour of the Females was the wrongest subject you could pitch upon. For you can come into no company of Ladies and Gentlemen, where you shall not hear an open and vehement exclamation against Learned Women'[2].

Yet it was respect for her learning alone which made Mrs. Chapone stir up her friends on her behalf. Mrs. Delany and her sister were anxious to provide for the scholar in distress, not the decayed gentlewoman, when they persuaded the Duchess of Portland to employ her. In her honoured old age at Bulstrode or the ducal establishment in London Elizabeth Elstob was a person on whom her own relatives were glad to wait. The story of her life illustrates how society was beginning to appreciate the capacities of women. It is surely remarkable that an obscure City parson's sister should be able to dedicate two learned works, one to the queen and the other to the Princess of Wales, that a chief justice should pay for the type-cutting for her *Grammar* and that the queen's bounty should be obtained for her work through the good offices of the chief minister of state. In choosing to write about learned women George

---

[1] Nichols, *Literary Anecdotes*, vol. iv, p. 133.   [2] Ballard MSS. XLIII, 89.

Ballard, though he did not realize it, was moving with the times. The long list of subscribers to his book, which, like the list of subscribers to Catherine Cockburn's works and to Elizabeth Elstob's *Homily*, contains a high proportion of women's names, shows that people of rank and culture were ready to be interested in women's achievements in the past. Such an interest could only arise in a society which is preparing to show respect to women's achievements in the future.

CHAPTER IX

The Eighteenth Century
Court and Society

For twelve years between 1702 and 1714 a queen was ruling in her own right and English arms were carrying on for most of this period a successful foreign war. It was possible for a woman to write of 'that GREAT QUEEN who has subdu'd the Proud, and made the pretended Invincible more than once fly before her; who has Rescu'd an Empire, Reduc'd a Kingdom, Conquered Provinces in as little time almost as one can Travel them, and seems to have Chain'd Victory to her Standard'[1]. She was clothed in the majesty of her office so that Thomas Madox, in dedicating to the queen his *History and Antiquities of the Exchequer*, addressed her as 'MOST DREAD SOVERAIGNE'[2] with no sense of incongruity. Her court was conducted with the formality and routine which centuries of use had made familiar. But Queen Anne was no Elizabeth I. She had not the wit to devise for herself a dangerous middle way, to play off one enemy against another, to determine the national policy herself and leave her ministers to follow. She was a simple, kindly, but obstinate, woman, devoted to the Church of England, uneasy about her own right to the throne, full of good intentions, over-involved in domesticities, often ill and in pain, and always anxious for a friend.

Whoever had been the queen's friend would have been drawn inevitably into politics. She would not have been able to prevent the leaders of opposing parties from trying to influence the queen through her. Long before she became queen, Anne had chosen as her closest friend and confidante Sarah Jennings, who in 1678 at the age of eighteen had married John Churchill, later the Duke of Marlborough. According to the duchess the queen's friendship for her went back to the days when

[1] Mary Astell, *Reflections on Marriage*, Preface, unpaged, last paragraph.
[2] London, 1711, The Dedication, unpaged, A 2.

she entered the household of the second Duchess of York to attend upon the Princess Anne, then a child. When in 1683 the princess married and a household was established for her, Lady Churchill, at the request of Anne herself, became one of the ladies of the bedchamber. In the early days of the princess's married life Lady Churchill came to such familiarity with her mistress that she was invited to address her as Mrs. Morley, and was called by the princess Mrs. Freeman. The friendship had momentous consequences, for it meant that Marlborough controlled the Government at home during the years of his great campaigns abroad. But it ended, as such friendships generally end, in the revolt of the weaker character against the overbearing authority of the stronger.

The Duchess of Marlborough long outlived her husband and the queen. She spent much time in her declining years in going over again and again the story of this friendship and its end. In 1742, two years before her death, she at last published an account of her conduct[1]. The final draft had the benefit of revision by a practised writer, Nathaniel Hooke, who is said to have been rewarded with £5,000 for his trouble. He certainly earned his fee, for the narrative is so seductive that the reader forgets to criticize it. According to the duchess she was supplanted in the queen's good graces by one who owed everything to the woman whose place she took. Abigail Hill, who was a first cousin of the duchess, had entered the service of Lady Rivers at Chafford, in Kent, when her parents died. The duchess took her into her own household at St. Albans, treated her like a sister, and eventually found her a place in the household of the Princess Anne. But Abigail Hill was also a kinswoman of Robert Harley and was inclined to the Tory side. She was a plain woman of considerable ability, who never made the mistake of trying to dominate the queen. The duchess only realized her danger when she learned some time in the spring of 1707 that Abigail had secretly married Samuel Masham—one of Damaris Masham's stepchildren—and that the queen had been present at the wedding.

The end of the story was never in doubt, for the duchess ruined her own cause by her untimely and incessant reproaches to the queen and reminders of their former friendship. She even talked of publishing the queen's letters. Anne at last, on 17 January 1711, requested the return of the duchess's key of office as groom of the stole within two days. It was

[1] *An account of the conduct of the Dowager Duchess of Marlborough, from her first coming to court, to the year 1710. In a letter from herself to My Lord ——,* London, 1742.

returned that evening. The Duchess of Somerset succeeded her as mistress of the robes and groom of the stole and Mrs. Masham was given the privy purse. In May Samuel Masham became cofferer of the household. Masham was one of the Tory peers created in 1712, but the queen only agreed to his elevation on condition that his wife, though now a peeress, remained a bedchamber-woman. She nursed the queen in her last illness and retired from court when she died.

The women about the bedchamber of a failing queen of necessity were the messengers between the queen and her ministers. Much depended on their integrity. They were ladies of position but were bound to perform the humblest offices about the queen's person. Their place and duties were ruled by a custom which had its roots in the medieval past. When Mrs. Howard, later Countess of Suffolk, was bedchamber-woman to Queen Caroline she enquired of Lady Masham through Dr. Arbuthnot about the duties of her position. Dr. Arbuthnot's letter of 29 May 1728 shows that Mrs. Howard was particularly interested in the relative position of the bedchamber-women and the bedchamber-ladies. 'The bedchamber-woman came in to waiting before the queen's prayers, which was before her majesty was dressed. The queen often shifted in a morning: if her majesty shifted at noon, the bedchamber-lady being by, the bedchamber-woman gave the shift to the lady without any ceremony, and the lady put it on. Sometimes, likewise, the bedchamber-woman gave the fan to the lady in the same manner; and this was all that the bedchamber-lady did about the queen at her dressing.

'When the queen washed her hands, the page of the back-stairs brought and set down on a side-table the basin and ewer; then the bedchamber-woman set it before the queen, and knelt on the other side of the table over-against the queen, the bedchamber-lady only looking on. The bed-chamber-woman poured the water out of the ewer upon the queen's hands.

'The bedchamber-woman pulled on the queen's gloves, when she could not do it herself.

'The page of the back-stairs was called in to put on the queen's shoes.

'When the queen dined in public, the page reached the glass to the bedchamber-woman, and she to the lady-in-waiting.

'The bedchamber-woman brought the chocolate and gave it without kneeling.

'In general the bedchamber-woman had no dependence on the lady of the bedchamber'[1]. There was certainly rivalry between the bedchamber-women and the ladies of the bedchamber. The bedchamber-women did so much more personal duty about the queen that the ladies of the bedchamber tended to be jealous of them. The etiquette here set out has the flavour of antiquity. Every servant about the queen kept jealous watch over her own rights and duties as each one had done in the time of every sovereign since the days when the duties and perquisites of the members of the royal household were first written down soon after the death of King Henry I.

Even when the sovereign was a woman the only department of the royal household which was wholly staffed by women was the queen's bedchamber. A place there was extremely valuable to its holder, not only for the salary, but also for the many perquisites which accompanied it. In 1707 there were ten ladies of the bedchamber, each with a salary of £1,000 a year. At their head was the Duchess of Marlborough, who also received £1,000 a year. Her offices were groom of the stole, privy purse, and first lady of the bedchamber. The queen gave the duchess £5,000 as a marriage portion for each of her four daughters and wished to double the duchess's salary. In the days of their friendship she refused this increase. But when the queen dismissed her the duchess wrote to ask whether the additional salary which the queen had proposed might now be allowed her on the privy purse accounts, a sum amounting by this time to £18,000. The queen allowed this[2]. The duchess herself admitted that her 'offices under the Queen were indeed considerable and I have ever acknowledged them to be so, amounting to 5,600 *l.* a year, deducting only for taxes and fees. But it is to be remembered, that they were only the same employments that I had executed when she was Princess at a salary of 400 *l.* a year'[3]. It would be impossible at this distance of time to find out just how much each of the other ten ladies of the queen's bedchamber received by way of perquisites, grants, and fees from their offices.

Whereas the ladies of the bedchamber were all wives of peers, the bedchamber-women were commoners. In 1707 there were four bedchamber-women, each receiving a salary of £500 a year, Mrs. Danvers,

[1] *Letters to and from Henrietta, Countess of Suffolk, and her second husband, the Hon. George Berkeley from 1712 to 1767*, London, 1824, vol. i, pp. 292–3.
[2] *Conduct*, pp. 293–5.   [3] *Ibid.*, p. 297.

Mrs. Cooper, Mrs. Fielding, and Mrs. Hill[1]. The contemporary habit of describing all women as Mrs., an abbreviation of Mistress, makes it difficult to be sure whether these women were, or were not, married. Abigail Hill was a spinster when, in 1707, she married Samuel Masham. In 1691 Queen Mary had only five ladies of the bedchamber, in addition to the Countess of Derby who was groom of the stole and lady of the robes, but she had six women of the bedchamber. Queen Mary's groom of the stole then received only £1,200, her five ladies of the bedchamber £500 each, and her six women of the bedchamber £200 each[2]. The bedchamber-women certainly earned their salaries by their attendance on the queen at her toilet and throughout the day and night.

Owing to the appointment of a novelist to a post about the person of George III's queen more is known about court routine in her day than in that of any of her predecessors. Fanny Burney, who had published *Evelina* anonymously in 1778, was provided for with the post of 'dresser to the queen' in 1786 in succession to one of the queen's German women-servants.[3] In reporting to a friend the terms of her appointment Fanny Burney said 'Her Majesty proposed giving me apartments in the palace; making me belong to the table of Mrs. Schwellenberg'—the senior dresser—'keeping me a footman, and settling on me £200 a year'[4]. She described her office to another friend as 'a place of being constantly about' the queen's 'own person, and assisting in her toilette,—a place of much confidence, and many comforts'[5]. She also found it a laborious place. She had to rise at six and await her first summons, which generally came at about half-past seven. The queen's German wardrobe woman, a Mrs. Thielky, had always dressed the queen's hair before Fanny Burney came. 'No maid', she recorded, 'ever enters the room while the Queen is in it. Mrs. Thielky hands the things to me, and I put them on'. After breakfast Fanny Burney had to arrange her own clothes and was free until a quarter to twelve, except that twice a week she was free only until a quarter to eleven, because of having her hair curled. At a quarter to one the queen began to dress for the day, an operation not concluded until three o'clock. Her dressers then had two hours free. They dined together at five and spent the evening together. Fanny Burney's last

[1] Chamberlayne, *Angliæ Notitia*, London, 1707, p. 545.

[2] Miege, *New State of England*, 1691, part 2, p. 176. Their names are on pp. 167–8.

[3] *Diary and Letters of Madame d'Arblay*, ed. Austin Dobson, London, 1904, vol. ii, p. 369 n.

[4] *Ibid.*, pp. 363–4.   [5] *Ibid.*, p. 370.

summons to the queen came between eleven and twelve, but her last period of duty seldom exceeded half an hour. 'The early rising and a long day's attention to new affairs and occupations cause a fatigue so bodily, that nothing mental stands against it, and to sleep I fall as soon as I have put out my candle and laid down my head'[1].

The queen was always attended by six maids of honour as had been Queen Elizabeth I herself[2]. *The Present State of England* of 1673 described the six maids of honour who attended the consort of Charles II as 'all Gentlewomen unmarried, over whom is placed a Governess called the Mother of the Maids; who is the Lady Sanderson'[3]. The mother of the maids, whose office was already established in the reign of Elizabeth[4], was both a chaperone and a guide to correct court behaviour. Lady Sanderson had been mother of the maids in the court of Charles I's queen. She died in 1681 at the age of eighty-nine. The salary of Queen Anne's maids of honour was £300, but in 1691 only the first of the maids received £300, the rest were paid £200 apiece[5]. Queen Elizabeth's maids had to be content with £40[6]. In her reminiscences, written in old age, Mrs. Delany, born Mary Granville, described how her aunt Anne Granville, the eldest sister of Lord Lansdowne, had been a maid of honour to Queen Mary II. She 'was particularly favoured and distinguished by her, and early attained all the advantages of such an education under so great and excellent a princess, without the least taint or blemish incident to that state of life, so dangerous to young minds'[7]. Anne Granville appears in the list of maids of honour of 1691 as Mrs. Anne Greenvill[8]. After Queen Mary died Anne Granville married Sir John Stanley and 'King William, who bestowed the usual addition to the Maid of Honour's portion, granted her the apartments in Whitehall which were afterwards the Duke of Dorset's'[9]. An annual salary, the opportunity of a good marriage, and a marriage portion from the crown were enough to make the post of maid of honour highly coveted.

---

[1] *Diary and Letters of Madame D'Arblay*, vol. ii, pp. 396–400.
[2] E.g. *Progresses*, vol. ii, p. 88.   [3] *Angliae Notitia*, London, 1673, p. 225.
[4] In the list of recipients of New Year's Gifts from the queen the 'Maydes of Honour' each have a piece of plate and their names are followed by that of the 'Mother of the Mades' who received a rather better piece. In 1578 she was 'Mrs. Hyde'; *Progresses, loc. cit.*
[5] *Angliæ Notitia*, 1707, p. 545.   [6] *Progresses*, vol. i, pp. 269–70.
[7] *Mrs. Delany*, vol. i, p. 8.
[8] Miege, *New State of England*, 1691, part 2, p. 168.
[9] *Mrs. Delany*, vol. i, p. 2.

None of Queen Anne's maids can have made a better match than Jane Warburton, who had entered the household by 1710[1]. Her companions found it hard to understand how she acquired the position, for she had spent her life in rustic retirement in Cheshire and brought with her to court the manners and speech of a simple country environment. Her family was an old one and by birth she was a gentlewoman. But she knew no language except her own and 'her rusticity, ignorance, and want of breeding' made her 'the standing jest of her companions in office.' To the end of her long life her 'Pug' and her 'Puss' were 'pronounced alike'[2]. Nevertheless, the Duke of Argyll fell in love with her, to the mortification of her companions. He had been separated from his wife, but she was still alive. He made offers to Jane Warburton, but she refused them though she remained friendly with him. So close was their friendship that when Queen Anne died, instead of being sent home to Cheshire with or without a small pension, Jane Warburton became one of the maids of honour to the Princess of Wales. When his duchess died the duke, even before she was buried, asked Jane to marry him. She made him wait the proper six months before she would consent.

Mrs. Delany recalled how she had herself been promised a place as maid of honour in Queen Anne's court. In the expectation of this she was carefully educated. When she was six she was placed in the care of Mlle Puelle, a French refugee, who received twenty pupils, but no more, at a time. It was a select academy, intended for the daughters of men of rank, wealth, or fashion. Among Mary Granville's twenty contemporaries were the daughters of an earl, a duke, 'a very considerable brewer'[3], and also 'the daughter of Mrs. Oldfield, the actress, who after leaving school was the *pink of fashion* in the beau monde, and married a nobleman'[4]. When she was eight Mary Granville left school to live at Whitehall with Lady Stanley. She remained there until Queen Anne's death in 1714 ended her hopes of a place at court, for the Tories were out of favour

[1] *Angliae Notitia*, 1710, p. 541.

[2] Lady Louisa Stuart's caustic account of Jane Warburton comes from 'Some account of John, Duke of Argyll and his family', privately printed in 1863 and reprinted as an introduction to *The Letters and Journals of Lady Mary Coke*, Edinburgh, 1889, vol. i, pp. xv ff.

[3] Brewing had ceased to be exclusively in women's hands since the Tudor period, when it was separated from the sale of beer to simplify the collection of excise duty. During the seventeenth century women were gradually put out of business and the trade passed into capitalists' hands. A. Clark, *The Working Life of Women in the Seventeenth Century*, pp. 221 ff.

[4] *Mrs. Delany*, vol. i, pp. 2–3.

in the new Hanoverian age. While she lived with Lady Stanley, Mary Granville's greatest friend was Catherine Hyde, daughter of one of the ladies of the bedchamber, Lady Hyde. The Hydes lived in the Gatehouse at Whitehall, in the household of the Earl of Rochester. Lord Hyde was his eldest son, grandson of the great Lord Clarendon. Lady Hyde was a kinswoman of the Granville's. Catherine Hyde grew up to become the beautiful Duchess of Queensberry who died in 1777 of eating too many cherries. Matthew Prior wrote a poem to 'Kitty beautiful and young' when she first came out as a girl. Horace Walpole added a verse to it when she was seventy-two. The duchess retained her beauty to old age and remained, in the words of Mrs. Delany 'to the end of a long life, a general object of animadversion, censure, and admiration'[1].

The accession of George I, which drove Mary Granville's father to remove his family from London to Gloucestershire, brought back to power the Whigs, who had been out of favour in the last years of Queen Anne. Among them was Lord Cowper, to whom Queen Anne had given the Great Seal in 1705 when, as the Duchess of Marlborough wrote, 'I prevailed upon her Majesty to take the great seal from Sir Nathan Wright, a man despised by all parties'. Of Lord Cowper the duchess said that 'he was not only of the whig party, but of such abilities and integrity as brought a new credit to it in the nation'[2]. Lord Cowper became Lord Chancellor in 1707, resigned in 1710, but was restored to office in 1715. He had married in 1706 as his second wife Mary Clavering of Chopwell, County Durham, who in 1714 began to keep a diary of her life at court. She determined to do it because of 'the perpetual Lies that one hears'[3]. Her diary was no more than a rough draft, which she intended 'to revise and digest into a better Method'. Fortunately she never did this, for her jottings give a vivid picture of the court of the Prince and Princess of Wales. Lady Cowper had been in correspondence with the princess for four years before the death of Queen Anne brought her to England as Princess of Wales. On the queen's death Lady Cowper wrote 'to offer her my Service, and to express the perfect Resignation I had to whatever she would think fit to do, were it to choose or refuse me'. She did not press for a place as she had 'resolved not to add to the Number of' the princess's 'Tormentors'[4]. She was delighted to learn

---

[1] Mrs. Delany, vol. i, p. 4.
[2] Conduct, pp. 147–8. The duchess meant that he brought credit to the Chancery.
[3] Diary of Mary, Countess Cowper, London, 1864, p. 1. Henceforward quoted as Lady Cowper.   [4] Lady Cowper, p. 2.

from the king's chief German minister, Baron Bernstorff, that he had orders to offer her a place as a lady of the bedchamber.

Since George I's wife had been for many years confined in the castle of Ahlen there could be no queen consort's court and all the ladies competed for a place in the court of the Princess of Wales. Lady Bristol, who went with Lady Cowper to the coronation, 'had still a greater mind to be a Lady of the Bed-chamber than I had'[1]. When Lady Cowper went to kiss the princess's hand on her appointment she found the Duchesses of St. Albans and Bolton there. The Duchess of Shrewsbury asked the king to get her a place, but he had to ask the princess three times before she agreed to take her. She was the daughter of an Italian marquis by an English mother, and had given up the Roman Catholic faith when, according to the gossip Lady Cowper recorded, her brother 'forced the Duke to marry her after an Intrigue together'. Even at the moment when the duchess secured her place Lady Cowper said that 'it was impossible to hate her so much as her Lord, though she had been engaged in the same ill Design', that is, in supporting the Tory party. 'She had a wonderful Art at entertaining and diverting People, though she would sometimes exceed the Bounds of Decency. She had a great Memory, had read a good deal, and spoke three languages to Perfection'[2]. The duchess had ignored Lady Cowper since her husband gave up the Great Seal in 1710, but 'upon coming into the Bedchamber all old Quarrels are laid aside for the Ease and Quiet of our Mistress'[3]. When Lady Cowper 'came mighty ill to court' she found that 'the Duchess of Shrewsbury had so much Humanity as to wait out my Week for me'[4]. The Duchess of St. Albans was made groom of the stole and the Duchess of Shrewsbury 'a Lady in Ordinary, as we all are'[5]. Lady Cowper records that the Duchess of St. Albans 'put on the Princess's Shift, according to the Court Rules, when I was by, she being Groom of the Stole'[6]. The Duchess of St. Albans had consulted the Duchess of Marlborough about the precedence of the ladies of the bedchamber. The Duchess of Marlborough wrote that 'in all the courts that I have seen the Groom of the Stole has the first place, and next to her the Lady in waiting, whatever quality she may be of, and after them two all the Ladies are placed according to their own titles'[7].

It was obviously important for politicians to get their wives into the

---

[1] *Lady Cowper*, p. 3.   [2] *Ibid.*, pp. 8–9.   [3] *Ibid.*, p. 10.
[4] *Ibid.*, p. 47.   [5] *Ibid.*, p. 13.   [6] *Ibid.*, p. 19.   [7] *Ibid.*, p. 177.

princess's bedchamber. Lord Cowper had prepared what his wife describes as 'a Treatise on the State of Parties' for the guidance of the new king and his instruction in the virtue of the Whigs and the faults of the Tories. Lady Cowper wrote it out and translated it into French so that the king and his German ministers could read it. She handed it to Baron Bernstorff when he waited upon her to tell her of her appointment to the bedchamber[1]. Before the end of the year she recorded that 'the king is as we wish upon the subject of Parties, and keeps my Lord's manuscript by him, which he has read several Times'[2]. Before this the princess told Lady Cowper that 'she had seen the Treatise on the State of Parties, already mentioned, and complimented me mightily on it'[3]. But the princess, who was a highly intelligent woman, realized that the Whig lords had no intention of allowing the king to have his own way if they could stop him. When Lady Cowper went into waiting on 2 February 1716 and the princess asked her for news she 'took the Opportunity of asking' the princess 'if she continued in her Resolution of being a Tory. She told me that she was till I could give her convincing Arguments that a Whig was more than a Tory for the King's Prerogative. I said I hoped to do so'[4]. In the following month she recorded that 'Baron Bernstorff made a Visit to my Lord and me. He is afraid of ill People that influence the Prince and Princess by telling Lies of the Whigs being against the King's Prerogative. Desired me to use Endeavours to prevent it'[5].

The zest with which Lady Cowper entered upon her position at court and the pleasure she took in using her influence to perform small services for others had passed when she wrote the last surviving portion of her diary in 1720. Lord Cowper was no longer chancellor, and although Lady Cowper was still a lady of the bedchamber she no longer felt at ease with the princess, who had not made her groom of the stole. In February 1724 Lady Cowper died at the age of thirty-nine, four months after the death of her husband. The editor of her diary describes her, justly, as 'an exemplary Wife and an attached Mother'. Although, as 'Mistress Mary Clavering', she had been one of the toasts of the Kit Cat Club, her time as a girl seems to have been passed in study and practising the harpsichord rather than in a continuous round of gaiety. When her diary was published in 1864 there were still at her country home at Panshanger 'a numerous Collection of Books belonging to her'. Many of

---

[1] *Lady Cowper*, p. 7.   [2] *Ibid.*, p. 32.   [3] *Ibid.*, p. 14.
[4] *Ibid.*, p. 65.   [5] *Ibid.*, p. 98.

them were 'on rather abstruse Subjects' and contained 'copious Annotations in her Handwriting'[1].

The appearance of the king's two middle-aged German mistresses at court cannot have pleased English ladies like Lady Cowper. She records the presence of the first to arrive, Madame Kielmansegge, at parties and at court. On 1 November 1714 Lady Cowper described a supper party at Lady Bristol's before waiting on the king, adding 'but though I was mightily diverted, and there was a great deal of Music yet I could not avoid being uneasy at the Repetition of some Words in French which the Duchess of Bolton said by Mistake, which convinced me that the two foreign Ladies were no better than they should be'[2]. A week later Madame Kielmansegge sent a book to the princess by the hand of Lady Cowper. One of the bedchamber-women, Mrs. Howard, warned Lady Cowper that 'there was a mortal Hatred between' the princess and Madame Kielmansegge and that 'the Princess thought her a wicked Woman'[3]. Madame Kielmansegge was the wife of Baron Kielmansegge, master of the horse to the king in Hanover. He died in 1721 when the king created his widow Countess of Darlington. Mademoiselle Schulenberg, the other royal mistress, soon followed the court to England. She had been a maid of honour to the king's mother, the Electress Sophia. In 1716 she was created Duchess of Munster and in 1719 Duchess of Kendal. Lady Cowper recorded without comment that with Lord Cowper she called on Mademoiselle Schulenberg 'to wish her Joy' after her elevation to the English peerage[4].

In the courts of Charles II and James II the open immorality of the kings, their mistresses and men of fashion shocked a generation which had grown up in days when the rulers of England had been faithful to their own wives. Between 1625 and 1660 no one could excuse his own infidelity by pointing to the king, the protector, or his chief advisers. After 1660 for a hundred years every King of England openly maintained at least one mistress. In that hundred years the Queens of England set a good example to their courts, but they could not prevent recurrent scandals. Maids of honour were subjected to many temptations, which most of them seem to have resisted. The follies of Sophia Howe, who

---

[1] *Lady Cowper*, p. ix.

[2] *Ibid.*, p. 12. The second foreign lady to whom Lady Cowper referred was the Duchess of Shrewsbury, who was Italian by birth.

[3] *Ibid.*, p. 13.   [4] *Ibid.*, p. 108.

died in 1725 'with a blemished reputation and a broken heart'[1], and of
Anne Vane, who gave birth to an illegitimate son in 1732[2], were condemned in their own day, though men were glad to take advantage of
them. No scandal was ever attached to the names of the two most beautiful
maids of honour in the court of the Princess of Wales. The wit and
beauty of Mary Lepell attracted the love of John, Lord Hervey, whom
she married in 1720. Mary Bellenden had no difficulty in keeping the
Prince of Wales in his place, but thought it best to marry without announcing her wedding until it was over. In 1721 she married Colonel John
Campbell, one of the grooms of the bedchamber, who long after his
wife's death became Duke of Argyll. The bedchamber-woman, Mrs.
Howard, was so discreet in her management of her intrigue with
George II that her many friends could affect to know nothing about
it[3]. When her husband succeeded to the earldom of Suffolk she was
made groom of the stole to the queen. Lord Suffolk died in 1733 and
Lady Suffolk retired from the court in the next year and married again.

   Men of position, who had always believed that they could make their
own rules of conduct, were beginning to regard it as unbecoming to
acknowledge their illegitimate children. Whether this was a step towards
a higher standard of conduct is doubtful. In his will John Sheffield, Duke
of Buckingham (1648–1721), provided for several children born out of
wedlock, 'a youth, commonly called Charles Herbert, who at present is
at Utrecht' and 'two Girls called Catherine Sophia, and Charlotte . . .
both of them having been for a great while educated at home by the
kindness of my Wife, and since put to a school at Chelsea; and I desire
still they may be under my Wife's care and direction'[4]. The author of the
contemporary character of the duke, published with his writings in 1723,
wrote of him: 'He left many natural children, which he had and own'd
before his third Marriage: and he has been often heard to say since he had
legitimate children, he wish'd he had never had the others, or at least had
not own'd them; it being in private families an ill example'[5]. The duke
had no children by his first two wives. His third wife was herself an
illegitimate daughter of James II. It is a curious reflection on the attitude

---

[1] *Letters to and from Henrietta, Countess of Suffolk, and her second husband,* London, 1824,
vol. i, pp. 35–6.   [2] *Ibid.,* p. 407.
   [3] The editor of Lady Suffolk's letters maintained that she was not the mistress of
George II, but his arguments hardly carry conviction.
   [4] *The Works of John Sheffield, Duke of Buckingham,* 2nd ed., London, 1729, vol. ii, *A Short
Character. . . .,* p. 39.   [5] *Ibid.,* p. 21.

of great men to their wives and families that it was regarded as a sign of merit in the Duke of Buckingham that 'he always took care to have an eminent physician to attend on his wife all the time she went with child, and during her lyings-in, having besides advis'd to secure his constant attendance upon his only son'. According to the writer, 'many people, esteem'd more generous than he, did not do this'[1].

Marriage was still a matter for parents to settle by treaty without regard to the wishes of daughters. Mary Granville, whose long life spanned the years from 1700 to 1788, writing in old age an account of her life for her friend the Duchess of Portland, still remembered bitterly her misery when she was forced at seventeen to marry Alexander Pendarves, a Cornish landowner of nearly sixty. The marriage was arranged by her uncle, Lord Lansdowne, 'who rejoiced at an opportunity of securing to his interest by such an alliance, one of some consequence in his county, whose services he at that time wanted'[2]. Although she loved someone else and dreaded the marriage she felt bound to agree to it. Lord Lansdowne threatened to have her lover dragged through the horsepond if he dared to appear. Her parents, who were dependent on Lord Lansdowne's charity, pretended that her tears were caused by sorrow at parting with her home. Pendarves had offered before marriage to settle all his property upon her, but when he died in 1725 she found herself left with only her jointure. Her married life, spent for the first two years in Cornwall and then, after a happy respite with her parents, in London, had been as unsatisfactory as she had expected. Her husband drank, was jealous, wasted his money, and suffered from gout. When he died she was only twenty-three. She was shocked at his death, 'but my natural good spirits, time, and finding myself freed from many vexations, soon brought me to a state of tranquillity I had not known for many years. As to my fortune, it was very mediocre, but it was *at my own command*'[3]. Mary Pendarves's second marriage in 1743 to the Reverend Patrick Delany was of her own making. Her kinsfolk disliked it, for he was of humble Irish birth, but it brought great happiness to both partners.

The liveliest and most intelligent of the young married women in society in the early years of George I's reign was Lady Mary Wortley Montagu, who, unlike Mary Granville, had refused to submit to her father's choice of a husband. She was born in 1689, the eldest daughter of

[1] *The Works of John Sheffield, Duke of Buckingham*, vol. ii, *A Short Character. . . .*, p. 23.
[2] *Mrs. Delany*, vol. i, p. 26.   [3] *Ibid.*, p. 109.

Evelyn Pierrepont, who was created Duke of Kingston in 1715. Lady
Mary had the run of her father's library at Thoresby and in London and
was fortunate enough to win the friendship of Bishop Burnet. He encouraged her in her classical studies, and corrected her translation of the
Enchiridion of Epictetus. In sending it to him in 1710 she wrote a curious
letter for a girl of twenty-one. 'My sex is usually forbid studies of this
nature, and folly reckoned so much our proper sphere, that we are
sooner pardoned any excesses of that, than the least pretensions to reading
or good sense. We are permitted no books but such as tend to the weaken-
ing and effeminating of the mind. Our natural defects are every way
indulged, and it is looked upon as in a degree criminal to improve our
reason, or fancy we have any. . . . There is hardly a character in the world
more despicable, or more liable to universal ridicule than that of a learned
woman; those words imply according to the received sense, a talking,
impertinent, vain, and conceited creature. . . . I am not now arguing for
an equality of the two sexes. I do not doubt but that God and nature
have thrown us into an inferior rank, we are a lower part of the creation,
we owe obedience and submission to the superior sex, and any woman
who suffers her vanity and folly to deny this rebels against the law of the
Creator'. She concluded a long letter with a quotation in Latin from
Erasmus in which he confutes the vulgar belief that a woman should not
learn Latin[1]. Nearly fifty years after this letter was written Lady Mary
recalled that she knew the bishop 'in my very early youth, and his condescension, in directing a girl in her studies, is an obligation I can never
forget'[2].

Lady Mary's condemnation of the way in which young women of
position were bred is reminiscent of the phrases of Mary Astell. Writing
to her daughter in 1752 Lady Mary recalled that the 'project of an English
monastery' was 'a favourite scheme of mine when I was fifteen; and had I
then been mistress of an independent fortune, would certainly have
executed it, and elected myself lady abbess'[3]. She possessed a sumptuously
bound copy of Mary Astell's treatise about a women's college, inscribed
'From the Author'. But her love affair with Edward Wortley Montagu,
a grandson of the Earl of Sandwich, soon drove such thoughts from her
head. He was eleven years her senior, was in the House of Commons, and

[1] *The Letters and Works of Lady Mary Wortley Montagu,* ed. by her great-grandson, Lord
Wharncliffe, Paris, 1837, vol. i, pp. 115-17.
[2] *Ibid.,* vol. ii, p. 173.   3 *Ibid.,* p. 105.

hoped for a career in the service of the crown. He was a good scholar and was first attracted by Lady Mary's interest in the classics. Addison was his friend and dedicated to him the second volume of the *Tatler*. The courtship began by letters supposedly written by Wortley Montagu's sister, Anne, and to her Lady Mary addressed her replies. After Anne died in September 1709 Wortley and Lady Mary wrote directly to each other. They were both individualists of strong character. Wortley Montagu feared her wit, admired her beauty, and doubted if she could be happy as his wife. 'You think if you married me, I should be passionately fond of you one month, and of somebody else the next: neither would happen. I can esteem, I can be a friend, but I don't know whether I can love', she wrote before he had approached her father[1]. If Wortley Montagu would have made the settlements usual in marriages between people of rank the duke would readily have accepted him as a suitor for his daughter. But Wortley Montagu refused to impoverish himself for the benefit of his heirs[2].

The duke therefore accepted another offer and preparations for the wedding were made: even the day was fixed and Lady Mary was sent into the country to be out of her lover's way. She eloped with him from an inn upon her journey. 'I tremble for what we are doing. Are you sure you shall love me for ever? Shall we never repent? I fear and I hope'[3] she wrote on the brink of her elopement. The marriage took place in August 1712. Lady Mary was obliged to spend the early years of her married life in the country and her letters show how much she disliked separation from her husband and the dull round of country life. At the accession of George I she was established in London and even after she had lost her eyelashes in the smallpox she could still play everybody else off the stage. 'Her ladyship is mighty gay and airy, and occasions a great deal of Discourse. Since her arrival the King has took but little Notice of any other Lady, not even of Madame Kielmansegg, which the Ladies of Hanover don't relish very well'[4], wrote a kinsman of Lady Cowper's, who had attended the king on a visit to his German duchy. With her husband Lady Mary was then on her way to Turkey, for Wortley Montagu had been appointed ambassador to the Porte in 1716.

[1] *Letters and Works*, vol. i, p. 124.

[2] George Paston, *Lady Mary Wortley Montagu and her Times*, London, 1907, p. 63, quoting an unpublished letter of Wortley Montagu's.

[3] *Letters and Works*, vol. i, p. 136.   [4] *Lady Cowper*, p. 195.

He was not a successful ambassador and was recalled in 1718, but Lady Mary, who had always wanted to travel, made the most of her adventures. She sent home a stream of carefully written letters, describing her journey, the country, its inhabitants and their customs. Among her correspondents were Lady Rich, Lady Bristol, and Alexander Pope, but most of her letters were sent to her sister, Lady Mar. Copies of her letters, with a few written to her, passed from hand to hand after her return. Mary Astell would have liked to see them in print and on one of the copies wrote a Preface, dated 1724, in which she confessed that she was 'malicious enough to desire that the world should see to how much better purpose LADIES travel than their LORDS'[1]. While she was in Turkey Lady Mary saw the process of inoculation for the smallpox and had her own son inoculated. Her daughter, born in Turkey, could not be treated, because her nurse had never had the smallpox. When the family reached home Lady Mary at once began to advocate inoculation, but met with strong opposition from the medical profession. Her daughter was inoculated with four leading doctors looking on to report on the process to the Government. Lady Mary said that they were so hostile that she dared not leave the child alone with them[2]. By 1724 the practice was generally accepted, despite its crudity and dangers. An article in *The Plaindealer* of that year, probably written by Mary Astell, declared that Lady Mary's introduction of inoculation justified the reflection '*That England has owed to Women the greatest blessings she has been distinguished by*'[3].

For the next twenty years Lady Mary and her husband lived in London. Wortley Montagu remained a Member of Parliament, but never held office. He must have been a disappointed man. He figures little in his wife's correspondence, but she showed great anxiety to conceal from him her financial troubles over the South Sea bubble. In all innocence she had taken money from a Frenchman to invest for him, but the stocks fell, his money was lost, and he accused Lady Mary of stealing it. Apart from this, Lady Mary's letters to Lady Mar suggest that she led a life devoted to heedless pleasure. It is possible that she exaggerated her devotion to amusements and her interest in the love affairs, lawful and unlawful, of the little group which made up high society. Lady Mar, whose husband had led the Scottish rebellion of 1715, was obliged to live abroad and gradually sank into melancholia until in March 1728 she was declared a

[1] *Letters and Works*, vol. i, p. 177.   [2] *Ibid.*, p. 65.
[3] Quoted by George Paston, *Lady Mary Wortley Montagu*, p. 306.

lunatic. Lady Mary probably hoped it would amuse her sister to read 'There are but three pretty men in England, and they are all in love with me, at this present writing. This will surprise you extremely; but if you were to see the reigning girls at present, I will assure you, there is little difference between them and the old women'[1]. This was in 1725. To her sister Lady Mary hardly ever wrote of books, but always of people, trying to rouse her with amusing bits of scandal. But it is noteworthy that she was silent about the private life of her own friends.

Mrs. Pendarves never approved of Lady Mary, who was too clever for many of her contemporaries. Her poems circulated from hand to hand and were touched up by professional writers like Gay and Pope. Malicious men of fashion, like the Duke of Wharton, put it about that their own scandalous verses were hers, and few accepted her denials[2]. She was impulsive, tactless, and her wit was often searing. But to the end she retained the affection of the virtuous, if dull, Lady Oxford, and the respect of her daughter, the Duchess of Portland. The old Duchess of Marlborough and her daughter, the Duchess of Montagu, were both Lady Mary's friends, although they had quarrelled with each other. There are hints in her letters to her sister that she wearied of the social round. 'I leave the great world to girls that know no better', she wrote in 1726, 'and do not think one bit the worst of myself for having out-lived a certain giddiness, which is sometimes excusable, but never pleasing'[3]. She wrote in some depression in the next year: 'Don't you remember how miserable we were in the little parlour at Thoresby? We then thought marrying would put us at once into possession of all we wanted. Then came being with child, etc., and you see what comes of being with child'[4]. Her son was a continual trouble: 'my young rogue of a son is the most ungovernable little rake that ever played truant'[5]. She consoled herself with her daughter, 'a small damsel, who is at present every thing I like'[6]. Her quarrel with Pope, which began in 1727, was embarrassing, for he mercilessly pursued her with his barbed pen. Lady Mary had kept the friendship of Lord Hervey, though she did not care for his wife. Together, Lady Mary and Lord Hervey wrote verses attacking Pope in reply to his attacks on them. Even her daughter displeased Lady Mary for a time by falling in love with Lord Bute. Since Lady Mary would not

---

[1] *Letters and Works*, vol. i, p. 365.   [2] E.g. *Ibid.*, p. 362.
[3] *Ibid.*, p. 372.   [4] *Ibid.*, p. 373.
[5] *Ibid.*, p. 379.   [6] *Ibid.*, p. 374.

agree to the marriage the young couple eloped, as she had done before them[1].

Already in 1727 Lady Mary was thinking of escaping abroad: 'I have a mind to cross the water, to try what effect a new heaven and a new earth will have upon my spirits', she wrote to Lady Mar[2]. In 1739 Lady Mary left England and only returned, after twenty-three years abroad, to die. She is the first of a long succession of English women who in modern times have found happiness in living in Italy. Her husband advised her about her journey, which she described in her letters to him stage by stage. To a friend she wrote that she hoped that he would follow her abroad. But they never met again, for even when Wortley Montagu went abroad he did not visit her. But their surviving letters to each other are friendly and she wrote of him to her daughter with respect. Since she had no settlement on marriage she could not have lived abroad without her husband's help and consent, although her father left her £6,000. She lived on what she described as an allowance, and never complained that it was insufficient. After visiting Venice, Rome, southern Italy, Geneva, Lyons, and Avignon, Lady Mary settled near Brescia, later moving to Padua and to Venice. Her occupations and amusements are vividly described in her letters to Lady Bute, who sent her news and books from England. Lady Mary was a second cousin of Henry and Sarah Fielding and read Henry Fielding's novels with delight. Sarah's came in for more tepid praise[3]. Although she wept over Richardson's stories, she had a poor opinion of their verisimilitude: 'I believe this author was never admitted into higher company, and should confine his pen to the amours of house-maids, and the conversation at the steward's table, where I imagine, he has sometimes intruded, though oftener in the servants' hall. . . . He has no idea of the manners of high life'[4]. She thought *Pamela* 'foolish stuff', which 'has met with very extraordinary, and (I think undeserved) success. It has been translated into French and into Italian: it was all the fashion at Paris and Versailles, and is still the joy of the chambermaids of all nations'[5].

Lady Mary found pleasure not only in reading, and in writing letters, but in gardening, dairy farming, and riding. She enjoyed the society of Italy, a country where 'the character of being a learned woman is far from being ridiculous'. From her wide experience she declared that 'there is no

---

[1] George Paston, *Lady Mary Wortley Montagu*, pp. 358-9, 374-6.
[2] *Letters and Works*, vol. i, p. 380.   [3] *Ibid.*, vol. ii, pp. 132-3 and 150.
[4] *Ibid.*, p. 104.   [5] *Ibid.*, p. 64.

part of the world where our sex is treated with so much contempt as in England'[1]. She urged Lady Bute, her daughter, to educate her own children well. 'Learning, if she', her eldest granddaughter, 'has a real taste for it, will not only make her contented, but happy in it. No entertainment is so cheap as reading, nor any pleasure so lasting'. Again, she says: 'If she has the same inclination (I should say passion) for learning I was born with, history, geography, and philosophy will furnish her with materials to pass away cheerfully a longer life than is allotted to mortals'. It is possible that Lady Bute may have been irritated to read that 'the ultimate end of your education was to make you a good wife (and I have the comfort to hear that you are one) hers ought to be, to make her happy in a virgin state'[2]. Lady Mary felt that Lord Bute must have been 'extremely shocked' at her recommendation of a learned education for his daughters and proceeded with her usual tactlessness to make matters rather worse by saying, 'I look upon my granddaughters as a sort of lay nuns: destiny may have laid up other things for them, but they have no reason to expect to pass their time otherwise than their aunts do at present; and I know by experience that it is in the power of study not only to make solitude tolerable, but agreeable'[3]. Only one of Lady Bute's six daughters remained unmarried and, curiously enough, she was the only one who inherited something of her grandmother's brains and ability. The introductory anecdotes to Lord Wharncliffe's edition of Lady Mary's works were written by Lady Louisa Stuart, who died at the age of ninety-five in 1851[4].

In 1761 Wortley Montagu died, leaving his large fortune to his daughter. His death was perhaps the sign for Lady Mary to prepare for her journey home to England. She reached London early in 1762 and people were surprised to find how little changed she was. 'When Nature is at the trouble of making a very singular person, Time does right in respecting it. Medals are preserved when common coin is worn out; and as great geniuses are rather matters of curiosity than of art, this lady seems reserved to be a wonder for more than our generation. She does not look older than when she went abroad, has more than the vivacity of fifteen, and a memory which, perhaps, is unique'. So wrote Mrs. Edward Montagu, the leader of the new cult of the learned lady. 'I visited her', she added,

---

[1] *Letters and Works*, vol. ii, p. 99.   [2] *Ibid.*, pp. 106–8.   [3] *Ibid.*, p. 111.
[4] Lady Louisa also wrote, completing her work in 1827, 'Some account of John, Duke of Argyll and his family', which has already been quoted, see p. 252.

'because her cousin and mine were cousin-germans. Tho' she has not any foolish partiality for her husband or his relations, I was very graciously received, and you may imagine entertained by one who neither thinks, speaks, acts nor dresses like anybody else'[1]. But Lady Mary was already smitten with the cancer which killed her on 21 August in the same year.

From time to time among the aristocratic families of this country a woman appears who is a portent among others of her class and generation. Such was Margaret, Duchess of Newcastle, in the seventeenth century, and such was Lady Mary Pierrepont. She was unfortunate in living in a time when the literary men used their wit at the expense of anyone who had offended them. Her very virtues meant that Horace Walpole was unfair to her, for she was the close friend of Maria Skerrett, his father's mistress and second wife[2]. When the malice of Pope and Walpole is discounted she remains the most brilliant of the great ladies of the first half of the eighteenth century, a faithful friend, an affectionate mother to her daughter, and a witty commentator on the world of her day.

The women whose names appear in Lady Mary's correspondence form a small but representative section of aristocratic society. Her daughter's marriage to Lord Bute had brought his kinsfolk, the Duke of Argyll and his duchess, formerly Jane Warburton, into the close range of Lady Mary's family connections. They were brought still closer when, soon after Lady Mary went abroad, Lord Bute's only brother, James Stuart Mackenzie, married Lady Elizabeth Campbell, one of the duke's five daughters. Her eldest sister had been happily married to the Earl of Dalkeith, who died in 1750, leaving her a rich widow of thirty-three. Five years later she married Charles Townshend, who was some eight years her junior. He was the second son of Lord Townshend and a rising politician. The news brought prophecies of woe from Lady Mary in a letter to her daughter. 'I pity poor Lady Dalkeith who, perhaps, thinks herself at present an object of envy: she will be soon undeceived: no rich widow can marry on prudential motives; and where passion is only on one side, every marriage must be miserable. If she thought justly, she would know that no man was ever in love with a woman of forty since the deluge. . . . All she can hope for is a cold complaisance, founded on

---

[1] Dr. Doran, *A Lady of the Last Century* (*Mrs. Elizabeth Montagu*), London, 1873, p. 129.

[2] A further reason for Horace Walpole's hostility was Lady Mary's friendship with Dolly Walpole, sister of Sir Robert Walpole and later the wife of Lord Townshend. Sir Robert's first wife, Horace Walpole's mother, did not get on well with her sister-in-law.

gratitude, which is the most uncertain of all foundations for a lasting union. . . . Lady Dalkeith had fond parents, and, as I have heard, an obliging husband. Her sorrowful hours are now coming on; they will be new to her, and 'tis a cruel addition to reflect (as she must do) that they have been her own purchasing'[1]. Townshend, described by Lady Hervey as 'an inexhaustible fund of entertainment in all company'[2], died at the age of forty-two in 1767. His widow did not marry again.

Lady Mary's favourite among the five sisters was the youngest, also named Mary, whose unhappy story occasioned much moralizing in letters to Lady Bute. The Duke of Argyll died in 1743 and the arrangement of Lady Mary Campbell's marriage fell to her mother. Although the duchess disliked Lord Leicester and knew that his son, Lord Coke, was addicted to 'play', she was persuaded that he would be a good match for her daughter. Lady Mary Campbell disliked and despised Lord Coke and plainly showed her feelings, but her pride and obstinacy made her go through with the marriage, which took place in 1747. Lord Coke retaliated as soon as they were married by ignoring her, and it seems that the marriage was never consummated. After Lady Mary Coke had endured two years of misery her relatives intervened. The duchess, accompanied by her son-in-law, Mr. Stuart Mackenzie, and a lawyer, went down to Holkham to see her daughter. She was refused admission, returned to London and obtained a writ of *Habeas corpus* from the Judges of the King's Bench commanding Lord Coke to produce his wife before them. Lady Mary Coke then instituted proceedings for divorce in the spiritual court on the grounds of ill usage, but a separation was arranged without the case coming to judgment. Lord Coke died three years later and Lady Mary was free to arrange her life as she wished. Her relatives were happy to note that she behaved with propriety on her husband's death, not pretending to grief but wearing mourning and abstaining from amusements for the appropriate period. She enjoyed an income of £2,500 a year[3].

Lady Mary Wortley Montagu, writing to her daughter, hope Lady Mary Coke 'may make use of her bitter experience to escape the ⸗nares laid for her: they are so various and so numerous, if she can avoid them I shall think she has some supernatural assistance'[4]. It seemed to the exile in

---

[1] *Letters and Works*, vol. ii, pp. 77–8.

[2] *Letters of Mary Lepel, Lady Hervey*, London, 1821, p. 325.

[3] *The Letters and Journals of Lady Mary Coke*, pp. lix–lxxii, from Lady Louisa Stuart's Introduction.   [4] *Letters and Works*, vol. ii, p. 78.

Italy that a young and rich widow was 'walking blindfold, upon stilts, amid precipices, though perhaps as little sensible of her danger as a child of a quarter old would be in the arms of a monkey leaping on the tiles of a house'. Lady Mary used this simile more than once when a rich widow was under discussion. It seemed to her, writing in 1755, that 'nothing but a miracle, or the support of her guardian angel' could protect Lady Mary Coke from the perils about her. Her one protection, thought Lady Mary, was that 'she had a great turn to economy'[1]. The daily life of Lady Mary Coke can be learned in detail, for she kept a diary in the form of letters which she despatched to her sisters Lady Stafford and Lady Betty Mackenzie. It is a naïve record of its author's passing hours and can only be read continuously with determination. It reveals something of the dangers which beset the rich and independent woman, but it also shows that Lady Mary Coke had enough strength of character to overcome at least some of them.

She loved gardening and she enjoyed reading history. She could spend an evening happily over Selden's *Titles of Honour* in the library at her mother's house[2] and she read Mrs. Macaulay's history[3]. She spent money on books and in 1769 noted 'I have laid out in books since I came to Town about fifty pounds'[4]. It gave her pleasure to meet the learned Miss Carter of Deal and she would have cultivated her society had they lived nearer to each other. But the social habit of spending the evening, even when a few ladies dined together, at loo or other games of chance was rigid. Lady Mary Coke always noted what she won or lost at 'lu'. On one occasion she 'had surprising luck, came off winning seventy-six guineas; and tho' I won all the money that was lost, the company was civil and good humoured, which does not always happen'[5]. Lady Mary once noted sadly after losing 'seven and thirty guineas', 'it might have been better imploy'd'. But she never played on Sundays and when she asked to be excused waiting on the Princess Amelia on Good Friday she was hurt to hear the princess murmur 'the Pharasee'[6].

Long after Lady Mary Coke was dead, Lady Louisa Stuart, the youngest daughter of Lady Bute, wrote her account of the family of John, Duke of Argyll, and without the author's intention, Lady Mary Coke occupied the centre of the stage. Her character was so firm and definite, her assurance

---

[1] *Letters and Works*, vol. ii, pp. 141, 143.   [2] *Lady Mary Coke*, vol. i, p. 51.
[3] *Ibid.*, vol. ii, pp. 155, 159.   [4] *Ibid.*, vol. iii, p. 53.
[5] *Ibid.*, p. 40.   [6] *Ibid.*, p. 49.

of rectitude so complete, her pride so invincible, that she inevitably created situations ridiculous to others though not to herself. Society was entertained at her assumption that Lord March, who as Old Q. came to symbolize the immorality of the eighteenth century, wished to marry her. Ignoring the fact that his mistress lived in his house and presided at his table, Lady Mary could assume that he intended marriage because, as he said to his friends, 'thinking her tolerably handsome . . . he supposed he might try his fortune in making a little love'[1]. Even greater amusement was caused by her assumption that the Duke of York, one of George II's unattractive sons, was in love with her and she with him. Her exaggerated grief when he died is recorded in her diary. Her fury at the marriages of the Dukes of Cumberland and Gloucester to women who were not of royal blood was greater than that of any member of the royal family. Lady Mary had a reverence for royalty which made her persuade herself that George II's mistress, Lady Yarmouth, was secretly married to him and that the beautiful, but illegitimate, Lady Waldegrave was degrading the royal family by her marriage with the Duke of Gloucester.

According to Lady Mary Coke the young king, George III, was concerned at the immorality of the age. In March 1769 she 'was told that the King had said to my Lord Chancellor that he was desirous that something should be thought of that might be likely to prevent the very bad conduct among the Ladys, of which there had been so many instances lately; that my Lord Chancellor answered that he should be very glad to second any such proposition, it being highly necessary that something should be done, and 'tis believed that the Arch Bishop will move in the House of Lords that Ladys who are guilty of Adultery should not be permitted to marry again'[2]. Early in his reign George III had been attracted by the charm and beauty of Lady Sarah Lennox, daughter of the Duke of Richmond, so that her kinsfolk at Holland House hoped that something might come of it[3]. But the king married a German princess and Lady Sarah married Sir Charles Bunbury in 1762. She was only seventeen and her husband was engrossed in horse-racing. Her daughter, born in December 1768, was the child of Lord William Gordon. She joined him in February 1769 and stayed with him until November, when she returned to her brother at Goodwood House. According to Lady Mary Coke, the duke

[1] *Lady Mary Coke*, vol. i, p. lxxvii.   [2] *Ibid.*, vol. iii, p. 52.
[3] *The Life and Letters of Lady Sarah Lennox, 1745–1826*, ed. the Countess of Ilchester and Lord Stavordale, London, 1902, vol. i, pp. 47–51.

had tried to prevent her from going to her lover, but 'she told him that she was determined to go to Lord William Gordon, tho' it was not her intention to marry him, when She was divorced from Sir Charles Bunbury, for that he had not a good temper, and perhaps she should not live with him six months'[1]. It is possible that George III's concern in March 1769 for the morals of the ladies was, in part at least, caused by this affair'[2].

It was not from the women of the great eighteenth-century families that attempts to improve the legal position of all women could come. Lady Mary Wortley Montagu might derisively call the unmarried women of such families 'a sort of lay nuns', but they were generally free to make what they liked of life. Miss Anne Pitt, Lord Chatham's sister, had her own establishment, was able to go to Bath or Tunbridge Wells, or to travel on the Continent as she chose. Wives were protected by elaborate marriage settlements and they would depend on their kinsfolk for help if they needed it. Even if they themselves failed to keep their marriage vows their own families stood by them. Widows were equally free to make their own lives. The happiness of widows, as of spinsters, depended entirely on the possession of enough money to buy not only necessities but luxuries, and enough intelligence to find interests. In her widowhood Lady Mary Coke was a decorative figure as she drove about London. In 1784 Lady Louisa Stuart wrote to a friend 'A loud knock at the door . . . has interrupted me and called me to the window. 'Tis a chaise with a magnificent red and silver postilion, and out of it, behold! jumps Queen Mary, as magnificent in green and silver'[3]. To a twentieth-century woman looking back on those times it seems that there were grievous limitations on the lives of all women, but few who belonged to the great families of England really noticed them. The cries of 'Wilkes and liberty' which they deplored were the precursors of an emancipation for all women which was beyond their imagining.

Moreover, the increasing urbanity of eighteenth-century life gave to aristocratic ladies importance of a kind which had not belonged to their predecessors. Those among them who enjoyed great wealth and were blessed with beauty and wit could wield immense influence. They were

---

[1] *Lady Mary Coke*, vol. iii, p. 31.
[2] Lady Sarah in 1781 married Colonel Napier and when in 1804 her husband died, was given a pension of £800 a year. *Lady Sarah Lennox*, vol. ii, p. 200.
[3] *Lady Mary Coke*, p. cxxxiii.

able to gather about them the most interesting people of the day, both of their own and of the rising middle class. A small group of such ladies succeeded in breaking down the fashion for large assemblies, too noisy for intimate talk, in which the only recreation was cards. Consciously imitating the salons of French hostesses, they set the fashion for parties at which people were expected to engage in conversation. The unfortunate name 'blue-stockings' which has been attached to them gives, through its later use, a false impression of the grace and charm of such women as Elizabeth Montagu, Elizabeth Vesey, and Frances Boscawen, to name only the leaders of the movement. Mrs. Montagu seems to have been the first to hold informal parties, for in 1750 she began to give 'literary breakfasts' at her husband's London house. Later she gave evening assemblies and called them conversation parties. She invited only intelligent people who were not expected to come in the elaborate dress of fashion. Blue worsted stockings instead of black silk did not affront any of these hostesses[1]. Lord Bath, Lord Lyttelton, and Horace Walpole were frequent guests, who welcomed the opportunity of meeting such men as Dr. Johnson, David Garrick, and Sir Joshua Reynolds.

Mrs. Vesey, whose friends called her 'the sylph', was the daughter of the Bishop of Ossory. Her second husband was her cousin, Agmodesham Vesey, who died in 1755. She caused amusement because to secure informal chat, she set her guests about the room in groups of two and three so that many had their backs to each other[2]. Mrs. Montagu arranged her guests in a semicircle. Mrs. Boscawen, the wife of Admiral Boscawen, was widowed in 1761, but had been holding parties for talk rather than play before her husband's death. She was a much-loved wife and mother.[3] Perhaps because of that she was easier in her personal relations than either of the other two ladies. She took literary folk into an inner room for talk, leaving rank and fashion to amuse itself in its accustomed way. Although these ladies and others like them admired learning they were in no sense scholars themselves. They were cultivated women of the

---

[1] A direct tradition of the origin of the term 'blue-stockings' is preserved by Montagu Pennington, *Memoirs of the Life of Mrs. Elizabeth Carter*, p. 315, who obtained his information from his aunt, Miss Carter. 'A foreign gentleman, who was to go there with an acquaintance, was told in jest that he might appear there, if he pleased, in his blue stockings. This he understood in the literal sense; and when he spoke of it in French called it the *Bas Bleu* meeting'.   [2] *Diary and Letters of Madame d'Arblay*, vol. i, p. 189.

[3] Brig.-General Cecil Aspinall-Oglander, *Admiral's Wife*, London, 1940, and *Admiral's Widow*, London, 1942.

world, rich enough to indulge their taste for the society of wits and scholars. Only Mrs. Montagu ventured into print. In 1760 she contributed three dialogues to George Lyttelton's *Dialogues of the Dead* and in 1769 published anonymously an essay defending Shakespeare from 'the Misrepresentations of Mons. de Voltaire'. With the fourth edition of this essay, her three dialogues were reprinted and the name 'Mrs. Montagu' appeared upon the title-page.

Of all the women who delighted to entertain the literary world of London the most intelligent was Mrs. Thrale, wife of Henry Thrale, the wealthy owner of the famous Southwark brewery. She was twenty years younger than Mrs. Montagu, and much livelier. Thrale was a masterful husband, who would not allow his wife to ride or take any part in the business of housekeeping. But he encouraged her to give parties, and it was as much by his invitation as hers that Dr. Johnson became for a time a member of their household at Streatham Park. Beside Johnson, the group of which she was the centre included Fanny Burney, whom she introduced into society when everyone was asking who had written *Evelina*. After Thrale's death in 1781 Mrs. Thrale fell in love with Gabriel Piozzi, an Italian singer, whom she married three years later. Although she had provided for the comfort and safety of her daughters by Thrale, her second marriage was received with violent criticism within her little world. Her friendship with Fanny Burney came to an end. Johnson wrote to her saying 'You have abandoned your children and your religion, God forgive your wickedness'[1]. In spite of all this unmerited disapproval the marriage was a singularly happy one. With her husband's encouragement, Mrs. Piozzi took to writing, and her first book—*Anecdotes of the late Samuel Johnson, LL.D.*—was successful in her own day and has secured her a place in literary history.

These ladies welcomed to their houses both to large parties and intimate dinners women of wit and learning as well as men. Miss Carter of Deal was their contemporary and became the close friend of them all. Young women also found no difficulty in entering their world. The young Hannah More, who first came up for the London season in 1774, soon found herself invited to Mrs. Montagu's parties. She became the poet who praised 'Vesey! of verse the Judge and Friend' and 'Boscawen sage, bright Montagu' in her poem *Bas Bleu*, written in 1782. When in 1778

---

[1] *Autobiography and Literary Remains of Mrs. Piozzi (Thrale)*, ed. A. Hayward, Q.C., 2nd ed., London, 1861, vol. i, p. 239.

Fanny Burney was 'invited to Mrs. Montagu's' she wrote in her diary 'I think the measure of my glory full'[1]. She was delighted to find Mrs. Montagu 'gratified by hearing' that *Evelina* 'is written by a woman'[2]. At a party given by Miss Monckton and her mother, Lady Galway, in 1782, Fanny Burney met Edmund Burke. He told her that she 'had done the most wonderful of wonders in pleasing the old wits, the Duchess of Portland and Mrs. Delany'[3]. The service done to the cause of women by such ladies has often been exaggerated. The givers of conversation parties were too secure to desire to change the accepted relations between men and women. But women owe them a measure of gratitude. They forced contemporary society to admit that there was something admirable in women aspiring to learning and that women who wrote plays and novels could be chaste.

While London society was enjoying, or laughing at conversation parties, there was growing up in the country a brilliant girl whose life was to display out of due season the eccentricity permissible to the great ladies of the eighteenth century. Lady Hester Stanhope was the daughter of the third Earl Stanhope by Lady Hester Pitt, one of the daughters of the great Lord Chatham[4]. Her father was something of a genius; an inventor of a steamship, a calculating machine, and a printing press he, almost alone in the English peerage, welcomed the French Revolution. For a time he called himself Citizen Stanhope and coronets no longer graced his iron gates. His children were the chief sufferers from this passing fad, for Lady Hester's three half-brothers were apprenticed to a trade. One of her own two sisters married the local surgeon when she was barely sixteen. The other left home and married a penniless army officer. Citizen Stanhope and old Governor Pitt were formidable ancestors and Lady Hester soon showed herself their true daughter. Alone of his children Lady Hester could manage her father, but she could only secure a proper education for her eldest half-brother by smuggling him out of the country to enter a German university under a false name so that his father could not find him. Lord Stanhope allowed his daughters to ride and hunt, and in the Kentish countryside round Chevening Lady Hester became a fine horsewoman. She was born in 1776 and until 1800 remained at

---

[1] *Diary and Letters of Madame d'Arblay*, vol. i, p. 125.
[2] *Ibid.*, p. 121.   [3] *Ibid.*, vol. ii, p. 140.
[4] *Life and Letters of Lady Hester Stanhope*, by her niece, the Duchess of Cleveland, London, 1914.

home. By that time her two sisters were married and Lady Hester went to live with her grandmother, Lady Chatham, at Burton Pynsent in Somerset. Her skill in breaking in the vicious horses of the neighbourhood was long remembered there[1].

When Lady Chatham died in April 1803 Lady Hester was enjoying a continental tour. On her return her uncle, William Pitt, received her into his house and she remained with him until he died. She acted as his hostess at Putney and at Walmer Castle, reviewed troops with him, riding with him to 'parade after parade, at fifteen or twenty miles distant from each other. . . . The hard riding I do not mind, but to remain *still* so many hours on horseback is an incomprehensible bore, and requires more patience than you can easily imagine', she wrote to a friend in November 1802 when preparations were being made to repel expected invasion[2]. Pitt showed great generosity to Lady Hester's two younger half-brothers, procuring them commissions in the army and opening his house to them. Until she died Lady Hester constantly recurred to these years of glory, when, as Pitt's niece, she was at the heart of politics and flattered by all. Her lively presence cheered her uncle, but she made enemies by her tactless wit. 'Lady Hester! Lady Hester! what are you saying?' Pitt was heard to exclaim after she had addressed a general who annoyed her as 'you nasty kangaroo'[3]. On his death-bed Pitt expressed the hope that a pension of £1,000 or £1,200 might be allowed to Lady Hester and smaller sums to her two sisters. Parliament accordingly granted £1,200 a year to her and £600 to each of her sisters for their several lives.

In the years between her uncle's death in 1806 and her own departure from England in 1810 Lady Hester tried to accustom herself to her new unimportance. General Moore became her friend, and ten years later she said that had he returned from Portugal they would have married. Both her brothers were with him there, and the elder was killed almost at the moment when the general was dying at Corunna. For consolation for her double loss she turned to the Welsh hills. For a year she lived in modest lodgings near Builth, keeping two saddle-horses and a cow. She made her own butter and lived as simply as her neighbours. The clergyman's youngest son and a 'sprightly, good-tempered girl of thirteen' attended her as she rode about the Welsh country-side[4]. There she made up her mind about the future. On 10 February 1810, she left England

---

[1] A. W. Kinglake, *Eothen*, Everyman's Library, p. 63.
[2] *Life and Letters of Lady Hester Stanhope*, p. 54.   3 *Ibid.*, p. 99.   4 *Ibid.*, p. 89.

taking with her a manservant, Elizabeth Williams, her maid, and her physician, Dr. Meryon. Her brother James and a friend of his accompanied her to Gibraltar. Thence the party moved on to Malta. The voyage was accomplished in a frigate, and when Lady Hester's party left Malta it was in a man-of-war. Elizabeth Williams stayed in Malta with her married sister, and another Englishwoman, Mrs. Fry, was engaged to attend Lady Hester.

Lady Hester's niece, the Duchess of Cleveland, was convinced that her aunt had no intention of leaving England for ever when she embarked at Plymouth in 1810. Her future life was determined by the love affair in which she engaged at Malta with a young man of good family and notable charm named Michael Bruce. Lady Hester had never cared for women. When she was staying with Pitt at Walmer Castle before her grandmother's death, she wrote to a man friend 'I am enchanted with everything here. I have never seen the face of a woman till today. Charming!—nothing but pleasant men'[1]. And again, after she had joined Pitt's establishment she wrote 'There are generally three or four men staying in the house, and we dine eight or ten almost every other day. Military and naval characters are constantly *welcome* here; women are not, I *suppose*, because they do not form part of our society. You may guess, then, what a pretty fuss they make with me'[2]. It was unfortunate for Lady Hester that she had no one to teach her that a woman needs friends of her own sex. Michael Bruce was eleven years younger than Lady Hester, who was thirty-four when they met at Malta. He was extremely handsome, with a temperament that made women love him. He wrote to tell his father that on his arrival at Malta he 'found Lady H. Stanhope and as I find her much cleverer and better informed than my companions, I have left them and adscribed myself to her party'[3].

Michael Bruce was completing his education by foreign travel before entering public life in England. His father, Patrick Crawford Bruce, the fifth son of a Scottish baronet, had entered the East India Company, founded a prosperous business in Bombay and returned to England to become a banker in London, the possessor of a country estate and a Member of Parliament. He had made his way by his own exertions and intended his eldest son to go still farther. No expense had been spared on his education and he was allowed to draw on his father freely for

[1] *Life and Letters of Lady Hester Stanhope*, p. 37.   [2] *Ibid.*, p. 53.
[3] Ian Bruce, *The Nun of Lebanon*, London, 1951, p. 56.

funds. The romance between Michael Bruce and Lady Hester ripened quickly. Before the end of June in 1810 they were living together and had determined to continue their travels in company. Lady Hester was by far the stronger character. She wrote to her lover's father of his son's 'elevated and Statesmanlike mind, his brilliant talents, to say nothing of his beautiful person'. She admitted her love, but declared that when the time came she would resign her lover to 'some thrice happy woman really worthy of him'[1]. At the same time Michael wrote to his father assuring him that his feelings for Lady Hester 'were not called forth by mere personal charms, but by the enlarged powers of her understanding and her most exalted mind'. In a letter to Michael's father written in December Lady Hester reiterated her determination to leave Michael free to make his own life when their affair should be over. She had made her choice and counted its cost. She declared that she would 'most scrupulously avoid ever setting eyes upon a modest woman' and concluded 'you must not imagine, Sir, because my conduct has been imprudent that my heart is either devoid of sentiments of real delicacy or honor'[2].

The association lasted three years, and though their letters show signs of strain, they never quarrelled. Michael's father, proud at first that so great a lady should fall in love with his son and flattered at her deference to himself, soon began to find their travels expensive. In one period of eight months alone he had to supply them with £3,500. His own affairs were not going well and he could not allow such expenditure to continue. Lady Hester had nothing but her pension. She was over-generous and had little idea of the value of money. The party had travelled through Greece and settled in Constantinople. They hired a ship in October 1811 to take them to Alexandria, but suffered shipwreck. Thereafter Lady Hester took to Turkish dress and never abandoned it. From Cairo they went by boat to Jaffa so that they might visit Palestine and the ruined city of Palmyra. It was characteristic of Lady Hester's attitude to Michael that she wrote a long letter to his father headed 'on board my boat upon the Nile'[3]. It is surprising that their association lasted so long. It was she who was in command during the dangerous journey through the desert to Palmyra, where, in her own words, 'I was crowned Queen of the Desert under the triumphal arch'[4].

After Bruce unwillingly left her in October 1813 Lady Hester's finances

---

[1] *The Nun of Lebanon*, p. 63.   [2] *Ibid.*, p. 77.   [3] *Ibid.*, p. 133.
[4] *Life and Letters of Lady Hester Stanhope*, p. 159.

gradually sank into hopeless confusion. Bruce would gladly have supplied her with money and in the months immediately after his departure expressed his intention of giving her half his income. But his father's financial troubles became so serious that no more help could be expected from that source. She wrote her last sad letter to her former lover in 1817. But she was undefeated, even when Mrs. Fry and Dr. Meryon had both left her. Elizabeth Williams, learning about her loneliness, came to her in 1816 and remained with her till death in 1828. Lady Hester spent the last twenty years of her life in a rambling house on Mount Lebanon, an object of reverence to the people of the mountains and of curiosity and interest to Europeans and the Syrian Christians of the East. She rarely received visitors, but in 1824 Captain Yorke, later Lord Hardwicke, was cruising in the Levant and asked permission to call. He was concerned at her condition and wrote to Lord Chatham: 'She is very forlorn, and her mind has taken a serious turn, much impaired, and full of magic and divination'. Obviously fearing that Lord Chatham would take no action, he added a postscript: 'I do sincerely hope some measures will be taken to make her comfortable. She has not very long to live, depend upon it.— C. Y.'[1] The traveller A. W. Kinglake, whose mother had known her as a girl, was also received by Lady Hester. By that time the doctor had returned to her service and Miss Williams was dead. Lady Hester could still amuse her guest by her powers of mimicry and appear 'full of audacious fun', but he found her also a prophetess: 'she carefully insinuated, without actually asserting, her heavenly rank'[2].

She died at last in 1839. She had sent Dr. Meryon away some months before her death. According to Kinglake the doctor 'had sunk into the complete Asiatic'[3] and it may be that Lady Hester wearied of his company. He left her as 'She was about to shut herself up alone, without money, without books, without a soul she could confide in; without a single European, male or female, about her; with winter coming on, beneath roofs certainly no longer waterproof, and that might fall in; with war at her doors, and without any means of defence except in her own undaunted courage'[4]. Nevertheless she did not die alone, for when the British consul came all Lady Hester's thirty-four native servants were in

---

[1] *Life and Letters of Lady Hester Stanhope*, pp. 235–7.
[2] *Eothen*, pp. 73–9.   [3] *Ibid.*, p. 79.
[4] *Memoirs of Lady Hester Stanhope as related by herself in conversations with her Physician*, London, 1845, vol. i, p. vii.

the house. Dr. Meryon, who found it hard to make a living at his own profession, had kept a record of Lady Hester's talk and copies of her letters, hoping one day to make a book about her. It appeared in 1845. To Dr. Meryon Lady Hester was a great lady whose memory should be preserved: 'Peace be with her remains, and honour to her memory! A surer friend, a more frank and generous enemy, never trod this earth. "Show me where the poor and needy are", she would say, "and let the rich shift for themselves!" As free from hypocrisy as the purest diamond from stain, she pursued her steady way, unaffected by the ridiculous reports that were spread about her by travellers, either malicious or misinformed, and not to be deterred from her noble, though somewhat Quixotic enterprises, by ridiculous abuse, by threats or opposition'[1]. Writing in 1850 of the eminent people who died between 1835 and 1841, Harriet Martineau recorded that when Lady Hester's death was announced in England 'There was a sense of relief—a sense of comfort that that restless and mysterious mind was asleep, and past the power of annoyance from without, and misgiving from within'[2].

[1] *Memoirs of Lady Hester Stanhope*, vol. i, p. x.
[2] Harriet Martineau, *The History of England during the Thirty Years' Peace*, London, 1850, vol. ii, p. 454.

CHAPTER X

The Eighteenth Century
The New Middle Class

The publication of a new edition of Ascham's *The Schoolmaster* in 1711 reflects the widespread interest in education which marked the turn of the seventeenth and eighteenth centuries[1]. The charity school movement, which many women fostered, was one result of this interest. The lively activity of dissenting academies in various parts of England was another. At these academies, many others than men intended for the dissenting ministry were educated, for in them a sound education could be acquired without subscription to the Articles of the Church of England and far more cheaply than at Oxford and Cambridge. Dissent was increasing in the early years of the century among the middle classes and critical congregations demanded the services of well-trained ministers. Women in middle-class families benefited by the quickening of intellectual interests in their male relations, although not even the dissenting academies were broadminded enough to contemplate receiving women students. It is certain that many of the girls' schools which flourished in this period were not particularly efficient. Hackney was the most popular suburb for girls' schools in the early eighteenth century as it had been a century earlier, and a glimpse of the girls at one of them gossiping with three boys at the back door is preserved in the diary of young Dudley Ryder, the Nonconformist draper's son who became Chief Justice of the King's Bench. The schoolmistress sharply rebuked the girls 'for their having held discourse with a man, and entertaining them upon the wall. One of the Lancashire girls talked very smartly to her again'[2].

Dudley Ryder, who was a grandson of a minister ejected in 1662, was

---

[1] Ed. with notes by James Upton; reissued in 1743.
[2] *The Diary of Dudley Ryder* (1715–16), ed. William Matthews, London, 1939, p. 84.

educated at the dissenting academy at Hackney, whence he had gone on to Edinburgh and Leyden to study civil law. His French, Latin and short-hand were good. The fragment of his diary which has survived was written when he was twenty-four. His sister's education is never mentioned, but she and her girl friend, a tailor's daughter, could hold their own in Bath society. Dudley Ryder easily fell in love, but found it hard to talk to girls. He greatly envied the young men of his acquaintance who could take liberties and tumble them about with impunity. He did not marry until he was forty-three and had made his mark in the law. One of his letters to his wife expresses a strikingly civilized attitude to marriage: 'I look upon matrimony as it really is not only as a society for life, in which our persons and fortunes in general are concerned, but as a partnership wherein our very passions and affections, our hopes and fears, our inclina-tions and aversions, all our good and ill Qualities are brought into one Common Stock'[1]. The women of the family, his mother, his aunts and sisters are constantly and affectionately mentioned in Dudley Ryder's youthful diary, though he was much concerned at the oddness of his grandmother: '. . . her continual finding fault, her appearing never obliged, her rash censuring upon every little occasion, and impregnable obstinacy in whatever she once asserts, though never so false or absurd, makes it a very uneasy thing to live in the house with her'. He could only agree with his Aunt Billio that it was the result of her husband's 'narrow way of living', which made her 'such a slave' that she did not know how to spend her 'plentiful fortune that is entirely at her own disposal'[2].

A glimpse into another middle-class dissenting circle is afforded by the letters of Philip Doddridge, who died in 1751 at the age of forty-nine[3]. Like Dudley Ryder he was a grandson of one of the ejected ministers of 1662. Philip Doddridge was the youngest of a family of twenty children, of whom he and one sister were the only survivors. Consumption carried his sister off when she was still a young woman and was the cause of his own early death. He was thirteen when his father died and only the help of a dissenting minister, Samuel Clark, enabled him to enter the dis-senting academy at Kibworth to study for the ministry under its head, Mr. Jennings. From that time to his death Doddridge kept up a close

---

[1] *The Diary of Dudley Ryder*, quoted in the Introduction by the editor, p. 20.
[2] *Ibid.*, pp. 54–5.
[3] *The Correspondence and Diary of Philip Doddridge*, ed. John Doddridge Humphries, London, 1829.

correspondence with an expanding circle of friends. In his early days he enjoyed writing playful letters to many young women, and often reverted to the relations between the sexes: 'too many of the sex are as empty and worthless as the generality of our own', he wrote to a Miss Farrington, whom he addressed as his 'dear mamma' or his 'best mamma in the world'[1]. Miss Hannah Clark, sister of Samuel Clark, he called Clio, once beginning his letter 'dear, sedate, methodical Clio'. He reproached her for suggesting that their friendship would end when she found a lover: 'Is there anything suspicious in such a platonic friendship as ours that you imagine your future husband will be offended? Pray tell him that my share in your friendship is one of the dearest things I have in the world and that I will never give it up: but shall expect to call you Clio when I cannot call you Clark'[2]. Clio embroidered for him 'turnovers', a curious article worn over the shoulders like a long collar, and was the recipient of his confidences about the young ladies with whom he fell in love, Miss Kitty Freeman[3] and 'the blooming Florella'[4], the sixteen-year-old daughter of Mr. Jennings. In 1730 he met and married Mercy Maris, of Upton-on-Severn. He wrote to Hannah Clark, by this time addressed as Cordelia, to describe his affection for 'that lovely Charmer', Mercy, whom he called 'Sabrina' and 'Cleora'[5]. The correspondence with Clio does not seem to have survived his marriage.

Doddridge kept up a more desultory correspondence with Hannah's sister, Elizabeth, whom he called Philomela. To both sisters he described himself as Celadon. Philomela was, perhaps, more critical than her sister, for Doddridge wrote to her with particular care: 'It is such an awful business', he declared in 1723, 'to write to a lady of so delicate a taste and so exact a judgment as Philomela, that I confess I have been seven weeks contriving how I should begin'[6]. In 1726 Philomela started a girls' school and Doddridge sent her his good wishes in a postscript to a letter to Hannah, adding 'I congratulate those young ladies who are to be under her care'[7]. In June Doddridge wrote to Philomela herself, for she had described 'teaching a large school' as 'a great undertaking' and asked him for advice. He agreed that the office of a schoolmistress was one 'of much labour and difficulty', but comforted her with the reflection that 'it is a post of the most honourable and important service that a member of

---

[1] *Doddridge*, vol. i, pp. 80–2, 89.   [2] *Ibid.*, pp. 49–52.
[3] *Ibid.*, pp. 257, 341 and 420.   [4] *Ibid.*, vol. iii, p. 34.   [5] *Ibid.*, p. 35.
[6] *Ibid.*, vol. i, p. 268.   [7] *Ibid.*, vol. ii, pp. 107–8.

your sex can be engaged in; nor are there many employments in our male world which can be compared with it'. He felt that her pupils might 'possibly have found some other mistress equally capable of instructing them in the dexterities of the needle, or in those other playful arts which it is generally expected they should learn; though I believe there are few who would have the vanity to pretend to rival you in these; but I conceive that they could not have found a more beautiful pattern of judicious taste, elegant sentiment, and polite behaviour; much less could they have fallen into the care of a person equally capable and equally solicitous to lead their dawning minds into the knowledge and love of practical religion, untainted by the awkward, though fashionable, mixture of affectation, censoriousness, superstition, and bigotry'[1]. Perhaps it would have been too much to expect the future head of the Northampton dissenting academy to recommend learning as well as religion to the attention of those who taught young women.

Doddridge's letters as he grew older display a patronizing attitude to women which was probably much that of other men less well educated than he. In his youth he had felt respect and affection for individual women, in particular his sister and Mrs. Jennings, the wife of the Principal of Kibworth. While at college he kept 'upon very civil terms with all', but was 'intimate with nobody but Mrs. Jennings'. She, he sadly told his sister, 'is always either tired or busy'[2]. The first young woman he wanted to marry he described to Samuel Clark as 'prudent, generous, cheerful, genteel, complaisant, and, above all, remarkably pious', but, he concluded, 'considering the family and neighbourhood in which she has been brought up, it is next to impossible that she should be the mistress of a great deal of politeness: but she has naturally a very good genius; and as I conceive that I have her education in my own hands, I will not be wanting on my part to form her more completely, at least to my own fancy'[3]. It is not perhaps surprising to learn that the young lady refused in the end to have any more to do with him. When any woman of his acquaintance criticized him in conversation he never replied in anger but went home and wrote to her kindly, but firmly, setting out her own faults. Mrs. Wingate, having been 'so kind as to tell' him 'of some things which' she 'thought amiss in' his behaviour, received a long letter written the next day accusing her of vanity, egoism, and jealousy. Having told her that her vanity had spoiled many a dish of chocolate drunk with her he had the effrontery to

---

[1] *Doddridge*, vol. ii, pp. 146–7.   [2] *Ibid.*, vol. i, p. 185.   [3] *Ibid.*, p. 375.

subscribe himself 'Your very great Admirer, your affectionate Friend, and obliged humble Servant'[1]. Even Mrs. Jennings, who, as his tutor's widow, might well have felt free to speak her mind, did not escape reproof. She was, he said in a letter written the day after she had told him of his own faults, 'pettish and morose', 'prone to contradict those with whom she was at all displeased', apt to treat the faults of those she loved 'with too great severity, and sometimes with an air of contempt'[2].

Doddridge wrote in a very different strain to aristocratic ladies. An early friend, with whom he corresponded until her death, was the widow of the sixth son of the Duke of Bedford. She had married again, but was always addressed by Doddridge as 'Lady Russell'. Their acquaintance began when Mr. Jennings, who attended at her home at Maidwell to teach her daughter astronomy and the globes, took Doddridge over with him from Kibworth in 1721. 'I lay there all night', he told his sister, 'and when I went away her ladyship gave me a guinea and told me that she hoped I should be no stranger to Maidwell while she continued on this side of the country'[3]. As he grew older he seems to have sent either a sermon or one of his volumes entitled *The Family Expositor* to individual ladies who might sympathize with his views. In this way he became acquainted with Lady Hardwicke, wife of the Lord Chancellor Hardwicke, with the Duchess of Somerset, and with Lady Huntingdon.

He found these ladies very kind and appreciative. The Countess of Hardwicke, thanking him for his books sent in 1748, expressed the wish that 'more of our writers employed their pens to better their own hearts and those of their readers, and then the press would not abound, as it does, with books calculated to destroy both our civil and religious liberties'[4]. The Duchess of Somerset, writing from Percy Lodge in 1750 after her husband's death, said that she 'had not the pleasure of being acquainted with any of your writings till I was at Bath three years ago, with my poor Lord, when an old acquaintance, the Dowager Lady Hyndford, recommended me to read the Rise and Progress of Religion in the Soul; and I may with great truth assure you that I never was so deeply affected with anything I ever met with as with that book, and I could not be easy till I had given one to every servant in my house who appeared to be of a serious turn of mind'. She added that her 'dear Lord read your former volumes with great attention and satisfaction, and frequently spoke of

---

[1] *Doddridge*, vol. ii, pp. 252–8.   [2] *Ibid.*, pp. 248–9.
[3] *Ibid.*, vol. i, p. 47.   [4] *Ibid.*, vol. v, p. 79.

them as the best books he had ever seen upon the subject'[1]. Doddridge's correspondence with the Countess of Huntingdon began in 1744, when he sent her a sermon asking 'that I would sit, with pen and paper by me, to mark all I could find amiss in it'. It must have given him pleasure when the Countess replied 'with all my care, I was not able to make a single objection, nor even to fear one from any mortal for you; and I must beg you will be so good to let me have a hundred sent, in order to give away'[2].

Selina, Countess of Huntingdon (1707–91), was one of the three co-heiresses of the second Earl Ferrars and married Theophilus, ninth Earl of Huntingdon, in 1728. This marriage brought her into the ambit of Lady Elizabeth Hastings, who, with her young half-sisters, was leading a life of piety and charity at Ledstone Hall[3]. References to Lady Huntingdon in contemporary letters before her conversion give no hint that she was to become the foundress of a religious connection, which has survived into the modern world. Mrs. Pendarves, in one of her letters to her sister, described Lady Huntingdon's dress before any of the others worn at the prince's birthday in January 1739 because it was the most impressive of them all. She wore a black velvet petticoat embroidered in chenille in a pattern of a large stone vase with ramping flowers and between each vase a pattern of gold shells. Her gown was of white satin, also embroidered with chenille and with gold ornaments. Mrs. Pendarves thought 'it was a most laboured piece of finery' and its wearer 'a mere shadow that tottered under every step she took under the load'[4]. In March of the same year Lady Huntingdon was one of the ladies who stormed the House of Lords when the Lords had ordered the gallery to be closed during a debate on the Spanish question. Mrs. Pendarves was there, too, and told her sister how 'the ladies bore the buffets of a stinking crowd from an hour after ten in the morning until five in the afternoon' without any food[5]. They learned that while they remained outside, the door would not be opened to the Members of the House of Commons so they allowed the Commons to come up and rushed in with them. Lady Mary Wortley Montagu described them as 'heroines', who had shown 'their zeal and appetite for knowledge in a most glorious manner'[6].

Soon after this exploit Lady Huntingdon was converted to Calvinistic

[1] *Doddridge*, vol. v, pp. 184–6.   [2] *Ibid.*, vol. iv, pp. 330–1.   [3] See above, p. 225.
[4] *Mrs. Delany*, vol. ii, p. 28.   [5] *Ibid.*, p. 44.
[6] *Letters and Works*, vol. i, p. 391.

Methodism by her sister-in-law, Lady Margaret Hastings, who herself went so far as to marry in 1741 one of the Methodist preachers, Benjamin Ingham. The death of two sons from smallpox in 1743 turned Lady Huntingdon's mind even more closely to religion. Lord Huntingdon died in 1746, leaving her a wealthy widow, able to make her own life. She lived until 1791, although she wrote to Doddridge in 1747 describing herself as 'weak and ill'[1]. In that year the Methodist preacher George Whitefield became her chaplain and, as she wrote to Doddridge, 'some of the great of this world hear with me the gospel patiently; and thus much seed is sown by Mr. Whitfield's preaching'[2]. The Methodists and Dissenters felt themselves in sympathy with each other, but inevitably the growth of Methodism drew people from the congregations of the Old Dissent. Lady Huntingdon never wished to leave the communion of the Church of England or abandoned her belief in episcopacy, but from the time of her conversion she was the friend and protector of many clergymen whose views were suspect to orthodox churchmen. She claimed and exercised the right as a peeress of appointing as many chaplains as she chose, and in 1761 sold her jewels to build her first regular chapel at Brighton. She thereafter built chapels in places frequented by people of fashion, such as Tunbridge and Bath.

She has been described as 'a child of emotion', and is said to have likened herself to 'a ship before the wind carried on by an impulse she could not resist or describe'[3]. Nevertheless she must have been a good woman of business. In 1768 she founded a seminary in North Wales to train young men for the ministry, making it plain that after three years of study they could enter the ministry of the Church of England or any other Protestant congregation. She believed in moving her chaplains from place to place every three years. If she came to disapprove of any one of them she dismissed him. This happened in the case of Thomas Wills, a Cornishman who had been a successful minister in the Church of England. At Bath he met Miss Selina Wheeler, a niece of Lady Huntingdon's. They were married in 1774 and Lady Huntingdon invited Wills to join her connection 'and change a stationary life for one of a more itinerant nature'. He therefore left his parish and after a time became incumbent of a new chapel which Lady Huntingdon had built at Spa Fields. The incumbent of Clerkenwell protested at this intrusion and after the case had come before the consistorial court of London many of

---

[1] *Doddridge*, vol. iv, p. 530.   [2] *Ibid.*, vol. v, p. 38.   [3] *Ibid.*, vol. iv, p. 328 *n*.

Lady Huntingdon's chaplains judged it expedient to secede from the Church of England. Wills seceded in 1782 and took out a licence as a Dissenting minister. He remained in Lady Huntingdon's connection until July 1788, when after he had preached at the Spa Fields chapel on 6 July he received during the following week a letter from Lady Huntingdon 'signifying that she had no further occasion for his services, and in consequence gave him his dimission'. Permission to preach a farewell sermon was denied him[1].

Lady Huntingdon was always ready to take on new responsibilities. When George Whitefield died in 1770 and left her his American property she had no hesitation in sending missionaries there. Her beliefs were clear-cut and she firmly made known her disapproval of developments in Wesleyan Methodism after 1770. Almost to the end of her life she kept the control of her connection in her own hands, but in 1790, when she felt her end approaching, she asked that an association should be formed to help her, and to carry on the work after her death. She died in 1791 and her place as head of the connection was taken by her friend, Lady Anne Erskine. Lady Huntingdon's administrative powers have always been recognized, but her humanity and her charity have perhaps been underestimated. The expenses of maintaining her chapels and her missionaries were so great that she reduced her own style of living and was not always able to respond to deserving requests for help. Her bequest to Lady Anne Erskine was simply an annuity of £100. But it was Lady Huntingdon who defrayed two-thirds of the cost of sending Doddridge to Portugal in a vain search for health. She never hesitated to undertake a distasteful task if she felt it was her duty. She visited her cousin Laurence, Earl Ferrars, while he was in prison awaiting execution for the murder of his steward. She was the life-long friend of her aunt, the beautiful Lady Frances Shirley, born like her in 1707, who made no secret of the fact that she was Lord Chesterfield's mistress. By 1750 the affair was over and Lady Frances became a Calvinistic Methodist like her niece. When she died in 1778 she left the bulk of her fortune to Lady Huntingdon and was buried in the cemetery attached to Lady Huntingdon's chapel at Bath[2].

Her social position enabled Lady Huntingdon to make full use of her faculties, and experience the delight of creating and dominating a large religious organization. For the middle-class woman with intellectual

[1] W. Wilson, *History of the Dissenting Churches of London*, London, 1810, vol. iii, pp. 118-21.   [2] E. Shirley, *Stemmata Shirleiana*, 2nd ed., 1873, pp. 217-19.

ambitions there remained the less exciting activities of correspondence with others of their kind, the construction of elegant verse, and modest adventures in scholarship. Before the middle of the century one such woman had won for herself a considerable reputation for learning. Elizabeth Carter was born in Deal in 1717, the eldest daughter of Nicholas Carter, perpetual curate of Deal. Her father, the son of a large farmer in the vale of Aylesbury, had been intended for his father's business but made such progress in his studies that he went to Cambridge and entered the Church. He gave a sound classical education to all his children, both boys and girls. Elizabeth was so slow at first in acquiring the ancient languages that her father besought her not to struggle further with them, but she persisted, and, reading early and late, taking snuff and chewing green tea to keep herself awake, she at length gained a sufficient mastery of both Latin and Greek. Like the women scholars of the Renaissance period she went on to acquire a smattering of Hebrew, French, Italian, and Spanish. In the hope of getting a place at court she began to learn German and in later life taught herself something of Arabic and Portuguese. Her father would have liked her to marry, for he had by his second wife an increasing family and was without private means. 'I will lay no commands upon you', he wrote in reference to the last proposal made for her, 'because it is more immediately your own affair, and for life: but you ought certainly to consider with great attention, before you reject an offer, far more advantageous in appearance than any other you can ever expect. You can always count on my indulgence; but do not let my indulgence mislead you. If you cannot bring your mind to a compliance, I and all your friends will be sorry for your missing so good a prospect'[1].

Great strength of mind must have been necessary to resist such anxious care. Elizabeth Carter remained single, bearing cheerfully the burdens which fell upon the eldest daughter of a long family. In 1747, when she was already famous, she wrote without complaint of 'labouring on in the beaten track through whole dozens of shirts and shifts' and, to amuse her correspondent, described how she once made a pudding 'so overcharged with pepper and brandy that it put the whole family in a flame'. She 'happily applied' herself 'to forming a special good sweet cake, with such success that the former mishap was forgot, and I was employed to make

[1] Montagu Pennington, *Memoirs of the Life of Mrs. Elizabeth Carter*, London, 1807, pp. 20–1.

every christening cake that happened in the family ever after. And though I say it, that should not say it, several grave notable gentlewomen of unquestionable good housewifery have applied to me for the receipt'[1]. She was delighted to be able to take sole charge of her youngest brother's education and prepare him for the university. She was a woman of happy disposition, interested in everything about her. She was sensitive to the beauty of the countryside around her home, and wrote of her long walks very much as a modern woman might. She wrote poetry and loved music and read every book that came her way. There is never a hint that she felt frustrated by the limitations custom imposed on a woman's ambition. She was, indeed, more fortunate than many other women, for she had kinsfolk in London and friends in the close of Canterbury who were glad to entertain her for the long visits customary in those leisurely days. Above all, owing to her father's friendship with Edward Cave, founder of the *Gentleman's Magazine*, she had the pleasure of seeing her work in print when she was seventeen.

Her first contribution to the *Gentleman's Magazine* appeared in 1734 and was followed by many others, although not everything under the name Eliza was from her pen. To Edward Cave Miss Carter owed both the production of her first slender volume of poems in 1738 and her introduction to Dr. Johnson in the same year. It was certainly Cave who suggested to her that it might be profitable to publish the translations she had made of two modern works: Crousaz's criticism of Pope's *Essay on Man* from French and Algarotti's explanation of Newton's philosophy for the ladies from Italian. Although these books appeared in 1739 without the name of the translator on the title-page Cave saw that it was well known who had done the work. Miss Carter herself had no exaggerated opinion of their value and in later life deprecated any reference to them. But they brought her much renown at the time of their publication, and in the *Gentleman's Magazine* Thomas Birch described her as 'a very extraordinary phenomenon in the republick of letters'. Cave understood, as a good business man, the interest which could be aroused by the spectacle of a learned and personable young woman who yet could write readable books and poems. He would have liked Miss Carter to write more, and in 1746 complained in a letter to her father 'I cannot persuade Miss to undertake anything, and the world wants to know what she is about'[2].

[1] *A series of Letters between Mrs. Elizabeth Carter and Miss Catherine Talbot*, ed. Montagu Pennington, London, 1809, vol. i, pp. 218–19.   [2] *Memoirs*, p. 71.

A new influence entered Elizabeth Carter's life in 1741 when she met Catherine Talbot, who was the granddaughter of William, Bishop of Durham. To the close friendship which grew up between them, Elizabeth Carter owed her introduction to a far wider circle than her own. Two of the most eminent ecclesiastics of the time, Joseph Butler, Bishop of Gloucester and later of Durham, and Thomas Secker, Bishop of Oxford, Dean of St. Paul's, and later Archbishop of Canterbury, had each been helped in the course of his promotion by Catherine Talbot's grandfather. Her mother had been left poorly off by her husband's early death and it was in keeping with the generosity of Thomas Secker's character that he invited Mrs. Talbot and her daughter to join his household. He superintended Catherine Talbot's education, and the letters she and Elizabeth Carter exchanged reveal two circles in which intelligent young women are leading active, useful, and innocently happy lives. Evenings were spent in reading aloud, sometimes Clarendon's *History of the Great Rebellion*, sometimes Steele's essays, sometimes Lady Mary Wortley Montagu's letters. The publication of Mrs. Cockburn's works was eagerly awaited, and both Catherine Talbot and her mother were subscribers.

It was at the impulse of Catherine Talbot that Elizabeth Carter began in 1749 to translate the works of Epictetus. Many young women had started on this before, but none had completed the work. Miss Carter sent the sheets to Miss Talbot as she wrote them and Miss Talbot told her what she and Bishop Secker thought of the work. In the bishop's opinion she was making too smooth and elegant a translation. He added a postscript to the letter, 'Let me speak a word for myself: Why would you change a plain, home, awakening preacher into a smooth, fine, polite writer, of what nobody will mind? Answer me that, dear Miss Carter'. Later he wrote 'Good Miss Carter' a long letter explaining his preference for 'a rough, almost literal translation, if it doth but relish strongly of that warm and practical spirit, which to me is the characteristick of this book'[1]. When the work was finished, and the bishop insisted that nothing should be omitted, he set about encouraging Miss Carter to write notes to the text and a life of Epictetus as an Introduction. At the same time he was looking for a publisher. He decided at last on publication by subscription, half a guinea to be paid on placing the order and half on receipt of the book.

The bishop's guidance did not end there, for he read the proofs and

[1] *Memoirs*, pp. 112–15.

found it necessary to reprove Miss Carter for carelessness. 'Do, dear Madam Carter, get yourself whipt, get yourself whipt. Indeed, it is quite necessary for you. I know you mean to be careful; but you cannot without this help. Everything else hath been tried, and proves ineffectual. Here are some sheets come down. I have this moment open'd them; and the first thing I have cast my eyes upon is *Epictetus* for *Epicurus*, p. 73. I will look over the whole in a day or two; but one needs go no further to see what prescription your case indicates'[1]. As the book was in the press more subscribers than were ever expected paid their half-guineas, so that an extra two hundred and fifty copies had to be printed. The printer was Mr. Richardson, the author of *Clarissa* and the friend of many contemporary women. His bill for the first edition, apart from the extra copies, was £67 7s. od. A thousand and thirty-one people subscribed and Miss Carter made 'nearly, if not quite, a thousand pounds'[2]. Miss Carter's nephew, in writing her life, described how 'some years after, Dr. Secker, then Archbishop of Canterbury, brought a bookseller's catalogue to her, saying "Here, Madam Carter, see how ill I am used by the world; here are my Sermons selling at half-price, while your Epictetus truly is not to be had under eighteen shillings, only three shillings less than the original subscription".'[3] Two more editions were published in Miss Carter's lifetime and another one after her death.

Miss Carter owed gratitude to Thomas Secker for financial help as well as for training in scholarship. In 1763 he noted in his diary 'This year I lent Miss Carter, to whom, I believe, I had given about fifty pounds before, £150 upon her note, without interest. And I do not intend that she shall repay it me'[4]. Secker had been translated to the see of Canterbury in 1758, the same year that *Epictetus* appeared, and it is probable that Elizabeth Carter's reputation as a scholar profited by her association with the archbishop's household. Thomas Secker was a Nottinghamshire man and was educated for the Nonconformist ministry at three Dissenting academies, but he came under the influence of Edward Talbot, Miss Talbot's father, and joined the Church of England. He deserves to be remembered, with Dr. George Hickes and Bishop Burnet, as a man great enough to realize a woman's capacity and generous enough to help her to develop it. Miss Carter preserved a revealing story about him. She was complaining one day in the palace at Lambeth about the unfair way in which the translators of the Bible had rendered I Corinthians vii.

---

[1] *Memoirs*, p. 140.   [2] *Ibid.*, p. 141.   [3] *Loc. cit.*   [4] *Ibid.*, p. 274.

12 and 13: 'that for the evident purpose of supporting the superiority of the husband they had translated the same verb as applied to the husband *put away* and as applied to the wife *leave: Let him not put her away* and *Let her not leave him*. The Archbishop denied the fact, and asserted that the words in the original were not the same; but finding his antagonist obstinate, "Come with me, Madam Carter", he said at length, "to my study, and be confuted". They went, and his Grace, on consulting the passage, instead of being angry that he was found to be in the wrong, said with the utmost good humour, "No, Madam Carter, 'tis I that must be confuted, and you are in the right".'[1]

The success of her book enabled Elizabeth Carter to spend longer periods in London, and in her own lodgings. Her home remained with her father at Deal, but she passed the early months of the year in London. She owed her introduction to London society to Miss Talbot, but her own quality made friends for her within it. The literary hostesses of the day, such as Mrs. Montagu and Mrs. Vesey, welcomed her to their houses. The letters that passed between Catherine Talbot and Elizabeth Carter often refer to aristocratic ladies in more revealing phrases than Lady Mary Coke or her young cousin, Lady Louisa Stuart, used. Lady Mary refers to Miss Anne Pitt frequently, sometimes as 'the old Virgin'. To Miss Talbot, Miss Anne Pitt was 'one of the liveliest, most friendly-looking persons' she saw when she attended the queen's drawing-room[2]. Nine months later Miss Talbot again mentioned Miss Anne Pitt as 'surely most inchantingly agreeable. There is with all her archness somewhat so natural and unaffected for the heart of me I cannot be afraid of her, though with that superiority of understanding to be sure I ought'[3]. Lady Mary Coke herself is not, in this correspondence, the figure of fun that Lady Louisa Stuart made her. Miss Carter 'was particularly charmed by Lady M. Coke's appearance and would have given' her 'ears to hear her talk' but she was shy and ran away[4]. In later years Elizabeth Carter often dined with Lady Holdernesse at Walmer Castle and on one occasion told Miss Talbot that she spent the greatest part of the afternoon walking on the seaside with Lady Holdernesse and Lady Mary Coke. On returning to the castle they saw a girl 'in stout contention with a cow, which she was lugging by the horns to pull her up the hill'. 'With the agility of a mountain nymph' Lady Mary went to the bottom and at once the cow

[1] *Memoirs*, p. 110.   [2] *Carter–Talbot Letters*, vol. iii, p. 19.
[3] *Ibid.*, p. 37.   [4] *Memoirs*, p. 153.

'gallopped up the hill before her Ladyship as hastily, though not as lightly, as a kid'[1]. Anyone who has tried to drive an unwilling cow will appreciate Lady Mary's skill.

Mrs. Montagu, as the wife of a rich husband, was able to do more for Miss Carter than merely invite her to parties. She took her to Lord Bath's country house near Maidenhead and in 1761 invited her to spend the season with her at Tunbridge. Lord Bath showed both kindness and delicacy of feeling by asking Mrs. Montagu to buy 'silk or damask or what you please' to make 'a small present to Mrs. Carter to make her fine when she comes to Tunbridge'. To persuade her to accept it he wrote saying that he had found some Greek books in his library, which were of no use to him, but might be to her, that he had also 'two pounds of very bad tea which he cannot take himself', also he has found 'in the drawer of an old India Cabinet a piece of silk with this wrote on it *Enough for a mantua and petty coat*', neither of which he could wear. At the same time he asked Mrs. Montagu to find some way of giving Miss Carter two twenty-pound notes which he enclosed, without letting her know from whom they came[2].

When Lord Bath died at the age of eighty-two in 1764 many people seem to have been surprised that he did not leave Miss Carter an annuity. Lady Hervey, writing to her sons' former tutor, said 'I wish he had left Mrs. Carter the forty pounds a year you mention, but she is not named in his will; whilst he lived he made her several presents, and, as I have been told, solicited a pension for her from the crown. She has great merit, but very little money, and as he saw her often, and profited by the one, 'tis pity he did not furnish her with the other'[3]. Lord Bath's heir was his brother, who died in 1767, when Mr. and Mrs. Pulteney, to whom the property passed, settled £100 a year on Miss Carter. About three years before she died the annuity was increased by £50[4]. Mrs. Montagu's husband died in 1775, leaving his large fortune to his wife. One of her first acts was to secure an annuity of £100 to Miss Carter. After Miss Talbot's death in 1770 her mother entrusted all her manuscripts to her friend, giving Miss Carter permission to deal with them as she wished. Miss Carter, in the same year, published at her own expense a volume of

[1] *Memoirs*, p. 272.
[2] E. J. Climenson, *Elizabeth Montagu, the Queen of the Blue-stockings*, London, 1906, vol. ii, pp. 235–6.
[3] *Letters of Mary Lepel, Lady Hervey*, p. 308.   [4] *Memoirs*, pp. 263–7.

religious reflections by Miss Talbot and again in 1772 a volume of Miss Talbot's essays. The reflections passed through many editions and the profits to Miss Carter 'were not inconsiderable'[1]. When Mrs. Talbot died she left Miss Carter a legacy of £200 and a few years later a childhood friend left her an annuity of £40. Through an unusual combination of personal charm and business sense she had come before the end of her life to a position of financial security and something more.

Her old age was spent in her own house at Deal. In 1763 she acquired several tenements held under the Archbishop of Canterbury by different leases. At her request Archbishop Secker allowed her to hold them all under a single lease and would take no fine from her on its renewal. While she was abroad repairs were carried out and her father was installed there. He rented the house from her and they lived there together, each with a separate study and meeting seldom, except at meals. His death in 1774 made little difference to her way of life. Her reputation increased with age. When she died in 1806 she had been 'the famous Miss Carter of Deal' for close on seventy years. Her teachers and guides had been old-fashioned classical scholars and ordained ministers of the Church of England. The study of the Bible was a lasting pleasure to her and she left many notes and criticisms of the accepted translation behind her. Perhaps the influence of her early friend Edward Cave may have helped her to become a good business woman. Her life was never that of the unworldly scholar who seeks to open new paths and advance the frontiers of knowledge. In this she differed to her own comfort from Elizabeth Elstob, thirty years her senior. But today Elizabeth Carter's *Epictetus* gathers dust on library shelves or is thrown away as salvage while Anglo-Saxon scholars are searching, often in vain, for the modest products of Elizabeth Elstob's scholarship.

The adulation poured out upon Miss Carter is an example of the interest in the capacities of women always latent in society, but always stronger in times when internal peace directs attention to the arts of civilization rather than the art of war. Tracts on the position of women had always sold well since Cornelius Agrippa's time, but women's achievements in the seventeenth century gave a new twist to the tracts of the succeeding age. The earlier tracts were written by men, but women were publishing their own views before the century was over. It was

[1] *Memoirs*, p. 281.

natural that journalists should exploit this situation and begin to write anonymous tracts, pretending to speak as women. The identity of 'Sophia, a person of Quality', who in 1739 wrote *Woman not inferior to Man*, has never been established, but it is unlikely that a woman wrote it[1]. On the title-page the author put a few lines from Rowe's play *The Fair Penitent*, beginning:

> 'How hard is the condition of our Sex
> Thro' every state of Life a Slave to Man'.

The argument of the tract was that woman should have equality of education and opportunity with man. Women should not be excluded from government, from public office, or the teaching of the sciences; 'with regard, however, to warlike employments, it seems to be a disposition of Providence that custom has exempted us from them'[2].

It seems unlikely that a woman who felt deeply about the exclusion of women from all professions would have written like the so-called Sophia. It is perhaps significant that the tract first appeared in the same year in which Miss Carter produced her popular translations from French and Italian. It enabled 'Sophia' to quote 'an *Eliza* not more to be envied for the towering superiority of her genius and judgment, than honour'd for the use she makes of them'. The author declared 'I shall forbear to characterize her; content to see the work already done to my hand, by that sex itself: and therefore refer my readers for a further account of this true Woman to what the *Reverend Mr. Birch* says of her in the History of the Works of the Learned: which is so much the more to be relied on as it comes from a Man'[3]. Surely such advertisement must have been inspired by Miss Carter's publisher, Edward Cave. The appearance in 1751 of *Beauty's Triumph or the superiority of the Fair Sex invincibly proved* strengthens the argument that 'Sophia' was a male journalist[4]. The book is in three parts, the first being a reprint, with a few additions, of 'Sophia's' tract. The second part is an answer to 'Sophia' setting out *The Natural Right of Men to Sovereignty over the other Sex*. The third part is 'Sophia's' rejoinder offering further proof that women are 'superior in excellence to men'. The whole book is of a piece and its style, to the present writer, seems to betray the masculine author. No woman to whom the accepted

1 London, for John Hawkins, price one shilling.
2 *Woman not inferior to Man*, p. 55.
3 *Ibid.*, p. 47.   4 London, for J. Robinson.

superiority of man was a burning injustice would write coyly about 'my fair partners in oppression'[1].

In 1753 William Kenrick, who has been described as 'the enemy of every decent and successful person'[2], had the temerity to put out a nasty little tract described on the title-page as *The Whole Duty of Woman*, by a Lady, written at the desire of a noble lord[3]. He wrote in flowery language and separated what he had to say into twenty-four sections, each dealing with a different subject, such as Knowledge, Elegance, Modesty, Affectation and so on. 'It is not for thee, O woman, to undergo the perils of the deep, to dig in the hollow mines of the earth, to trace the dark springs of science, or to number the thick stars of the heavens.

'Let the kingdom rule itself, let the wise-men and the councellors enact laws and correct them: the policy of government is a hidden thing, like a well of water in the bottom of a deep pit.

'Thy kingdom is thine own house, and thy government the care of thy family.

'Let the laws of thy condition be thy study, and learn only to govern thyself and thy dependants'[4]. These pearls of wisdom are part of the section on knowledge. That a third edition of this tract was required in the year of its publication is a warning against assuming that the fulsome praise given to Miss Carter indicates a fundamental change in the attitude of men to women.

Miss Carter herself was always conscious of the inert mass of opinion hostile to women moving out of their domestic duties into a wider sphere. According to her nephew she never made any efforts to cultivate the society of men of letters largely because she felt 'an extreme partiality for writers of her own sex. She was much inclined to believe, that women had not their proper station in society, and that their mental powers were not rated sufficiently high'. Nevertheless 'she detested the principles displayed in Mrs. Woolstonecroft's wild theory concerning the "Rights of Women", and never wished to interfere with the privileges and occupations of the other sex, yet she thought that men exercised too

---

[1] A similar work to 'Sophia's' is *Female Rights Vindicated; or the Equality of the Sexes morally and physically proved*, by a Lady, London, 1758. This appeared again in 1780 under a new title *Female Restoration, by a moral and physical vindication of Female Talents*, by a Lady, with no indication that it was merely a reprint of an earlier tract. Without saying dogmatically that these tracts are written by a man, the present writer much suspects they were.

[2] *Dictionary of National Biography.*

[3] London, for R. Baldwin.   [4] *Ibid.*, pp. 17–18.

arbitrary a power over them as too inferior to themselves'[1]. The attitude
of mind set out in these sentences was shared by all the ladies who met at
London parties and wrote each other long letters from their country
homes. They were not revolutionaries, but they believed in the capacity
of their own sex.

This attitude appears again in the writings of Hester Mulso, better
known as Mrs. Chapone, who was born in 1727 at Twywall, Northamptonshire. Her early promise was checked by her mother's jealousy, and
it was not until 1750, when her mother was dead, that she was free to choose
her own way of life. She made use of her new freedom to gain the
acquaintance of Miss Carter, and of Samuel Richardson, with whom she
corresponded at length. He liked and understood women and his successful
novels owed much to the love-letters he had written for three young
girls in Derby when he was a young man. At his house, Hester Mulso
met a poor attorney and fell in love with him. He is chiefly remarkable
because he was the son of Sally Chapone—the Sappho of Mrs. Delany's
youth—and became Hester Mulso's husband. Their marriage was delayed
for some six years because her father withheld his consent. Her letters to
Richardson about the relationship between parents and children are
forcibly expressed. It was not God, she argued, who made daughters
more dependent on their parents than sons. 'Custom, indeed, allows
not the daughters of people of fashion to leave their father's family to seek
their own subsistence, and there is no way for them to gain a creditable
livelihood, as gentlemen may. But amongst the lower ranks of people,
daughters are as soon independent as sons. The girls and boys are alike
sent out to provide for themselves'[2]. Before her marriage Hester Mulso
carefully thought out and sent to Richardson a statement of her beliefs
about the married state. She did not question the husband's 'divine right
to the absolute obedience of his wife', although she remarked with a touch
of asperity 'in many marriages the natural superiority in all mental
excellencies, is evidently on the woman's side'[3]. Her own married life was
soon cut short by her husband's death.

Hester Chapone won a high reputation among her contemporaries
for her *Letters on the Improvement of the Mind*, which had been written
for the benefit of her niece. Fifteen hundred copies of the first edition

[1] *Memoirs*, p. 303.
[2] *Bluestocking Letters*, ed. R. Brimley Johnson, London, 1926, p. 193.
[3] *Ibid.*, pp. 197–8.

were sold out at once and a second edition was being set up within a year of publication. The absolute correctness of the advice made the book popular. Girls should consult their parents before giving a lover the least encouragement[1]. Mrs. Chapone advised her niece not to try to acquire the learned languages. 'The danger of pedantry and presumption in a woman, of her exacting envy in one sex and jealousy in the other—of her exchanging the graces of imagination for the severity and preciseness of a scholar, would be, I own, sufficient to frighten me from the ambition of seeing my girl remarkable for learning. Such objections are perhaps still stronger with regard to the abstruse sciences'[2]. Mrs. Chapone urged her niece to be careful in her choice of friends. 'Your equals in rank are most proper for intimacy, but to be sometimes among your superiors is in every way desirable and advantageous, unless it should inspire you with pride, or with the foolish desire of emulating their grandeur and expense. Above all avoid intimacy with those of low birth and education! nor think it a mark of humility to delight in such society; for it much oftener proceeds from the meanest kind of pride, that of being the head of the company, and seeing your companions subservient to you'[3]. If any married friend 'encourages or tolerates the addresses of a lover . . . I can only say that, after proper remonstrances, you must immediately withdraw from all intimacy and confidence with her'[4]. The prudential morality of the Victorian age is already implicit in the writings of Mrs. Chapone.

It is a remarkable sign of the improvement in the education generally given to girls that from the 'forties of the eighteenth century a continually increasing number of women won for themselves a modest place in the national memory by their intellectual achievements. Without considering such a giant in her own day as Hannah More, born in 1745, or such a best-selling novelist as Fanny Burney, her junior by seven years, it is easy to compile a list of remarkable women, born in widely separated parts of England, who in different ways illustrate this release of the female intellect. Before these women had time to prove their quality the Reverend John Duncombe had written, as part of his courtship of Susanna Highmore, a poem in praise of women called *The Feminiad*[5]. Though an indifferent

---

[1] *Letters on the improvement of the mind addressed to a Lady*, London, 1810, p. 96.
[2] *Ibid.*, pp. 156–7.   [3] *Ibid.*, p. 81.   [4] *Ibid.*, pp. 90–1.
[5] London, 1754, price one shilling. The poem is generally quoted as *The Feminead*, but in the copy I have used the word is spelt *Feminiad*.

poem it deserves to be remembered for its excellent sentiments and the
pleasure they gave to women.

> 'To these weak strains, O thou! the sex's friend
> And constant patron Richardson attend'

sang Duncombe. He praised his own love as Eugenia:

> 'With lovely mien Eugenia now appears
> The muse's pupil from her earliest years'.

Susanna Highmore could turn verses, but she is best known as the artist
who sketched the picture of Richardson reading *Sir Charles Grandison* to
his friends in his grotto at North End, Hammersmith, with Hester
Chapone sitting in the middle of the circle. Duncombe, although celebrating eminent women, declared

> 'Nor mean we here to blame that father's care
> Who guards from learned wives his booby heir . . .
> The wise themselves should with discretion chuse
> Since letter'd nymphs their knowledge may abuse
> And husbands oft experience to their cost
> The prudent housewife in the scholar lost.'

Mrs. Cockburn's collected works had recently been published by subscription and Duncombe's father had taken a copy. His son described her as
'Philosopher, Divine and Poet'. But with all his desire to praise women,

> 'The modest muse a veil of pity throws
> O'er Vice's friends and Virtue's female foes
> Abashed she views the bold unblushing mien
> Of modern Manley, Centlivre, and Behn,'

Duncombe did not subscribe to Ballard's book, nor does he seem to have
seen it.

Twenty years after *The Feminiad* appeared a Miss Mary Scott wrote a
poem called *The Female Advocate*, which was 'occasioned by reading
Mr. Duncombe's *Feminead*'[1]. In her dedicatory letter 'To a Lady' Mary
Scott recalled how they had both often read Mr. Duncombe's *Feminiad*
with grateful pleasure, but regretting that 'it was only on a small number
of Female Geniuses that Gentleman bestowed the wreath of Fame'[2].

---

[1] For Joseph Johnson, London, 1774, price two shillings.   [2] *Ibid.*, p. v.

'Prompted by a most fervent zeal for their privileges' Mary Scott therefore set out to supply verses celebrating other women deserving of renown. Like Duncombe she had not subscribed to Ballard's book, but the women she wrote about are generally those whom Ballard also described. She began her researches with Katherine Parr and continued them into her own lifetime. Footnotes to the verses tell the reader something about each woman who is being praised. The poem represents much devoted work by a woman 'in whom years of ill health have impaired every faculty of my mind'. Its interest lies in the author's indignation at the limitations imposed on women's education. Do not men, she asks, 'regard the woman who suffers her faculties to rust in a state of listless indolence, with a more favourable eye, than her who engages in a dispassionate search for truth?' Mary Scott believed 'that it is a duty absolutely incumbent on every woman whom nature hath blest with talents, of what kind soever they may be, to improve them; and that is much oftener the case than it is usually supposed to be'[1].

Among her own contemporaries Miss Scott found many women whose works she could praise. She even saw resemblances to Pope in the *Essays in Prose and Verse* by Miss Mary Jones, of Oxford:

'Her wit so keen, her sentiments so true
Like him the charming maid, with skill refined
Hath pierced the deep recesses of the mind'[2].

The most remarkable feature of Miss Jones's book is a fifty-page list of subscribers; among them Miss Scott herself, described as of Barham, Kent[3], and Mr. Christopher Smart, M.A., Fellow of Pembroke Hall, Cambridge. It is unlikely that the great precursor of William Blake drew much satisfaction from the mild verses in which Miss Jones attributed human feelings to D'oman, her cat. But it was possible for Miss Scott to find two other men whom she could praise as 'generous pleaders of the female cause'. One, whom she called Philander, was probably her own father. The other was Dr. Seward, Canon of Lichfield, who earned her commendation by the poem which he printed in Dodsley's *Miscellanies* called *The female right to Literature, in a Letter to a young Lady from Florence.* He was the father of Anna Seward (1747–1809), who as a child was encouraged to write poetry by Erasmus Darwin. She spent her life at

[1] *The Female Advocate*, p. viii.   [2] *Ibid.*, p. 19.
[3] She dated the Preface to *The Female Advocate* at Milborne Port, 10 May 1774.

Lichfield and was able to supply Boswell with anecdotes of Dr. Johnson. She nursed her father through his slow decay, wrote poems on national occasions, corresponded with an ever-growing circle of friends and became to a younger generation 'The Swan of Lichfield'[1]. The neglect of later generations has perhaps justified Horace Walpole's condemnation of 'the harmonious virgins' of his day. But they deserve credit for trying to cultivate their modest gifts in an indifferent world.

Anna Letitia Aikin, better known as Mrs. Barbauld (1743–1825), is particularly interesting from her early environment. She was the daughter of John Aikin, who was a pupil of Philip Doddridge at Kibworth and succeeded him as head of the academy there. He married Jane Jennings, daughter of the founder of Kibworth and one of the girls whom Doddridge had thought of marrying. Anna was born at Kibworth, but her father left it to teach in the newly established dissenting academy at Warrington when she was fifteen. She was a clever and diligent girl, but her father was only with difficulty persuaded to teach her the ancient languages. Her brother encouraged her early attempts to write and persuaded her to print a volume of poems in 1773. She was greatly cheered when Mrs. Montagu wrote to her appreciatively about them. In the next year she married Rochemont Barbauld, who had been a student at the Warrington academy and had entered the Dissenting ministry. Mrs. Barbauld enjoyed teaching and helped her husband while he kept a school in Suffolk. They had no children of their own, but adopted a nephew for whom Mrs. Barbauld wrote *Early Lessons for Children* and published it in 1778. After Barbauld died his widow produced a fifty-volume edition of the best English novelists, with an historical introduction and biographies of each author. It is, perhaps, Anna Barbauld's chief distinction that she carried far into the nineteenth century a living tradition of the Dissenting academies which arose in answer to the Great Ejection of 1662.

The inspiration of Mrs. Barbauld's *Early Lessons* encouraged Mrs. Sarah Trimmer (1741–1810) to make a book of the early lessons she had given to her own children. *An Easy introduction to the Knowledge of Nature* appeared in 1782 with a sketch of Scripture History, which Mrs. Trimmer afterwards enlarged into a separate work. Mrs. Trimmer was the daughter of John Kirby, a Suffolk artist, who became clerk of the works at Kew Palace, a connection with court which was useful to his daughter. Her

[1] A good impression of Miss Seward can be gained from *The Swan of Lichfield, being a Selection from the Correspondence of Anna Seward*, ed. Hesketh Pearson, London, 1936.

first fourteen years were spent at Ipswich where she attended a good school kept by a lady who had been cast off by her family because of 'an imprudent marriage'[1]. When her parents moved to London they were accepted in the literary circle dominated by Dr. Johnson and Sarah was able on one occasion to produce a copy of *Paradise Lost* from her pocket for the settlement of a textual point disputed by the company. Sarah married when she was twenty-one and settled with her husband at Brentford. She educated her six daughters entirely herself and directed the education of her six sons, except for their classical studies. She said herself that in those years she 'could find but little leisure for reading; the needle was my principal occupation when I was not nursing or teaching'[2]. As her elder children grew up Mrs. Trimmer anticipated the methods afterwards most used in the education of the masses by allowing the older children to instruct the younger in their own newly acquired knowledge. She was in this way 'at length released from every part of education, except casual advice or admonition'[3].

In 1785 Mrs. Trimmer began to keep a journal after reading Dr. Johnson's *Prayers and Meditations*. For her own improvement she examined her behaviour minutely and meditated on God and her soul. A modern reader may be allowed to regret that she omitted so much about the ordinary business of her life. The Vicar of Ealing, Mr. Sturgess, was responsible for drawing Mrs. Trimmer's attention to the work of Robert Raikes at Gloucester, where he had started his first Sunday-school in 1780. Mrs. Trimmer's long practice in teaching her own children and her pity for the ignorance of the poor combined to make her welcome the opportunity and Sunday-schools were opened at Brentford on 18 June 1786. 'My attendance at them', she wrote on 2 July, 'prevented the continuing of my Journal. It is a most interesting employment to assist in instructing the poor children. To see them hunger after spiritual food,— who would not exert his best endeavours for their benefit'[4]. On 15 August she noted 'The Sunday-schools engross all the time I used to spend on my Journal'[5]. In November of the same year Queen Charlotte consulted Mrs. Trimmer about establishing Sunday-schools at Windsor and as a result of this interview Mrs. Trimmer wrote a guide for those who wished to undertake such work, entitled *The Œconomy of Charity*.

Mrs. Trimmer's activities soon became widely known and in 1786

[1] *Some Account of the Life and Writings of Mrs. Trimmer*, London, 1814, vol. i, p. 2.
[2] *Ibid.*, p. 16.   [3] *Ibid.*, p. 15.   [4] *Ibid.*, p. 111.   [5] *Ibid.*, p. 112.

Mrs. Denward, a charitable gentlewoman who was looking for an almoner, wrote to Elizabeth Carter and asked to be introduced to Mrs. Trimmer[1]. At Mrs. Denward's suggestion Mrs. Trimmer started a School of Industry at Brentford. In November 1786 Mrs. Denward wrote saying, 'I met the other day with an account in a newspaper, of a spinning wheel so constructed that eighteen small children might spin at the same time, which twists the thread of itself, at the pleasure of each spinstress. It was invented about twenty years ago ... it cost at first only five pounds and is very seldom out of repair; now dearest Madam, you are so prone to do good, that I will make no apology, but wish you to get one of them, and present it as your own gift to the poor of your parish. I think it will be of infinite service, as it will inure them early in life to industry. I have therefore taken the liberty of enclosing a little draft to purchase the spinning wheel'[2]. It was also at Mrs. Denward's suggestion that Mrs. Trimmer wrote a story called *The Two Farmers*, to persuade the children of the poor to be kinder to animals, and introduced descriptions of animals into her *Charity School Spelling Book*. Many of Mrs. Trimmer's books remained for years on the list of works recommended by the Society for the Promotion of Christian Knowledge. *The Story of the Robins* remained popular almost to the present generation.

Little seems known of Mr. Trimmer, though his illnesses and recoveries are mentioned in his wife's journal. He helped the education of his family by gathering the children together in the evening and setting one of them to read aloud[3]. On 22 May 1792 Mrs. Trimmer wrote in her journal, 'This day the silent tomb is closed upon the remains of my dear departed husband'[4]. Mr. Sturgess, writing from St. Mary's Vicarage at Reading, recommended to her 'immediate perusal the affectionate letter of the pious Mrs. Doddridge to her children' informing them of Philip Doddridge's death at Lisbon[5]. Hannah More delayed her condolences until August 'rather out of tenderness and apprehension, than from unkindness and neglect'[6]. Although the recorded facts of Mrs. Trimmer's life show that she was more than competent to manage her own affairs she had no sympathy with the views of Mary Wollstonecraft, of whom she spoke as 'a woman of extraordinary abilities', adding 'I cannot help thinking they might be employed to more advantage to society'. In regard to the Rights of Woman she declared 'I found so much happiness

---

[1] *Some Account of the Life and Writings of Mrs. Trimmer*, p. 153.   [2] *Ibid.*, p. 169.
[3] *Ibid.*, p. 16.   [4] *Ibid.*, p. 301.   [5] *Ibid.*, p. 353.   [6] *Ibid.*, p. 356.

in having a husband to assist me in forming a proper judgment and in taking upon him the chief labour of providing for a family, that I never wished for a further degree of liberty or consequence than I enjoyed'[1].

Mary Wollstonecraft and Sarah Trimmer belonged to different worlds of thought and action. Mrs. Trimmer is important in social history because of the part she played in stemming the revolutionary forces represented by Mary Wollstonecraft. The labours of Mrs. Trimmer in the cause of popular education, her intercourse with influential persons, and the controversies in which she was involved were all inspired by a determination that the teaching of the children of the poor must be based on religion interpreted by the principles of the Church of England. Her example was an encouragement to all who wished that popular education, however widely it might be extended, should still be controlled by the framework of thought and organization inherited from the Anglican past.

A writer of a different quality from these literary ladies of the eighteenth century, with an independent mind denied to Mrs. Trimmer, is Mrs. Catharine Cappe (1744–1821), who has received less than her due both from her contemporaries and from historians of literature. Her memoirs, written in her old age and published after her death by the pious care of her stepdaughter, form a document of the first importance for the lives of ordinary people in the north of England. They also indicate the mental activity possible in this age to a woman who had received no education of any formal sort[2]. Her account of rustic society at Long Preston in Craven, where she was born, has already been quoted[3]. While Catharine was still a girl her father accepted the living of Catterick and moved his family there. Although she was brought up in the Church of England Catherine Harrison comes into the story of the Dissenting academies, for her husband, Newcome Cappe, had been educated for the Dissenting ministry for one year under Aikin at Kibworth and for three years under Doddridge at Northampton. In her old age Mrs. Cappe herself was largely responsible for arranging the removal of the Manchester academy to York.

---

[1] *Some Account of the Life and Writings of Mrs. Trimmer*, p. 355.

[2] *Memoirs of the Life of Mrs. Catharine Cappe*, written by herself, 2nd ed., London, 1823; with a portrait. First published in 1822. A list of Mrs. Cappe's writings is printed at the end of the book.   [3] Above, pp. 113–14.

Her early education was neglected, for her father 'had imbibed some of the prejudices of that day, in respect to the cultivation of the female mind'[1]. He spent fruitless hours teaching his son, who had also the advantage of going to Cambridge, whereas Catharine's teaching was left to a female dependant of the family. 'Far from recommending or pointing out to me', she wrote, 'any little plan of mental cultivation he frequently insinuated incidentally in conversation, that domestic occupations and household duties, were the proper province of women. This, indeed, I was ready to admit, but I would have added, if I could have taken courage, "Surely not exclusively".'[2] When she was twelve Catharine was sent to a school in York, where her schoolfellows mocked at her because her father did not keep a coach, her parents had only four servants, and her mother had not supplied her with 'a gauze suit of linen'[3].

Catharine's two 'worthy aunts' lived in York and continually warned her against spending her time reading. 'They never knew it come to any good', was their argument, for they had 'a great horror of learned ladies'[4]. When Catharine's father died his widow and daughter were left poorly off and the follies of Catharine's brother made their position worse. She thought of keeping a school in York, but her aunts 'could not endure the thought that a niece of theirs, who was well known to have been in the habit of associating with some of the first families, in the city where they lived, should engage in an undertaking, which in their estimation, would remove her from the rank of a gentlewoman'[5]. It is curious that this should have been felt in York while Hannah More and her four sisters were making a fortune out of an efficient girls' school at Bristol. But they had no position to lose, whereas Catharine Harrison was descended on her mother's side from the younger son of a baronet and her maiden aunts could not forget it. Catharine's cousin was Sir Roland Winn, of Nostell Park.

Catharine Harrison's way of life was determined by her admiration for Theophilus Lindsey, her father's successor at Catterick. His pastoral work was in advance of his time. Before Robert Raikes had begun his work at Gloucester, Lindsey was holding a Sunday-school at Catterick, which Catharine Harrison imitated at Bedales in the back kitchen of the cottage in which she and her mother lived. But in 1773, after some four years of mental struggle, Lindsey resigned the living of Catterick to become an

---

[1] *Mrs. Cappe's Memoirs*, p. 19.   [2] *Ibid.*, p. 55.
[3] *Ibid.*, p. 46.   [4] *Ibid.*, p. 53.   [5] *Ibid.*, pp. 196–8.

independent Unitarian minister[1]. It was an heroic decision, for his whole future would depend on his success in attracting a congregation to the preacher of an unfashionable doctrine which had no emotional appeal. When he left Catterick he was uncertain whether to go to Bristol or to London. His early friendship with Lady Elizabeth Hastings, in whose house he had spent his holidays from school, and his consequent acquaintance with Selina, Countess of Huntingdon, may have prepared the way for his change of opinion, although in becoming a Unitarian he took a path which each of these ladies would certainly have condemned[2]. Catharine Harrison, after thinking out the whole question for herself, followed him out of the Church of England.

For some twenty years, Catharine Harrison engaged herself in every form of charitable work open to the unmarried daughter of a widow of narrow means. For a time, she and her mother lived in a mining village, where she established a Female Benefit Club for the wives and daughters of the colliers. In 1782 they moved to York, where Catharine helped to found a similar association—the first of its kind in the city. She brought into being a spinning school for the employment of children who had been working in a rope factory, and she persuaded the governors of the Grey-coat School for Girls to improve the regulations under which it was managed. Scarcely a day passed on which she did not visit one or other of these schools. On coming to York, she joined a Unitarian congregation under the Rev. Newcome Cappe, a leader in the varied activities which made York at that time a local capital. In 1788 she and Newcome Cappe were married. Mr. Cappe's health had already begun to decline. The first of a series of strokes came on him in 1791 and he died in 1800. Mrs. Cappe helped him to prepare for the press his sermons on the providence and government of God, which appeared in 1795. In her widowhood she brought out more of her husband's sermons and wrote a memoir of his life to serve as Preface. Her interest in charity schools remained as keen as ever, and she published an account of her own experiences to help others in the work. Three years before her death she wrote a pamphlet advocating the appointment of female visitors to women confined in public hospitals and asylums for the insane. To the end of her life, every movement for the benefit of helpless persons, from

[1] *The Apology of Theophilus Lindsey, M.A., on resigning the Vicarage of Catterick, Yorkshire*, London, for J. Johnson, 1774, is a book of 508 pages.
[2] *Mrs. Cappe's Memoirs*, p. 116.

chimney boys to pauper lunatics, received her warm and most efficient support.

Mrs. Cappe kept an almost childlike simplicity and directness of outlook which enabled her to express herself with clarity. She felt no envy of those who escaped financial difficulties and her own never embittered her. When she wrote her memoirs in old age she made a particular effort to describe the people she had met in order that others might share with her the lessons of her experience. The pages of her autobiography contain vignettes of many girls and women, whose careers always show virtue triumphant and vice or indifference bringing its due reward. The lives of two sisters who were at school with her become in her hands a cautionary tale. One of them thought of nothing but dressing finely and making conquests. At one time she could count twenty admirers, but to get away from an uncomfortable home she married 'a dignitary of the Church, having become such by the interest of his near connexions; for in himself he was a very poor creature in every respect, but good tempered'. They lived in a secluded part of the country and saw few people. She made no effort to amuse her husband, but spoiled her only son, who 'grew up insolent and tyrannical, became early the slave of depraved appetite and passion, and died a victim to disease, brought on by his vices, at the age of nineteen or twenty. The unhappy father did not long survive him'. His widow married a man of whom she knew nothing. He would never settle anywhere, and she led a wretched wandering life. The other sister, who had always been industrious, married happily and had a large family. She retained her habits of industry to the end, constantly helping people poorer than herself. 'She was attended most assiduously and affectionately by her exemplary daughter, and is most deeply lamented by her friends, and by all the poor in the village where she resided'[1].

Like other women of her generation, Mrs. Cappe accepted the established relationship between the sexes without any apparent repining. She would certainly have agreed with Miss Scott that women ought to develop their talents, and her experience had brought her into contact with many women of ability, engaged in charitable works in York and elsewhere in the north. She made no comment on, and had probably never read, Mary Wollstonecraft's *Rights of Woman*. Nor were her thoughts stirred by the French Revolution. Like many other excellent women she lived from day to day doing the work to her hand to the best

[1] *Mrs. Cappe's Memoirs*, pp. 57–64.

of her abilities. Her religion was her overriding interest. Her adoption of the Unitarian creed had carried her away from the mental region in which most of her contemporaries lived happily. It limited her range of friends, but it did not limit her capacity for social service. Unlike Hannah More, she had never attempted to enter the fashionable world of London or tried her hand at popular or didactic writing. Hannah More was an Evangelical churchwoman in close touch with many influential friends, but in their attitude to the education of the poor, in their hatred of the slave trade, and in their sense of social responsibility Catharine Cappe and Hannah More were of one mind.

They both lived on into a new age in which their eighteenth-century attitude to politics and religion was out of date. The woman born before 1750 who challenged most directly the prevalent conceptions of her time died before the mass of Englishmen had felt the full impact of the revolutionary ideas which stemmed from France. Catharine Macaulay (1731–91) is described in the *Dictionary of National Biography* as 'historian and controversialist', a description which could have been given to no Englishwoman before her. She was the first woman to attempt the writing of history on a large scale, based on materials, in manuscript as well as in print. Over a period of twenty years she published eight massive volumes covering the history of England from the accession of James I to the coming of the Hanoverian kings. Her narrative is supported with ample footnotes, giving the sources of her information and extracts from them. A century later, Lecky, writing with supreme impartiality a history of the age in which she lived, described her as 'the ablest writer of the New Radical School'[1]. In her Preface to the first volume she set out her reasons 'for undertaking a subject which has already been treated of by several ingenious and learned men. From my early youth I have read with delight those histories which exhibit liberty in its most exalted state, the annals of the Roman and Greek republics. Studies like these excite that natural love of freedom which lies latent in the breast of every rational being, till it is nipped by the frost of prejudice, or blasted by the influence of vice'[2]. To her, 'liberty became the object of a secondary worship' and she determined to write a history of England in which justice should be

---

[1] W. E. H. Lecky, *The History of England in the Eighteenth Century*, 3rd ed., London, 1883–90, vol. iii, p. 256.

[2] Catharine Macaulay, *The History of England from the accession of James I to that of the Brunswick Line*, London, 1763, vol. i, p. vii.

done 'to the memory of our illustrious ancestors, . . . still having an eye to public liberty, the standard by which I have endeavoured to measure the virtue of those characters which are treated of in this history'[1].

Catharine Macaulay's republican attitude is sufficiently indicated by her constant reference to Cromwell as a 'usurper'[2] and her description of Ludlow as 'vigilant and sagacious' and 'brave and honest'[3]. She shared this outlook with her brother John Sawbridge, of Olantigh Park in Wye, Kent, who figured on the popular side in the controversy between John Wilkes and the Government, and was described by a contemporary memoir writer as 'a stern republican'[4]. A description of Catharine Sawbridge at the age of twenty-six is preserved in a letter to Catherine Talbot from Elizabeth Carter who met at Canterbury 'a very fine lady, who after curtseying to me for several years past with more civility than I had any title to, and with much more than fine ladies usually show to such awkward-looking folks as me, did me the honour this year to take to me mightily by way of conversation, which she introduced by subscribing in a very handsome manner to *me*' (that is, Epictetus), 'and railing very heartily at the *Stoics*. She is a very sensible and agreeable woman, and much more deeply learned than beseems a fine lady; but between the Spartan Laws, the Roman politics, the philosophy of Epicurus, and the wit of St. Evremond, she seems to have formed a most extraordinary system'. Miss Carter concluded that she would have hesitated to hold such a conversation at a party 'with a professed philosopher or scholar, but as it was with a fine fashionable well-dressed lady, whose train was longer than anybody's train, I had no manner of scruple'[5]. It is a pleasant impression of the first English woman to write history.

When she was twenty-nine in 1760 Catharine Sawbridge married Dr. Macaulay, a Scottish doctor, who was a friend of Smollett and had helped him in his financial difficulties. The first volume of her history, which covered the years 1603 to 1628, appeared in 1763 and showed that she had a contemporary purpose in writing. 'Whosoever attempts to remove the limitations necessary to render monarchy consistent with liberty', she wrote, 'are rebels in the worst sense; rebels to the laws of

---

[1] *The History of England from the accession of James I to that of the Brunswick Line,* pp. vii and ix.   [2] *Ibid.*, e.g. vol. v, p. 190.
[3] *Ibid.*, vol. v, pp. 275, 159. The owner of the manuscript of Mrs. Hutchinson's life of her husband had been often solicited for permission to publish it 'particularly by Mrs. Catharine Macaulay'. *Memoirs of the Life of Colonel Hutchinson,* ed. C. H. Firth, p. ix.
[4] Wraxall, *Memoirs,* vol. i, p. 105.   [5] *Carter–Talbot Letters,* vol. ii, pp. 260-1.

their country, the law of nature, the law of reason, and the law of God. Can there be such men? was I to put the question to my own heart, it would answer that it was impossible there should be such. But the annals of this country have a shameful tale to tell, that such a faction has ever existed in this state, from the earliest period of our present constitution. This faction has not only prevented the establishing any regular system to preserve or improve our liberties; but lies at this time in wait for the first opportunity that the imperfections of this government may give them, to destroy those rights, which have been purchased by the toil and blood of the most exalted individuals that have ever adorned humanity'[1]. Such words brought her under attack as a political writer, and in the eighteenth century no holds were barred.

Dr. Macaulay died in 1766, the year in which his wife published her second volume. The last volume appeared in 1783. Despite party criticism she rapidly attained a high reputation. In 1774 Mary Scott addressed her thus:

'But thou Macaulay, say, canst thou excuse
The fond presumption of a youthful Muse?
A Muse, that, raptured with thy growing fame,
Wishes (at least) to celebrate thy name;
A name to every son of freedom dear,
Which patriots yet unborn shall long revere'[2].

In the year this poem appeared Mrs. Macaulay moved to Bath. There she became 'the centre of a little circle of politicians, to whom she was accustomed to give lessons on general politics and constitutional history'[3]. Dr. Wilson, the non-resident rector of St. Stephen's, Walbrook, placed his house[4] and library in Alfred Street at Mrs. Macaulay's disposal. He even set up a white marble statue of her in the character of History within the altar-rails of his London church. On 2 April 1777 he organized a magnificent birthday party at which six odes written in her praise were 'read with great propriety and expression'[5]. The day was 'ushered in by

[1] *Mrs. Macaulay's History*, vol. i, p. xi.   [2] *The Female Advocate*, p. 27.
[3] Joseph Hunter, *The Connection of Bath with the Literature and Science of England*, London, 1853, p. 57.
[4] Alfred House, so called from the bust of King Alfred still to be seen over the door in Joseph Hunter's time. *Ibid.*, p. 56.
[5] *Six Odes presented to the justly-celebrated Historian Mrs. Catharine Macaulay* on her Birthday, and publicly read to a polite and brilliant Audience, Assembled April the second, at Alfred House, Bath, to congratulate that Lady on the happy Occasion. Bath, price one shilling and sixpence.

the ringing of bells and other public demonstrations of joy'. 'Mrs.
Macaulay, very elegantly dressed, was seated in a conspicuous, elevated
situation in front of the company'. After the 'poetic offerings' Dr. Wilson
presented her with a gold medal struck in Queen Anne's reign and her
doctor presented her with a copy of his own works with a dedication to
her in which he advertised his remarkable success in curing her of a
serious illness. At the conclusion of 'these solemnities', wines were served
and Mrs. Macaulay moved about among the company until nine o'clock
when 'the doors of another apartment were thrown open, in which
sideboards were ranged round, and covered in a sumptuous manner,
with syllabubs, jellies, creams, and ices, wines, cakes, and a variety of dry
and fresh fruits, particularly grapes and pineapples'[1]. The story of this
happy day was printed and sold at Bath for the benefit of a distressed
clergyman 'in the eastern counties', who 'has had fifteen children, eight
of which are still living and mostly small'[2].

Mrs. Macaulay visited Paris in 1775 and again in 1777 and was received
with great honour by the leading men and women of the day. Her
marriage in December 1778 to William Graham, a younger brother of
her doctor, shocked her friends and delighted her enemies, for he was
only twenty-one and not half her age. Dr. Wilson removed her statue
from his church and declared that he would hold Alfred House against
her, although he had to admit that he had given it to her. Mrs. Macaulay
Graham, as she was thereafter known, gave up her home in Bath and
settled with her husband at Binfield, Berkshire. Her *History*, despite its
length, by no means absorbed all her energies. She found time in 1769 to
comment on Hobbes's *Philosophical Rudiments concerning Government and
Society*, and to draft 'a short sketch of a democratical form of Government' for the benefit of Pasquale Paoli and the republicans of Corsica[3].
In 1770 she replied to Burke's *Thoughts on the Cause of the Present Discon-
tents*, and in 1774 she wrote *A modest Plea for the property of Copyright*.
Her sympathies were naturally with the colonists in the War of American
Independence, and in 1784 she sailed for America to see for herself the
new republican state. She and her husband spent ten days with George
Washington in 1785, and she corresponded with him until her death.

[1] *Six Odes presented to the justly-celebrated Historian Mrs. Catharine Macaulay*, pp. vii–xv.
[2] From the title-page.
[3] *Loose Remarks on certain positions to be found in Mr. Hobbes' Philosophical Rudiments . . .*,
2nd ed., 1769.

Washington's careful letters show that to him she represented radical opinion in England. In reply to a letter congratulating him on his achievements, Washington set out at length his own diffidence and his hopes for the future happiness of his country. 'There is scarcely any part of my conduct', he wrote from New York on 9 January 1790, 'which may not hereafter be drawn into precedent. Under such a view of the duties inherent in my arduous office, I could not but feel a diffidence in myself on the one hand; and an anxiety for the Community that every new arrangement should be made in the best possible manner on the other'. Washington concluded his long letter: 'Mrs. Washington is well and desires her compliments may be presented to you. We wish the happiness of your fireside, as we also long to enjoy that of our own at Mount Vernon. Our wishes, you know, were limited; and I think that our plans of living will now be deemed reasonable by the considerate part of our species. Her wishes coincide with my own as to simplicity of dress, and everything which can tend to support propriety of character without partaking of the follies of luxury and ostentation. I am, with great regard, Madam, Your most obedient and humble servant Geo. Washington'[1]. It would seem that Catharine Macaulay had been advocating the antique simplicity of Roman manners to her illustrious host.

It may perhaps be argued that in approaching history as a lover of liberty to point a moral to her own generation Catharine Macaulay forgot that the true historian should come to his subject with a mind cleared from every prejudice, even in favour of virtue. But such impartiality was impossible to an eighteenth-century writer about events almost within living memory. If the title of historian is denied to Catharine Macaulay on this account, her contemporaries and successors must lose it too. Mary Wollstonecraft, indicating to younger women the path to the new age, saw Mrs. Macaulay as 'the woman of the greatest abilities that this country has ever produced', and thought it shocking that her death had passed almost without notice. She rightly pointed out that in Mrs. Macaulay's style of writing 'no sex appears, for it is like the sense it conveys, strong and clear. I will not call hers', she continues, 'a masculine understanding, because I admit not of such an arrogant assumption of reason; but I contend that it was a sound one, and that her judgment, the matured fruit of profound thinking, was a proof that a woman can

[1] *Notes and Queries*, 5th series, vol. ix, Jan.–June 1878, pp. 421–2.

acquire judgment in the full extent of the word'[1]. With this opinion on the potentialities of women, expressed by the first of modern feminists, the nineteenth century was to find good reason to agree. But Catharine Macaulay's successors quickly passed beyond the principles of eighteenth-century radicalism for which she had stood, and within a generation of her death she had become little more than a half-remembered name. In Binfield Church a marble memorial to Catharine Macaulay Graham, inscribed *moerens conjux posuit*, bears a medallion of her head, showing strong clear features and thick rippling hair. Above her head, Minerva's owl looks out into the dark church.

[1] Mary Wollstonecraft, *A Vindication of the Rights of Woman*, 3rd ed., London, 1796, p. 235.

CHAPTER XI

Reaction and the Rise of Modern Feminism

A genuine revolution of many women supported by many men was necessary before any effective change in the legal and social position of the mass of women could be secured. The complete dependence of the married woman on her husband, the impossibility of divorce, the scorn of the foolish at the woman who did not marry, the impossibility of a woman entering any learned profession were barriers to achievement which only the most exceptional woman would surmount. In moments of despair those who were trying to enlarge the opportunities of women must have felt that they were fighting a hopeless struggle against the general indifference of their own sex and the active hostility of many men. All through the nineteenth century and, indeed, on into living memory, a considerable body of feminine opinion satisfied with things as they were, hampered the movement towards greater freedom in which other women spent their lives. It was by no means only the women of poor intelligence who would not join in the battle. The very success of some outstanding women made them singularly obtuse when it came to considering the position of women in general. Hannah More, who had been a complete success as a school teacher, much praised as a dramatist and poet, highly successful as a writer in more than one vein, and busy in the work of teaching the poor could declare that 'they little understand the true interests of woman who would lift her from the important duties of her allotted station, to fill with fantastic dignity a loftier but less appropriate niche'[1]. She accepted without question that for other women than herself 'their knowledge is not often like the learning of men, to be reproduced in some literary composition, nor ever in any learned profession; but it is to come out in conduct'[2].

[1] *Strictures on the Modern System of Female Education*, London, 1799, vol. ii, pp. 21–2.
[2] *Ibid.*, p. 1.

She wrote these words in 1799, seven years after Mary Wollstonecraft (1759-97) had published her famous book, *A Vindication of the Rights of Woman*. This book was already in its third edition in 1796 and found many admirers among women of the middle class, who lacked the protection of the aristocratic marriage settlement and could never hope for divorce from a bad husband. Harriet Martineau, born in 1802, remembered that the book had been much admired in her parents' Unitarian circle in Norwich when she was a child[1]. But Hannah More in 1793 wrote to Lord Orford, 'I have been much pestered to read the *Rights of Women*, but I am invincibly resolved not to do it. Of all jargon, I hate metaphysical jargon: besides there is something fantastic and absurd in the very title. How many ways there are of being ridiculous! I am sure I have as much liberty as I can make good use of, now I am an old maid: and when I was a young one, I had, I dare say, more than was good for me'. This contemptuous rejection of Mary Wollstonecraft's plea on behalf of all women by one who had, as she admits, always enjoyed a high degree of liberty, shows a crass indifference to the possibility of other women's sufferings. 'Old maids' who were well enough off to live in comfort and intelligent enough to find something to do were, of all women save perhaps widows, those who suffered least from the attitude of the law and the Church to women.

Hannah More was sufficiently intelligent to realize that in writing thus she was betraying her own sex; for she admitted that if she had still been young she might perhaps have written differently. Nevertheless, she continued in the same letter 'so many women are fond of government, I suppose, because they are not fit for it. To be unstable and capricious, I really think, is but too characteristic of our sex; and there is no animal so much indebted to subordination for its good behaviour as woman'[2]. It is suggestive to compare this lamentable generalization with Catharine Macaulay's words written in 1790: 'The great difference that is observable in the character of the sexes as they display themselves in the scenes of social life, has given rise to much false speculation on the natural qualities of the female mind'[3]. The follies of women came, she was convinced,

---

[1] *Harriet Martineau's Autobiography*, ed. Maria Weston Chapman, 2nd ed., London, 1877, vol. i, p. 399, quoted hereafter as *Harriet Martineau*.

[2] *Memoirs of the Life and Correspondence of Mrs. Hannah More*, ed. William Roberts, 3rd ed., London, 1835, vol. ii, p. 372.

[3] Catharine Macaulay Graham, *Letters on Education*, London, 1790, p. 203. This book was lent to me by Mr. Arnold Muirhead, of St. Albans.

from their physical and moral education as girls. She took a very different view of female subordination from that of Hannah More. 'Though the situation of women in modern Europe', she wrote, 'when compared with that condition of abject slavery in which the women have always been held in the east may be considered as brilliant, yet if we withhold comparison, and take the matter in a positive sense, we shall have no great reason to boast of our privileges, or of the candour and indulgence of the men towards us. For with a total and absolute exclusion from every political right to the sex in general, married women, whose situation demands a particular indulgence, have hardly a civil right to save them from the grossest injuries; and though the gallantry of some of the European societies have necessarily produced indulgence, yet in others the faults of women are treated with a severity and a rancour which militates against every principle of religion and common sense'[1].

Catharine Macaulay's 'warmth in the vindication of female nature'[2], to use her own phrase, has been forgotten, for her arguments, clear and cogent though they were, were never widely read, She wrote as a scholar writes who does not try to appeal to a large audience. But there can be no doubt that her words inspired Mary Wollstonecraft to write *A Vindication of the Rights of Woman*. 'When I first thought of writing these strictures', she recorded, 'I anticipated Mrs. Macaulay's approbation, with a little of that sanguine ardour it has been the business of my life to suppress; but soon heard with a sickly qualm of disappointed hope; and the still seriousness of regret—that she was no more'[3]. After Mary Wollstonecraft's death in 1797, her husband, William Godwin, author of *An Enquiry concerning Political Justice*, wrote a brief account of her life. He declared that the *Vindication* 'was begun, carried on, and finished in the state it now appears, in a period of no more than six weeks'[4]. This haste accounts for the uneven character of the work and may also account for the note of rough eloquence which rises from time to time.

Both Catharine Macaulay and Mary Wollstonecraft had been moved to indignation by Burke's *Reflections on the French Revolution* and had printed an immediate reply. Catharine Macaulay addressed her *Observations* to Lord Stanhope, almost the only peer to welcome the revolution.

---

[1] *Letters on Education*, p. 210.   [2] *Ibid.*, p. 214.
[3] London, by J. Johnson, 3rd ed., 1796, p. 236. First printed 1792.
[4] William Godwin, *Memoirs of the author of A Vindication of the Rights of Woman*, 2nd ed., London, 1798, p. 84.

Mary Wollstonecraft called her work *A Vindication of the Rights of Man* and, indeed, it became an impassioned plea for human rights in general. The evils of the slave trade, the greed of great landlords, the misery and degradation of unemployment are set out in this tract with an explosive violence of rhetoric remote from Catharine Macaulay's cool argument that the French people have the right to choose their own form of government. 'If the French people', wrote Catharine Macaulay, 'therefore should be so capricious as to fling off their new constitution, and subject themselves to more unequal forms of government, or even to tyranny, it will be agreeable to the course of past experience: but such an exertion of power can not injure their right; and whatever form or complexion any future government in France may bear, it can have no legitimate source, but in the will of the people'[1]. This is the voice of the historian and contrasts sharply with Mary Wollstonecraft's concluding paragraphs: 'Why is our fancy to be appalled by terrific perspectives of a hell beyond the grave?—Hell stalks abroad;—the lash resounds on the slave's naked sides; and the sick wretch, who can no longer earn the sour bread of unremitting labour, steals to a ditch to bid the world a long good night— or, neglected in some ostentatious hospital, breathes his last amidst the laugh of mercenary attendants. Such misery demands more than tears— I pause to recollect myself; and smother the contempt I feel rising for your rhetorical flourishes and infantine sensibility'[2].

In similar fashion when Mary Wollstonecraft wrote *A Vindication of the Rights of Woman* her quick intelligence and command of words enabled her to drive home the fact of woman's subjection and the folly of her education, which neglected her understanding while providing her with accomplishments. It was the emphasis of the writing which impressed the book on the public mind. She attacked the sentiments expressed by those who had written about women. Most girls were given a copy of Dr. Gregory's *Legacy to his Daughters*. 'I respect his heart', wrote Mary Wollstonecraft, 'but entirely disapprove of his celebrated legacy to his daughters'[3]. Mrs. Piozzi was quoted scornfully for her arch letter of advice to a newly married man urging him never to let his wife know if, and when, his love for her grew less. 'All our attainments, all our arts,

---

[1] *Observations on the Reflections of the Right Hon. Edmund Burke on the Revolution in France. In a Letter to the Right Hon. the Earl of Stanhope,* London, 1790, p. 95.

[2] *A Vindication of the Rights of Man in a Letter to the Right Honourable Edmund Burke,* 2nd ed., London, 1790, pp. 152–3.

[3] *Vindication,* 3rd ed., p. 53. Dr. Gregory's arguments are disposed of on pp. 215–24.

are employed to gain and keep the heart of man' were sentiments which displeased Mary Wollstonecraft[1]. The *Vindication* was written at a white heat of passion. As thoughts rose in her mind she put them on paper, without weighing them and considering all their implications. She had no reserves and her very generosity of spirit meant that she wrote with a force shocking to many who would have agreed wholeheartedly with the same ideas more moderately expressed. She herself clearly felt that she was writing to Mrs. Macaulay's text and she inveighed against the foolish treatment given to women without formulating her claims for them more definitely than Catharine Macaulay had done. 'Let woman share the rights and she will emulate the virtues of man; for she must grow more perfect when emancipated, or justify the authority which chains such a weak being to her duty' are the opening words of her penultimate paragraph. She continued 'If the latter, it will be expedient to open a fresh trade with Russia for whips: a present which a father should always make to his son-in-law on his wedding day, that a husband may keep his whole family in order by the same means'[2]. Beyond this, she never defined emancipation or set out the rights women should share.

Some of the bitterness in this book which offended milder people was due to the harsh experiences of the author's own life. Her father was a spendthrift, who dissipated his inheritance, drank, and beat his wife. He moved his household every few years, so that as a girl Mary lived sometimes in Essex, sometimes in Yorkshire, and for a little time in Wales. She had no proper education and was only taught to write neatly and spell correctly when she was sixteen by a friend, two years older than herself, named Fanny Blood. It was evident to Mary that she would have to get her own living, and when she was nineteen she became a companion to the widow of a London merchant living in Bath. She kept the post two years, but was called home to nurse her mother, whose dying words, 'A little patience, and all will be over', haunted her daughter through life[3]. Her mother's death in 1782 left her physically exhausted, but she went on to nurse her married sister through a dangerous illness. In 1783, with her friend, Fanny Blood, and her two unmarried sisters, she started a school at Newington Green. In the next two years her school prospered and she made friends with several men and women of liberal tendencies, among them the Nonconformist preacher and writer on economics, Dr. Price, who also lived at Newington Green. She met Dr. Johnson

---

[1] *Vindication*, p. 228.   [2] *Ibid.*, p. 451.   [3] Godwin's *Memoirs*, p. 28.

not long before his death. But by 1785 Fanny was far gone in consumption and was ordered to Lisbon. An Irish merchant living there proposed marriage to her. Mary persuaded her to accept him and herself followed Fanny to Lisbon to nurse her, borrowing money for her fare. Fanny died before the year was out and Mary returned to find most of her pupils had left the school. At the suggestion of a friend she turned to writing for a living and sold her first book, *Thoughts on the Education of Daughters*, to Joseph Johnson, in 1787[1].

J. Johnson's imprint often appears on women's books; both Maria Edgeworth and Mrs. Barbauld were among his authors. He gave Mary ten guineas for her tract which contains sensible advice on the upbringing of daughters, but no hint of the tempestuous mind which was later to produce the vindications of the rights of man and woman. The fact that the tract was pirated in the next year by a Dublin printer and put out by him in the same volume with Fénélon's instructions to a governess and an address to mothers confirms the absolute propriety of its contents[2]. Mary's employment for about a year as governess to the daughters of an Irish peer shows that she was not yet regarded as a revolutionary. Encouraged by Johnson she gave up her post in 1790 to engage in literary work in London. He invited her to stay in his own house until she had found herself a lodging and employed her as a reader and translator. In his house she met his liberal friends, Thomas Paine and William Godwin among them. It was in these years that her best work was done. At the end of 1792 she went alone to Paris, possibly, as her friends said, to free herself from her love for the painter, Fuseli, who was a married man. There she met Gilbert Imlay, an American in business, and agreed to live with him as his wife. Her daughter by him was born in 1794 and called Fanny. Imlay's business called him often from home and Mary began to mistrust his fidelity. She followed him to England in 1795, but agreed to undertake a journey for him to Norway. When she returned before the end of the year she found him living with another woman and tried to drown herself by jumping off Putney Bridge. She was saved by a passing boat and returned to her literary work for Johnson. In the course of 1796 she became friendly with William Godwin, and the friendship ripened quickly into love. In his most famous work Godwin had set out his

---

[1] *Thoughts on the Education of Daughters with Reflections on Female Conduct in the more important Duties of Life*, London, 1787.
[2] Dublin, by W. Sleater, 1788.

considered reasons for disapproving of the institution of marriage[1], but when Mary became pregnant he married her. She died in childbirth at the age of thirty-eight. Her daughter by Godwin has a place in literary history as the wife of Shelley rather than for her own talent as a writer.

Mary Wollstonecraft will always hold an honoured place in the history of the movement by which women threw off their age-long subjection, but she is often credited with more than the *Vindication* will bear. 'In this book the whole extent of the feminist ideal is set out, and the whole claim for equal human rights is made'[2]. This statement can only be accepted in the most vague and general sense. Mrs. Macaulay, whose words, already quoted, inspired Mary Wollstonecraft to write this book, was the first woman to draw attention to the 'total and absolute exclusion from every political right' suffered by all women[3]. Mary Wollstonecraft was a creature of emotion, as her own sad story shows. Her generosity was boundless, and her friends were the founders of the English socialist creed. Her personal conduct offended rigid moralists, although as Godwin records, she maintained her circle of friends until she married him, for people could affect to believe that she was Imlay's wife. In her simplicity she thought that when she married Godwin she would regain the respect which her previous conduct may have lost her, but she found the reverse was the case. Some women, among them Mrs. Siddons, refused to continue her acquaintance[4].

After her death Godwin assuaged his grief by writing an account of Mary Wollstonecraft which was already in its second edition by 1798. It appeared under the title *Memoirs of the Author of A Vindication of the Rights of Woman*. It is possible that it stimulated interest in Mary Wollstonecraft's writings, for Godwin concealed nothing. Mary's love for Fuseli, her association with Imlay, the birth of her first child and her attempted suicide were all disclosed. Nor did Godwin conceal the fact that only her pregnancy persuaded them to marry. Those women, like Elizabeth Carter, who shrank from the violence of the *Vindication* must have been confirmed in their dislike by the appearance of this book. But in 1803 there appeared a defence of Mary Wollstonecraft written by a man in the form of a series of letters to a lady. He tried as 'an advocate and a

---

[1] *Enquiry concerning Political Justice by William Godwin*, ed. F. E. L. Priestley, Toronto, 1946, vol. ii, pp. 507–8.   [2] Ray Strachey, *The Cause*, London, 1928, p. 12.
[3] *Letters on Education*, p. 210.   [4] Godwin's *Memoirs*, p. 168.

friend' to vindicate one whom he regarded as 'an incomparable woman'[1]. 'On the correctness of her judgment in certain cases, most men will probably be disposed to demur;' he wrote, 'individual parts of her private conduct lie still more open to the disapprobation of the systematic moralist; but the purity of her intentions, both in her private and public concerns, must be considered as unimpeachable. More genuine benevolence, more enlarged philanthropy, more solicitude for the interests of her fellow creatures, and more deference to the dictates of duty, as far as she could make a clear discovery of them, never warmed a human breast'[2]. He could only palliate her attempted suicide by stressing the misery of her situation. 'My surprize is not at all excited by her hurrying into an act of desperation; but rather that her whole mental economy was not totally and for ever disarranged'[3]. To the writer she 'was much too intelligent, too independent, too good, and too great' for a world which 'was not worthy of her'[4].

The irregularity of Mary Wollstonecraft's own life inevitably reduced the effectiveness of her teaching. The reaction of contemporary liberal opinion produced from Thomas Gisborne *An Enquiry into the Duties of the Female Sex* in 1797, which had reached its ninth edition by 1810. For almost a generation after the *Vindication* appeared there was little more deliberate propaganda for the liberation of women. Two books which fall within this period were each written, as the authors state in their Prefaces, some years before publication. The woman who wrote *An Appeal to the Men of Great Britain on behalf of Women*, published by Johnson in 1798, laid aside her own work when a friend sent her Mary Wollstonecraft's book. Afterwards she took it up again, hoping that 'by managing and sympathizing with the prejudices of mankind' she would make the cause of women more acceptable to men. This appeal fell on deaf ears, for the author lacked fire. When in 1825 a man again took up the cause of women he referred to 'the timidity and impotence of conclusion accompanying the gentle eloquence of Mary Hays, addressed about the same time that Mary Wollstonecraft wrote, in the shape of an "Appeal" to the then closed ears of unreasoning men'[5]. Nothing more about Mary Hays can be discovered[6].

---

[1] *A Defence of the Character and Conduct of the late Mary Wollstonecraft Godwin founded on principles of Nature and Reason*, London, 1803, p. 143.   [2] *Ibid.*, pp. 27–8.
[3] *Ibid.*, p. 127.   [4] *Ibid.*, p. 148.
[5] William Thompson, *Appeal of one half of the human race*, London, 1825, p. vii.
[6] Halkett and Lang give, without evidence, 'D. Geddes' as the author of this *Appeal*, but Thompson's statement cannot be ignored. It is possible that Mary Hays may be identified

Mary Hays's anonymous *Appeal* was followed in 1799 by *The Female Advocate or an Attempt to recover the Rights of Women from Male Usurpation* written seven years before publication by Mary Anne Radcliffe[1], who was deeply concerned with the fate of women driven by poverty to vice. She pointed out in her Introduction that since the advantages of education were in Britain 'monopolized by the male sex' it was surely the duty of men to protect women, who 'are so perfectly tamed, either through custom or compulsive submission, that, let but the lenient hand of protection be stretched out to their aid, and, doubtless, content and happiness will resume their seat'[2]. The first part of the book dealt with 'the fatal consequences of men traders engrossing women's occupations', in particular, 'what can be said in favour of men-milliners, men-mantua-makers, and men-stay-makers, besides all the numerous train of other professions, such as hair-dressers, etc., etc.; all of which occupations are much more calculated for women than men'[3]. The author dated her Preface from Kennington Cross and undoubtedly knew what she was writing about when she stressed the large numbers of women, uneducated for earning their own living, who were driven to poverty by the death of their husbands or fathers. Since begging was forbidden by law it was not surprising that such women, often brought up in a luxurious home, fell into a vicious way of life. The second part of the book 'demonstrates that the Frailty of Female Virtue more frequently originates from embarrassed Circumstances, than from a depravity of Disposition'[4]. It is a sign of a developing social conscience that one of their own sex has at last come forward to take up the cause of the unfortunate women who have not been trained for the honest labour market and therefore have been forced into the market for vice.

The first book which set out a coherent argument for the full emancipation of women and for their admission even to the legislature, appeared in 1825. Its author was William Thompson, of Cork, an important figure in the early history of modern socialism. He was moved to write by resentment at a passage in the article on Government contributed by James Mill to the *Encyclopaedia Britannica* in 1820. The title of his book, *Appeal of one half of the human race, Women, against the pretensions of the*

with Mrs. Mary Hay, evidently the daughter of Mrs. Hay, of Hartrow, Somerset. Both women subscribed to the poems of Miss Mary Jones in 1750. In her Preface to the *Appeal* the author describes herself as 'living in an obscure corner of the kingdom'.

[1] London, 1799, p. 1.
[2] *The Female Advocate*, pp. x–xi.   [3] *Ibid.*, p. 20.   [4] *Ibid.*, p. 77.

other half, Men, to retain them in political, and thence in civil and domestic, slavery; in reply to a paragraph in Mr. Mill's celebrated 'Article on Government', is contentious. Thompson printed James Mill's offending paragraph on his title-page: 'One thing is pretty clear, that all those individuals whose interests are indisputably included in those of other individuals may be struck off from political rights without inconvenience. In this light may be viewed all children up to a certain age, whose interests are involved in those of their parents. In this light also women may be regarded, the interest of almost all of them is involved either in that of their fathers, or in that of their husbands'. As his frontispiece, Thompson inserted a picture of Mrs. Anna D. Wheeler, who appears to be beautiful and is dressed in the height of fashion. To her he addressed a long introductory letter beginning 'Honoured with your acquaintance, ambitious of your friendship, I have endeavoured to arrange the expression of those feelings, sentiments, and reasonings, which have emanated from your mind. In the following pages you will find discussed on paper, what you have so often discussed in conversation—a branch of that high and important subject of morals and legislation, the condition of women, of one half of the human race, in what is called civilised society'[1]. Thompson hoped that Mrs. Wheeler would write the book. 'Anxious that you should take up the cause of your proscribed sex, and state to the world in writing, in your own name, what you have so often and so well stated in conversation and under feigned names in such periodical publications of the day as would tolerate such a theme, I long hesitated to arrange our common ideas. . . . Anxious that the hand of a woman should have the honour of raising from the dust that neglected banner which a woman's hand nearly thirty years ago unfolded boldly in the face of the pre-judicies of thousands of years, and for which a woman's heart bled, and her life was all but the sacrifice—I long hesitated to write'. He thought that 'narrow views . . . too often marred Mary Wolstonecroft's pages'. Since Mrs. Wheeler lacked the 'leisure and resolution to undertake the drudgery of the task' Thompson undertook it himself, declaring that 'A few only of the following pages are the exclusive property of your mind and pen, and written with your own hand. The remainder are our joint property, I being your interpreter and the scribe of your sentiments[2].

The elegant Mrs. Wheeler (born in 1785) belonged to the family of Doyle of Bramblestown, Kilkenny. Her husband, Francis Massy Wheeler,

[1] Thompson, *Appeal*, p. v.   [2] *Ibid.*, pp. vi–vii.

a grandson of Lord Massy, had seen Anna Doyle at the local races and fallen in love with her. She was fifteen and her husband nineteen when they married. Wheeler drank and neglected his estate and his wife, who turned to reading as a refuge from unhappiness. She found her own thoughts reflected in the work of the socialist thinkers and poets. In 1812 she left her husband, taking her two daughters with her[1]. One of them, Rosina, later became the wife of Edward Bulwer-Lytton. For a few years Mrs. Wheeler lived with her uncle, Sir John Doyle, then Governor of Guernsey. In 1816 she went to London and thence for a time to Caen, before returning to settle in London. Wherever she went, her beauty, charm and revolutionary ideas made an immediate impression. Thompson's violent championship of women was the result of his friendship with Mrs. Wheeler, who, like him, was an ardent believer in the early form of communism which they knew as 'Co-operation'. In his history of the co-operative movement, G. J. Holyoake referred to Mrs. Wheeler as 'a familiar name in co-operative literature of a lady who very sensibly advocated the usefulness of women taking part in public affairs'[2]. Again, when describing the early advocates of co-operation, he states: 'Mrs. Wheeler attracted considerable attention by well-reasoned lectures, delivered in 1829 in a chapel near Finsbury Square'[3]. Thompson's *Appeal* was printed by Longman and his partners, 'and sold at the London Co-operative Society's offices, 18 Pickett-Street, Temple Bar'.

Co-operation was a new idea in 1825. To its founder, Robert Owen, it seemed the means by which social justice could be secured, and William Thompson was one of the early adherents to this view. He had resided for some years with Jeremy Bentham, of whom he spoke with reverence in the introductory letter to the *Appeal*. If James Mill had complied with Bentham's request that he should remove the offending words about women from his article on government Thompson might never have written this book. He wrote with the fervour of a man who is teaching his countrymen a new religion. Godwin, in his consideration of political

---

[1] Richard K. P. Pankhurst, *William Thompson*, pp. 70–8.

[2] George Jacob Holyoake, *The History of Co-operation in England*, London, 1875, vol. i, p. 140.

[3] *Ibid.*, p. 379. Holyoake mentioned Miss Reynolds as a 'lady lecturer who excited great admiration', also Kate, wife of Goodwyn Barmby, and Mary Hennell, who wrote for the same cause. 'The most notable of all the ladies who have been lecturers among this party was Mrs. Emma Martin, who had the wit and courage of several men'. She was 'the most womanly woman of all the lecturesses of those times'. *Ibid.*, pp. 379–80.

justice, had rejected the institution of marriage, but he had not gone on to consider the place women should fill in society. In demanding for them absolute equality with men, Thompson pointed out that women must have equal political rights to be assured of their civil rights. It was unfortunate for his cause that he could see no way of securing for women the rights he was convinced were their due save in a co-operative form of social order, in which, apparently, marriage should not exist. It seemed to him that in the present form of society men could not allow women equal opportunities with men, for 'men dread the competition of other men, of each other, in every line of industry. How much more will they dread your additional competition'[1]. He looked hopefully towards a happy state: 'Large numbers of men and women co-operating together for mutual happiness, all their possessions and means of enjoyment being the equal property of all. . . . Here no dread of being deserted by a husband with a helpless and pining family, could compel a woman to submit to the barbarities of an exclusive master. The whole Association educate and provide for the children of all: the children are independent of the exertions or the bounty of any individual parent: the whole wealth and beneficence of the community support woman against the enormous wrongs of such casualties: they affect her not'[2].

Such words as these, implying that English family life must be abandoned to secure the chimera of equality for women, offset the argument for emancipation which might have been based on the achievements of women in the recent past. The support of the feminist cause by the new socialism imported a dangerous element of fear into the instinctive reaction against new ideas felt by the great mass of ordinary people. All the generosity of Mary Wollstonecraft weighed as nothing in the balance against the irregularities of her life. The unpractical idealism of Thompson and his kind confirmed in their doubts those whose friendship to the cause of women had already been shaken by her story. Nothing could keep exceptional women from the public work for which they were fitted and nothing could prevent women who could write from publishing their books. But for every one of them the way was harder because of the preaching of those who felt themselves their best friends. A massive force of opposition moved originally by fear lay behind the repression of women by virtuous and kindly fathers and husbands in the reign of Queen Victoria.

[1] Thompson, *Appeal*, p. 197.   [2] *Ibid.*, pp. 199–200.

But this was still in the future when the distinguished group of women born in the 1760's were reaching maturity. Joanna Baillie, born in 1762, Mary Berry in 1763, Maria Edgeworth in 1767 and Jane Marcet in 1769 were a brilliant quartette of woman writers, each in a different vein. They all lived long and carried the eighteenth-century tradition into the heart of a new age[1]. Mary Berry and her younger sister, Agnes, brightened the declining years of Horace Walpole with their company when they were in England and with their letters when they were abroad. They had little formal education, for their mother died when Mary was four and to save expense, Robert Berry, their father, did not engage a successor to their first governess when she married in 1775. Through sheer weakness of character Robert Berry had lost his chance of inheriting a fortune. Mary Berry was conscious both of her own ability and of the weakness of her father and sister. 'I soon found', she wrote in old age, 'that I had to lead those who ought to have led me; and that I must be a protecting mother instead of a gay companion to my sister; and to my father a guide and monitor, instead of finding in him a tutor and protector'[2]. Neither sister married, though each was for a time engaged. Horace Walpole, who had succeeded to the earldom of Orford in 1791, is said to have desired to marry one of them in order that the rank of a countess and the jointure of £2,000 a year for one would make the future of both secure. When he died he left each of them £4,000 and, jointly for their lives, Little Strawberry Hill, the house they were then occupying, with its furniture and the garden and the meadow in front of it. To Robert Berry and his daughters jointly Lord Orford left all his printed works and manuscripts to be published at their discretion and for their benefit.

This bequest started Mary Berry on her literary work, for the five-volume edition of Horace Walpole's works which appeared under the nominal editorship of Robert Berry in 1798 was prepared for the press by her. She tried her hand at play-writing, but without success. She had for some time studied Latin and Greek with private tutors and she read everything that came her way. In a letter written in 1798 she expressed the pleasure she had derived from reading Malthus's *Essay on the Principles*

[1] Another woman, older than these, deserves a note: Mrs. Anne Seymour Damer (1749-1828), daughter of Field-Marshal Conway, was Horace Walpole's executrix and residuary legatee. She was described by Harriet Martineau as 'the acknowledged head of amateur sculpture in Europe', *The Thirty Years' Peace*, vol. i, p. 586.

[2] *Extracts from the Journals and Correspondence of Miss Berry*, ed. Lady Theresa Lewis, London, 1865, vol. i, p. 12.

of Population[1]. In 1810 she published in four volumes the letters of Madame du Deffand which had come into her hands with Walpole's papers. Most of the letters were addressed to Horace Walpole, but some, addressed to Voltaire, had been bequeathed to Walpole with the rest of her manuscripts by their writer. Miss Berry wrote an Introduction and identified in footnotes the people whose names are mentioned in the letters[2]. The work was well received and Professor John Playfair, on 1 January 1811, wrote assuring Miss Berry that her work would meet with 'great commendation' in the *Edinburgh Review*[3]. At his suggestion she turned her attention to social history. In 1828 she published *A Comparative View of the social life of England and France* from the Restoration of Charles II to the French Revolution.[4] A second volume continuing the history to the fall of Charles X in 1830 appeared in 1831. Before she began these books, which she regarded as her most important works, she had issued a volume containing the letters of Rachel, Lady Russell, which were in the possession of the Duke of Devonshire, together with a few letters, also in the duke's possession, written by Lady Sunderland—Waller's Sacharissa—to Lord Halifax. In a long Introduction to this book Miss Berry 'endeavoured to develope and hold up to the admiration of her countrywomen' the character of Lady Russell, 'a character whose celebrity was purchased by the sacrifice of no feminine virtue, and whose principles, conduct and sentiments, equally well adapted to every condition of her sex, will in all be found the surest guides to peace, honour, and happiness'[5]. A collected edition of Mary Berry's works appeared in 1844.

When in 1865 Lady Theresa Lewis published in three volumes selections from Miss Berry's journals and correspondence, she described her as a woman who 'longed to be great; she was fired with ambition in the best sense of the word, but there was no career. To the merely vain woman there is in every country a large arena for display, with its rich harvest of triumphs chequered by mortification; but to the ambitious woman, in this country at least, there is rarely the power of earning distinction

---

[1] *Miss Berry's Journals*, vol. ii, pp. 74–5.

[2] An engraving of a delightful drawing of the Marquise du Deffand, then preserved at Strawberry Hill, forms the frontispiece to vol. i.

[3] *Miss Berry's Journals*, vol. ii, pp. 458–9.

[4] A beautifully printed volume, on the best paper, by A. and R. Spottiswoode, New-Street-Square.

[5] *Some Account of the Life of Rachel Wriothesley, Lady Russell . . . followed by a series of Letters . . .*, London, 1819, p. c. This also is a beautiful piece of printing.

but as a reflection of the stronger, greater light of man. Miss Berry was amongst the few who would have received that light, and would have shone by it: she was fitted to be the partner of greatness, and she missed a participation in the serious realities of life'[1]. This observation of one who knew Miss Berry in her old age deserves respect. But even if Miss Berry felt that as a spinster she was shut out from affairs she must have realized that she had won an unusual position in society. Lady Theresa makes the point that Miss Berry 'owed not the position she occupied to the distinction of birth or of wealth, but to the result of personal character, of peculiar social habits, of literary tastes and pursuits, and of a modest but generous hospitality'[2]. Although in 1819 Miss Berry referred to herself as 'fast sinking to the grave that must shortly close for ever on an insignificant existence'[3], she lived until November 1852, and was privately presented to Queen Victoria a few months before her death. To Harriet Martineau, going every evening to at least one party, 'the Miss Berrys and their inseparable friend, Lady Charlotte Lindsey (the youngest daughter of Lord North), whose presence seemed to carry one back almost a century, were the main attraction of these parties. While up to all the modern interests, the old-fashioned rouge and pearl-powder, and false hair, and the use of the feminine oaths of a hundred years ago were odd and striking. e.g.: a footman tells his mistress that Lady So-and-so begs she will not wait dinner, as she is drying her shoes which got wet between the carriage and the door. The response is "O! Christ! if she should catch cold! Tell her she is a dear soul and we would not have her hurry for the world" etc., etc. My mother heard an exclamation at our door, when the carriage door would not open, "My God! I can't get out".' The earnest young Harriet Martineau felt that 'they were all three so cheerful, so full of knowledge and sympathy for good ideas, and so evidently fit for higher pursuits than the social pleasures amidst which one met them that though their parties were rather blue they were exceedingly agreeable'[4].

Miss Berry's friend, Joanna Baillie, lived until 1851 and her elder sister lasted ten years longer and reached her hundredth year. Most of Joanna's working life was passed in London, but she came on both sides of learned Scottish families. Her mother was a sister of William Hunter, whose name is preserved in the Hunterian Museum at Glasgow, where Joanna's

---

[1] *Miss Berry's Journals*, vol. i, p. xvi.   [2] *Ibid.*, p. xv.
[3] *Lady Russell*, p. c.   [4] *Autobiography*, vol. i, pp. 369–70.

father was professor of divinity from 1769 until his death in 1771. When she was ten Joanna was sent to a good school in Glasgow and she was bred in the cultivated society of a university city. When William Hunter died in 1793 he left his London house to Joanna's brother, Matthew, whose mother and sisters went to live with him. After Matthew's marriage, Mrs. Baillie and her daughters moved to Hampstead, where Mrs. Barbauld was a neighbour. In 1798 Joanna published a volume of plays anonymously. She had written a comedy and a tragedy on each of the stronger passions of the human mind. The work was reviewed as that of a man and was extravagantly praised, but her plays were not successful on the stage. Joanna sent a copy of the plays to Miss Berry, without disclosing her name. 'This winter the first question on everybody's lips', wrote Miss Berry in March 1799, 'is "Have you read the series of plays?" Everybody talks in the raptures I have always thought they deserved of the tragedies and of the introduction as of a new and admirable piece of criticism'[1]. Miss Carter of Deal, now an old woman, saw 'more of the genuine spirit of Shakespeare revive in the tragedies of Miss Joanna Baillie than has inspired any author since his time'[2]. Joanna Baillie, wrote Harriet Martineau, 'had enjoyed a fame almost without parallel, and had outlived it. She had been told every day for years, through every possible channel, that she was second only to Shakespeare,—if second; and then she had seen her works drop out of notice so that, of the generation who grew up before her eyes, not one in a thousand had read a line of her plays:—yet was her serenity never disturbed, nor her merry humour in the least dimmed'[3].

Maria Edgeworth, too, had to some extent outlived current taste when she died in 1849, but her stories influenced greater writers in her own time and retain a faint vitality today. Mrs. Jane Marcet, the last of this group of women writers, is more remarkable because she is the first woman who attempted to understand something of the contemporary movements of scientific thought and transmute them into simple language for the young. She was the only daughter of a Swiss merchant, Anthony Haldimand, who lived in London and had married an English wife. Alexander Marcet, Jane's husband, was born and brought up at Geneva, and after studying at Edinburgh set up as a doctor in London. The Marcets had a house in Russell Square where they staged theatrical performances,

[1] *Miss Berry's Journals*, vol. ii, p. 88.
[2] *Miss Carter's Memoirs*, p. 300.   [3] *Autobiography*, vol. i, p. 358.

with foreign professional actors, for the amusement of London society. Jane Marcet survived her husband for thirty years and died in 1858. To the end of her long life she was writing children's books on a variety of topics, history and grammar, as well as stories and simplified science. Her first book, *Conversations on Chemistry intended more especially for the Female Sex*, appeared in 1806 and was in its sixteenth edition in 1853. Her most famous book, *Conversations on Political Science*, was described by J. R. McCulloch in 1845 as 'on the whole the best introduction to the science that has yet appeared'[1]. It was Mrs. Marcet's book which suggested to Harriet Martineau the possibility of writing a series of stories to illustrate the truths of political economy.

Jane Marcet was not a scholar and cannot be called a scientist, but her work facilitated the great expansion in scientific knowledge which marked the nineteenth century. Her books stimulated the curiosity of children who became the scientists of the next generation. Michael Faraday himself bore witness to the effect of her *Conversations on Chemistry* on his own mental development: 'at the height of his fame he always mentioned Mrs. Marcet with deep reverence'[2]. This is recorded in her own autobiography by a woman who may fairly be described as the first woman scientist in English history. Mary Somerville's long life (1780–1872) covered a period of intense scientific activity and excitement, in which she herself shared both as an investigator and as a popularizer. Her autobiography was written in extreme old age, but her struggles to win a knowledge of mathematics were still fresh in her memory. She was born at the manse at Jedburgh, the home of her uncle and future father-in-law, Dr. Thomas Somerville, but most of her girlhood was spent at Burntisland, on the coast of Fife, opposite Edinburgh. She was not taught to write until after she was eight, though she already enjoyed reading. A year at an expensive school at Musselburgh did little except supply her with the rudiments of writing and a little French and English grammar. Her mother let her read as much as she liked, despite a maiden aunt's complaint 'I wonder you let Mary waste her time in reading, she never sews more than if she were a man'[3].

But Mary acquired all the feminine graces. She could cook, sew,

[1] Quoted in the *D.N.B.*

[2] 'So many books have now been published for young people that no one at this time can duly estimate the importance of Mrs. Marcet's scientific work', Martha Somerville, *Personal Recollections from early life to old age of Mary Somerville*, London, 1874, p. 114.

[3] *Ibid.*, p. 28.

paint and play the piano. She was called 'the rose of Jedwood' for her delicate beauty when she was a girl, and was still beautiful in old age. Her uncle, Dr. Somerville, encouraged her desire for knowledge and, when she stayed at Jedburgh, read Latin with her before breakfast. At home she read Latin and Greek with her younger brother's tutor, and through him obtained textbooks of algebra and geometry. She rose early and studied these subjects before the household stirred. In 1804 she married Samuel Grieg, son of a Scottish sailor who became a Russian admiral. Her first husband 'took no interest in science or literature, and possessed in full the prejudice against learned women which was common at that time'[1]. His death after three years meant that his widow returned with two little boys to her father's house. She was more free to pursue her studies as a widow than she had been as a girl. She started on Newton's *Principia*, which she found 'extremely difficult', but she persisted. She began to work out the problems which appeared in a mathematical journal published from the Royal Military College at Great Marlow, where William Wallace, later professor of mathematics at Edinburgh, was a teacher. With his advice she was able to provide herself with 'an excellent little library' by the time she was thirty-three. She no longer concealed her interests. 'I was considered eccentric and foolish, and my conduct was highly disapproved of by many, especially by some members of my own family. . . . As I was quite independent, I did not care for their criticism'[2].

As a charming widow she had several suitors, one of whom 'whilst he was paying court to me, sent me a volume of sermons with the page ostentatiously turned down at a sermon on the Duties of a Wife, which were expatiated upon in the most illiberal and narrow-minded language. I thought this as impertinent as it was premature; sent back the book and refused the proposal'[3]. In 1812 she married her cousin, Dr. William Somerville. Although marriage interrupted her studies for a time, she was able to take them up again with her husband's full sympathy. He was appointed a member of the Army Medical Board in 1816 and they moved to London. Through Professor Wallace, the Somervilles were put in touch with 'the illustrious family of the Herschels'[4]. Sir William Herschel was born in Hanover in 1738 and entered the Hanoverian guards as an oboist, but came to England in 1757. After some years of struggle he became organist at the Octagon chapel at Bath. He earned his living by music, but mathematics and astronomy were his recreation. In

[1] *Personal Recollections*, p. 3.   [2] *Ibid.*, pp. 79–80.   [3] *Ibid.*, p. 88.   [4] *Ibid.*, p. 104.

1772 he was joined in England by his sister, Caroline, who had been trained as a musician, but was diverted to astronomy by helping her brother. He set himself to construct his own instruments and discovered the planet Uranus by means of his own reflectors. The king settled £50 a year on Caroline Herschel as her brother's assistant in 1787. When Mrs. Somerville first visited the Herschels Caroline was abroad, but she met Sir William's son, later Sir John Herschel, whom she described as 'my dear friend for many years'. Sir William died in 1822 and Caroline went back to Germany, where she lived in great honour until the age of ninety-eight. It is possible that her skill and ability as an astronomer made Sir William and his son the readier to welcome a woman scientist into their friendship. Mrs. Somerville persisted in her studies despite the recurrent births of children and the long illness and death in 1823 of her eldest girl. She never allowed her work to keep her from a full social life, and she remembered Mary Berry's luncheon parties with strawberries and cream at Twickenham across the gulf of years.

In 1827, to use her own words, 'the whole character and course of my life was changed'. On 27 March Lord Brougham wrote to Dr. Somerville asking him to persuade his wife to translate a famous French book about the structure of the universe, the *Mécanique Céleste*, of Laplace, for publication by his new Society for Diffusing Useful Knowledge. Brougham followed up the letter by a visit and, in spite of her diffidence, Mrs. Somerville agreed to undertake the task. She rose early to deal with household matters so that she could spend the day in writing. She was subject to many interruptions. Her own little room had no fireplace, so that in cold weather she worked in the drawing-room and she learned to concentrate so closely on her work that she was oblivious to what was happening around her. When a visitor came she hid her work so that no one should discover what she was about. When the book was finished she 'was equally surprised and gratified that Sir John Herschel, our greatest astronomer, and perfectly versed in the calculus, should have found so few errors'. He wrote to her saying that he had read her manuscript with 'the highest admiration. Go on thus and you will leave a memorial of no common kind to posterity'[1]. Mrs. Somerville's book appeared in 1831 under the title *Mechanism of the Heavens*, and the whole first printing of 750 copies was sold at once, chiefly at Cambridge. 'I was', she wrote, 'astonished at the success of my book'. The Royal Astronomical

[1] *Personal Recollections*, p. 167.

Society elected her an honorary member together with Miss Caroline Herschel, and the Royal Society unanimously voted that Mary Somerville's bust, which they commissioned Chantrey to execute, should be placed in their great hall. She recorded that 'our relations and others who had so severely criticized and ridiculed me, astonished at my success, were now loud in my praise'[1].

The publication of Mary Somerville's first book coincided in time with the foundation of the British Association for the advancement of science. An intelligent public without technical knowledge was stimulated by the scientific achievement of an attractive woman, who was playing her full part as a wife and mother. Cambridge laid itself out to do her honour. In April 1834 she and her husband were entertained for a week at Trinity by the Master, and Adam Sedgwick arranged a series of parties. Her second book, *The Connexion of the Physical Sciences*, came out in that year. It was a summary of research into physical phenomena, lucidly set out. Its appearance was followed by public recognition of her achievement. In March 1835 Sir Robert Peel wrote to inform her that 'to encourage others to follow the bright example which you have set, and to prove that great scientific attainments are recognized among public claims' he was advising His Majesty to grant her a pension on the civil list of £200 a year. This was later increased to £300. The loss of her husband's private fortune made this pension of particular value. After 1838 Dr. Somerville's health compelled him to spend the winter in a warmer climate and the delay caused by journeys abroad meant that Mrs. Somerville's *Physical Geography* did not appear until 1848. Dr. Somerville died in 1860 and his widow turned to her work for solace. She prepared a summary of recent discoveries in chemistry and physics, under the title *Molecular and Microscopic Science* in 1869, the year in which she reached the age of eighty-nine. She died in Italy in 1872 at the age of ninety-two. Her daughter recorded that 'it was with intense delight that she pursued her intricate calculations after her ninetieth and ninety-first years'. She repeatedly said 'how she rejoiced to find that she had the same readiness and facility in comprehending and developing these extremely difficult formulae which she possessed when young'[2].

Two of Mary Somerville's four major works passed through many editions. The *Connexion of the Physical Sciences* was in its ninth edition in 1858 and *Physical Geography* in its sixth in 1870. Nor were new editions

---

[1] *Personal Recollections*, p. 176.   [2] *Ibid.*, p. 177.

mere reprints of the first. In the Preface to the new edition of the *Physical Geography* which appeared in 1849 the author informed her readers that she had corrected many inaccuracies in the first edition and collected much new information 'from the scientific periodicals of Europe, America, and India'. All her work was of the highest order. There is the authority of Adams himself for the statement that it was her prediction of a planet to be discovered by calculation from the motions of Uranus which set him upon the investigations afterwards confirmed by the discovery of the planet Neptune'[1]. A masterly popularizer of acquired knowledge, she might, under other conditions, have been one of the few who in any generation have changed the atmosphere of a subject. The greatest scientists of her day saw in her their peer.

Mary Somerville was the only woman born before the French Revolution who took part in the movement for the political enfranchisement of women. She signed the petition presented to the University of London in 1862 praying that women might be allowed to sit for degree examinations. Although it was rejected, George Grote, then treasurer of University College, told those who organized it that the name of 'Mrs. Somerville was the one that made the greatest impression', and he went on to urge 'that women should do things, showing their capacity'[2]. Writing in her eighty-ninth year Mrs. Somerville recorded that she had 'frequently signed petitions to Parliament for the Female Suffrage, and have the honour now to be a member of the General Committee for Women Suffrage in London'. When John Stuart Mill published *The Subjection of Women* in 1869 Mrs. Somerville wrote to him expressing her gratitude for his exposure of the 'iniquity and injustice' of the laws for women in England. In his reply J. S. Mill described her praise of the book as 'the approbation of one who has rendered such an inestimable service to the cause of women by affording in her own person so high an example of their intellectual capabilities'. 'Age', wrote Mrs. Somerville, when she was approaching her eighty-ninth year, 'has not abated my zeal for the emancipation of my sex from the unreasonable prejudice too prevalent in Great Britain against a literary and scientific education for women'[3].

The years between the first fully argued appeal for the complete emancipation of women set out by William Thompson in 1825 and the

[1] *Personal Recollections*, pp. 289–90.
[2] Barbara Stephen, *Emily Davies and Girton College*, London, 1927, pp. 73–4.
[3] *Personal Recollections*, pp. 344–6.

publication of *The Subjection of Women* in 1869 had seen a change of opinion about the place of women in English society. Women themselves were slow to follow up William Thompson's arguments with their own demands, for they realized the danger of associating themselves with his eccentricities. Nor did many go all the way with him in his description of the ideal relationship between men and women. Moreover, the sympathy with women shown by the early Socialists tended to alarm even the ultra-Radicals. Some of the skilled craftsmen, who resented their own exclusion from any political influence and formulated a charter of their demands, sympathized with women's aspirations, but dared not go farther in their charter than ask for universal male suffrage. But the question of female suffrage did not entirely drop out of view and in 1831 a motion was proposed in Parliament by the formidable Radical, Henry Hunt, that 'every unmarried female possessing the necessary pecuniary qualifications should be entitled to vote for Members of Parliament'[1]. The stream of propagandist literature began to flow freely in the eighteen-forties, and in 1848 the young Disraeli, in supporting a motion to extend the vote to all householders, said 'In a country governed by a woman, where you allow women to form part of the estates of the Realm—Peeresses in their own right, for example—where you allow women not only to hold land but to be ladies of the manor and to hold legal courts—where a woman by law may be a churchwarden and overseer of the poor—I do not see, where she has so much right to do with State and Church, on what reasons, if you come to right, she has not the right to vote'[2].

More urgent matters affecting the welfare of women than their admission to the polling booths agitated their friends during these years. The inequality of the law which governed the relations between husband and wife had been exposed by a lawyer more than two hundred years before[3]. His advice to wives to appeal to Parliament for relief was premature in 1632, but it remained the fact that only legislative action could correct the law's injustice to married women. The exposure by Caroline Norton (1808–77) of her own sad story was hardly necessary to make plain the need for action, but lawyers would perhaps have moved more slowly if Mrs. Norton had born her troubles in silence. She was one of the three beautiful and highly gifted granddaughters of Richard Brinsley Sheridan and had married George Chappel Norton, a brother of the third Lord Grantley. The contemptuous rejection by the jury of his action of criminal

[1] *The Cause*, p. 32. [2] *Ibid.*, p. 43 *n*. [3] See above, p. 149.

conversation brought against Lord Melbourne in 1836 left Mrs. Norton still tied to her husband by the unbreakable marriage bond and unable to get access to her own children. She had begun her literary career in 1829, two years after her marriage, with the publication of a volume of poems. Its success meant that she could earn a handsome income by contributing to and editing the literary annuals popular in the nineteenth century. She said that in one year she made as much as £1,400. Her husband withheld her allowance and claimed the money she earned by writing. Their financial arrangements were complicated by a trust fund which had been created for Mrs. Norton and her children, and her husband's attempts to raise money on it. Norton wrote to *The Times* setting out his side of the case and Mrs. Norton replied in a pamphlet entitled *English Laws for Women*, published in 1854[1]. In the next year she published a tract in the form of *A Letter to the Queen on the Lord Chancellor Cranworth's Marriage and Divorce Bill*[2].

Mrs. Norton's social position, her popularity as an author, and the fact that Lord Melbourne had been implicated made her case famous, but it was by no means the only one in which the hard usage of a wife caused public scandal in the first half of the century. Two other instances of cruelty to married women in these generations may be quoted here. John Paget, the Lord Chancellor's secretary, was moved to take up the case of Mrs. Talbot, against whom her husband had obtained, on perjured evidence, a divorce in the consistorial court of Dublin. The case of Mrs. Talbot, who had lost her reason in the course of the proceedings, was treated by Paget in a series of pamphlets which called public attention to the whole practice of ecclesiastical courts in matrimonial causes[3]. The second instance is that of the Marchioness of Westmeath, who published an account of her own case in 1857 while the Divorce Bill was going through Parliament. It was then an old story, which Lady Westmeath deliberately brought up at this time as material to be used by the supporters of the Bill. In dedicating her work to the Lords Lyndhurst and Brougham, she expressed the hope 'that exertions they are disinterestedly making to obtain justice for a suffering class, may be further stimulated by this Narrative, published with a view to the exposure of such cruelties,

---

[1] C. Norton, *English Laws for Women in the Nineteenth Century*, London, 1854.

[2] Quoting on the title-page from Thackeray's Lecture on Swift, 'Only a Woman's Hair'.

[3] *Talbot v. Talbot, A Letter to the Hon. Justice Torrens*, 1855. *A Report on the Judgment of Dr. Radcliffe in the case of Talbot v. Talbot*, 1855. *Talbot v. Talbot, A Report of the Speech of Wm. Keogh, Esq.*, 1855.

legal and personal in my own case, as may, I trust, lead to a mitigation of persecution against others, by providing a remedy for all'[1]. As a conclusion to her long and confusing narrative, Lady Westmeath wrote: 'If I shall have assisted the spirit of enquiry now aroused, as to the dreadful state of the laws, respecting married women in this country in any degree, my object is answered'[2].

Lady Westmeath's case illustrates most clearly the fact that a divorce from bed and board granted to either husband or wife by an ecclesiastical court left the parties still married in law. This situation had given rise to the most celebrated matrimonial case of the eighteenth century. The Duke of Kingston married in March 1769 Elizabeth Chudleigh, who had been his mistress for about ten years. She had made a secret marriage in 1744 with the second son of Lord Hervey and had a child by him in 1747. Just before Elizabeth Chudleigh became the duke's mistress she had gone to the trouble of establishing the fact of her former marriage by causing a record of it to be entered in the register of the chapel where the marriage had taken place. She did this because her husband's elder brother, by this time Earl of Bristol, was in poor health and she wished to make sure of becoming a countess. Her connection with the Duke of Kingston opened to her the opportunity of becoming a duchess and, since her husband was also anxious to be free, she instituted proceedings against him in the consistory court and sentence was given in her favour. After her marriage to the duke she was accepted as his wife, although her conduct did not commend itself to ladies. The duke died in 1773 leaving all that he could leave to her as his widow. It is possible that no action would have been taken against her had the duke been less generous. As it was, the duke's nephew, Mr. Evelyn Medows, caused a Bill of Indictment for bigamy to be drawn up against the supposititious duchess. The case was heard before the House of Lords, where she was convicted, the Duke of Newcastle, her neighbour in Nottinghamshire, alone adding to his sentence of 'Guilty' the words 'but not intentionally'. Elizabeth Chudleigh escaped corporal punishment by pleading the privilege of peerage which was allowed her[3]. An intolerable possibility of scandal was removed in 1857 when the Matrimonial Causes

[1] *A Narrative of the Case of the Marchioness of Westmeath*, London, 1857, Dedication.
[2] *Ibid.*, p. 213.
[3] *The Whole of the Evidence of the Trial of Her Grace Elizabeth, Duchess Dowager of Kingston . . . together with an authentic copy of Her Grace's Defence as Spoken by Herself.* This was published by order of the duchess and sold for two shillings and sixpence.

Act at last ended the jurisdiction of the Church courts in matrimonial causes and established the Divorce Court for all suits touching marriage.

A society which aimed at a general reform of abuses in the law had been formed in 1844 as the Law Amendment Society. Ten years later, a young woman of twenty-seven, Barbara Leigh Smith, persuaded the society to consider the disabilities of married women. She herself belonged to a highly intelligent Unitarian family. Her grandfather represented Norwich in Parliament from 1802 to 1830 and her father from 1841 to 1847. When Barbara came of age in 1848 he settled on her £300 a year, so that she was unusually independent. In 1845 she produced *A brief Summary in Plain Language, of the most important Laws concerning Women*, which was all the more impressive because the author herself was not a sufferer. A family friend who was one of the founders of the Law Amendment Society helped her in preparing this tract. After a public discussion in 1856, which women attended although they did not speak, the Society promoted a Bill to provide that married women should be free to own property on the same terms as unmarried women and that they should be able to make wills touching other property than their personal possessions. The Bill was introduced in May 1857, but got no farther than a second reading owing to the simultaneous passage of the Divorce Bill through the House. During the course of the debates on the Divorce Bill Lord Lyndhurst secured the insertion of a clause affording protection to the property acquired by married women separated from their husbands[1]. The *Saturday Review*, the persistent enemy of women, declared that the proposals put forward by the Law Amendment Society 'were enough to remove the whole discussion from the region of reality to that of burlesque'[2].

Divorce, which before this Act could only be obtained by a private Act of Parliament, was now placed under the jurisdiction of a court erected for the purpose. The Act of 1857 opened a regular procedure for divorce to both men and women, though on unequal terms. Equality was not secured until 1923. It is hard at this distance of time to look back into the minds of those who opposed the changes in the law of husband

[1] An Act to amend the Law relating to Divorce and Matrimonial Causes in England [28 August 1857], Clause xxv. The wife in case of judicial separation is to be considered a *femme sole* with respect to any property she may acquire and [Clause xxvi] for the purposes of contracting and suing. *The Statutes at Large*, London, 1857, pp. 532–46.

[2] Quoted by Barbara Stephen, *Emily Davies and Girton College*, pp. 40–3.

and wife now set in motion. The considered opinion of an outstanding Anglican churchman of the time may fairly be taken as representative. In 1857, Christopher Wordsworth, Canon of Westminster, afterwards Bishop of Lincoln, delivered a series of discourses in the Abbey on the subject of divorce. After examining the Scriptures, the Fathers of the Church and later canonists, he came to the reluctant conclusion that after a woman had been divorced for adultery her husband might be allowed to marry again, though he pleaded that the clergy might be relieved from the obligation to perform such marriage ceremonies. In 1879, when he republished the discourses in his collected works, he described the social and religious evils which in his opinion had followed inevitably upon the operation of the Act. 'The apprehensions expressed in these Discourses', he wrote, 'have been realized. Divorce before that time'—that is, 1857—'was scarcely mentioned in Christian Society among us, without a feeling of shame and a shudder. But the newspaper reports of the proceedings in the Divorce Court—then constituted by Law—have now made it familiar. And the examples of conjugal infidelity in fashionable society and high rank—displayed to public view with all their loathsome details—have destroyed much of that salutory abhorrence with which men recoiled from such things, as too revolting to be named. . . . It is too much to expect the Divorce Act will be repealed, for some time to come. But it is possible to create a more wholesome public opinion on the subject, and so either to prepare the way for repeal, or at least to diminish greatly the number of cases in which it is applied. This is the work for the Clergy and Laity of the Church'[1].

In 1859, Wordsworth made the introduction of a Bill to legalize the marriage of a widower to his deceased wife's sister the occasion of a sermon which calls to mind the rhetoric of a robuster age. 'And let us not', he cried, 'inflict an injury on those sisters of a wife, who are now received into the most confidential and endearing intercourse in the home of their sister's husband. All those tender relationships, which impart an inexpressible charm and delicate sanctity to our English homes, would be scattered to the winds by the repeal of the law of God, which requires a husband to regard his wife's sisters as his own sisters, and to honour and love them as such'. After a rhapsody on the delights of

---

[1] Chr. Wordsworth, D.D., *Miscellanies, Literary and Religious*, 1879, vol. iii, pp. 202 ff. 'On Marriage and Divorce'. The copy of the bishop's works which I have used was given by him to my husband's father at the time of publication.

gaining a sister, he continued: 'But, let this law be repealed, and all these blessings are gone—gone for ever. The morrow after its repeal, the sisters of all the wives in England, and the wives who have sisters, and the husbands of such wives, and the children of such husbands and wives will find their position changed. The husband will have lost the sister whom he gained by marriage. The wife will have lost the sister whom she had by blood. The wife's sister will have ceased to be a sister, and have become almost a stranger. She can no longer enter the house with the same freedom and familiarity as before. Or, if she does, what jealousies and heartburnings may arise! The wife may be less fair than her sister. . . .' The bishop pursued this unprofitable theme to see divorce easier still and the wife's sister 'set up in her sister's house, at her sister's table, and in her sister's place', so that 'the wife's children may loathe their own home and may hate their mother's sister, and their own father, as the authors of their mother's misery and of their mother's disgrace'[1].

These discourses, reprinted in 1879 with ample footnotes, obviously represent the mature views of the Bishop of Lincoln as well as the opinions of the Canon of Westminster of twenty years before. They must have been widespread, for Parliament did not legalize the marriage of a man with his deceased wife's sister until 1907 and that of a woman with her deceased husband's brother until 1921. Christopher Wordsworth was himself a fine scholar, he had been an exemplary parish priest and he became a venerated bishop. He sympathized with women's aspirations towards scholarship, and rejoiced when his daughter became the first Principal of Lady Margaret Hall at Oxford. The attitude of such a man to these problems of conduct may help to explain the slow progress of emancipation in the later nineteenth century, at a time when a large number of eminent people desired it to come. To Christopher Wordsworth, and to a great multitude of Englishmen, both clergy and laity, the views of the reformers threatened the end of all that was of good repute in life.

The women who led the movement for the reform of English laws relating to their sex were not those whose own achievements had brought them contemporary fame. Harriet Martineau (1802–74) and Florence Nightingale (1820–1910) were in the years after 1855 perhaps the two most famous of contemporary women. Mary Ann Evans, better known

---

[1] *Miscellanies*, vol. iii, pp. 237 ff. 'On Marriage with a Deceased Wife's Sister'. The passage quoted is on pp. 253–5.

as George Eliot, was still at the beginning of her career for she started
on her first novel in 1856. Mrs. Somerville was famous only among
intelligent people and she lived much abroad. Harriet Martineau came
of a Unitarian family of Huguenot descent settled in Norwich since the
late seventeenth century. She had been well educated according to the
standards of the day which did not envisage a professional career for
women. In 1826 her father, a Norwich manufacturer of bombazines,
was ruined in the widespread financial troubles of that year. The market
for his products failed, and he died. Harriet had already earned £5 for a
story and determined to be a writer. In 1827 Mrs. Marcet's *Conversations
on Political Economy* came into her hands and she realized that a story she
had written about machine-breaking was an illustration of one of the
principles which Mrs. Marcet expounded. The idea of a series of such
stories at once occurred to her, and her mother and brother encouraged
her to write it. It was not easy to find a publisher, as she sets out in her
autobiography, and if her struggles sound harsher and her triumphs
more splendid than either can have been, Miss Martineau may be pardoned
for her slight exaggeration. Her autobiography is a vivid document
although her friends felt that she did herself no justice by her plain-spoken
criticism of those with whom she had disagreed. Her brother was hurt
by her attitude towards members of her own family. But the autobiography reveals a woman of generous Radical sympathies and complete
intellectual honesty. She scorned to conceal her Unitarianism for social
reasons when she began her literary career in London, nor would she
conceal her doubts about revealed religion in her later years.

Harriet Martineau trained herself to become a first-rate political
journalist. She could master a wide range of related matter and reduce
it to a clear narrative which the intelligent reading public could understand. Her power is well displayed in *The Thirty Years' Peace*, a massive
work in two volumes treating contemporary history in the form of
annals[1]. Neat obituary notices of the famous people recently dead appear
at regular intervals and the modern reader feels that he is enjoying the
'review of the year' in the leading journal of the day. Harriet Martineau
wrote as a Radical, and her political outlook helps to preserve the freshness
of her work. She had the enthusiasm of a reformer and was not burdened
by the overwhelming mass of material which the modern scholar writing
of the same period would feel obliged to consult. Her powers as a novelist

[1] Covering the years 1816–46, London, 1849.

were small, for she had no understanding of the passions which sway ordinary men and women. Her friendship with Charlotte Brontë did not long survive candid criticism of each other's books, but her stories on political economy were followed by stories illustrating the Forest and Game Laws, which delighted a Westmorland poacher so much that he made her an anonymous present of turf for her garden at Ambleside. Her faith in 'mesmerism', for which she has often been criticized, was based on the fact that her own temporary recovery from painful illness coincided with hypnotic treatment. In 1855 she began to prepare for death, but she lived nearly twenty years longer, contributing from her Westmorland cottage innumerable articles to the *Daily News* and other journals of an advanced tendency.

Her attitude to the women's movement, as revealed in her autobiography, was that of a woman strong enough to make her own way, but lacking imaginative insight into the feelings of others: 'It seemed to me, from the earliest times when I could think on the subject of Woman's Rights and condition, that the first requisite to advancement is self-reliance, which results from self-discipline'. She had therefore little sympathy with Mary Wollstonecraft, whom she described as 'with all her powers, a poor victim of passion, with no control over her own peace, and no calmness or content, except when the needs of her individual nature were satisfied'. 'I felt', she continued, 'forty years ago, in regard to her, just what I feel now in regard to some of the most conspicuous denouncers of the wrongs of women at this day;—that their advocacy of Woman's cause becomes mere detriment, precisely in proportion to their personal reasons for unhappiness, unless they have fortitude enough (which loud complainants usually have not) to get their own troubles under their feet, and leave them wholly out of the account in stating the state of their sex. Nobody can be further than I am from being satisfied with the condition of my own sex, under the law and custom of my own country; but I decline all fellowship and co-operation with women of genius or otherwise favourable position, who injure the cause by their personal tendencies. When I see an eloquent writer insinuating to everybody who comes across her that she is the victim of her husband's carelessness and cruelty, while he never spoke in his own defence: when I see her violating all good taste by her obtrusiveness in society, and oppressing everybody about her with her epicurean selfishness every day, while raising in print an eloquent cry on behalf of the oppressed; I feel to the bottom of my heart that she is the worst enemy of the cause she professes to plead'.

'The best friends of that cause', continued Miss Martineau, 'are women who are morally as well as intellectually competent to the most serious business of life, and who must be clearly seen to speak from the conviction of the truth, and not from personal unhappiness. The best friends of the cause are the happy wives and the busy, cheerful, satisfied single women, who have no injuries of their own to avenge, and no painful vanity or mortification to relieve. The best advocates are yet to come,—in the persons of women who are obtaining access to real social business,—the female physicians and other professors in America, the women of business and the female artists of France; and the hospital administrators, the nurses, the educators and substantially successful authors of our own country. Often as I am appealed to to speak, or otherwise assist in the promotion of the cause of Woman, my answer is always the same:—that women, like men, can obtain whatever they show themselves fit for. Let them be educated,—let their powers be cultivated to the extent for which the means are already provided, and all that is wanted or ought to be desired will follow of course. Whatever a woman proves herself able to do, society will be thankful to see her do,—just as if she were a man. If she is scientific, science will welcome her, as it has welcomed every woman so qualified. I believe no scientific woman complains of wrongs. If capable of political thought and action, women will obtain even that. . . . I have no vote at elections, though I am a tax-paying housekeeper and responsible citizen; and I regard the disability as an absurdity, seeing that I have for a long course of years influenced public affairs to an extent not professed or attempted by many men. But I do not see that I could do much good by personal complaints, which always have some suggestion of passion in them. I think the better way is for us all to learn and to try to the utmost what we can do, and thus win for ourselves the consideration which alone can secure us rational treatment'[1].

Harriet Martineau was a better friend to the women's movement than this arrogant statement suggests. In 1857 she supported in the Press the abortive Married Woman's Property Bill of that year[2]. As a woman journalist, she could not resist the opportunity of writing a comprehensive review of recent publications illustrating the different ways in

---

[1] *Autobiography*, pp. 400–2.
[2] Barbara Stephen, *Emily Davies*, pp. 41–2.

which women were earning their own living. Her long article on 'Female Industry', written anonymously as if by a man, appeared in the *Edinburgh Review* for April 1859[1]. It informed a wide circle of influential readers that a vital change had come over the position of women as a result of the industrial expansion of recent generations. Far more women, instead of being supported by some man, husband or father, were now economically independent. The accuracy of many of Miss Martineau's historical generalizations is open to doubt, but she proved her main thesis beyond question. 'So far from our countrywomen being all maintained as a matter of course by us "the breadwinners" three millions out of six of adult English women work for subsistence; and two out of the three in independence. With this new condition of affairs, new duties and new views must be accepted. Old obstructions must be removed and the aim must be set before us, as a nation as well as in private life, to provide for the free development and full use of the powers of every member of the community'[2].

In spite of the masculine disguise which she had assumed when writing this article the robustly successful *femme sole* impatient of incompetence is clearly in the background. 'Wearied as some of us are with the incessant repetition of the dreary story of spirit-broken governesses and starving needlewomen, we rarely obtain a glimpse of the full breadth of the area of female labour in Great Britain'[3]. 'The proceedings in the new Divorce Court', she wrote, 'and in matrimonial cases before the police magistrates, have caused a widespread astonishment at the amount of female industry they have disclosed. Almost every aggrieved wife who has sought protection, has proved that she has supported her household, and has acquired property by her effective exertions'. All this in itself might be satisfactory, but it meant that Harriet Martineau could no longer, as sometimes in the past, feel complacent about the attitude which men were likely to take when confronted by a further expansion of women's activities. She admitted in this article that there might be difficulty in the way of women who wish to be doctors and surgeons. 'The jealousy of the medical profession is, to be sure, proverbial'. Although Dr. Elizabeth Blackwell had secured her qualifications in America 'in our country, more time will, no doubt, be required. Prejudices are stronger; the capabilities of women are less tested and understood[4].

---

[1] Vol. cix, pp. 293–336.   [2] *Ibid.*, p. 336.
[3] *Ibid.*, p. 294.   [4] *Ibid.*, pp. 331 and 332.

The obstruction which Florence Nightingale had met in the Crimea had already shown that Harriet Martineau's apprehensions were well-founded[1]. Miss Nightingale had learned how policy could be directed to her ends by the force of public opinion and she realized that opinion could be moulded by the Press. She, naturally, sent her report on her experiences in the Crimea to Harriet Martineau, who responded by lending her influence to the causes in which Miss Nightingale was engaged. In 1858 she based a series of articles for the *Daily News* on Miss Nightingale's report, and in the next year she published them in a book, *England and her Soldiers*. The alliance between these two outstanding women thus formed continued to the end of Harriet Martineau's life. Her pen was always ready to support Florence Nightingale's schemes, whether directed at the reform of the Army Medical Board, the prevention of state brothels for the army in India, or the training of nurses. In the article on 'Female Industry' Harriet Martineau wrote 'The function of industry which might be supposed to be standing wide for women is not in fact so,—the nursing function in all its directions, in private dwellings, in workhouses, in hospitals, in lunatic asylums, where it is at least as much wanted as anywhere else. We shall not argue or plead for it here. Florence Nightingale and her disciples have inaugurated a new period in the history of working women, and the manifest destiny of the nursing class will fulfil itself'[2].

In her youth Florence Nightingale had been bitterly resentful of the emptiness of her life as a well-bred young lady, but as she grew older she disclaimed all interest in the movement to widen the opportunities before women. 'I am brutally indifferent to the right and wrongs of my sex', she wrote to Harriet Martineau in 1858[3]. She had never felt that her sex hindered her work in the Crimea or afterwards. She hardly realized how much she owed to her secure social position. Only a woman with friends in high places and a wide acquaintanceship could have harried the Government into the reform of army hygiene. 'The more chattering and noise there is about Women's Missions', she wrote in 1865, 'the less of efficient women can we find'[4]. She was convinced that if women were unemployed it was because they would not work. Her difficulties in finding the right women to train as matrons made her unsympathetic with women who wanted to be doctors. It was embarrassing to those

---

[1] Cecil Woodham-Smith, *Florence Nightingale*, first published in 1951 and now available in Penguin Books, No. 1110.   [2] 'Female Industry', p. 331.
[3] Quoted by Cecil Woodham-Smith, p. 245.   [4] *Ibid.*, p. 359.

who were trying to further the cause of women that a woman whose own life had been so conspicuously successful should show no interest in their work. Even John Stuart Mill could not induce her to join Harriet Martineau, Mrs. Somerville, and 1,498 other women in signing the first general petition for women's suffrage, which he presented to Parliament in 1866[1].

[1] A printed copy of the petition and signatures can be consulted at the Women's Service Library, Fawcett House, 27 Wilfred Street, Westminster, S.W.1.

Epilogue

If the emancipation of women from the last traces of their feudal subjection seems to have been achieved slowly it should be remembered that
it was but one aspect of the great movement for reform which swept
majestically, but with irregular momentum, through the nineteenth
century. Those aspects of the reforming movement which specifically
concerned the welfare of women advanced more surely as an ever-increasing number of well-educated women came forward to share in the work.
As early as 1847 Tennyson in *The Princess* had written about a women's
college, and although his playful nonsense reads oddly today, it shows
that the idea of the higher education of women was already in the public
mind. In 1848 Frederick Maurice, the leader of the Christian Socialists,
secured the establishment of Queen's College to be a training school for
governesses. The foundation of Bedford College by Mrs. Reid in the
next year gave additional opportunities for the education of young
women. Mrs. Reid was the widow of a doctor and a friend of Harriet
Martineau. In 1860 she provided for the future of Bedford College by
establishing a trust specifically for the higher education of women there.
One of the trustees whom she chose was Miss Jane Martineau, Harriet's
niece. Women trained in these colleges could teach in schools where a
standard of education inconceivable to previous generations was constantly
improved as students from the new women's colleges at Cambridge and
Oxford came to join in the work. North London Collegiate School
was founded in 1850 by Frances Mary Buss (1827–94), who had begun
her teaching life at fourteen in her mother's school. She prepared herself
for her life's work by earning her living teaching in the daytime and
attending classes at Queen's College in the evenings. Dorothea Beale
(1831–1906) entered Queen's College as a student in 1848 and became
mathematical tutor in the following year. In 1858 she was chosen as
principal of Cheltenham Ladies' College, founded four years before. In
1865 girls' schools as well as boys' schools were the subject of an enquiry
by royal commission and two women were summoned to give evidence.
The way was slowly opening for the Girls' High Schools of the late
nineteenth century and the Grammar Schools for the girls of today.

The fight for the admission of women to the examinations for university degrees went on side by side with the struggle to create good girls' schools and persuade parents to send their daughters to them. The most effective woman associated with both movements who was not herself a schoolmistress was Emily Davies (1830–1921). Her brother, Llewelyn Davies, was ordained to a Limehouse curacy in 1851 and moved on to a London living in 1856. He had become a follower and friend of Frederick Maurice and a member of his Christian Socialist group. When Emily Davies came to visit him from her father's Gateshead rectory she found herself among people who believed in the capacity of women and were working for their better education. In 1858 Emily Davies went to Algiers to accompany her invalid brother home and there she met Barbara Leigh Smith, now Madame Bodichon, who spent every winter there with her husband. Emily Davies had already met Elizabeth Garret in the north and their friendship grew closer in London. In 1859 Dr. Elizabeth Blackwell, the only Englishwoman who had acquired a medical degree, visited London and lectured on her work. Elizabeth Garret was interested and Emily Davies urged her to begin her training for a doctor. The first approach to London University about the admission of women to its degree examinations was made with Miss Garret in mind. Its failure meant that she approached her end by way of private study for the qualifying examination of the Society of Apothecaries, which she passed in 1865. This enabled her to practise as a doctor, but the Society in 1868 refused to allow candidates to enter for the examination after private study, so that no other woman could qualify for the medical profession in London until the medical schools of the university were opened to receive them after 1878.

In assisting the campaign which ended with Elizabeth Garret's acquisition of her medical qualifications Emily Davies found her vocation. She realized that the universities must be approached with caution and tact. And she understood and sympathized with the attitude of the London senate, which felt diffident about being the first university to open its degrees to women. Miss Davies desired the full emancipation of women as strongly as Barbara Bodichon, but she realized that she would be more likely to secure the future of women in the universities if she held aloof from the Radical activities of those who were working to secure the vote for women. She secured the admission of girls to the Cambridge local examinations, a victory won after a real campaign. Leslie Stephen, asked to go up to Cambridge to vote for the proposal, refused on the ground that he was writing against it in the *Saturday Review*[1]. After considering and abandoning the possibility of converting Queen's College into an institution for higher education where girls sent on by the schools might hope in the future to work for a degree, Miss Davies turned to Cambridge and began to plan for the creation of a women's college there. The little group of students from which Girton College grew started work at Hitchin in 1869.

Before his election to Parliament in 1865 J. S. Mill had openly expressed his desire to see the franchise extended to women. His candidature at Westminster was supported by young women working in the interests of women, such as Madame Bodichon, Emily Davies, Bessie Parkes and Isa Craig, who drove about the constituency in a hired carriage covered with election posters. In 1865, Mill was at the height of his reputation. A whole generation of men engaged in public affairs had grown to maturity under the influence of his writings. His advocacy secured for the women's cause a degree of respect which could have come to it in no other way. Behind the closely reasoned arguments of his famous books on philosophy and economics there had always lain a passionate desire for justice in human relationships. In the tract entitled *The Subjection of Women* which he published after long reflection in 1869, the passion comes to the surface with a force which carries the argument from the sphere of practical politics into the wider region of public morality. The tract cannot have been pleasant reading in the family circles, typical of the age, where it was felt that women needed protection rather than independence. But it would be hard to name a single event more significant in the history of women's emancipation than the appearance of the *Subjection of Women* in 1869.

The effect of this book on public opinion was less marked in the campaign for women's suffrage which individual reformers intermittently maintained than in the new momentum which came over the women's cause as a whole during the following years. In the same year the municipal franchise was granted to all ratepayers. The first woman entered the higher branches of the civil service when James Stansfield appointed Mrs. Nassau Senior as a poor-law inspector in 1872. Stansfield was not only a courageous supporter of causes which concerned women, but also sacrificed his political career in their interest. In 1874 he abandoned

---

[1] Barbara Stephen, *Emily Davies*, p. 100.

Cabinet office to give his support to Josephine Butler's campaign for the repeal of the Contagious Diseases Acts. In 1883, after a long struggle, the reformers carried a resolution in favour of repeal through the House of Commons and in April 1886 a repealing statute became law. A Bill to secure married women in the possession of their own property was introduced in 1870, and although in its passage through the Lords its provisions were limited, it allowed married women to own whatever they themselves had earned. In 1882 married women were given for the first time since the Norman Conquest rights of separate ownership over every kind of property so that at last their position was again assimilated to that of the *femme sole*. Four years before this momentous Act London University had opened its degrees to women. The new university colleges growing up under the shadow and protection of London were now able to enter all their students, women as well as men, for the external degrees of London University. Young women of modest means all over England owed gratitude to London University for the opportunity which it had given them.

A review of the fortunes of women through the centuries of English history reveals certain landmarks pointing on the one hand towards full participation in the rights and duties of the social order, and on the other towards a state of irresponsible subjection to men. The evidence which has survived from Anglo-Saxon England indicates that women were then more nearly the equal companions of their husbands and brothers than at any other period before the modern age. In the higher ranges of society, this rough and ready partnership was ended by the Norman Conquest, which introduced into England a military society relegating women in general to a position honourable, but essentially unimportant. With all allowance for the efforts of individual churchmen to help individual women, it must be confessed that the teaching of the medieval Church reinforced the subjection which feudal law imposed on all wives. Nevertheless some traces of the Anglo-Saxon attitude towards women lingered through the Middle Ages, notably among the farming families of the country-side and in the towns. But the homilies and sermons of the Reformed Church, insisting that subjection was the natural lot of wives, created an atmosphere in which the least intelligent male could feel superior to all women. On the other hand, even feudal law had never been able to force the widow or the unmarried woman of full age into complete subjection to any man. English history provides a continuous line of women who have left their mark on English life. Their growing influence was checked by a general reaction against the too eager advocacy of the women's cause by the founders of modern socialism. But the succession of women eminent in literature and affairs was never broken. If J. S. Mill's argument seems overstrained to a modern reader, it is because he ignored the achievements of English women in history. They deserve a salute today.

Index